Instructional Design for ELearning:
Essential guide to creating successful eLearning courses

Marina Arshavskiy

Trademarks

All brand names and product names used in this book are trademarks of their respective owners. The author is not associated with any product or vendor in this book.

Table of Contents

Introduction

When I first entered the field of instructional design, I reviewed a lot of literature and read many books on the subject. However, I did not find a single guide that offered a combination of theoretical and practical information. As a result, I had to supplement the theoretical knowledge I gained from these books and other resources with on-the-job experience. *Instructional Design for ELearning: Essential guide to creating successful eLearning courses* combines both theoretical aspects of instructional systems design and practical information from field experience to help instructional designers create the most compelling and effective courses. In this text, you will find the best knowledge, skills, and tools I could glean from the market. In addition to introducing theory and providing practical advice, this book aims to offer best practices drawn from many years of personal experience in the field of learning and development.

The Instructional Design for eLearning book can serve as a desk guide for instructional designers at any level and of any professional experience. Whether you are an aspiring instructional designer looking for a career change, a novice instructional designer trying to learn the basics of eLearning course development, a seasoned instructional designer needing a desk reference guide, or a human resources professional designing professional development training programs for employees, this book is your new go-to resource. Even though it concentrates primarily on designing eLearning courses for the workplace, curriculum developers and instructional designers who create face-to-face training programs can also benefit from it, as it covers all the important elements of course design regardless of the context.

The book is divided into four sections:

Part I - Basic Elements of Instructional Design
Part II – Designing Instructionally Sound ELearning Courses
Part III - Interactive Elements in ELearning Courses
Part IV - Advancing Your Skills

This text includes 26 exercises that will help you put your newly acquired knowledge into practice. Even though the activities will not be graded or reviewed, they are an excellent way to recap the information from each chapter and put it into perspective. Note that the first exercise sets the foundation for your project but does not provide all the content needed to create a project. Therefore, to complete the exercises, you will have to make certain assumptions about the topic and its content. Alternatively, you can use a project you are currently working on or simply invent one to complete these exercises.

Read each chapter, apply the knowledge you gain, and enjoy your learning quest!

Part I - Basic Elements of Instructional Design

"If you think training is expensive, try ignorance".

Peter Drucker

Chapter 1:
Instructional Design for ELearning

This chapter will cover:

- Definitions of instructional systems design, eLearning, and blended learning
- Definitions of CBT and WBT
- Advantages and disadvantages of eLearning
- Situations when eLearning is an appropriate solution

Instructional Systems Design

Instructional Systems Design, also known as ISD, is a systematic approach to creating effective courses. ISD is both a science and an art – a science because it is based on learning theories, and an art because of the creativity involved in the design process. Furthermore, ISD is a tool that guides the structure of any course and promotes meaningful and active learning.

ISD follows standards similar to curriculum design; the chief difference being that ISD is mainly practiced in the workplace and concentrates on the *how*, while curriculum design applies to academic settings and concentrates on the *why*.

Even though there are many different approaches to designing courses, experienced instructional designers typically combine a variety of methods and incorporate technology and multimedia to enhance instruction.

Instructional designers are interested in knowing how people learn and retain information. According to Marc Rosenberg, a leader in the world of training, performance is ultimately more important than training. There are many factors involved in creating eLearning materials that enable learners to retain information and, more importantly, transfer their newly acquired knowledge and skills to their jobs.

To people new to the field, ISD may appear easy. In reality, however, creating effective courses is rather complex. Skilled instructional designers focus on creating learning solutions that bring value to the organization by managing a project's time and cost. The success of their learning solution is measured by the performance improvement of their learners.

ELearning

ELearning is a form of learning conducted via Internet, intranet, network, or CD-ROM. Successful eLearning courses are interactive, energetic, dynamic, and appealing to the learner's auditory, visual, and tactile senses.

ELearning can be synchronous or asynchronous. Synchronous eLearning is done in real-time with a live instructor. The synchronous eLearning experience is similar to that of a regular classroom, except learners can take courses anywhere in the world as long as they have a computer, Internet connection, and access to audio or video conferencing. Some of the tools associated with synchronous eLearning are instant messaging, application sharing, and polling. While synchronous eLearning has the value of having a real instructor and ability to communicate with other participants in the course, it requires learners to virtually attend the course at a specific time.

Because adult learners are busy, many of them find synchronous eLearning impractical. To address this problem and to target a wider audience, instructional systems designers began recording synchronous eLearning courses and making them available to learners unable to attend live sessions. This is where asynchronous eLearning originates. Asynchronous eLearning is self-paced. It allows learners to go through courses as quickly or as slowly as they desire at their convenience. Some of the most commonly used tools in asynchronous eLearning are forums, blogs, and webcasts.

Computer-Based Training vs. Web-Based Training

Computer-Based Training (CBT) and Web-Based Training (WBT) are among the most popular eLearning delivery methods. CBT is a form of education in which learners take training courses on the computer. CBT courses are typically packaged into a CD or DVD format, and are intended for asynchronous delivery. WBT courses, on the other hand, operate on the Internet and are intended for both synchronous and asynchronous delivery.

Blended Learning

Even though eLearning is a popular solution for many performance problems, it is mostly appropriate for increasing knowledge and developing cognitive skills.

Even if the course follows the most solid instructional design principles, it cannot teach people how to drive a car, for example, because driving is a psychomotor skill, which requires real-life practice for best results.

Teaching interpersonal skills that change learners' attitudes and behaviors can be effective through eLearning if instructional designers add simulations, serious games, and role-plays. This is where the blended learning approach comes into play. The ultimate goal of this method is to combine several media in one course. In most cases, blended learning is a combination of face-to-face delivery with eLearning activities. For example, learners might have to complete the lecture part of a particular course via eLearning, followed by the instructor-led training for practice and hands-on activities. This blended instructional approach is becoming popular in higher education and can help instructional designers address different learning styles as it combines the needs of more traditional learners with the needs of the net generation.

So, to give you an example of a blended learning approach, let's assume an instructional designer needs to create a professional development course for physical therapists. For maximum effectiveness, the course will be divided into two parts. The first part will be delivered via eLearning, and consist of mostly theoretical content. It will include many real-life examples along with high-level games and simulations. The second part will be conducted in the classroom. Participants will complete applicable hands-on activities that will help them acquire psychomotor skills.

Advantages and Disadvantages of ELearning

When stakeholders identify the need for a training course, they often wonder whether they should choose eLearning over traditional learning. As an instructional designer, you should be aware of advantages and disadvantages that eLearning provides and share them with your clients. Some of these advantages include being able to:

- access courses at any time;
- take courses anywhere;
- learn at any pace;
- go back and review course materials as needed.

Although eLearning can be suitable for some courses, it is not always a substitute for traditional classroom training. The disadvantages of eLearning include:

- low retention levels by learners with limited motivation;
- lack of immediate assistance when ambiguous information is presented; and
- low computer literacy may prevent learners from fully benefitting from the learning experience.

While the development of eLearning is much more expensive than the development of classroom training solutions, the implementation costs are significantly lower than those for the instructor-led training (ILT). For classroom training, some of the implementation costs are typically associated with paying the trainer, renting a training room, printing hard copies of all course materials, and many more. Alternatively, expenses associated with implementation of eLearning are typically limited to the costs of web servers and technical support.

When Will ELearning Work?

The questions below should help you determine whether eLearning is the appropriate solution for the content and requirements that stakeholders provide.

- What types of skills does the training address?
- What are the goals of the training?
- What is the motivation level of your target audience?
- What is the learners' level of computer literacy?
- Which generation do most learners come from?
- What is the geographic location of your learners?
- How many learners will the training course target?
- How much money is available for the training?

Exercise 1

Your company has just signed a contract to develop an eLearning course for the department of finance in a large business firm. Your program manager has assigned this project to you. The client wants to train employees on a new salary-calculating tool. The stakeholders believe that they know exactly what they need and do not want you to spend time, money, or resources on needs analysis. You have six months to complete the project. Based on the information you have so far, which approach (synchronous, asynchronous, or blended) should you most likely use, and why?

Chapter 2:
Instructional Design History

This chapter will cover:

- Evolution of instructional design
- Major contributors to the field of instructional design
- Innovations in the ISD field

The study of how people learn began with Ebbinghaus and Pavlov's studies on the effects of classical conditioning and how people forget. Then, B.F. Skinner, an American psychologist and behaviorist, built upon their studies and developed the behaviorist approach to learning. Well-known psychologists, including Piaget and Vygotsky, studied learners' development stages as well as the cognitive processes associated with learning. As a result of their studies, the cognitive theory of learning evolved. This theory included the role of metacognition and the importance of connecting learners' background knowledge with newly acquired knowledge.

Even though the aforementioned psychologists played a vital role in the development of ISD, actual instructional design is a fairly new field. It was founded during World War II when the U.S. military needed to mass train people to perform complex technical tasks as quickly as possible. Training programs created for these people were based on B.F. Skinner's theory on operant conditioning and observable behaviors. Specifically, large tasks were broken down into subtasks. Then, each subtask was treated as a separate learning objective. The training focused on rewarding correct performance and remediating incorrect performance. Many researchers, psychologists, and educators worked together to create an efficient and effective training program. Together, they discovered the importance of designing a form of instruction that met learners' needs. After the war, many of these researchers continued their work and developed a systematic approach to learning. This approach included the three major aspects of course design – analysis, design, and evaluation – which became the foundation for the popular ADDIE model.

Later, in the late 1950s and early 1960s, B.F. Skinner's studies on learning influenced instructional design. Short, to-the-point lessons with frequent questions and instant feedback were introduced into the education. Because these lessons were measurable and could easily be revised based on the assessments, formative evaluation became part of the design process. This behavioristic approach to learning required clear, instructional objectives. Robert Mager taught educators how to write measurable and observable objectives. Later, Benjamin Bloom used Mager's guide to develop his taxonomies of learning. He created key verbs for instructors to use when writing objectives, known as Bloom's taxonomy. The purpose of these verbs is to help learners move toward the highest possible learning domain.

Robert Gagné also played an important role in instructional design. His work described the five domains of learning outcomes, including verbal information, intellectual skills, attitudes, motor skills, and cognitive strategies. He then determined specific conditions for each of these domains.

Additionally, Gagné developed the Nine Events of Instructions, which became a major part of effective lesson design.

As time went on, other theories emerged. Educators and researchers created their own instructional theories for developing effective learning materials. Some of the popular models that emerged as a result of their efforts are the Dick and Carey Systems Approach to instructional design, and the Seels and Glasgow ISD model.

With the emergence of the computer age, instructional design experienced major changes that resulted in new theories, models, and learning modes. Many organizations decided that traditional learning was no longer the answer to their training needs. They wanted their learners to have access to training at any time and any place. Therefore, they began using eLearning and blended learning approaches.

Today, more and more people use social networking tools such as Facebook, Twitter, and LinkedIn not only for socializing, but also for education purposes. It is becoming obvious that instructional design is an ever-changing field highly dependent upon technological innovations.

Chapter 3:
Instructional Design Models

This chapter will cover:

- ADDIE model
- Seels and Glasgow ISD model
- Dick and Carey Systems Approach model
- ASSURE model
- Rapid ISD model
- Four-Door (4D) ELearning model
- SAM model

There are as many instructional design theories, techniques, and models as there are instructional designers. This chapter describes the most popular ones.

As you read, please keep in mind that top instructional designers do not adhere to any one approach, but instead choose whatever technique best suits the specifics of a course's audience and content.

The ADDIE Model

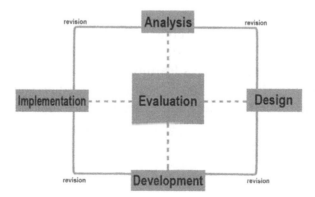

ADDIE is the classic model. All other instructional design models are rooted in the ADDIE model. While critics of the model state that the design is too linear, it still remains the most popular model among instructional designers. ADDIE stands for

A- *Analysis*

D - *Design*

D - *Development*

I - *Implementation*

E - *Evaluation*

In the *Analysis* phase you clarify problems, define goals and objectives, and collect necessary data. You also define audience characteristics, the content to be included, the learning environment, and the technical requirements. For example, you may find that training is not the best solution for the problems you have been asked to solve; or that computer-based training will be a better fit for your audience than web-based training. Your findings might not meet your stakeholders' expectations, so it is important to capture the details of your research and back up your training suggestions with solid data.

In the *Design* phase you write objectives, and craft the structure and sequencing of the course. You also create a project management plan with deadlines, milestones, implementation details, and possibly budgeting. When you are done, you will have a blueprint for your course and its delivery methods.

In the *Development* phase, you bring your design to life by using text, storyboards, graphics, audio, and/or video, and by assembling all these elements into a compelling course.

In the *Implementation* phase, your course is delivered to its audience.

And, in the *Evaluation* phase, the effectiveness of your course is assessed by measuring the level of your audience's learning and retention, as well as how well your project's goals have been met. Although this is the final stage of the ADDIE model, you should actually be performing evaluation throughout the design process.

Seels and Glasgow ISD Model

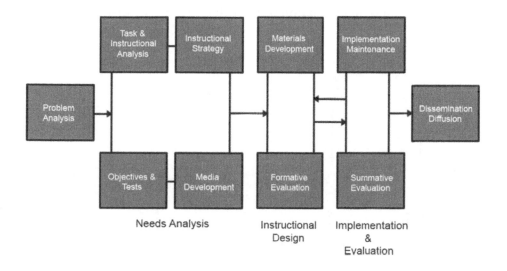

The *Seels and Glasgow ISD model* places design within the context of project management to ensure a course stays within time and budget constraints. Under this model, you conduct front-end analysis, develop the course, and perform evaluations.

The Seels and Glasgow ISD model consists of three phases:

- *Needs Analysis Management Phase* – Analyzing and documenting instructional requirements and goals.
- *Instructional Design Management Phase* – Formulating instructional strategies, breaking down development into tasks, selecting delivery systems, and performing formative evaluations.
- *Implementation and Evaluation Management Phase* – Developing and producing the course materials, delivering, and evaluating the results of the course.

Dick and Carey Systems Approach Model

The *Dick and Carey Systems Approach model* focuses on selecting and organizing the appropriate content for each module. This model incorporates the learner's needs, skills, and learning context into the course design. The Dick and Carey Systems Approach is based on theoretical principles of learning and Robert

Gagné's conditions of learning. This model is widely implemented by curriculum developers in higher education.

The Dick and Carey Systems Approach is composed of ten steps, which include nine basic steps and an evaluation of the effectiveness of instruction.

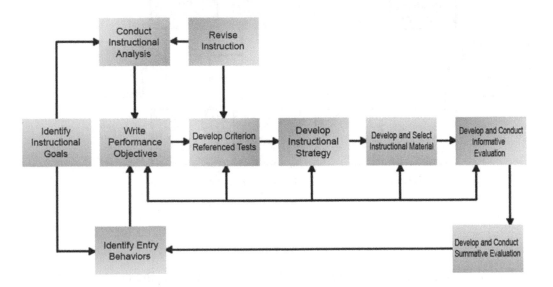

Step 1– During the first step, you conduct needs assessment to identify instructional goals.

Step 2– Instructional Analyses are conducted to determine the skills and knowledge required for the goal.

Step 3 – During the third step you analyze learners in terms of skills, attitudes, prior knowledge, and motivation.

Step 4 – After collecting and analyzing all the required information, you begin writing performance objectives specifying the skills, the conditions, and the criteria for learning.

Step 5 – The fifth step involves the development of assessment instruments.

Step 6 – The sixth step requires you to develop an instructional strategy for presenting the information, testing, and learning activities.

Step 7 – Now that there is strategy in place, you can develop and produce instruction.

Step 8 – The eighth step involves collecting data for conducting a formative evaluation.

Step 9 – The ninth step requires you to revise the lesson using the data collected from the formative evaluation, analysis, objectives, assessment instruments, and instructional strategies and content.

Step 10 – The final step involves conducting a summative evaluation to measure success of the instruction.

ASSURE Model

The *ASSURE model*, developed by Heinich, Molenda, Russell, and Smaldino, is based on Gagné's Nine Events of Instruction. The model assumes that the course design uses different types of media and is especially useful for designing eLearning courses. ASSURE stands for:

A - Analyze Learners – You research the general characteristics of learners, including their gender and age. Additionally, you learn more about participants' learning styles and preferences focusing on the motivational aspects of learning.

S - State Objectives – You develop specific and measurable objectives for the course.

S - Select Media and Materials – You select the materials and media for the course and develop and modify already existing materials.

U - Utilize Media and Materials – You implement the selected materials. However, prior to the implementation, you should pilot test them to ensure that the selections meet your objectives. In this phase, you also confirm that the course works the way it should and that the learners can easily access all materials.

R- Require Learner Participation – You elicit participation. You can do this through discussions, games, simulations, or assessments. You should ensure that all the activities allow learners to apply their knowledge and understanding of the content.

E- Evaluate and Revise – You evaluate whether or not the objectives were met. You can do this by revisiting presentation methods to see if the media and materials selected are appropriate for the lesson. After conducting a thorough evaluation, you should consider editing your materials and revising the course based on your findings during this process.

Rapid ISD Model

Today, instructional designers are searching for ways to create their courses quickly and effectively. At the same time, they want the learning to be engaging and interactive. The *Accelerated Learning Rapid Instructional Design (RID)*

Model, created by David Meier, is ideal for those who work with tight deadlines, a limited budget, and constantly changing content. This model is all about accelerated learning design strategies and shortcuts. Meier believes that traditional ISD models are too time-consuming and controlling. He also believes that these models are presentation-based rather than activity-based. According to RID, people learn more from application with feedback than from presentations. It replaces media-heavy courses with activity-based courses. Even though the RID model makes courses more interactive and engaging, it does not incorporate analysis and evaluation phases, which are crucial in the development of an eLearning course. There are four phases in the RID model.

- *Preparation* – Arouse interest and motivate learners by stating goals and removing learners' barriers
- *Presentation* – Encounter new knowledge and skills by appealing to all learning styles and incorporating interactive presentations and discovery activities into the learning experience
- *Practice* – Integrate new knowledge and skills by incorporating games, hands-on activities, and skill building practice exercises as well as providing substantial corrective feedback to the learner
- *Performance* – Allow time to apply the new knowledge and skills and reward the use of these skills.

The Four-Door (4D) ELearning Model

The *Four-Door (4D) ELearning Model* was developed by Dr. Sivasailam "Thiagi" Thiagarajan. This is a simple model that allows professionals to develop eLearning courses cheaply and rapidly while addressing different types of learners. According to this model, learners have full control of course navigation. The four doors in this model are the Library, Café, Playground, and Evaluation Center. However, you can change these names depending on the training needs. Learners can enter any of the doors they want based on their personal preference, background knowledge, and experience.

Library – In this area, learners will find all the information and resources they need to master objectives and to complete the assessment. Some of the materials that can be found here are presentations, slideshows, videos, and audio recordings.

Café – The social learning takes place here. Discussion boards, blogs, and wikis are types of tools found in the café. This area includes open-ended questions that help learners apply content presented in the library.

Playground – In this area, learners can play games to recall and apply the content they learned in the Library. The games can be played as many times as necessary until the content is mastered.

Evaluation Center – In this area, learners take assessments and performance tests. Most of the time, instead of giving regular assessments with multiple choice questions, learners have to complete real assignments related to the job.

Successive Approximation Model (SAM)

Successive Approximation Model (SAM) is an agile instructional design model created by Michael Allen, a recognized pioneer and leader in the design of interactive multimedia learning tools and applications. The model emphasizes collaboration, efficiency, and repetition. According to Allen, there is no perfect project; therefore, to create the best possible outcome, instructional designers should focus on producing usable products as quickly as possible. The model focuses on prototyping more heavily than other instructional design models do. With SAM, the goal is to take smaller, more flexible steps within a larger framework to achieve high quality in training and learning, as opposed to following the step-by-step process. SAM expects that mistakes will be made throughout the project. It also expects that stakeholders will change their minds or decide to make corrections along the way. Because of all these issues, SAM considers collaboration and early evaluation important to successful completion of any project. The model enables instructional designers to move quickly through the initial phases of course design to a rapid prototyping. There are essentially two SAM models.

SAM1 is for small simple projects that do not require extensive development or any specialized skills such as programming or graphic design. SAM 1 is composed of the following three steps:

- *Evaluation / Analysis*
- *Design*
- *Development*

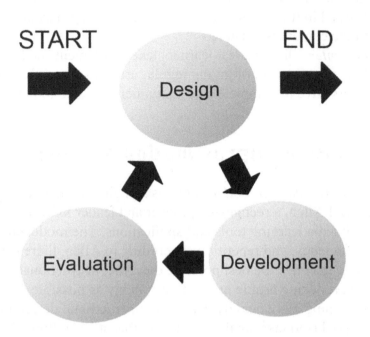

The process cycles through three iterations, modifying and testing prototypes along the way. Because ideas are frequently evaluated, instructional designers can create usable courses relatively quickly and effectively while avoiding costly mistakes.

SAM 2 is for large projects that require advanced development skills. This model is divided into the following three phases:

- *Preparation Phase* – Instructional designers gather background information and brainstorm ideas about the project together with stakeholders and their entire team.

- *Iterative Design Phase* – Further broken into the following three steps:

    - *Prototype*
    - *Evaluate*
    - *Design*

During this phase, instructional designers and their teams rotate through design, prototype, and review, making decisions and refining their prototype prior to making critical mistakes.

- *Iterative Development Phase* – Further broken into the following three steps:

  - *Develop*
  - *Implement*
  - *Evaluate*

The Iterative Development phase begins with the design proof, and produces three deliverables known as alpha, beta, and gold releases.

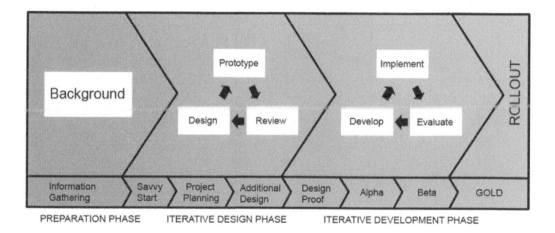

Exercise 2

Select an instructional design model for your new salary-calculating tool training course. Explain why you think the model you selected fits your project's needs.

Chapter 4:
Learning Theories

This chapter will cover:

- The principles of behaviorism, cognitivism, and constructivism
- The concept of andragogy
- Malcolm Knowles's six principles of adult learning

While Instructional Systems Design (ISD) models are essential tools that help instructional designers create effective courses, knowing how to apply learning theories to course design is equally important. There are three learning theories typically addressed within the scope of effective instructional design. These theories are behaviorism, cognitivism, and constructivism. Each learning theory has its strengths and weaknesses; therefore, to choose the theory that suits the needs of a specific course, you should take multiple aspects of learning into consideration, including your goals, learners, and situations.

Behaviorism

Behaviorism is based on observable and measurable changes in behavior. It assumes that the learner's behavior is shaped through positive or negative reinforcement. Both positive and negative reinforcement increase the probability that the behavior will reoccur. Punishment, on the other hand, decreases the likelihood that the behavior will happen again.

So, what role does behaviorisms play in instructional design? The development of objectives is the main area where behaviorism affects instructional design. According to behaviorists, objectives indicate whether learners mastered the knowledge presented in the course. In other words, if the learner mastered the objectives, then their behavior changed, and learning took place.

Cognitivism

According to cognitivists, learning involves the reorganization of experiences. It is considered an active learning process. Cognitivism assumes that an existing knowledge structure is used to process new information. This theory believes that the information is received, stored, and retrieved. When cognitivists design their courses, they focus primarily on the learner. As opposed to behaviorists, who focus mainly on learning objectives, cognitivists concentrate on making learning meaningful through using learners' background knowledge. Cognitivists also believe that it is easier to remember items mentioned at the beginning or at the end rather than somewhere in the middle. Therefore, instructional designers who follow this theory focus on presenting the "must-know" content both at the beginning and at the end of the course.

Constructivism

Constructivists focus on how learners construct knowledge based on prior experience. They believe in experiential, self-directed learning. Therefore, instructional designers who follow this theory should understand what learners bring to the table in terms of prior knowledge and interests.

Adult Learning Theories

To create truly beneficial training courses, you need to understand adult learning theories and methodologies. Andragogy, or adult learning, is an adult learning theory that describes assumptions about the learners. The concept of andragogy was pioneered by Malcolm Knowles, a theorist of adult education. He defined andragogy as "the art and science of helping adults learn." Knowles identified six principles of adult learning. According to him:

Adults are internally motivated. Typical adult learners are satisfied with such extrinsic motivators as promotions and bonuses. However, satisfying intrinsic motivators such as self-esteem, power, and achievement is equally important. As an instructional designer, you should create learning activities that nourish those intrinsic motivators by demonstrating how the new knowledge and skills would be beneficial for the job.

Adults bring life experiences to new learning situations. Adults have more experience than young learners do. Most adult learners bring a lot of experience to the training, and apply this background knowledge to the new learning that they acquire. Your training activities should reflect the actual work the learners perform and provide exercises that allow learners to apply their prior knowledge and experience to the theoretical aspects of the training.

Adults are goal-oriented. Adults must have a need for learning. If an employee is expected to have certain skills or knowledge, the level of interest in training will be higher than if the same skill is not required for successful job performance. Providing just-in-time training is very important for the success of the course.

Adults are relevancy-oriented. Adults must know the reason for learning. They want to know the benefits of acquiring, and the cost of not acquiring new knowledge. For this exact reason, you should base your courses on the intended audience and include all objectives and goal statements in the lesson plans and activities as well as on real work experiences.

Adults are practical. Adults have a task-centered orientation to learning. Most school-age children have a subject-centered orientation to learning and focus on the content just to pass the test. Additionally, most children are not interested in retaining the information they learned in class. The ultimate goal for adult learners, however, is to retain as much information as possible from the training course; therefore, adults seek task-centered training experiences. If you satisfy this need and develop your courses around problem solving, then adult learners will most likely learn the content with the intention of actually applying it to the job. Your eLearning courses should allow learners to solve problems or perform tasks similar to those encountered on the job. This can be done through games, simulations, and various problem-solving activities. It is important to avoid information dumping and design activities that focus on practicing the information rather than simply memorizing it.

Adults like to be respected. Adults like to be self-directing. In other words, they need other people, such as management, to see that they are capable of taking responsibility for themselves. Incorporating "search and discovery" elements in training courses can address this need.

Exercise 3

Explain how you will adhere to the six principles of adult learning in your new salary-calculating tool course.

Chapter 5:
Learning Styles

This chapter will cover:

- The VAK model
- David Kolb's Four Learning Styles
- Howard Gardner's Nine Multiple Intelligences
- Generational learning styles
- Presentation methods that address multiple learning styles

Targeting as many learning styles as possible is necessary for designing solid eLearning experiences. Even though all people have a preferred learning style, to maximize the efficiency and quality of learning, all learners must be exposed to all learning styles to one extent or another.

VAK Model

To better process new information or learn a new skill, one must hear it, see it, or try it. Most learners' preferences fall into one of the three categories. There are people who learn better through seeing; there are also people who prefer to learn by hearing; yet, there are other learners who must do hands-on activities to understand and retain new information. These three learning preferences are known as the visual, auditory, and kinesthetic learning styles and are part of the VAK model.

- *Visual Learning Style* – These learners learn best by seeing. If you design courses that have no visual aids, they will be lost. In order to satisfy visual learners, you should include images, handouts, videos, slides, and demonstrations in your courses.

- *Auditory Learning Style* – As opposed to visual learners, auditory learners understand and retain information by hearing it. To accommodate their needs, you should include lectures, discussion groups, and presentations as part of your course design.

- *Kinesthetic Learning Style* – Kinesthetic learners learn best by doing. To accommodate these learners, you should consider adding hands-on activities to your courses. You may also incorporate board games, experiments, and role-plays in your training.

To ensure better retention among learners, you should accommodate all three learning styles by adding at least one activity that fits each style.

David Kolb's Four Learning Styles

David Kolb, an American educational theorist, developed the learning style inventory. His inventory is comprised of a four-stage cycle of learning and four learning styles. The stages of Kolb's learning cycle are as follows:

- *Concrete Experience* – These learners are intuitive, they take an artistic approach to learning, are open-minded, and do not like structure. To accommodate these learners, training instructors or eLearning presenters should serve as motivators.

- *Reflective Observation* – These learners are good at understanding different points of view, they understand the meaning of situations by observing and describing them. To accommodate these learners, training instructors or eLearning presenters should serve as experts.

- *Abstract Conceptualization* – These learners analyze information to formulate theories and take a scientific, systematic approach. To accommodate these learners, training instructors or eLearning presenters should serve as coaches.

- *Active Experimentation* – These learners like to learn actively. To accommodate these learners, training instructors or eLearning presenters should serve as facilitators and allow them to learn through experimentation and discovery.

Based on the four-stage cycle, Kolb developed the following learning styles:

- *Convergers* – Prefer to learn through games and simulations
- *Divergers* – Prefer to learn through hands-on exploration followed by constructive feedback
- *Assimilators* – Prefer to learn through lectures, experiments, and conceptual models
- *Accomodators* – Prefer to learn through hands-on activities, presentations, role-plays, and debates

Howard Gardner's Nine Multiple Intelligences

The psychologist Dr. Howard Gardner pioneered the Multiple Intelligences theory. Based on his theory, people are born with certain aptitudes for learning new information and solving problems. According to Gardner, most people are only comfortable in three or four intelligences.

The table below lists and describes these intelligences and learners' preferences for each one of them.

Table 1 Howard Gardner's Nine Multiple Intelligences

Intelligence	Description	Learners' Preferences
Linguistic Intelligence	Aptitude for writing and speaking	Learners prefer to learn through written and oral communication.
Logical/Mathematical Intelligence	Aptitude for math and logic	Learners prefer to learn through logical analysis, strategizing, and creating a process.
Musical Rhythmic Intelligence	Aptitude for music and sounds	Learners prefer to learn through music and sounds.
Bodily/Kinesthetic Intelligence	Aptitude for physical movement	Learners prefer to learn through movement, touch, and feel as well as through physical experience.

Spatial/Visual Intelligence	Aptitude for visualizing things	Learners prefer to learn through images, shapes, and visual designs.
Naturalistic Intelligence	Aptitude for being with nature	Learners prefer to learn through working with living things as well as with different features of the natural world. This aptitude is especially valuable among biologists, botanists, and farmers.
Intrapersonal Intelligence	Aptitude for working alone	Learners with this aptitude learn best through self-discovery.
Interpersonal Intelligence	Aptitude for working with others	Learners prefer to learn through team work and communication.
Existential Intelligence	Aptitude for understanding one's purpose	Learners prefer to learn through posing and answering questions about existential realities such as life and death.

While it is not always possible to address all of these intelligences in one lesson, you should aim towards including activities for as many intelligences as possible. For example, you can create both oral and written activities that require learners to "think outside the box" and analyze the information presented in the lesson. You can encourage collaboration through setting aside time for group work or participation in chats or forums. Presenting information visually through images, diagrams, skits, and videos can also help you address the needs of learners. At the end of each lesson, you should consider providing written summary of main points, keeping in mind that learners may interpret the same concept differently based on their background knowledge and skills. Providing clear objectives and evaluation methods at the beginning of the training can minimize misinterpretation of the intended message in the lesson. Whenever possible, consider giving your learners an option between writing, illustrating, or giving an oral report on the same topic.

Generational Learning Styles

Cultural changes influence people's tastes, preferences, and beliefs. As a result, a generational gap between older and younger generations occurs. Because of a rapidly changing culture and wide generational gap, instructional designers have realized the need for taking different generational learning styles into consideration. While all generations are able to learn through a variety of media, each generation has certain preferences. The four generational learning styles are

- Traditionalists
- Baby Boomers
- Generations X
- Generations Y or Millennials

The table below illustrates the learning preferences of each generation.

Table 2 Generational Learning Styles

Traditionalists	Baby Boomers	Generations X	Generations Y or Millennials
• Ages 66 and over • Prefer learning through lectures • Dislike role-plays and games	• Ages 47-65 • Like to learn through lectures and workshops • Enjoy small group activities	• Ages 29-46 • Prefer eLearning to traditional learning • Enjoy experiential learning activities • Prefer self-studying	• Ages 18-28 • Prefer eLearning to traditional learning • Prefer hands-on learning • Prefer learning through social networking tools such as wikis, blogs, podcasts, and mobile applications.

As an instructional designer, one of the main challenges that you will face is creating a successful learning experience geared towards all generations. While it is nearly impossible to create one perfect solution that would close the gap between generations, there are certainly ways to build courses that satisfy most learners' needs. Understanding the VAK model is one way to cover the needs of most generations. According to studies, traditionalists prefer an auditory approach to learning because most of them grew up listening to the radio. Baby Boomers, on the other hand, prefer visuals because they grew up watching TV. Most learners who fall under Generation X and Y are both kinesthetic and visual as they grew up playing video games, writing emails, and using different types of social media tools such as Facebook and Twitter. As you create your courses, you should consider incorporating a variety of activities that appeal to all learning styles. Additionally, you should focus on making your courses meaningful by choosing a blended approach to learning and mixing strategies to accommodate both younger and older generations.

Exercise 4

What types of activities will you include in your eLearning course to ensure that you address the auditory, visual, kinesthetic, and generational learning styles?

Chapter 6:
Motivation

This chapter will cover:

- Intrinsic and extrinsic motivation
- Abraham Maslow's Hierarchy of Needs and its influence on training courses
- The WIIFM principle
- John Keller's ARCS Model of Motivational Design and its application to course design

Designing highly motivational learning experiences is the challenge that most instructional designers face. After all, each learner has different goals, desires, and needs. Therefore, creating a course that motivates all learners is nearly impossible. However, certain aspects of motivation must be considered to ensure the effectiveness of course design. Motivation can be either intrinsic or extrinsic. Intrinsic motivation refers to internal drives. Specifically, learners take the course because they enjoy it or because they want to develop a particular skill. This is the type of motivation you should aim for when creating your courses. Extrinsic motivation, on the other hand, refers to performing activities to get something in exchange such as monetary rewards, certificates, or good grades.

Abraham Maslow's Hierarchy of Needs

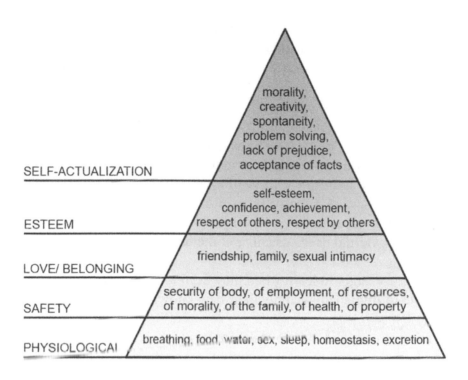

Abraham Maslow is known for developing a hierarchy of human needs. According to Maslow, five basic human needs must be satisfied in order for internal motivation to occur. *Physiological needs* are considered the lower level needs and must be met first. They include the need for food and sleep. *Safety needs* come into play when all the physiological needs are met. When both physiological and safety needs are satisfied, the *need to belong* becomes important. This involves the need for family and friends as well as the need to feel like one belongs somewhere. Typical eLearning courses satisfy the need to belong by offering a safe environment for answering questions, receiving feedback, and making decisions. Once the lower levels have been satisfied, the *need for esteem* surfaces. This involves the need to be highly regarded by others. Finally, when all four levels are completely satisfied, people begin looking for *self-actualization*, or the need to be "all that they can be."

Even if you create the most fascinating course, if learners' physiological needs are not met, they will not gain much from it. This is why it is highly recommended that learners get enough sleep and eat a good breakfast prior to the training. Establishing a safe learning environment is an important factor in training success. Additionally, the learning environment should satisfy participants' needs to belong. Learners also expect to be respected by the trainer and other participants. Once the training is completed, learners expect to be able to utilize their newly acquired knowledge to grow on either a personal or professional level. In other words, the need for self-actualization typically takes place after completing the training course.

When designing, consider motivation, goals, experience, and culture of learners as these four elements play a crucial role in course development. Successful trainings are designed with the question *What's in it for me?* or *WIIFM*, in mind. You should aim to combine internal and external needs and motivators. Internal motivators arise from the sense of accomplishment people feel from learning something new. Alternatively, external motivators are associated with tangible outcomes such as money or awards. Creating training courses that satisfy both internal and external needs usually get the best results and receive good evaluations.

Most adults are eager to learn when they need to achieve a goal. Adult learners want to be able to immediately apply their new knowledge and skills to real-life situations.

As we have already discussed, adult learners bring a lot of experience and background knowledge and expect to apply them to the new material. Most adults are kinesthetic learners; therefore, whenever possible, you should incorporate hands-on activities into your lessons.

Even if you take WIIFM, goals, and experience into consideration, the course will not be successful unless cultural aspects are incorporated into the design. It is important to remember that designing training requires a lot of initial research as organizational culture varies from department to department, and even from team to team.

ARCS Model

John Keller's ARCS Model of Motivational Design is a systematic approach to designing motivational learning. It consists of the following four steps for promoting motivation in the learning process:

- *Attention* – Elicit learners' interest and curiosity
- *Relevance* – Show the importance and usefulness of the content
- *Confidence* – Include challenging but doable activities
- *Satisfaction* – Make the overall experience positive and worthwhile

The table below illustrates how you can apply the steps from the ARCS model.

Table 3 ARCS Model

Attention	Relevance	Confidence	Satisfaction
• Include games and role-plays • Use a variety of presentation methods • Use a small amount of humor • Add visuals • Ask questions • Have learners solve problems	• Use examples that learners are familiar with • Provide reasons why the content is relevant • Explain learning goals • Ask about learners' goals	• Provide performance requirements and evaluation • Provide feedback • Allow learners to control their learning	• Reward learners • Provide opportunities to practice what has been learned • Provide reinforcement

Even the most interesting and useful content will neither increase learners' motivation nor guarantee information retention. While instructional designers have no control over learners' motivation, they do have control over the design of their course. Providing motivational rewards such as giving an opportunity to move to the next section of the course after successful completion of the first section or even allowing learners to take a pre-test to determine whether they can go directly to the next level can work effectively. Adult learners do not like to take eLearning courses that have absolutely no value for them. Therefore, by clearly outlining the benefits associated with taking the course, learners' success levels will increase. That is why providing learning objectives at the beginning of the course and asking thought-provoking questions enable learners to clearly see the benefit of taking the course. Evaluating learners' performance and providing constructive feedback are also ways to motivate learners. Obviously, the content will determine which elements to incorporate into the course to increase its motivational value.

Exercise 5

Think about the motivational factor in your eLearning course. How will you address each level of Maslow's hierarchy of needs? Using the ARCS model, think of some motivational activities to include in your course.

Chapter 7:
Memory

This chapter will cover:

- The role memory plays in learning
- Long-term, short-term, and working memory
- George Miller's magical number
- Cognitive load theory and ways to avoid it in your course design

---

The ultimate goal of any training course is performance improvement. Understanding how memory works and designing eLearning courses accordingly is a big step towards that ultimate goal. If, at the end of the course, learners do not remember a single thing, then learning has not taken place, performance has not improved, and the course design was ineffective. To design truly effective courses, you need to understand the characteristics of memory.

Short-term memory refers to "the temporary storage for manipulation and processing of information." According to George Miller's magical number, "seven, plus or minus two," short-term memory is only able to hold about seven bits of information. To ensure better retention, it is best to break lessons up so that they contain even fewer pieces of content. The exact amount of information provided in the course should depend on the content and its complexity. For instance, most people can remember numbers more easily than words. Therefore, if the course requires learners to memorize numbers, you can create lessons that contain as many as seven pieces of information. On the other hand, if the lesson requires memorization or retention of terminology, smaller lessons featuring only four bits of information should be created. Each time new information is presented, it is temporarily stored in the short-term memory. Thereafter, it can either be encoded into long-term memory or completely disappear from the memory. Whether or not learners retain the content from the lesson depends on the lesson design. Experienced instructional designers always aim to avoid cognitive overload and create interactive and memorable learning experiences.

Cognitive Load

Cognitive load theory states that traditional instructional techniques can load working memory. However, the point at which cognitive overload occurs depends on each individual's experience, background, and age. John Sweller, an Australian educational psychologist, developed cognitive load theory or CLT, a set of principles proven to result in better course design. This theory is the scientific basis for efficiency in learning and it applies to all learners and delivery methods. Information overload is a serious issue when it comes to learning, as it causes poor retention. For example, a medical student who crams the information for the exam and forgets it quickly afterwards will not be able to accurately diagnose his patients. Today, many organizations want instructional designers to create quick training solutions for their employees. Most of the time, clients are set on a specific type of training without ever realizing that there are better solutions to their problem. Keep in mind that most stakeholders do not know much about effective instructional design principles, and the only desire they have is to reach their ultimate goal, which is improve their employees' performance. Performance improvement can mean increased sales, better customer service, or anything else pertinent to a particular organization. What clients do not realize is that retention and mastery of skills and information is the real solution to performance improvement.

When you design learning experiences, there are three types of cognitive loads that should be considered. These types are intrinsic load, germane load, and extraneous load. To maximize learning efficiency, you, as an instructional designer, should find a good balance between all three of them.

Intrinsic load – Determined by instructional goals and element of interactivity. For example, if you are teaching French and want your students to learn vocabulary, the element of interactivity is low. Therefore, the intrinsic load is also low. Remember the "seven, plus or minus two" rule, and keep in mind that shorter words are easier to remember, while longer words may require greater effort from learners. After learners memorize the words, they are ready to begin constructing sentences using these words. In addition to retrieving the newly acquired vocabulary words from memory, your learners will have to apply what they know about sentence structure and grammar in French. Now, learners know vocabulary words and can construct sentences. The next goal is to have them carry out a conversation in French using correct vocabulary, sentence structure, and grammar. At this point, the intrinsic cognitive load becomes even greater as the learner has to be able to understand the question quickly, and come up with the answer in French using appropriate vocabulary, grammar, and pronunciation. As a result, the element of interactivity becomes significantly higher. What does this mean for the instructional designer? Simply put, in order for your lesson to be effective, it needs to be split into small segments. Creating a number of relevant prerequisite tasks and distributing them over the lessons can help instructional designers break information into manageable pieces.

Germane load – The germane load is the demand placed on short-term memory while the learner obtains new knowledge and skills. A germane cognitive load is one of the most effective cognitive loads, primarily because it requires learners to successfully construct schemata. A schema, or schemata, is a term used in cognitive psychology that describes structures that organize our knowledge about something for interpreting and processing information.

Extraneous load – Also known as irrelevant load, is the third type of cognitive load, which refers to unnecessary information that wastes mental resources. Everything that distracts learners from the main objective is part of the extraneous load.

Finding a balance between all three types of cognitive loads is key to effective course design. However, you should always aim towards maximizing the germane cognitive load and minimizing the extraneous, or irrelevant, cognitive load.

John Sweller has recommended guidelines for reducing the cognitive load. According to him, when designing courses, you need to focus primarily on objectives and avoid adding "filler" information. One way to lower the cognitive load is to remove irrelevant visual elements. Moreover, when designing courses, you should break information into meaningful portions less than thirty minutes in length. If there is a lot of the *must-know* content, spreading it throughout different modules or lessons can be beneficial. Additionally, when you create simulations or multiple choice questions, try to limit the number of options. This will eliminate unnecessary mental work for learners and consequently lower their cognitive load. When designing eLearning courses, consider dividing content into beginning and expert level sections. This way, the expert level learners will not have to go through extensive examples that increase their cognitive load, and novice learners will get all the necessary exposure to step-by-step explanations and examples.

Long-Term Memory

Long-term memory is the target destination where newly acquired knowledge assimilates. The information is stored permanently here. One of the main roles of long-term memory is providing the background knowledge needed to understand new concepts. This is done through the retrieval of appropriate information from long-term memory into short-term memory. Encoding, storage, and retrieval are the three operations that long-term memory performs. Encoding is when new information is transferred to long-term memory. Storage is when the information is stored into the long-term memory, and retrieval is when the information is actually activated and used.

So, what are some ways to enhance encoding and retrieval of information from the long-term memory? The answer is repetition, repetition, repetition. You should structure your courses in ways that force learners to tie that information together and create mental images of the material. Additionally, consider distributing practice activities throughout the lesson as opposed to placing them at the end of the module. If the course is separated into multiple chunks, offering practice in each module can help learners put information from each individual module into perspective. Some of the best ways to repeat important points include:

- showing a video that explains the concept;
- adding a case study or a skit to the lesson;
- presenting the information in a form of graph; and
- paraphrasing or finding another way to explain the same idea.

Another way to ensure the content presented in the course makes its way to the long-term memory is by offering quizzes and self-checks throughout the lesson. According to Confucius, "I hear and I forget. I see and I remember. I do and I understand." In other words, application is key to successful retention. Quizzes should give learners a chance to apply their knowledge and recall information from the lesson. Adding short *Check Your Knowledge* quizzes after each section of the course as opposed to offering a long test at the end helps with long-term retention.

Exercise 6

Taking George Miller's magical number and short-term memory into consideration, how will you ensure that your learners retain the content presented in the course? How will you find a balance between the intrinsic, germane, and extraneous loads?

Chapter 8:
Six Principles of Effective eLearning

This chapter will cover Ruth Clark's six principles of effective eLearning courses.

When designing eLearning courses, it is important to consider the following six principles developed by Ruth Colvin Clark, an instructional design and workforce learning specialist, and Richard E. Mayer, an American educational psychologist. All of these principles have been researched extensively and are backed up by science. Below is a short overview of them.

Principle 1: Multimedia Principle

According to the multimedia principle, when designing learning experiences, you should use both text and graphics. Relevant graphics help learners understand and organize the material. Courses that have both text and appropriate visuals help learners engage in active learning through constructing and connecting visual and verbal representations of the material.

Principle 2: Contiguity Principle

The contiguity principle states that text should appear near graphics on the screen. When text and images are separated on the screen, learners use their cognitive resources to match them. This creates extraneous processing unrelated to the instructional goal. As a result, learners have less capacity for mentally organizing and integrating the material.

Principle 3: Modality Principle

The modality principle refers to the fact that eLearning courses should have audio narration instead of on-screen text. People have separate processing channels for visual/pictorial processing and for auditory/verbal processing. When learners have to watch something and read it at the same time, their visual channels may become overloaded. For example, when there is a list of steps, it is best to present them visually and add audio to the presentation.

Principle 4: Redundancy Principle

According to the redundancy principle, eLearning courses should not have both on-screen text and audio added to the multimedia presentation. When there is a visual illustration on the screen, it is best to avoid audio narration of the text. On the other hand, when there are no visual illustrations, the information should be presented as both text and audio.

Principle 5: Coherence Principle

The coherence principle refers to adding extraneous visuals, text, and sounds to the eLearning courses. Incorporating these elements distracts the learner and activates irrelevant prior knowledge. Therefore, non-essential visuals, text, and sounds should be avoided. Music is one example of an extraneous sound that distracts learners and promotes emotional as opposed to cognitive interest.

Principle 6: Personalization Principle

This principle states that using first and second person constructions in eLearning courses make them more personable and create a feeling of social presence. To address this principle, you should use a conversational style when scripting your eLearning materials. This will help learners better process the information. As a result, their level of retention will increase.

Exercise 7

Using the six principles for creating effective eLearning materials, decide how you will address them in your eLearning course for the department of finance.

Part II - Designing Instructionally Sound ELearning Courses

"Change is the end result of all true learning."
— Leo Buscaglia

Chapter 9:
Needs Analysis and Data Collection Methods

This chapter will cover:

- The importance of analysis in instructional design
- Audience analysis, performance gap analysis, and task analysis
- Data collection methods and techniques
- Steps in conducting needs analysis

The analysis phase is an essential part of instructional design. After all, without conducting a needs analysis, you have no way of knowing the reason for creating the course. Needs analysis discovers the target audience for the course as well as the true purpose for creating it. Based on data collected during this phase, you will be able to determine the approach you need to take in designing the course. You will also be able to decide on media and delivery method based on the findings. Moreover, the analysis phase will help you figure out what content should be included in the lesson, whether the training is for beginners or more advanced learners, or whether it is just a refreshment or a job aid. In addition to answering all these questions, the analysis phase helps to find out if the training is really a viable solution.

Oftentimes, instructional designers conduct a thorough needs analysis just to realize that there is a performance issue, which cannot be solved by a training course. Alternatively, some instructional designers do not conduct needs analysis at all. This approach can be detrimental to designing an effective solution to a problem. In real life, clients underestimate the value of needs analysis; therefore, they do not dedicate the budget for this phase. If you face this situation, you can either try to convince your client of the importance of doing analysis by explaining the risks associated with avoiding it, or conduct minimal analysis to get the information needed to design the course. Oftentimes, stakeholders already have most of the required information; therefore, conducting extensive needs analysis becomes unnecessary.

There are three major types of analyses. They are:

- audience analysis
- performance analysis
- task analysis

Audience Analysis

Conducting audience analysis is a critical step because knowing your audience is necessary to effectively present training material. Audience analysis should include information on demographics as well as on learners' motivation and background knowledge. Below are some questions you should consider during the audience analysis.

- Who is the target audience for this course?
- What is the average age of learners?
- Are learners mostly men or women?
- What is their cultural background?
- What is their education level?
- What experience do learners have?
- What is their motivation level?
- Why do learners need this course?
- How much time can they devote to training?
- Do they have any specific needs?
- What is their learning preference?

Performance, Gap and Root Cause Analysis

The ultimate goal of an eLearning course is to close the gap between the current and the desired performance. To identify and close that gap, you need to conduct gap analysis. Before conducting gap analysis and identifying the real reason for training, assumptions about training needs and requirements should not be made. Only after carrying out gap analysis will instructional designers be able to draw conclusions and propose solutions. To conduct gap analysis, you should have your goals in place, as they indicate the desired state. Not only should you find a solution to close the existing gap, but you should also figure out the reason the gap exists. By conducting a root cause analysis, you should be able to address the actual root cause of the gap and therefore treat the real problem instead of its symptoms. One of the best ways to collect information about performance gap and root causes is by using the *Five Why Technique*. The essence of this technique is to repeatedly ask *Why* until you arrive at the root cause of the problem.

During the performance gap analysis, you may discover that people in the organization do not achieve the desired performance because they lack necessary knowledge or skills. However, you may also discover that poor performance is due to the lack of motivation, appropriate tools, resources, or organizational support in the company. If your analysis shows that the problem lies in knowledge and skills, then you can safely proceed with training. However, if the problem is with motivation, lack of tools, or organizational support, then it is a performance improvement issue, and training will not be helpful. Training does not solve all problems associated with inadequate information, lack of resources, poor process, or management issues. If, during performance analysis, you discover the problem is not related to knowledge or skills, you should advise the client that even the most innovative training course will not effectively address the need.

Task Analysis

Task analysis identifies knowledge and skills needed to accomplish instructional goals. It helps you describe the tasks and sub-tasks that learners will perform as well as prioritize the sequence of these tasks and create appropriate terminal and enabling objectives based on the results. Below is a list of questions that should be considered during the task analysis.

- What is the complexity of the task?
- How often is the task performed?
- Is the task critical to the performance of the job?
- Is this task performed separately or as part of other tasks?
- What is the relationship between all the tasks?
- What is the risk associated with not being able to perform the task?
- What background knowledge and skills are needed to perform the task?

In addition to performance, audience, and task analyses, there are other types of analyses including instructional, environment, and technical analyses.

The *instructional analysis* breaks down the tasks of each goal and helps designers eliminate extraneous information. To conduct an instructional analysis, ISD specialists should work together with the Subject Matter Expert (SME) designated for that course.

The *resource analysis* collects information on the learning context to ensure that the instructional designer does not go beyond the available resources dedicated to the project.

The *environment analysis* identifies the environment in which the learning should occur. It can range from watching an instructional video to listening to an educational podcast.

Technical analysis identifies technical specifications needed to develop and implement the course.

As you collect specific data about the type of eLearning course the client is looking for, you should consider asking the stakeholder the following questions:

- Is your content already available?
- Do you have any materials developed?
- How many SMEs will work on this project, and what is their availability?
- Do you have already existing visuals that you would like to include in the course?
- How long do you expect this course to be?
- Do you want to include assessments?
- Do you have a Learning Management System? If not, how do you expect the course to be launched? (We will cover Learning Management Systems in Chapter 16.)

Data Collection Methods

There are many information-gathering strategies you can use to conduct your analyses. These strategies range from review of relevant literature and direct observations to conducting interviews and focus groups. All strategies have advantages and disadvantages. The method that suits the specific needs analysis depends on many different factors, including the intensity of analysis and the amount of time dedicated to the analysis. Whenever possible choose several different methods to ensure accurate data collection.

Literature and Document Reviews

When there is no budget for needs analysis, you should at least review relevant documents. This approach is inexpensive compared to most other methods and provides the background information necessary for carrying out a project. However, before choosing this method, it is necessary to understand that the information found in documents can be outdated, inaccurate, incomplete and disorganized.

Observations

This is an excellent way to collect data when the training goal is to teach a new skill or change a behavior. You can simply sit and observe the performance of the best, average, and worst employees in the organization. Then, document your observations of both the current and desired performance. The observation method works well primarily because it allows instructional designers to see for themselves what people do and how they perform. However, there are also disadvantages to this method. One of them is that people typically perform better when they know they are being observed.

Interviews

Interviews work very well for gathering information about current business needs, performance, and audience analyses. They are also useful for gathering stories for learning scenarios and simulations. The interviewing method can help you clarify confusing information collected by either observations or literature reviews. Unlike observations, interviews can be done over the phone, which is very convenient for both you and your interviewee. The main problem with interviews, however, is that they can be biased as they rely on the reactions and opinions of respondents. Further drawbacks to interviews are that they can be costly and time consuming.

Focus Groups

Focus groups are a good way to collect information from many different people without meeting with each one of them individually. Using this data gathering method has many of the same advantages and disadvantages as interviews. In addition to being resource intensive, it takes a lot of time to analyze the information gathered from the entire group. Therefore, it is best to limit focus groups to ten participants. Moreover, there are typically participants who dominate the discussion, leaving the opinions of less outspoken group members unheard. The most important drawback to focus groups is the lack of anonymity, which can lead participants to not sharing their opinions.

Surveys

Surveys are the most commonly used tool for conducting needs analysis. Surveys vary greatly in the amount of time and money they require. While they can help instructional designers obtain both qualitative and quantitative data, there are still many problems associated with them. First, oftentimes people mark their answers without even reading the questions. As a result, data gathered from this source is not always precise. Surveys also require clear and accurate wording of each question. In interviews and focus groups, participants have an opportunity to clarify questions, and instructional designers can even provide examples that describe the meaning of each question. With surveys, participants do not have the luxury of asking questions or clarifying ambiguous statements. Therefore, if they do not interpret the question correctly, the results will be skewed. There are different types of questions and rating scales used in surveys. Some of the most popular ones are the following:

- Likert Scale
- Dichotomous questions
- Multiple choice questions
- Semantic differential
- Open-ended questions

Likert Scales

Likert Scales are linear rating scales. These scales are typically used to rate attitudes. You provide statements that you want participants to evaluate along with the definitions of the scale. In most cases, Likert Scale ranges from 1 to 10 with 1 being the worst and 10 being the best possible option.

Example of a Likert Scale:

Question / Statement	Strongly agree	Agree	Disagree	Strongly Disagree
I am satisfied with my job				

Dichotomous Questions

Dichotomous questions are yes/no questions. While they do not provide enough information for analysis, they work well as screening tools to identify people eligible to participate in the survey.

Example of a dichotomous question: Have you ever had on-the-job training before?

- *Yes*

- *No*

Multiple Choice Questions

Multiple choice questions can ask for one or more answers. This question type can be used to analyze attitudes and behaviors, as well as personal preferences and styles. However, multiple choice items are difficult to construct, and oftentimes people circle the response without reading the question.

Example of a multiple choice question: What is your preferred learning style?

A. *Visual*

B. *Auditory*

C. *Kinesthetic*

Semantic Differential

This survey is used to measure the meaning of concepts, events, and objects based on peoples' perceptions and attitudes. The scale typically provides two or more contrasting ideas and asks people to rate them as important – not important, valuable – useless, interesting – boring, etc.

Example of semantic differential: What do you think about this training course?

> (5) Relevant to my job

> (4)

> (3)

> (2)

> (1) Completely irrelevant

Open-Ended Questions

Open-ended questions are very effective because participants have to think about their answers before responding. These questions can provide a lot of valuable, qualitative information for analysis. However, it can be very difficult to elicit only pertinent information and avoid useless irrelevant comments and responses. In addition, open-ended questions require a lot of time for participants to complete and for instructional designers to analyze.

Example of an open-ended question: *What type of training are you looking for to improve your overall performance?*

Steps for Conducting Needs Analysis

To conduct a thorough needs analysis for your course, you should do the following:

1. *Define objectives* – This step answers the following questions:

   - What is the purpose of the course?
   - What are the performance issues?
   - What are the root causes for performance issues?
   - Is training solution to the problem?

2. *Identify Data* – This step answers the following questions:

    - What is the training need?
    - Who needs this training?
    - What are some of the strategies for designing and delivering this training?

3. *Select Data-Collection Method* – This step answers the following question:

    Which data collection approach will be used for needs analyses?

4. *Collect Data* – During this step, you gather the information using selected methods.

5. *Analyze Data* – In this step, you use the data you collected and compare, organize, and analyze it.

6. *Prepare Analysis Report* – During this step, you document both the data you collected and your analyses of that data in the analysis report. In addition, your report should include conclusions made as a result of data analysis. Typical analysis report includes the following sections:

    - Overview of the project
    - Performance analysis
    - Tools used to collect data
    - Training needs analysis
    - Conclusions or recommendations made based on the analysis

Exercise 8

Keeping in mind that stakeholders do not have budgets allocated for needs analysis, think about the information you need to find out about the course to address the clients' needs. Are you going to convince them that needs analysis is an important part of course design? If so, how? What questions will you ask? Which data-gathering tools will you use in your needs analysis? Once you made your decisions, design an interview, survey, or focus group questionnaires.

Chapter 10:
Learning Objectives

This chapter will cover:

- Role of learning objectives in course design
- The A-B-C-D format of learning objectives
- Terminal and enabling objectives
- SMART objectives
- Bloom's Taxonomy and three learning domains
- Revised Bloom's Taxonomy
- SOLO Taxonomy and five stages of understanding
- New approach to writing learning objectives

Learning objectives are an indispensable part of any course. They describe what the learners will be able to do upon completion of the course. Learning objectives are also sometimes called behavioral objectives, performance objectives, or course objectives. The main goal of objectives is to define the scope of the course and help learners focus on specific outcomes. Prior to writing objectives, you should determine the overall goal for the course. Objectives should always be written after conducting a thorough needs analysis. The main difference between goals and objectives is that goals provide information about the purpose of the course while objectives are measurable instructional outcomes of the course. Objectives describe the knowledge, skills, or attitudes learners should demonstrate after completing the training.

Robert Mager is a key contributor to the field of instructional design and to objectives in particular. He believed that all objectives should be measurable and observable, as those that cannot be measured and observed will have little chance for evaluation.

All objectives should include four components, known as the A-B-C-D format. These components are:

- Audience
- Behavior
- Condition
- Degree

Audience

When writing objectives, it is crucial to know the target audience. For instance, if you are creating a course on Teaching English as a Second Language (TESL), the *audience* component of the objective is the TESL learner.

Behavior

The *behavior* element of the objective should state what the learner will be doing using action verbs to describe the behavior. Most behavior statements are worded *should be able to*. However, many instructional designers prefer the *will be able to* statement. While both statements are correct, it is highly recommended you use *should be able to* in your objectives. The *will be able to* statement automatically makes a promise while the *should be able to* statement does not promise any definite results. Whether or not learners achieve the objectives depends on many different aspects not always under your control. For instance, your learners may be distracted while taking your course.

When writing behavioral statements in objectives, you should avoid using such verbs as *know* and *understand* as they are not measurable and observable. Instead, consider using *apply, identify,* and *explain*.

Condition

Objectives should include the *condition* under which the tasks are performed. Conditions should provide context that supports all other elements of the objective. For example:

- given a desk reference guide, or
- after completing a real-life simulation

Degree

The last element of effective objectives is *degree*. It is the level at which learners must perform the task. Some examples of degree statements are:

- without error
- successfully five times
- within one hour
- by giving facts

- on two different issues

All of these degree statements are measurable and observable. After seeing them, learners should be clear of what they need to do to meet the objectives.

Terminal and Enabling Objectives

Each course should include both terminal and enabling objectives. Terminal objectives describe what the learners are expected to be able to do by the end of the course. They focus on the result, not the process.

Example of a terminal objective:

Given realistic scenarios depicting the most common writing problems of high school graduates, you should be able to write essays without errors.

Enabling objectives support terminal objectives. They define the skills, knowledge, or attitudes learners must obtain to successfully complete terminal objectives. Enabling objectives are more specific than terminal.

Example of an enabling objective:

Given handouts and videos related to essay writing, you should be able to complete essay-writing activities with 100% accuracy.

Developing SMART Objectives

To ensure that your objectives are well-written, you should use the SMART approach. SMART objectives focus on the result rather than the activities and allow learners to measure their own success. SMART stands for Specific, Measurable, Attainable, Relevant, and Timely.

- *Specific* – Objectives should clearly state the knowledge or skill the learners need to demonstrate as a result of training. Specific objectives define what needs to be done by answering the *What*, *Why*, and *How* questions. Even individuals without any background knowledge about the topic should be able to read the objective and interpret it correctly.

Example – *Increase enrollment of ISD students in X University through participation in the local job fair*

- *Measurable* – Focuses on the evaluation standards and includes some type of quantifiable measurement such as standards or parameters. Instructional designers should be able to evaluate this element through assessment.

Example – *by 15%*

- *Attainable* – Even though your objective can be both specific and measurable, it may not be feasible during the proposed period or with the limited resources available. The attainable part of your objective is responsible for the capability of satisfying the expectation. Action verbs such as *observe, identify, participate, demonstrate,* and *communicate* can help represent the behavior the objective is trying to measure.

Example – *Participate in the local job fair*

- *Relevant* – Emphasizes the practicality of the objective and clarifies why something should be done.

Example – *Increase enrollment of ISD students in X University over the next three months through participation in the local job fair*

- *Time-bound* – Identifies the time when something will be done.

Example – *Over the next three months*

Bloom's Taxonomy

In 1956, educational psychologist Benjamin Bloom identified three learning domains. These domains are:

- Cognitive (knowledge)
- Affective (attitude)
- Psychomotor (skills)

When you write your objectives for any of the three domains, you should always aim towards the most complex behavior.

Cognitive Domain

The cognitive domain includes content knowledge, which involves the ability to recall specific facts that help learners develop new skills and abilities. There are six levels in this domain. The lowest level is knowledge, and the highest level is evaluation. The table below describes each of these levels and provides action verbs associated with each learning outcome.

Table 4 Bloom's Taxonomy – Cognitive Domain

Level	Description	Verbs
Knowledge	Being able to recall applicable knowledge from the memory	• Define • Describe • Identify • Label • List • Name • Recall • Recite • State
Comprehension	Being able to construct meaning from written, oral, and graphic messages	• Convert • Distinguish • Estimate • Explain • Predict • Summarize
Application	Being able to apply previous knowledge to carry out a procedure	• Compute • Demonstrate • Develop • Organize • Solve • Use

Analysis	Being able to identify the relationships among content elements	• Diagram • Differentiate • Illustrate • Infer • Outline • Relate
Synthesis	Being able to combine the elements learned in a lesson to produce something completely new	• Categorize • Compose • Create • Formulate • Predict • Produce
Evaluation	Being able to make judgments or suggestions based on specific criteria	• Compare • Contrast • Criticize • Justify • Support

Affective Domain

The affective domain includes feelings, emotions, motivations, and attitudes. The table below illustrates the five categories in this domain and the action verbs that describe learning outcomes. The receiving level is the simplest behavior; the internalizing level the most complex. The table below describes each of these levels and provides action verbs associated with each learning outcome.

Table 5 Bloom's Taxonomy – Affective Domain

Level	Description	Verbs
Receiving	Being aware of something in the environment	• Attend • Control • Listen • Notice • Share

Responding	Showing new behavior as a result of experience	<ul><li>Comply</li><li>Follow</li><li>Obey</li><li>Participate</li><li>Practice</li></ul>
Valuing	Showing commitment	<ul><li>Act</li><li>Argue</li><li>Debate</li><li>Express</li><li>Organize</li></ul>
Organization	Integrating a new value into an already existing set of values	<ul><li>Abstract</li><li>Balance</li><li>Define</li><li>Systematize</li><li>Theorize</li></ul>
Characterization by Value	Acting regularly with the new value	<ul><li>Avoid</li><li>Exhibit</li><li>Manage</li><li>Resolve</li><li>Revise</li></ul>

Psychomotor Domain

The psychomotor domain includes movements, coordination, and motor skills. Developing skills in this domain requires practice. The psychomotor domain consists of seven categories. Perception, the simplest behavior; and origination, the most complex. The table below describes each of these levels and provides action verbs associated with each learning outcome.

Table 6 Bloom's Taxonomy – Psychomotor Domain

Level	Description	Verbs
Perception	Being able to use sensory cues to guide motor activity	• Choose • Detect • Isolate • Relate • Select
Set	Mental, physical, and emotional readiness to act	• Display • Explain • Move • React • State
Guided Response	Attempting the physical skill	• Copy • Follow • React • Reproduce
Mechanism	Learned responses of a physical skill become habitual	• Assemble • Construct • Fix • Measure • Sketch
Complex Overt Response	Skillful performance of physical activities	• Build • Display • Grind • Manipulate
Adaption	Modifying movements for special situations	• Adapt • Alter • Change • Rearrange • Revise

Origination	Creating new movement patterns to fit specific situation	<ul><li>Arrange</li><li>Combine</li><li>Compose</li><li>Initiate</li></ul>

Revised Bloom's Taxonomy

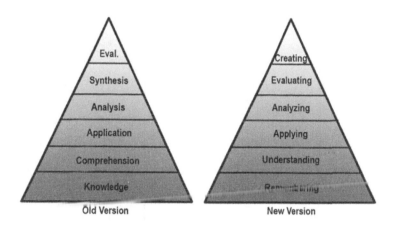

Old Version — New Version

In the mid-90s, Lorin Anderson, Bloom's former student, revised the learning domain to reflect a more active form of thinking and make it more relevant to modern needs. The two major modifications are:

- change of names from noun to verb forms, and
- rearrangement of the levels

Table 7 illustrates the updated version of Bloom's Taxonomy.

Table 7 Revised Bloom's Taxonomy

Level	Description	Verbs
Remembering	Being able to recall, recognize or retrieve information such as definitions, facts, or lists	• Acquire • Define • Duplicate • Label • List • Memorize • Recall • Recognize • Repeat • Reproduce • Retrieve
Understanding	Being able to construct meaning by correctly interpreting, classifying, summarizing, explaining, or comparing information	• Classify • Describe • Give examples • Interpret • Locate • Paraphrase • Predict • Select • Summarize • Translate
Applying	Being able to use knowledge in new situations such as applying concepts to simulations or procedures	• Apply • Carry out • Choose • Diagram • Employ • Execute • Implement • Modify • Prepare • Solve • Use

Analyzing	Being able to break materials or concepts into parts	<ul><li>Break down</li><li>Contrast</li><li>Compare</li><li>Deconstruct</li><li>Differentiate</li><li>Examine</li><li>Find</li><li>Illustrate</li><li>Outline</li><li>Separate</li></ul>
Evaluating	Being able to make judgments about materials, concepts or ideas	<ul><li>Appraise</li><li>Argue</li><li>Categorize</li><li>Critique</li><li>Compare</li><li>Conclude</li><li>Experiment</li><li>Hypothesize</li><li>Justify</li><li>Judge</li><li>Summarize</li><li>Support</li></ul>
Creating	Being able to combine elements to form a new meaning	<ul><li>Assemble</li><li>Categorize</li><li>Combine</li><li>Compile</li><li>Formulate</li><li>Generate</li><li>Invent</li><li>Plan</li><li>Produce</li><li>Rearrange</li><li>Reconstruct</li><li>Write</li></ul>

SOLO Taxonomy

SOLO stands for the Structure of Observed Learning Outcomes. It is a hierarchical taxonomy, developed by John Biggs and Kevin Collis, to help instructional designers and educators create objectives and evaluate learning outcomes. The main difference between Bloom's taxonomy and SOLO taxonomy is that SOLO focuses on teaching and learning while Bloom's taxonomy mainly concentrates on knowledge. SOLO is comprised of five stages of understanding. The lowest level is pre-structural and the highest level is extended abstract. The table below describes each of these levels and provides action verbs associated with each learning outcome.

Table 8 SOLO Taxonomy

Level of Understanding	Description	Verbs
Pre-structural	The learner acquires bits and pieces of unconnected and disorganized information that do not make any sense	No understanding is demonstrated; the learner misses the point; instructional designers want to avoid this stage; therefore, there are no verbs associated with this level.
Uni-structural	The learner shows basic understanding about a topic and is only able to make obvious, very simple connections concentrating on one issue.	• Do simple procedure • Identify • Memorize

Multi-structural	The learner understands several concepts or ideas, but they are still disorganized and unclear.	• Classify • Combine • Describe • Do algorithms • Enumerate • List
Relational	The learner demonstrates understanding of how bits and pieces contribute to the whole and is able to apply this understanding to familiar situations	• Analyze • Apply • Compare • Contrast • Explain causes • Integrate • Relate
Extended abstract	The learner can make connections and transfer learning to a new situation and develop new ideas based on new knowledge	• Generalize • Generate • Hypothesize • Reflect • Theorize

Learning Objectives Makeover

There is no doubt that learning objectives play a very important role in course design. Typically, instructional designers use a classical approach to writing their objectives. As a result, the first element learners see when they start a course is the objectives. Even though the purpose of objectives is to help learners focus on their learning experience, most learners do not like to read the objective list and skip it whenever possible. Because of this, the value of objectives is diminished. However, if learners do not know the objectives, they cannot truly benefit from the course. The dilemma that instructional designers face lies in approaching learning objectives in the most interactive way possible while avoiding long and boring bulleted lists. So, what can you do to turn objectives into motivators?

First, before writing objectives, you need to identify a business goal for the course. Then, think about the actions necessary to reach that goal. Once a list of actions is compiled, the objective makeover can begin. Not only should objectives be measurable and observable, but they should also be motivational and relevant. Remember, you design courses for adults, and most adults are busy people. Therefore, you need to ensure that objectives meet your learners' needs. For example, even though the objective with an action verb *define* is measurable, it is most likely useless as in most cases people do not need to be able to define something to solve a problem or master a skill. While it is still a good idea to include definitions in training courses, turning them into objectives may be impractical for adult learners.

Incorporating scenarios will add meaning to your learning objectives. The goal of the objectives is to help learners understand the benefits of learning the content in the course as well as the risks associated with not learning it. Objectives that use the pronoun *you* instead of the word *learner* are more personal as they speak directly to the learner. For example, saying: *By the end of the module, you should be able to...* is more personal than saying: *By the end of the module, the learner should be able to....* Also, turning abstract concepts into real situations that learners will experience on the job adds meaning to objectives. For example, instead of, *After completing this module, you should be able to describe the four stages of the ARCS model of Motivational Design,* consider, *After completing this module, you should be able to design motivational courses for your learners.*

Exercise 9

Write terminal and enabling objectives for your course. Ensure that your objectives are SMART and include the A-B-C-D components.

Chapter 11:
Designing the Learning Experience:
Gagné's Nine Events of Instruction

> This chapter will cover:
>
> - Robert Gagné and his levels of learning
> - Nine Events of Instruction
> - Presentation methods that adhere to the Nine Events of Instruction

Gagné's Theory of Instruction

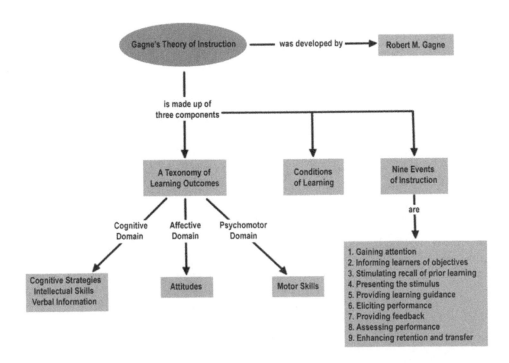

Robert Gagné is an American educational psychologist best known for his "conditions of learning for training applications." In 1965, Gagné published the book titled *The Conditions of Learning*. In this book, he explained the relationship between learning objectives and instructional design principles. According to Gagné's theory, there are five major levels of learning, including verbal information, intellectual skills, cognitive strategies, motor skills, and attitudes. Each of these levels requires a different type of instruction.

Table 9 Gagné's Five Levels of Learning

Learning Outcome	Example
Verbal Information	Retrieve stored information such as poem recitation
Intellectual Skills	Perform mental operations such as problem-solving and rule-using
Cognitive Strategies	Develop new solutions to problems
Motor Skills	Perform a sequence of physical movements such as correct reproduction of musical pieces
Attitude	Hear persuasive arguments about a certain topic

Even though Gagné's levels of instruction cover all aspects of learning, his theory mostly focuses on intellectual skills. Based on this theoretical framework, Gagné developed a nine-step process known as the Events of Instruction. Together with the five levels of learning and learning outcomes, these events provide the necessary conditions of learning and play an important role in the development of instruction.

Below are the Gagné's Nine Events of Instruction along with a description of each one.

1. **Gain attention** – Start by gaining your learners' attention. This gives learners a framework into which they can organize the content that will be presented in the lesson. This instructional event is also used to motivate learners.
2. **Inform learners of objectives** – During this phase, designers should describe what learners should be able to do at the end of the course and

what tools they may be using to achieve learning objectives. Objectives should create expectancy and describe the structure of the lecture.

3. **Stimulate recall of prior learning** – Here, the instructional designer should relate the new lesson to situations that the learners are familiar with. For example, the previous lesson.

4. **Present the content** – In this stage, the instructional designer should describe the key points of the lesson using a variety of techniques. Designers should try to vary the format in order to keep the learners' attention and increase comprehension of the material.

5. **Provide guidance** – At this point, the instructional designer should present the lesson in small steps leading from simple to complex. It is important to begin the lesson with easy to understand information and add more difficult information as the lesson progresses. This gives learners an opportunity to build on their existing knowledge. As a result, they will understand the material better and retain more content.

6. **Elicit performance** – Here, the instructional designer should involve learners in discussion and questioning to confirm that they have learned the material. Learners' active participation should increase understanding and retention of the material.

7. **Provide feedback** – As learners respond to questions, instructional designers should provide them with reinforcement and remediation.

8. **Assess performance** – To confirm mastery of the objectives, instructional designers should include quizzes or other assignments in their lessons.

9. **Enhance retention and learning transfer** – At this point, instructional designers should provide the opportunity for learners to apply the outcome of their training to a real world situation. For instance, they might give learners some type of realistic assignment or provide a desk guide that learners can refer to at any time when they perform the tasks presented in the lesson.

The Nine Events of Instruction is an excellent framework for any lesson. Even though it is not always possible to incorporate all Nine Events into the lesson plan, instructional designers should at least consider them when creating their courses. Table 10 illustrates how you can use the Events of Instruction in your eLearning materials.

Table 10 Gagné's Nine Events of Instruction

Instructional Event	Application Methods
Gain attention	icebreakers, slideshows, case studies, YouTube videos, podcasts, demonstrations, Flash presentations, storytelling, polls, images, analogy, paradox, anecdote, articles, charts, and diagrams
Inform learners of objectives	slides, instructions, discussion boards
Stimulate recall of prior learning	review previous lectures, integrate previous information into activities using slides, use discussion boards, YouTube videos, audio recordings, graphics
Present the content	lectures, articles, activities, discussion boards, wikis, blogs, podcasts, YouTube videos, storytelling
Provide learning guidance	activities that include rubrics and state clear expectations, demonstration of principles in action, discussion of common errors, case studies, analogies
Elicit performance	discussions, written assignments, case studies, simulations, drills, role plays, interactive questions
Provide feedback	immediate and detailed corrective feedback

Assess performance	assessments, written projects, games
Enhance retention and transfer to the job	additional practice activities, exercises, job aids, manuals, desk guides, forums

The real-life example below illustrates the application of the Nine Events of Instruction to a hypothetical situation.

Scenario

Mrs. Rosario is a Human Resource Specialist at the X Corporation. Upper management made a decision to purchase the SnagIt screen-capturing tool, and Mrs. Rosario is now responsible for ensuring that all technical writers know how to use it. Mrs. Rosario has many other responsibilities; therefore, she decided to make this training available in the asynchronous eLearning format. She followed the Nine Events of Instruction to create her course.

Gain attention – When learners access the lesson, the senior technical writer appears on the screen and introduces the course. She discusses the importance of staying on the cutting edge of technology and explains how the SnagIt tool will be beneficial for technical writers.

Inform learners of objectives – After the introduction, the objective slide with the voiceover appears. One of the objectives on that slide is "Upon completing this training, you should be able to use all features of the SnagIt tool without further assistance."

Stimulate recall of prior knowledge – At this point, learners are called upon to use their prior knowledge of other similar tools to understand the basic functionality of SnagIt.

Present the content – Next, using screen images, Camtasia demonstration, and audio narration, the training program describes the basic features of SnagIt.

Guide learning – *With each new feature, learners are shown a variety of ways to use them. Complex sequences are chunked into short, step-by-step lists for easier storage in long-term memory.*

Elicit performance – *After each function is demonstrated, learners are asked to practice with realistic simulations.*

Provide feedback – *During the simulation, learners are given guidance and feedback as needed.*

Assess performance – *After all lessons are completed, learners are required to take a post-test. The assessment questions are tied directly to the learning objectives displayed in the lessons.*

Enhance retention and learning transfer – *Upon completion of the course, learners are presented with a downloadable desk guide, which includes step-by-step instructions on how to use the SnagIt tool.*

Exercise 10

Follow the Nine Events of Instruction to create a lesson plan for your eLearning course. Remember to include motivational examples and activities.

Chapter 12:
Creating a Design Document

This chapter will cover:

- The role of the design document
- Sections of the design document
- Information included in each section of the design document

As the name implies, the design document is created during the design phase of the instructional design process. Its purpose is to document the entire design process for a specific project. The document provides all the necessary information about the course to instructional designers, graphic artists, multimedia specialists, programmers, project managers, and all other team members. Just like all other documents created for the eLearning project, the sections included in your design document will differ depending on course requirements. For example, if you are creating a linear course using the rapid instructional systems design model, the design document will not have as many sections compared to a full-fledged eLearning course filled with interactions, simulations, and games.

Generally, all design documents are based on the thorough needs analysis and include all the objectives and assessment items for the course. In addition, these documents provide information about media and supplemental materials that will be included in the training as well as the screenshots of the layout of the course. The table below illustrates some major sections that a typical design document should include.

Table 11 Sections of a Design Document

Section	Information
Background Information	<ul><li>Course overview</li><li>Major topics</li><li>Overall goals</li></ul>

Scope	• Short statement about the scope of the course
Target Audience	• Who is this course designed for?
Prerequisites	• What should the learners already know before taking this course? • Which courses should the learners take prior to this one?
Interface of the Course	• Navigation • "Look and feel"
Compliance Considerations	• SCORM • Section 508
Project Management	• Development timeline maintenance requirements for this course • Project sign-off names and contact information
Objectives	• Terminal objectives • Enabling objectives
Evaluation Strategy	• Assessments • Kirkpatrick's Levels of Evaluation • ROI
Delivery Methods	• WBT • CBT • CD-ROM • ILT
Development Tools	• Tools used to create this course
Interactions	• Detailed description of interactions

Testing and Assessments	<ul><li>Questions</li><li>Answers</li><li>Corrective feedback</li></ul>
Technical Requirements	<ul><li>Plugins/players</li><li>Memory</li><li>Operating system</li></ul>
Media elements	<ul><li>Graphics</li><li>Animations</li><li>Video</li><li>Audio</li></ul>
Course Outline	<ul><li>Outline of course structure</li><li>Screenshots</li><li>Content</li></ul>

Exercise 11

Draft a design document for your course. Remember to include detailed descriptions and examples.

Chapter 13:
Storyboarding and Rapid Prototyping

This chapter will cover:

- Origin of storyboarding and storyboarding components
- Ways to storyboard and prototype
- Benefits of storyboarding and prototyping
- Rapid prototyping
- Difference between storyboarding and prototyping

The development phase of an eLearning course involves many complex steps and activities to guarantee a quality product. To ensure the outcome of all efforts meets the highest standards, ISD professionals use storyboards and prototypes to illustrate and communicate their ideas to team members and stakeholders.

Storyboarding

Storyboards are visual organizers that illustrate and communicate ideas to other professionals on the team such as graphic artists, multimedia specialists, and programmers. Typical storyboards include text, visual, and audio elements for every screen of an eLearning course. Instructional designers incorporate interactions, assessments, demonstrations, simulations, and games in their storyboards.

Historically, in the early 1930s, Walt Disney Studios started using storyboards to draw the scenes for their cartoons. By the late 1930s, all major studios had adopted the concept. *Gone with the Wind* was the first live-action film that was completely storyboarded. Nowadays, eLearning professionals use storyboarding as an aid to develop instructionally sound courses and learning materials. Many instructional designers provide storyboarding templates to Subject Matter Experts (SMEs), who use them to populate the content. It is then much easier for instructional designers to use the pre-populated template to rearrange the content and add interactivities and assessments.

There is no single way to storyboard. In fact, every organization uses its own template based on its unique needs. Even though many tools can be used to create storyboards, most templates are built in either PowerPoint or Word. Some instructional designers like to use multiple storyboards and choose the appropriate one based on their content. For instance, the template used to design a game or simulation would be different from a template for video development. Nevertheless, there are certain elements common to most storyboards. These elements include the following:

- *Content* – This is the information that will appear on the screen. In addition to the on-screen text, this section contains instructions for learners such as *Click Next for more information.*
- *Audio* – This is the narrator's script for each screen. In this section, the instructional designer writes out the pronunciation of terms and acronyms that might be unfamiliar to the narrator.
- *Graphics* – This is where instructional designers either place images that they want to appear on each screen or, if they cannot find the image they are looking for, or need the graphic artist to create an original one, simply explain what they want. Alternatively, they can find a visual that conveys the message but is not exactly what is needed. This sample visual will guide graphic artists as they develop graphics or search for appropriate images.
- *Programming Instructions or Developer's Notes* – This is the most complex element of a storyboard, primarily because it incorporates many sub-elements. In this area, instructional designers need to provide clear instructions about navigation. For instance, they should explain to the programmer where each screen should take learners and provide names for each button that appears on the screen. Additionally, in the *programming instructions* area, ISD specialists should provide detailed explanations of interactions, assessments, and feedback. It is important to keep in mind, however, that developers will be creating all the interactions, test questions, and remediation screens based on these descriptions; therefore, being very accurate and including as many details as possible is key. If the developer is responsible for creating assessment items, storyboards should include the question type and the question itself along with all answer choices. Instructions and corrective feedback that would appear on the screen must also be included in the storyboard.

In addition to the above elements, storyboards often include:

- *the name of the module*
- *page numbers*
- *screen references*

These elements help instructional designers and developers communicate more efficiently when discussing specific screens. Most of the elements mentioned above are common to storyboards; however, because there is no single way to storyboard your eLearning courses, you should choose the elements that suit your specific needs.

Below is an example of an eLearning storyboard.

Course Name:	Screen Number:	Module Name:	
On-Screen Text			Graphics
Audio Narration			Programming Notes

Even though storyboarding is very time consuming, it is a major time saver at the end. Storyboarding makes it easy for the SME to review projects, and allow instructional designers to avoid rework.

Prototyping

While storyboards are very useful for visualizing a course, they only work well for linear courses. Because many eLearning lessons are non-linear, storyboards can be rather confusing to both SMEs and programmers. Sometimes it is excessively difficult or even impossible to describe all the interactions, non-linear navigations, scenarios, simulations, and other media-rich content in words. Storyboards do not always allow to fully capture all the nuances of the design, especially when it comes to games and interactions. Therefore, many instructional designers turn to rapid prototyping to develop an interactive model of their eLearning course. In addition to all the information found in storyboards, prototypes contain the overall course layout including buttons and navigation. When you have many projects on your plate and a very short timeframe to complete them, rapid prototyping can save a lot of time as some of the elements created previously for other projects can be reused.

There are three prototyping styles:

- *Nonfunctional prototypes* – Do not have any functional elements but still have the look and feel that effectively communicates functionality of the future course.
- *Semi-functional prototypes* – Contain interactions and can be used as screenshots in storyboards.
- *Fully functional prototypes* – Include most of the content, interactions, and assessments and clearly demonstrate the functionality of the entire course.

Just like with storyboarding, there is no single way to prototype. Therefore, you should choose the prototyping approach that works best for your specific needs. There are many different tools that can be used to build prototypes; Articulate Storyline and Adobe Captivate are just some examples. If, however, rapid eLearning tools are not available, you can use PowerPoint to build your prototypes. ISD specialists who are technologically savvy and want to create a fully functional prototype with advanced interactions can turn to Adobe Flash to lay out their lesson. Prototypes are not meant to be complete. Furthermore, having the exact content is not required for building prototypes. Their sole purpose is to visualize the functionality and usability of the course.

When instructional designers submit their prototypes to stakeholders, they typically review them for the following:

Functionality and Navigation

- Do all elements of the course including videos and interactions play well at their workstation?
- Is the load time of all content and interactions acceptable?
- Do all buttons take the user to the correct place in the course?

Look and Feel of the Course

- Does the layout work for the purpose of this training course?
- Is the color scheme of the course appropriate?
- Are the fonts easy to read?

Interactions and Audio

- Are the videos and interactions appropriate?
- Do all interactions and videos play correctly?
- Do they meet instructional goals of the course?
- Are the voiceovers professional and audible?
- Is the tone of voice appropriate?
- Is the dialect easy to understand?

Nowadays, many instructional designers choose to use the rapid prototyping method in place of the ADDIE model. Rapid prototyping goes hand in hand with the rapid ISD model and allows you to create learning solutions quickly and effectively. This model focuses on developing a training solution rather than simply preparing for its development. In this model, you can immediately jump into prototyping and gather necessary information about learners' needs as you build your course and interact with SMEs.

Exercise 12

Using the example provided in this chapter, create your own storyboarding template.

Chapter 14:
Scripting Your ELearning Course

This chapter will cover:

- Basics of scriptwriting
- Plain language principles
- Style guides

By now, you have analyzed learners, developed learning objectives, selected appropriate media, created a design document, and even built a prototype. Now, it is time to write a voiceover script. Even for experienced writers, voiceover scripting can be difficult as writing for audio differs from other types of writing and requires a unique set of skills.

To write a script that will bring all the points across and engage learners with the material, you must understand the content. Logical organization is the key to effective scriptwriting. To turn the content into the chronological, well-written script, it is essential to be able to follow the material. Most instructional designers work on projects they know very little about. Conducting additional research and communicating with Subject Matter Experts (SMEs) is the essential first step in making sense out of the information that will be included in the lesson.

Even though clients often believe one has to be an expert in the subject area to write a good script, this is not true. In fact, not being an SME can be advantageous primarily because most SMEs know so much about the topic that they often leave the important information out, forget to mention crucial steps in the process, or provide unnecessary content that confuses learners. Instructional designers unfamiliar with the material will ask questions and clarify statements to get all the information needed for creating a clear and effective script. Alternatively, if instructional designers appear to be experts in the topic, finding a non-expert to review the script and provide feedback is recommended. Remember, as you seek clarification and answers to questions, you prevent learners from having the same questions and concerns about the content.

One of the most important rules in script writing is informality. Scripts are written to be heard, not read. Therefore, the writing style should be conversational.

To add a conversational tone to the script, consider using contractions (e.g., *isn't* instead of *is not*) and pronouns to make the eLearning content more personal (e.g., *you* instead of *learner*). You should also consider the plain language principles as you write your scripts. Some of these principles include:

- using active voice over passive voice

Example:
Active voice: Amy wrote the letter to her boss.
Passive voice: The letter to the boss was written by Amy.

- avoiding run-on sentences

Example:
Run-on sentence: *Amy is a great writer she writes well.*
Corrected sentence: *Amy is a great writer. She writes well.*

- avoiding sentences that express more than one idea

Example:
Sentence with more than one idea: *Amy likes writing letters and editing audio narration.*
Corrected sentence: *Amy loves writing letters. She also enjoys editing audio narration.*

- avoiding misplaced modifiers

Example:
Sentence with misplaced modifier: *If you only have time to write one letter, do it professionally.*
Corrected sentence: *If you have time to write only one letter, do it professionally.*

- avoiding double negatives

Example:
Sentence with double negative: *If Amy does not write a letter, she cannot send it to her boss.*
Corrected sentence: *Amy can send a letter to her boss if she writes it.*

- keeping subject and objects close to the verb

Example:
Sentence with subject and object far from the verb: Amy, anticipating salary increase, wrote a letter to her boss.
Corrected sentence: Anticipating salary increase, Amy wrote a letter to her boss.

If, in the script, you use word combinations that are difficult to pronounce together, the talent may have a hard time reading them, and learners may have problems understanding what they hear. One way to avoid tongue twisters is to reread the script multiple times and make relevant changes to wording and grammar.

Remember, eLearning courses should address multiple learning styles and meet accessibility requirements. When your learners hear the audio recording, they should be able to tell when the topic is changing. To achieve this goal, instructional designers should check their script for appropriate transitions.

Another good practice for scriptwriting dictates that pauses should be incorporated into the script to indicate where the talent should stop and to give learners a chance to absorb the information. Additionally, using 12-point font and double-spacing the script will help the talent go through it more easily. Double-spaced scripts provide enough room for narrator to make notes when necessary. If the talent will be reading from a hard copy, it is best to use a serif font such as Times New Roman. Alternatively, using a sans-serif font such as Arial is preferred when reading from a computer screen. Another way to help the talent is to spell out all URLs as well as terms or acronyms that are difficult to pronounce. The same principle applies to dollar amounts and dates. By following these simple rules, you will save a lot of time for both your talent and yourself as the audio recording session will not be interrupted for questions and clarifications.

Lastly, proofread, proofread, and proofread. There is nothing worse than noticing errors in the script after recording it.

Style Guide

When you work with other professionals such as editors, graphic artists, and programmers, maintaining a consistent style can be problematic. Therefore, it is important to create a standardized guide for each project that all team members will use. The content included in that guide will depend on the specific course. However, there are certain elements common to most style guides. They are:

- List of acronyms and their meanings
- List of abbreviations
- Capitalization rules
- Specific terminology and definitions
- Punctuation rules
- Spacing rules
- Active and passive voice rules
- Specific elements such as *bulleted or numbered lists*
- Font formatting such as *bolding, underlining, or italicizing certain key words*
- Specific commands such as *Click the OK button*
- Graphic format such as *.jpg, .png, or .gif*
- Consistent color scheme
- Consistent graphic elements such as *boxes, symbols,* and *shapes*
- Consistent page layout elements such as *buttons*
- Consistent file naming conventions

Exercise 12

Based on what you know about the topic for your eLearning course (new salary calculating tool for the department of finance), brainstorm the elements that will be included in the style guide.

Chapter 15:
Quality Assurance

This chapter will cover:

- Alpha, beta, and pilot testing
- Error log
- Checklists for identifying errors

Once you have developed your course, you should alpha and beta test it before submitting it to the client. Alpha testing involves interface testing to confirm that the course functions the way it should. Very often, alpha testing reveals misspelled words, ambiguous directions, broken links, poorly developed interactions, and unsynchronized audio and video.

The second phase of testing is known as Pilot or Beta testing. During this time, the course is released to the small group of target audience, most likely Subject Matter Experts (SMEs), to ensure its quality and functionality. It is important to have the pilot testing participants avoid making on-the-spot changes to the problems they encounter. Instead, ask them to focus on the course itself and keep an error log of all the issues they want to address. Once the pilot testing is complete, instructional designers and testing participants can meet to discuss desired changes.

Below is a sample error log template that you can use for piloting courses.

Reviewer's Name	Module #	Screen Title	Issue Type (e.g., text, font, graphic, navigation)	Explanation	Assigned to	Date completed

Table 12 should help you identify errors as you test your courses. This quality assurance checklist can also be given to the SMEs to guide them through the problems they should keep an eye on as they conduct course review.

Table 12 Quality Assurance Checklist

Question	Yes	No	N/A
Do all buttons work correctly and take learners where they should?			
Are all feedback statements programmed correctly?			
What happens if the learner answers correctly/incorrectly?			
Do all games and simulations work correctly?			
Are the directions clear?			
Do all videos play correctly?			
Are all videos placed correctly in the course?			
Is the audio level similar across the entire course?			
Are visuals relevant to the topic of the course?			
Is there a good balance of text, images, and multimedia?			
Is navigation simple and intuitive?			
Is design clean and there is a lot of white space on the screen?			
Is the content relevant to learners' needs?			

Is the content presented in an interactive way?			
Do interactions, games, and simulations support learning objectives?			
Are interactions, games, and simulations practical and realistic?			
Are the titles of all lessons clear and accurate?			
Does the course launch properly?			
Are all screens present?			
Are examples clear and easy to understand?			
Does each screen contain enough information?			

Exercise 13

Brainstorm ideas for alpha and beta testing your course. Then, using the example in this chapter, create your own error log template.

Chapter 16:
Implementation

This chapter will cover:

- Implementation of eLearning courses
- Learning Management System and Content Management System
- SCORM and guidelines for creating SCORM-compliant content
- Reusable Learning Objects (RLOs)
- Section 508

So, the course has been designed and developed, and it is now time to think about implementing it. During implementation, you upload all the content into the Learning Management System (LMS), Content Management System (CMS), or use another appropriate distribution method. Implementation also involves uploading the SCORM package and ensuring that it is tracking properly. Once you launch the course, you should test it to make sure it is fully functional.

During the eLearning implementation phase, you need to ensure that

- all the tools and equipment are readily available and work properly, and
- the learning application is fully operational.

This means all slides, interactions, games, assessments, and external links provided in the course should be tested. Some instructional designers upload their course and fail to review it again. Many of them are either too busy or do not consider this an important step primarily because they have already reviewed the course many times before uploading it to the learning platform. The importance of testing the eLearning course after uploading cannot be stressed enough. Once the course is launched, the operating system, web browser, and even the display settings on the computer may change the appearance and functionality of the course. Furthermore, there are can be many other technical reasons why the lesson may appear different after it is uploaded to the learning platform. Some of these reasons may go beyond the capability of an ISD specialist. However, it is still your responsibility to review the course for any possible errors, and have someone with the right skill set fix the issues.

Once an eLearning course is implemented, it will require continuous maintenance to ensure it functions effectively on the regular basis. In most cases, however, once you develop the course and confirm that it functions properly, you are no longer responsible for it unless the client comes back and asks for additional changes or upgrades.

The log should be kept throughout the implementation phase to record and fix errors. Below is a checklist that will guide you through major functionality questions that should be addressed during that time. While it is not exhaustive, it covers most major elements that you should look for when implementing your projects.

Table 13 Implementation Phase Checklist

Question	Yes / No / Not Applicable
Does the course launch properly?	
Are the learning results updated upon completion of the course?	
Does the menu play properly?	
Do all external links work properly?	
Do all attachments open?	
Does the scroll bar works correctly?	
Do all interactions in the course play correctly?	
Do all buttons take learners where they are supposed to take them?	
Is the load time of all screens including interactions and quizzes relatively quick?	
Are all buttons, links and objects displayed correctly on the screen?	

Do all videos play smoothly?	
Is the video quality acceptable?	
Is the audio audible?	
Do all audio pieces sound the same?	
Are all on screen elements such as text and graphics aligned correctly?	
Do all animations play smoothly and appear in the appropriate time and place?	
Is the color scheme consistent?	
Are the fonts easy to read?	
Is the spacing of paragraphs consistent?	

Learning Management System (LMS) and Content Management System (CMS)

A Learning Management System (LMS) is a software application used to plan, implement, and assess the learning process. LMS allows instructors and administrators to create and deliver content to the maximum number of people, monitor participation, and assess performance. Among some of the most popular LMSs are:

- Moodle
- Edmodo
- SumTotal Systems

Content Management System (CMS) is often the main function of a Learning Management System (LMS). Most LMSs encompass a CMS. As opposed to

LMSs, CMSs do not have to be SCORM-compliant and act more like databases. Among some of the most popular CMSs are:

- WordPress
- Joomla
- Drupal

There are countless LMSs and CMSs on the market. To choose the option that best suits the needs of a specific organization, you should consider your target audience, budget, and requirements. The following questions should guide you through the process of selecting the LMS and CMS for your needs.

- What are the organizational goals?
- What are the organizational business needs?
- How many learners will have access to the LMS?
- Is content relatively stable?
- Is the LMS SCORM-compliant?
- How would the LMS fit in the overall structure of the organization?
- What tracking features do you need?
- How much money can the organization spend on LMS?
- What kind of technical support is available?

SCORM

SCORM stands for Shareable Content Object Reference Model. SCORM is a set of technical standards that ensure the course works well with other eLearning software. SCORM also ensures that the learning content and the Learning Management System (LMS) communicate with each other. Even though SCORM does not speak directly to instructional designers, as it only relates to technical standards, you should be familiar with it.

SCORM governs how content communicates with an LMS and how the user is allowed to navigate between parts of the content. SCORM speaks only to the interface between content and LMS. ELearning content that is SCORM-compliant should be:

- *Accessible* – The content should be easy to find and access from one location and deliver to another location.

- *Adaptable* – The content should be adapted to organizational needs and new content should be able to be added easily and cost effectively.
- *Affordable* – The time and costs involved in training delivery should be minimized while production should be maximized.
- *Durable* – New content should be added without having to redesign or recode the course.
- *Interoperable* – ELearning courses should easily run in any location and on any CMS regardless of the location and set of tools used to develop the training.
- *Reusable* – Instructional designers should be able to reuse any part of the course to create other courses or to present contents as standalone modules.

The best way to ensure SCORM compliance is to use a SCORM-compliant authoring tool. Among these tools are Adobe Captivate, Adobe Presenter, Camtasia, Articulate Studio, and Articulate Storyline.

Reusable Learning Objects

Instructional designers always look for techniques to develop their courses quickly and inexpensively. One of the best ways to save time and money is by reusing course components. Course pieces that can be used again in a different context such as another course are known as Reusable Learning Objects (RLOs). For instance, if the lesson contains graphics, instructional designers can save and reuse them when developing other courses. For course pieces to be reusable, they must be designed as standalone objects. For example, reusable objects should not have transitions, summaries, or information presented in another part of the course. Additionally, truly reusable objects should all be created using the same style.

So, where should the reusable content be stored? You can create folders that everyone on the team or in the organization would have access to and save your reusable objects there. Alternatively, RLOs can be stored in a Content Management System (CMS).

Section 508

Section 508 is part of the Rehabilitation Act of 1973 amended in 1998. According to Section 508, all electronic and information technology must be accessible by people with disabilities. In other words, all eLearning courses must meet the needs of people with visual, auditory, and motor disabilities. The output of most eLearning courses, even those created with rapid tools, is Flash, which is not Section 508-compliant. Therefore, to meet the accessibility standards, ISD professionals should consider other ways to comply with the law. Some of these ways include the following:

- Providing a text equivalent for every non-text element;
- Offering synchronized captions for all audio and video files;
- Ensuring that all the information presented with color is also available without color;
- Avoiding elements that flash, whether text, graphics, or objects;
- Identifying row and column headers for all tables;
- Providing a text-only page with information equivalent to that on the non-text version;
- Adding alternative text for all images;
- Designing accessible and consistent navigation;
- Making a Camtasia movie of all interactive slides and elements.

There are many assistive technologies available to accommodate people with disabilities and give them an opportunity to benefit from eLearning courses. For example, JAWS (**J**ob **A**ccess **W**ith **S**peech) is a screen reader that allows visually impaired users to read the screen with a text-to-speech output or on a refreshable Braille display. Braille displays, screen magnification devices, and speech recognition software such as Dragon Naturally Speaking, all help people with visual or movement disabilities receive a similar experience to that of learners who take the interactive version of the course.

Obviously, assistive technology can merely replicate the content from the course, not its interactive elements. However, when developing eLearning, instructional designers should strive to increase the accessibility of their courses by using the above-mentioned strategies.

Exercise 14

Think about the implementation of your course. Which questions are you going to ask your stakeholder? How are you going to ensure your course is SCORM and Section 508-compliant? Are you going to have any reusable learning objects? How are you going to create them?

Chapter 17: Evaluation

This chapter will cover:

- Formative and summative evaluation
- Kirkpatrick's Four Levels of Evaluation
- Application of Kirkpatrick's model to eLearning courses
- Relationship between Needs Analysis and Kirkpatrick's Four Levels of Evaluation
- Level 5 evaluation: ROI model

Evaluation plays a vital role in training. It ensures that courses stay on track while they are being developed. It also ensures that training meets standards and expectations and helps instructional designers identify the strengths and weaknesses of their materials. Furthermore, evaluation ensures that all learning objectives have been met and the business goal has been achieved. A good system of evaluating training provides valuable information for the learner, management, and, ultimately, the instructional designer. Most training decisions such as those on additions, deletions, or modifications to the training programs are based on the information collected during the evaluation phase. Evaluations also help prioritize training needs at the organizational level. As a result of evaluation, resources can be shifted from training that has less impact on business goals to training that has a more promising cost-benefit ratio. In other words, evaluation ensures that training programs improve performance, which is the ultimate goal of all courses.

Formative and Summative Evaluation

The evaluation phase consists of two parts: formative and summative.
Formative evaluation occurs in all phases of the design process and ensures that the training course stays on track while it is being developed. Some of the questions that instructional designers should ask as they evaluate each phase of the ADDIE model are:

Analysis – Is this a training problem? What must learners be able to do to ensure the desired change in performance?

Design – What must participants learn that will enable them to fulfill the goal? Are all objectives measurable and observable?

Development – What activities and interactions will result in the required performance?

Implementation – Have learners become performers?

During formative evaluation, instructional designers should conduct delivery method, content, and usability reviews.

Summative evaluation, on the other hand, is the process of reviewing a course after implementation. It measures training outcomes in terms of learners' opinions about the course, assessment results, job performance, and return of investment (ROI) to the organization.

Donald Kirkpatrick's Four Levels of Evaluation

In the 1950s, Donald Kirkpatrick established the Four Levels of Evaluation model:

- *Level 1: Reaction*
- *Level 2: Learning*
- *Level 3: Behavior*
- *Level 4: Results*

Level 1: Reaction

Reaction is the first level of evaluation. It is the easiest way to evaluate any training program. At this level, you find out what learners think about the training. Reaction is typically measured through surveys, questionnaires, and verbal feedback. It is a fairly inexpensive way to gather information about the quality of the course. This level of evaluation is conducted immediately after the training event. Donald Kirkpatrick suggests asking for learners' feelings on all aspects of the course, including content and presentation methods. He also recommends making the reaction form anonymous to encourage honest feedback. When creating evaluation questions, consider including open-ended questions that allow learners to put their feelings and attitudes toward the course in writing.

Level 2: Learning

Learning is the second level of evaluation. It assesses the extent to which learners gained knowledge and skills and whether they learned what was expected of them. Pre-tests and post-tests are typical tools used to evaluate learning. If, however, the course is intended for beginners, there is no need for a pre-test. Instead, you should assess learners in different ways throughout the entire course. For instance, you can create a game or simulation that would allow learners to evaluate their knowledge, skills, and attitudes in an interactive way.

Level 3: Behavior

The third level of evaluation measures the extent to which change in behavior actually occurred. It measures whether or not learners apply the knowledge and skills they gained at the training to their job. Whenever possible, measure the before-and-after behavior to determine whether the change took place. To ensure more accurate results, Kirkpatrick suggests allowing sufficient time for a change to occur. Then, conduct surveys or interviews with learners, their management, and with the other people who constantly observe the learners' on-the-job performance. Before drawing the conclusion that the desired change has not occurred, and therefore no learning has taken place, keep in mind that several factors can contribute to learners' behavior. For instance, even though learners may have learned a lot from the course, their supervisor may not have given them an opportunity to apply their new knowledge and skills. In addition, because of the lack of on-the-job rewards, learners may simply be unmotivated to use what they learned in the training session. Even though interviews and focus groups can provide a lot of valuable data, the recommended practice is to conduct surveys to measure the real change in behavior. Being able to provide anonymous responses is key to honest feedback, especially when it comes to a change in behavior. Surveys will allow you to get the feedback you need without intimidating training participants.

Level 4: Results

Results are the fourth level of evaluation. This final level is the main reason for taking the training course and is considered the most important of all levels. It measures whether the employee's performance improved as a result of completing the training, and whether the organization benefited from it. Like the third level, the forth level of evaluation should be measured both before and after the session. It is also advisable to measure results several times after the training has taken place. Before measuring the results, however, you need to measure the third level and determine whether the desired change in behavior has occurred. If the change in behavior has not occurred and training participants have not been applying new knowledge and skills to the job, then conducting the fourth level of evaluation is unnecessary. Some ways to collect information for the results level of evaluation include conducting follow-up needs assessments, interviewing managers, leading focus groups, and sending out surveys.

When conducting the Four Levels of Evaluation, aligning each level with a needs analysis is important. Table 14 illustrates the relationship between the needs analysis and Kirkpatrick's Four Levels of Evaluation.

Table 14 Relationship between Needs Analysis and Kirkpatrick's Four Levels of Evaluation

Levels of Evaluation	Needs Analysis
Level 1- Reaction	Learners' Needs
Level 2 - Learning	Learners' Needs
Level 3 - Behavior	Performance Needs
Level 4 - Results	Business Needs

Level 5: The ROI model

Since Donald Kirkpatrick created his Four Levels of Evaluation, theorists including Kirkpatrick himself have modified the original version to better suit modern requirements. Jack Phillips added a fifth step to the already existing four levels of evaluation. His fifth level is known as Return-of-Investment or ROI. It compares the monetary program benefits with the program costs. According to Phillips, ROI should be measured between three and twelve months after the training. The evaluation of ROI is, in essence, a conversion of the Level 4 results into the monetary value and comparison of the monetary value with the cost of the training. When calculating ROI, you must keep in mind the analysis, design, development, implementation, and evaluation costs as well as acquisition and overhead costs. Interviews with supervisors and managers can provide an estimate for ROI calculations. In some cases, however, you may have to review extant data to get more accurate results. Use the following formula to calculate ROI:

$$\text{ROI\% = } \frac{\text{Benefits} - \text{Costs of Training x 100}}{\text{Costs of Training}}$$

Exercise 15

How are you going to evaluate your course? What methods are you going to use to evaluate learners' reaction, learning, behavior, and results? How are you going to measure ROI?

Chapter 18:
Assessments

This chapter will cover:

- Reasons for including assessments in eLearning courses
- Validity and reliability of assessment items
- Writing effective assessment items
- Types of assessment questions
- Scoring assessments
- Providing corrective feedback
- Intrinsic vs. extrinsic feedback

Assessments

At this stage, you would have conducted the necessary analysis, written learning objectives for the course, created storyboards, and even identified opportunities for interactivity, games, and simulations. The next step is to create effective assessment methods. Assessments allow both learners and their management to see whether they mastered the knowledge and skills presented in the course.

Below are some of the major reasons for including assessments in your training.

Assessments help to:
- draw attention to the most important elements in the content of the course;
- determine the effectiveness of the course;
- measure the extent to which learners have mastered course objectives;
- reinforce learning through corrective feedback;
- identify learners' strengths and weaknesses; and
- keep track of learners' progress.

Effective test questions must cover the objectives of the course; in addition, they must
- be valid and reliable;
- have correctly written stems;

- include appropriate distractors; and
- provide constructive feedback.

The assessment instrument you select should be appropriate to the specific situation. When creating assessment items, concentrate on the learners' ability to apply content rather than their ability to recall facts. While recall questions are much easier to construct, they are not nearly as effective as questions that allow learners to analyze and apply what they have learned in the lesson. In addition, recall questions typically promote lower-order learning while assessment items geared towards application and analysis promote higher-order learning. Although memorizing facts and obtaining passive knowledge are important parts of learning, true learning and the ability to perform tasks come from higher-order learning. Learning is a process of acquiring new knowledge and skills and transferring them to the next level, known as application. The goal of training courses should be to promote higher-order learning through proper activities, hands-on exercises, and assessments that allow learners to analyze and apply new information.

Validity and Reliability of Assessment Items

Validity refers to the extent to which the assessment instruments measure the outcomes they are intended to measure. To ensure validity, assessment questions should be clearly written and easy to understand. If, for example, learners misinterpret the intended meaning of a test question, the results would no longer be valid. When writing test questions, the goal is to accurately assess the knowledge and skills specified in the learning objectives. To improve validity, you should write assessment items that focus on the application of knowledge rather than just comprehension level. As you create assessment instruments, consider having professional colleagues review them. Then, if necessary, revise your questions based on the reviewers' feedback.

Reliability refers to the ability of the measured items to produce consistent results over a period of time. While test validity determines whether the assessment accurately measures what it is intended to measure, test reliability determines how frequently it succeeds in doing so. Providing clear and specific instructions for each assessment item can significantly improve its validity. To increase reliability, tests should not be too short in length as short tests can influence the overall results whereas longer tests will not affect the results as much. However, since the primary goal of assessments is to measure learning objectives, the nature of these objectives may influence the duration of a test.

Therefore, the number of assessment items included in the test and thus the reliability of that assessment strongly depends on learning objectives.

When it comes to the multiple choice questions, which typically consist of a stem, correct answer choice and incorrect options known as distractors, creating reliable items can be especially challenging. Distractors should still make sense, but at the same time, they must be decidedly incorrect.

You should also keep in mind that the difficulty level of all test questions should not be the same. Otherwise, the reliability of your items will significantly decrease.

Writing Effective Assessment Items

There are three major types of assessment items. They are

- *Diagnostic assessments* – Also known as pretests. Some of the reasons for conducting diagnostic assessments include:
  - finding out how much learners already know about a given topic;
  - delivering various versions or levels of a course to the needs of learners based on their performance in such tests;
  - allowing learners to test out if they already possess adequate knowledge of the content to be presented in the course; and
  - helping to shape learners' expectations about the course coverage.
- *Formative assessments* – Include questions after each topic or module, and allow measurement of learners' understanding of each unit of content.
- *Summative assessments* – Also known as post-tests. They are given at the end of a training session to check learners' understanding of the overall content.

The most common types of assessment questions are:

- multiple choice
- true/false
- fill-in-the-blank
- matching
- free responses/short answers/essays

Multiple Choice Questions

Multiple choice questions are probably the most popular type of assessment in eLearning. These questions require learners to choose the best response from several options. When creating multiple choice questions, you should indicate in the instructions area the number of possible correct responses. This step will avoid confusion among learners. Multiple choice questions are composed of three parts:

- question stems,
- correct answer or answers, and
- distractors.

You should create your assessment items in such a way that learners only have to read the stem once to begin formulating their answers. Stems can include either complete direct questions such as, *What is Instructional Design?* or statement completions items, such as, *Instructional Design is....* The second type requires that the correct answers are inserted into the blank to complete the statement. When writing question stems, you should try to keep them short and, if possible, choose complete direct questions over statement completion items. Longer stems can be easily misinterpreted. Therefore, the results gathered from such questions will not be accurate indicators of learning, and the question itself will not be reliable. If the question is in the incomplete statement format, the stem must end with a word common to all answer options so that each option flows logically from it. The example below illustrates this concept.

Example:
The role of an instructional designer is to design:
  a. *graphics*
  b. *courses*
  c. *houses*
  d. *clothes*

Instead of repeating the word *design* in each option, it was included in the question stem. While most incomplete question stems should have a verb, you should consider the grammatical structure of both stems and answer options when constructing your assessments.

Another suggestion for ensuring the clarity of questions or statement stems is to avoid negatives. Oftentimes, learners overlook the word *not* and, as a result, choose an incorrect response. Rewording negative question stems will make assessment items more reliable. If the stem cannot be reworded, bolding, underlining, or capitalizing the negatives will draw the learners' attention to these negatives and help them concentrate on the actual question. It is also suggested to add negatives at the end of the question stem and use capital letters to bring attention to them. The example below illustrates this concept.

Example:
All of the following are Gagné's Events of Instruction EXCEPT:

The stems should be written in a way that does not automatically reveal the correct response to any of the questions on the assessment. This can be accomplished by including only the information needed to answer each specific question and avoiding information that can be used to answer another question on the test. For example, using the same word in both the stem and the option can easily reveal the correct response. Another way to avoid the unintentional revelation of correct responses is to eliminate such grammatical cues as a/an. This can be done by including both options in the stem. The example below illustrates this concept.

Example:
A/An_____ about instructional design is now available on the Amazon Kindle.

 a. *eBook*
 b. *Report*

If, on the other hand, the stem had included only "an" instead of "a/an," the learner would be able to easily guess the correct response.

While correctly written stems are crucial for developing reliable test questions, it is equally important to choose appropriate distractors for each item. You should include no more than five answer choices in each question that is one correct answer and three or four distractors. Unless it is a multiple-answer question, there should only be one correct response. While all other options are distractors, they should still be plausible, meaning that they should make perfect sense in the context of the question. The best way to come up with distractors for assessment questions is to think of common errors that learners make and turn these errors into distractors. The following example illustrates this concept.

Example:

According to Robert Gagné's Nine Events of Instruction, *the first step in creating an effective lesson is:*
     A. *Gaining learners' attention*
     B. *Analyzing learners' current performance*
     C. *Stimulating recall of prior knowledge*
     D. *Eliciting performance*

While this question makes perfect sense and the correct answer choice is clearly *A*, the first distractor is not plausible because analyzing learners' performance is not part of Gagné's Nine Events of Instruction.

All the answer choices included in the question should be consistent in terms of content, form, and grammatical structure. In other words, all options should be logically derived from the stem so that test-takers would not be able to guess the correct answer based on the fact that the other options do not flow logically or grammatically from the stem. Additionally, all answer choices should be either nouns, verbs, or adjectives, not a mixture of three depending on the sentence construction and its relationship to the answer options provided. Otherwise, the item will appear confusing and may unintentionally reveal the correct response. Keeping both the correct response and distractors similar in length will also prevent learners from guessing the correct answer.

Many assessments use qualifiers such as *always* and *never* as well as absolutes such as *all of the above,* or *none of the above.* While it is tempting to include these phrases in your distracters, they make the options too easy, as they are often the correct response. The same principle applies to the "*Both A and B are correct*" option.

If learners do not know the answers to the questions, they often use guesswork. When learners do not know which option to pick, they frequently select option *B* as their answer. The reason for this is that when instructional designers create questions, they often make *B* the correct response. To improve reliability of the assessment, you should consider varying the placement of correct responses.

True/False Questions

True/false questions typically measure understanding of facts such as names, dates, and definitions. This type of question requires learners to choose between the two options, leaving them with a 50/50 chance of guessing the correct response. True/false questions are also difficult to construct without making the correct response too obvious. The main downside to this type of question, however, is that it only assesses learning at the knowledge level. If, however, you want to test at the application level, these items will not give adequate and reliable results. To avoid confusion, only include one idea in each statement. Just like with multiple choice items, true/false questions should be clearly worded and should not include negatives, broad statements, qualifiers, and absolutes.

Fill-in-the-Blank Questions

Fill-in-the-blank questions are also known as completion items. This type of question requires learners to finish a sentence by filling the correct word or phrase in a blank. While fill-in-the-blank questions are beneficial to learners, they are difficult to construct as they must be written in a way that significantly reduces guessing the correct response.

Matching Questions

The matching type of assessment consists of a list of questions or statements and a list of responses. Learners should find a match or association between each question and response. This type of exercise can be very effective because it can cover a lot of content at the same time and test learners' understanding of the material at the application level. However, constructing matching exercises can be challenging. While all of the options should be plausible, there should be only one correct answer choice. In addition, when constructing matching exercises, ensuring that both columns or lists are similar in content is important. A good practice is having the questions/statements on the left side as a numbered list and answer choices on the right side as a lettered list. Another practice is to include more answer choices than questions. Otherwise, learners will easily respond to the last question using the process of elimination.

Free response/Short answer/Essay Questions

While free response questions are less commonly used compared to multiple choice, true/false, and fill-in-the-blank assessment items, there are many benefits associated with this type of question. Free response questions require learners to understand the content in order to answer the question. It is nearly impossible for learners to answer this type of question correctly by guessing or eliminating incorrect responses. In addition, free response questions require a higher level of thinking, analyzing, and logically presenting information. At the same time, because instructional designers do not have to worry about plausible distractors, free response questions are easier to construct compared to other question types. For learners, these questions help put their newly acquired knowledge in perspective. For instance, instructional designers can present realistic scenarios that enable learners to apply what they have learned in the course to solve a problem. However, free response questions should be used sparingly as they can be difficult to score. In synchronous eLearning courses, trainers can grade questions or provide corrective feedback to each participant, but grading free response questions in asynchronous eLearning is impossible. Therefore, the only way to provide constructive feedback is by restating the points that learners should have covered in their responses.

To Score or Not to Score

There is no one correct answer to whether or not instructional designers should score assessments. Most people, however, prefer to see how well they did on the test. Scores motivate them to learn and master the content. However, some learners are afraid of failure and tend to avoid taking scored assessments. There are also learners who feel that scored tests are a pedagogical approach to learning not suitable for adult learners who simply need guidance to achieve better performance results, not scores. In spite of negative attitudes towards scores, scored assessments provide information to management about learners' progress and determine whether the learner is ready to move on to the next, more advanced level. When it comes to assessments, you should consider the nature and requirements of each training course as well as the organizational culture to determine whether the lesson will benefit from scored assessments. Whenever possible, involve stakeholders in the decision making process as they are typically more familiar with organizational culture and values than you are.

Corrective Feedback

Providing corrective feedback is imperative as it allows learners to progress toward their goal and tells them whether they have mastered the content from the course. Feedback also shows learners the parts of the course that need to be revisited or reviewed. When providing feedback to learners, you need to ensure that the overall tone is friendly and supportive even if the question was answered incorrectly. The goal of corrective feedback is not to embarrass or scold learners but to provide remediation and promote learning.

Most feedback statements should be composed of the following four parts:

1. *Acknowledgment of learners' response.* For example: *"That's correct"* or *"Sorry, that's incorrect."*
2. *Statement of the correct response.* For example: *"The correct answer is 'True.'"* Note that this statement should only be included if the learner chose the incorrect response.
3. *Repetition of the correct response.* Instead of saying *"The correct answer is B,"* consider repeating the entire statement. For example: *The correct answer is B. Instructional designers create prototypes during the development phase of the ADDIE model..."*
4. *Explanation of why the response is correct.* For example: *"...because prototypes are typically developed after conducting thorough needs analysis and writing learning objectives."*

To offer further remediation for incorrect responses, the course can branch back to the sections that provide information for the question that was answered incorrectly.

Intrinsic and Extrinsic Feedback

The feedback that learners receive can be either intrinsic or extrinsic. Intrinsic feedback is an indirect type of feedback. It immediately lets learners know they made a mistake and allows them to make adjustments based on that feedback. An example of intrinsic feedback is showing a person shaking head whenever the learner answers incorrectly.

Extrinsic feedback, on the other hand, is a direct type of feedback that comments on the learner's performance in a straightforward way. For example: "That's correct" or "No, that's incorrect."

The type of course, presentation methods, and assessment instruments chosen determine the type of feedback you provide. For example, while extrinsic feedback may be a good choice for multiple choice questions, it may not work well for a game. When learners play a game, they do not want to be interrupted; therefore, intrinsic feedback will guide their learning and provide information on how their response should be adjusted.

Exercise 16

Decide on the assessment instruments you are going to use to test your learners. Think about how you are going to ensure the validity and reliability of your assessment. Then, create one effective assessment item and the appropriate corrective feedback for it.

Part III - Interactive Elements in the ELearning Course

"Tell me and I forget, teach me and I may remember, involve me and I learn."
— Benjamin Franklin

Chapter 19:
Interactivity in ELearning

This chapter will cover:

- The role of interactivity in eLearning
- The four levels of interactivity
- Navigation and layout

The best way to lose your learners is to offer them a click-and-read course with lots of text on the pages. Adding interactivity to courses can help you avoid this problem. Interactivity is an exercise or activity that allows the learner to become more involved with the content by discovering information and checking knowledge through assessments, simulations, and games as opposed to simply reading text on the computer screen. To avoid text-heavy pages, you can add popup text boxes. Expandable charts, graphs, tables, and animations that appear in small chunks can also help you avoid having a large amount of text on the screen.

An interaction can be a scenario where the learner is presented with a problem that needs to be worked out to achieve a certain outcome. It can also take a form of a role-play, content revelation after selecting a specific object, or a game that puts learners in realistic setting and allows them to explore, try, succeed, and fail in a safe environment.

For example, if you are developing a new eLearning course for legal assistants, it may include some videos that present relevant information as well as some *clicking on the objects to reveal information* activities. Then, to test learners' understanding, you can add a game where future legal assistants would have to make decisions and answer questions related to certain on-the-job situations in a virtual world environment. If they answer incorrectly, the game would bring them to the remediation page. The game could also address possible consequences if people get that same question wrong in real life. While the game would illustrate situations legal assistants may come across at their job, no one will judge them for selecting incorrect responses. When learners actively perform tasks rather than passively sit and read or listen to something, they tend to retain more information. Additionally, when learners learn new material through trial and error, they are less likely to make the same mistake again. Remember, learners do not want to take courses that contain screen after screen of information. They do not want to read textbooks. All they want is to take a course that will help them address their current problems by providing relevant information in the most interactive and engaging manner. Instead of having learners go through bulleted lists, instructional designers should put them in realistic situations and force them to learn by making decisions.

Interactivity allows learners to become more involved with the content. The goal of any interaction is to process, encode, and store the material in memory. Most instructional designers sprinkle in one interaction for every 10 to 15 minutes of learning. It is important to keep the type of content in mind when deciding on the amount of interactivity. If the content is dry and boring, adding more interactions may spice it up and make the lesson more exciting and motivational.

Most eLearning courses can be classified according to four levels of interactivity:

Level 1 – Passive Interactions. Involve very limited interactivity such as assessment at the end of the lesson or module. The content is mostly linear and static. In this level, learners do not have control over the course. They can only passively sit and either read or watch the lesson. This type of eLearning is inexpensive compared to the other types and can be effective when communicating simple concepts and facts. However, passive courses are not very motivational for learners.

Level 2 – Limited Interactions. Give learners more control over the sequence of a course. The course may contain some multiple choice questions, hyperlinks to additional resources, simple activities such as matching and drag-and-drop, audio, and video. This type of eLearning can be effective when teaching facts or systematic procedures.

Level 3 – Complex Interactions. Give learners even more control of the course. The course may include animations, complex simulations, and scenarios. Most eLearning lessons fit into this category because this level of interactivity finds a balance between reasonable development time and active learning. This type of eLearning can be used to improve proficiency, to learn physical or mental skills, or to solve problems.

Level 4 – Real-Time Interactions. Involve all the elements of Levels 1, 2, and 3, plus very complex content, serious games, and 3D simulations. This level of interactivity often uses avatars, custom videos, and interactive objects. Real-time interactions can be used to have learners solve problems or apply their knowledge to real life situations. Even though real-time interactions are highly effective and motivational, they are very time consuming and expensive to develop.

Many factors can influence instructional designers' decision to select one level of interactivity over the other. Some of these factors are target audience, budget, content, and available resources. You should know that most courses that involve complex and real-time interactions are not 508-compliant. Therefore, if your eLearning course has to meet accessibility requirements, the choices will be limited to Level 1 and 2 interactions.

Navigation

ELearning courses can be either linear or non-linear. Linear courses are set up in a way where learners must go through the entire section before they can move to the next one. Linear courses require learners to complete the entire training. Typically, all mandatory courses including compliance-training have linear navigation. Non-linear navigation, also known as branched navigation, allows learners to jump from one section to the next in any desired order. There are some pitfalls and benefits to each type of navigation. Even though linear navigation is a good way to make learners go through the entire training, many learners find it boring and ineffective. Additionally, because the navigation is locked, learners cannot go back and review those sections that were not clear to them. As a result, their level of understanding and retention goes down. Moreover, according to adult learning principles, adults learn better when they can make their own decisions; therefore, locking navigation will not motivate them to take the course. Non-linear navigation, however, permits learners to go through the course in any order that they want, allowing them to skip or review sections. This, however, can be problematic because learners often treat such courses as "click through," which results in minimal understanding, retention, and application of the material. In contrast, with non-linear courses, learners have an option to go back and review any section that they want and therefore increase their retention rate. While there is no single best answer as to what type of navigation is better, it is suggested that you treat each course separately and design navigation based on course content and requirements. Using non-linear navigation whenever possible and motivating learners to complete the entire course by offering vivid and interactive presentation is more effective than having learners go through the course in a linear manner. During the analysis phase, explain all the benefits and pitfalls of linear and non-linear navigation to the client to ensure the end-result matches the stakeholder's vision.

Exercise 17

Think about the look and feel of your course. Will it be linear or non-linear?

Now, based on what you know about your course, decide on the level of interactivity you will include, and state your reasons for choosing one over the other.

Chapter 20:
Simulations and Games

This chapter will cover:

- The difference between games and simulations
- Types of learning games
- Elements of learning games
- Creating a story for the learning game
- Games as assessments
- Structure of the game
- Virtual Worlds
- Avatars
- Storytelling and scenario-based learning
- Choosing a game for the eLearning course

Today, many instructional designers use simulations and games in their training courses because they believe games help learners understand and retain the content. However, to create a learning experience, you should be familiar with different types of games as well as the process of effective game design.

What is a learning game? The learning game is an activity inserted into any eLearning course with the goal of improving the learning process and motivating the learner to complete the course.

A professionally designed game is an excellent learning aid. It helps learners clarify difficult concepts and practice the newly acquired knowledge and skills. When you incorporate games into your courses, you provide learners with an opportunity to practice and apply what they have learned in the lesson. Games also spark interest in learners, which leads to increased motivation, and as a result, better understanding and retention.

Types of Learning Games

Before getting into the design process, you must be able to choose the type of game you want to create. Some of the popular games in eLearning are:

- *Casual games*
- *Serious games*
- *Advergames*
- *Simulation games*
- *Assessment games*

Casual games

Casual games engage learners in a fun way. The purpose of such games is to reinforce the learning objectives through play. Some of the casual games include drag and drop, sequencing, and matching. These games can be easily created with a rapid eLearning tool and do not require any programming or technical skills.

Serious games

Serious games are typically simulations with other elements of game design. The intention of serious games is to improve a specific aspect of learning. Serious games are very popular in health care, military training, and in corporate education. The main goal of serious games is to achieve measurable and sustainable changes in learners' performance or behavior.

Advergames

Advergames include elements of both casual and serious games. These games are often used for advertisement and marketing purposes. Many times, they are designed in such a way that players do not even realize there is an advertisement involved.

Simulations

Simulations or branching scenarios are typically scenarios that allow learners to go through situations they will most likely encounter in real life. Simulations expose learners to many different choices they have to make and continue to the next step based on the decisions they make. Branching scenarios can either be a part of a serious game or a standalone activity in the eLearning course.

Assessments

As instructional designers look for new and engaging ways to present content, many of them want to test learners' knowledge without adding traditional true/false and multiple choice types of questions. Instead, they hide tests behind a game skin. Some examples of games used purely for assessment purposes are snakes and ladders, hangman, and popular game show variations. While these games are fun to play, they are neither engaging nor task-oriented. The sole purpose of such games is to test the content using a different approach.

Game Structure

The simplest way to approach the learning game design is to mimic the elements found in typical video games. The elements of a good game include the following:

- *Rules* – This is an important element of any game. Rules add structure as well as a sense of expectation. If learners do not know the rules, they will not know how to play the game and will soon become frustrated and disinterested.

- *Score* – This element adds excitement and forces learners to continue with the game. Players want to know if they are winning or losing.

- *Rewards* – Just like scores, this element adds excitement to the learning experience. Medals, badges, and points are some examples of rewards that can be given to learners as they complete each level of the game or provide correct responses to questions.

- *Strategy* – This element allows players to manipulate the game to maximize their score. Giving learners rewards and bonus points for completing a level or achieving certain milestones are ways to add strategy to the game design.

- *Message* – This element is responsible for communicating the objectives and goals of a lesson. Hide your messages in the game and allow players to discover them as they go.

- *Challenge* – You should aim to provide clear goals and feedback to engage learners in the game. It is important to make sure the goals are immediate. In other words, learners are much more likely to succeed if they know that they will achieve their goal instantly rather than a few days after playing the game. In addition to clear goals and appropriate feedback, learners should experience a certain degree of curiosity or surprise. You should give them control by providing enough but not too many options. If exposed to many choices, learners may become frustrated and refuse to continue exploring the game.

- *Risk* – This is a very important part of game design, especially when it comes to serious games. Learners want to have a sense of risk. Design your games to make the failure possible but avoidable and ensure that, regardless of how players move, failure is not their final result.

- *Levels and Titles* – This element allows you to split the course into sections providing learners with the opportunity to move on to Level 2 after completing Level 1. As learners move through the levels, their titles can change from Novice to Expert. Assigning levels and titles will motivate learners to complete the course.

- *Feedback* – This is an important motivational element in any game. As learners progress through the course, they expect appropriate motivational feedback. Corrective feedback can be either direct or indirect. *Great job! You are well on your way to becoming a superstar* is an example of a direct type of feedback while assigning scores is an indirect type of feedback. Regardless of the type of feedback provided, it should not interrupt the flow of the game.

Always keep in mind that learning games should align with your objectives and be based on a relevant, interesting, and meaningful story. To add a motivational factor to the story, the game can have learners go on a journey, discover a secret, or conquer the opponent. While being creative can add a spark to the plot, the story should not be unreasonably complex. Otherwise, the game will increase the extraneous load. The following questions should help you plan your learning game.

- Who are the characters?

- What are the genders, ages, and physical characteristics of characters?
- What happens to the characters in the game?
- How does that affect the players in the game?
- What learning objectives will the story cover?
- What content should the story cover?
- What will motivate learners to continue playing?
- What type of feedback will be provided?
- When would the learners win and when would they lose the game?
- What will happen at the beginning, in the middle, and at the end of the story?
- Where does the story take place?

The success of any learning game depends on instructional sequencing and methods as well as on the plot and motivational factors included in the game.

Virtual Worlds

Virtual Worlds are immersive 3D online environments where users can interact with any other users and characters. In a Virtual World, learners can experiment, plan, solve problems, negotiate, collaborate, evaluate, learn from mistakes, and take risks while learning new skills. The environment of Virtual World is three-dimensional, which allows users to choose an "avatar." While there are many virtual worlds, some of the most popular are *Second Life, Active Worlds*, and *There*.

Many instructional designers like to include Virtual Worlds in their courses for the purpose of collaboration. They also design their lectures, demonstrations, simulations, and experiences in the Virtual World environment. Additionally, Virtual Worlds work well for distance learning where trainers can post slides, audio, video presentations, and even self-paced tutorials. Virtual Worlds are a good platform for group projects. Designing one requires a lot of planning and understanding of how these environments work. In Virtual Worlds, you can create both synchronous and asynchronous learning experiences. The first step in designing the 3D environment is ensuring that learners are comfortable with the Virtual World, keeping in mind that different people learn differently depending on their background, experience, personal preference, and motivation. While some people will immerse themselves almost immediately in this 3D environment, others will need months to become comfortable and be able to fully concentrate on the learning experience.

Avatars

An avatar is a graphical representation of a character. Avatars are an effective way to engage learners. They often provide feedback and remediation to learners. In addition, avatars can ask questions and lead discussions, helping learners progress. The avatar can act as an instructor or a learning mate depending on the purpose of the game. As you plan the game, you should think about the role the avatar will play and how it will support learners.

Storytelling and Scenario-based Learning

Storytelling is a learning tool that teaches, motivates, and entertains at the same time. Well-crafted stories provide learners with necessary facts using realistic situations and at the same time evoke an emotional response. As a result, learners can easily relate to the content, better retain it, and transfer their new skills to the job.

Some of the reasons to add stories to the eLearning courses include helping learners to

- memorize facts,
- relate to an incident, or
- reflect on a situation.

Stories should contain the following elements:

- *Setting* – Where the story takes place
- *Characters* – The actors in the story
- *Problem* – The purpose of the story
- *Development* – Outcomes of correct and incorrect performance
- *Climax* – Lessons learned from the outcomes
- *Ending* – Conclusion, summary, or review of the key points

You can present stories using text, audio, or video elements, but you do not have to construct the stories yourself. Instead, consider delegating this task to Subject Matter Experts (SMEs) and have them provide stories related to the content. To help SMEs come up with relevant stories, you can ask related questions such as, *Think about a time when…*, or *What happened when….*

There are multiple ways to incorporate stories into eLearning courses. The most commonly used approach is making them part of a learning scenario. Typical learning scenarios include a realistic situation or story followed by questions that require learners to react to the story. In addition, storytelling can complement courses that include social learning elements in them. For instance, you can create a story and ask questions based on it. Then, have learners react or respond to the questions in the social media environment.

Choosing a Game for Your ELearning Course

Most of the time the type of game selected for the course will depend on the content and objectives associated with it. However, before making the decision to add a game to the course, you must determine its overall purpose. If the game does not communicate an instructional message or motivate learners, then it most likely lacks any instructional value. In addition, because game development requires significant time and resources, you must consider the shelf life of the information and skills in the game. While it may be worthwhile dedicating resources to create games for mostly static content, if the information is constantly changing and updating, it may not be worth the investment.

The large variety of learning games makes the process of picking the appropriate one challenging. To decide which game suits the needs of your specific course, you should answer the following questions:

- Who is the target audience?
- What is the learning objective?
- How will this objective be evaluated?
- What type of content will be included in the game?
- What are the intended results?

Exercise 18

Decide whether your eLearning course will include games, simulations, or scenarios. Then, using the guidelines from this chapter, outline their essential elements.

Chapter 21:
ELearning Tools

This chapter will cover:

- Adobe eLearning Suite authoring tools
- Rapid eLearning tools
- Screencasting, screenshot capturing, and interactivity development tools
- Choosing the right tool for your needs

There are many different eLearning authoring tools on the market that help instructional designers assemble their courses. Authoring tools are software used to build eLearning courses. These tools allow for the developing, editing, testing, and arranging of eLearning experiences. Authoring tools range from basic applications that have almost no learning curve to sophisticated software programs that involve coding. Earlier, when we talked about rapid eLearning design and custom eLearning design, we concluded that you should use rapid authoring tools whenever possible. Rapid authoring tools can save time, money, and resources while allowing you to produce highly effective learning experiences. Authoring tools vary in price and complexity.

Adobe eLearning Suite software is a toolbox for creating eLearning courses. These programs allow developers to create fully SCORM –compliant simulations, demonstrations, rich animation and digital imaging. Adobe eLearning Suite includes the following software:

Adobe Captivate for creating software demonstrations, simulations, branched scenarios, randomized quizzes, screencasts, and podcasts
Adobe Flash for authoring vector graphics, animation, games, and Rich Internet Applications (RIAs) which can be viewed, played, and executed in Adobe Flash Player
Adobe Dreamweaver for website development
Adobe Photoshop for editing graphics
Adobe Acrobat for viewing, creating, printing, and managing PDF files
Adobe Presenter for creating professional-quality videos and converting courses into interactive eLearning presentations
Adobe Audition for audio recording, editing, mixing, restoration and effects

Because there is programming involved, eLearning Suite allows ISD professionals to create almost anything they can possibly think of. However, course development with these tools is quite expensive and time consuming.

Nowadays, more and more instructional designers lean towards rapid eLearning tools. It is nearly impossible to cover all of them in just one chapter; therefore, we will focus on the most popular programs on the market.

There are three types of rapid eLearning authoring tools. They include PowerPoint plugin authoring tools, desktop authoring tools, and server-based authoring tools.

PowerPoint Plugin Authoring Tools

The PowerPoint plugin authoring tools use PowerPoint as the authoring environment. However, in addition to all the bells and whistles that PowerPoint offers, these tools allow instructional designers to add interactivities and assessments. Since most people are familiar with PowerPoint, they find these tools easy to use. Articulate Studio is one example of a PowerPoint plugin tool and is one of the most popular rapid eLearning tools on the market.

Articulate Studio

Articulate Studio allows instructional designers to quickly produce high-quality eLearning courses. It is comprised of Articulate Presenter, Articulate Quizmaker, Articulate Engage, and Articulate Replay. In Articulate Presenter, you can record and synchronize narration, add web objects, quizzes, interactivity, attachments, and flash movies. Articulate also offers highly customizable player templates, slide properties, and presentation options. Articulate Engage allows instructional designers to develop interactivities using pre-programmed templates in minutes. In Quizmaker, you can create both free form and form-based quizzes and scenarios. Articulate Replay is a tool for recording screencasts with your webcam and adding any media with just a few clicks. Once completed, Engage interactions, Quizmaker quizzes, and Replay videos can be easily incorporated into Articulate Presenter.

Desktop Authoring Tools

Desktop authoring tools are installed on the desktop. These tools offer more flexibility to eLearning designers, but at the same time, there is a learning curve. Some of the most popular desktop authoring tools are Articulate Storyline, Adobe Captivate, and Lectora.

Articulate Storyline

Unlike Articulate Studio, Storyline is a standalone application. Even though Storyline has templates for creating eLearning courses, the tool also allows instructional designers to create unique, fully customizable courses. Additionally, Storyline lets you import already created PowerPoint slides as well as Engage interactions and Quizmaker assessments from Articulate Studio. Storyline is known as a scenario/simulation type of tool. With this software, you can record screens and add captions, pointers, and images that can be edited externally. In addition, Storyline offers a library of both illustrated and photographic characters in different poses and with different expressions. The tool has full-fledged support for branching. More advanced users of Storyline will benefit from using variables to create courses that remember information such as learners' names.

Adobe Captivate

Even though Adobe Captivate is part of the eLearning Suite, it is still considered a rapid eLearning tool. With Captivate, you can create multimedia presentations in the form of movies. Captivate enables you to create step-by-step tutorials and animated help file enhancements. Usually, Captivate presentations contain mouse cursor movements with accompanying captioned text. They may also include multimedia elements, such as voice-overs and music. In more advanced applications, Captivate can be set up to prompt the learner for input. Just like Storyline, Captivate allows you to record software demonstrations and simulations as well as create presentations, quizzes, and screencasts. The new version of Captivate comes with a suite of characters and pre-programmed interactions that can be easily customized to meet the needs of each individual course.

Lectora

Lectora is a very powerful rapid eLearning tool by Trivantis. Because it is capable of producing high quality interactions and because there is a higher learning curve than with other rapid eLearning tools, some people do not consider Lectora a rapid authoring tool. However, once you learn how to use it, you can begin developing high-level eLearning courses very quickly. Lectora comes with image, audio, and video editing tools. This software allows you to create true/false, multiple choice, matching, hot spot, drag and drop, essay, and short answer assessments. With Lectora, you can create interactive learning objects such as mouse overs to engage learners with onscreen activities. Moreover, the tool allows designers to create branched learning scenarios. More advanced users of Lectora can add external elements as well as incorporate additional code to create custom applications.

Server-based Tools

The server-based tools are tools hosted on the server and accessible through Internet. Generally, these tools are very user friendly. Many organizations choose them because they are located on the server, and everyone on the team can easily access them and update the course when necessary. One example of a server-based authoring tool is CourseBuilder.

CourseBuilder

CourseBuilder is an easy to use, flexible authoring tool. This software comes with visual tools that allow instructional designers with limited technical skills to create groundbreaking eLearning courses and assessments. It also has a built-in comments function, which works well when other team members or SMEs want to review the project and comment on it.

Other Tools to Consider

In addition to the eLearning Suite and rapid eLearning tools, there are other software programs that do not belong in either of these categories, as they are not authoring tools. However, familiarizing yourself with these programs can be extremely advantageous for creating powerful eLearning content.

Camtasia

Camtasia Studio from TechSmith is a video-based screen capturing software program. The software is installed on the computer, so the screen captures are directly recorded in a digital video format with high quality audio. Camtasia can be customized to capture the entire screen, a specific window, or a user-defined region. Screen capture videos can be recorded with or without voice narration and annotated after recording. With Camtasia, you can create demonstrations, web site tours, narrated PowerPoint presentations, and explanations of lecture notes. Camtasia also allows the production of podcasts and vodcasts.

SnagIt

SnagIt is another software from TechSmith. This screen-capturing tool allows instructional designers to create highly engaging images, presentation videos, tutorials, and training documents. SnagIt is especially useful for developing technical training.

Raptivity

Raptivity is a tool that lets eLearning designers create a wide range of learning interactions that they can publish as .swf files. These interactions can be used as standalone learning objects or you can insert them into learning programs developed in tools such as Articulate, Lectora, or Captivate. Raptivity provides a pre-built library of more than 225 rapidly customizable interaction models including 3D, games, videos, scenario-based simulations, branching simulations, interactive diagrams, surveys, puzzles, animations, and many more. These interactions are based on the best practices in instructional design. The tool allows instructional designers to select the learning theory they want to use to create their training, such as Bloom's taxonomy, Gagné's Nine Events, or Keller's ARCS model. Once selected, Raptivity suggests a number of interactions for each step of the learning theory. With this option, even novice instructional designers can create instructionally sound eLearning courses. More experienced ISD specialists do not have to select learning interactions by learning theory and can simply browse by type of interaction instead.

Selecting the Right Tool

Before making a decision about the appropriate development tool, you should take budget, learning curve, and content requirements into consideration. Even though one tool may be perfect for creating simulations, it may not work for software demonstrations. It is suggested that instructional designers add as many eLearning tools to their arsenal as possible and use each one based on the needs and requirements of each course they develop.

The following questions should help you pick the eLearning tools that best suit your needs.

- What type of eLearning are you creating: synchronous or asynchronous?
- Does your course have social learning components such as wikis or forums?
- What type of media will your course have?
- What is the level of interactivity in your course?
- Do you need a specific output file format?
- How much money can you spend on the authoring tool?
- Does your course have to be Section 508-compliant?

Exercise 19

Based on what you know about the timeframe and budget for this project, select the tools that best suit your needs. Explain your decision.

Chapter 22:
Video in ELearning

This chapter will cover:

- When to include video in the eLearning course
- Three types of videos in eLearning
- Selecting your talent
- Screencasts in eLearning

Adding videos to your eLearning courses can either benefit or hinder the learning process. Prior to including a video recording in the course, you should review objectives to see if they lend themselves to video. Just like anything else in the course, videos must have a goal. All videos included in eLearning need a hook. They must be interesting, engaging, and educational at the same time. Commercials only have couple of seconds to get people's attention. They are short and to the point. This is exactly what all eLearning videos should be like. They should include important information and avoid superficial and irrelevant content. Long videos tend to be boring and take a lot of time to load. Instructional designers should always let the learners know that the program is loading; otherwise, learners will get frustrated and exit the course.

There are many types of videos that can be used in eLearning. However, most instructional designers use short video clips, talking heads, or scenarios.

- *Short video clips* – These are video clips from YouTube or any other source that are relevant to the content. Instructional designers should keep in mind that most courses benefit from short videos of no more than five minutes. If the video is longer, breaking it into a number of shorter chunks needs to be considered. This can be done by pausing after each clip to ask questions or presenting opportunities for learners to actively interact with the content instead of passively watch a video.
- *Talking heads* – The main problem with talking heads is that they often appear uninteresting and dull. Therefore, in general, it is recommended to avoid this type of video in eLearning. However, there are certain situations when a talking head video can be beneficial. For instance, your talking

head can briefly introduce the course, or serve as a guide and appear for a brief period of time to guide or coach learners, then disappear from the scene and reappear when necessary.

- *Scenarios* – Video scenarios are a perfect way to assess learning. One way to add scenarios to courses is to have learners watch a role-play or a situation that illustrates certain points from the course. Then, ask learners what they would do in this situation, or have them identify what went wrong. Using scenarios to get learners' attention at the beginning of the course and building the entire lesson based on that scenario is also a common practice.

Producing eLearning Videos

To effectively convey learning messages, eLearning videos must be done in a professional way. Hiring a professional videographer can be very expensive, so if money is an issue, you should consider self-producing your video.

The camera is the most important piece of equipment for shooting videos. There are many options to choose from, starting from the webcam built into the laptop to the expensive professional cameras. While the camera selected will mainly depend on your budget, the following questions should be considered:

- What resolution do you need? The options are 480i, 720p, and 1080i. Remember, higher resolution equals higher quality.
- What kind of zoom do you want? The answer to this question depends on your budget. While optical zoom costs more than digital zoom, the video quality with optical zoom will be much better than with digital zoom.
- What kinds of controls do you want? There are manual and automatic controls.
- What battery life are you looking for?
- Do you need a night vision?
- What kind of lighting do you need? There are built-in and external lighting options.

Once the camera and script are ready for the shoot, you can choose actors and assign roles to them. Hiring professional actors is rather expensive, but it will give the most professional results. If the budget for the project is low, using people on your team or other volunteers should be considered. Presenters who are not professional actors may feel uncomfortable being on camera. Leaving plenty of time for rehearsal is the best way to bring their comfort level up. As eLearning professionals guide actors through production, they should pay attention to their tone of voice, facial expressions, speech rate, and gestures as well as their attire and overall appearance. The way of acting and presenting in front of camera should fit the subject matter as well as the target audience for the course. The presentation should not be offensive in any way.

Obviously, it is unrealistic to ask the talent to memorize the script. This is where a teleprompter comes handy. The teleprompter is a device that displays the script to allow presenters concentrate on their delivery rather than the material they present. Reading from a teleprompter, however, requires practice. The goal is to sound as natural as possible. Learners should not notice that the presenter is reading. Rehearsals and practice should help actors achieve the most natural result.

When it comes to video development, file size becomes a major issue. This is especially true if the video is high quality. To keep file sizes under control, instructional designers should consider splitting them into smaller segments and compressing as much as possible. Uploading a video on YouTube and taking it down will automatically compress it.

Even if you are fully satisfied with the video and believe it fits the lesson well, it is still a good idea to receive client's approval before implementing it into the course.

Screencasts in eLearning

Screencasts are the recordings of a computer screen converted into a movie. Even though screencasting is a relatively new addition to eLearning, it is becoming increasingly popular for the development of software and information technology-related training courses. Training that includes demonstrations of the use of online tools such as websites or catalogues can also benefit from screencasts.

When it comes to designing screencasts, you should treat them as videos. There are both free and paid tools for creating screencasts. Camtasia Studio and Adobe Captivate are the most popular commercial tools for recording screens. Screenr and Jing are among the most commonly used, free, screencasting tools that have similar features to Camtasia and Captivate. The drawback to most free tools is that later editing of recordings is not possible; therefore, every time you make a mistake, you will have to go back to the beginning and rerecord the entire presentation. Commercial tools, on the other hand, allow for editing out any mistakes made during recording. In addition, both Camtasia and Captivate are desktop tools, meaning the screencasts can be saved to the desktop as opposed to having to publish them online as is the case with free, non-commercial tools.

Because screencasts are typically used for tutorials that teach how to use tools or programs, it is especially important that they cover all the steps. Oftentimes, Subject Matter Experts (SMEs) are so familiar with the topic and have used the tool so many times that they omit small steps important for learners seeing the program or tool for the first time. Therefore, after receiving the script for a screencast from an SME, you should ask for access to the tool they are doing the screencast on, and walk through the steps. As you review the script, note any inconsistencies or missing steps, and discuss them during the meeting with your SME. If the SME refuses to provide access to the tool or if there are privacy concerns, schedule a time to follow the navigational process in the SME's presence. Before recording the final version, you should walk through the steps in the script as many times as possible. This will help you catch problems early in the process, before editing and embedding the screencast into your eLearning course.

Also, prior to recording the screencast, it is necessary to ensure the desktop that will be recorded is clean and all documents, websites, and other windows are closed. Once the screencast has been recorded, video editors should go in and remove dead space and Personally Identifiable Information (PII) such as names, addresses, and social security numbers. In addition, they can add voiceovers, transitions, as well as highlight and zoom in features.

When recording voiceovers for screencasts, there are several things to keep in mind. First, even though it is possible to record audio using screencasting tools, the quality of the voiceover will not be the best. Therefore, if the project's budget allows for the use of professional audio recording services, use them. Otherwise, self-recording audio with a good quality microphone, editing it, and then importing into the screencast should be considered.

When recording audio for screencasts, the talent should read as slowly as possible. If the narrator's pace is fast, it will be hard to match the voiceovers with screen recordings. In addition, fast pace narration makes it difficult for learners to follow the screencasts. In the next chapter, we will cover audio and voiceover recording in detail.

Exercise 20

Based on the topic of your course, do you think it will be beneficial to include videos and screencasts? If so, are you going to record your own video or hire a professional? Explain your reasoning.

Chapter 23:
Audio in eLearning

This chapter will cover:

- Role of audio in eLearning
- Recording audio narration
- Quality of audio
- Equipment needed for audio recording
- Voice-over narration

Audio is a critical element in the eLearning course. The quality of audio narration should be clear, easy to understand, and free of any ambient noise that distracts from the learning process. Professional recording studios have walls that absorb all the noise. Therefore, the quality of the recording done in a studio with an audio engineer is much higher than a self-recorded audio. However, professional recordings are very expensive. If the budget for your project is low or if the course is intended for a small audience, it may not be practical to record a professional quality audio narration. Currently, most rapid eLearning tools allow to record and edit audio quickly and easily without the need for more expensive editing tools. While the quality of such recordings will be nowhere near professional, it will be decent enough for most eLearning courses.

Investing in a good quality microphone is necessary for obtaining optimum quality of audio. When recording narration for eLearning courses, it is best to use a unidirectional microphone because it does not pick up distractions from other directions, only recording the sounds coming from the narrator. If the lesson includes a scenario where voices and sounds come from various directions, the omnidirectional microphone is recommended. Regardless of the quality of a microphone, it is always wise to start the recording session with a sound check. Usually microphones pick up all kinds of noise; therefore, narrators should avoid turning pages as they are reading. The best way to do this is to break the script in a way that does not require the narrator to turn pages in the middle of a paragraph. Advising talent to pause for a while before turning the page is another common practice that allows instructional designers or media specialists to easily edit out the noise.

Recording audio in house is often associated with ambient noise, which adds distraction to the learning experience. The environment where voiceovers are recorded should be as quiet as possible. This can partially be accomplished by unplugging all machines and putting a *Do Not Disturb* sign on your door. Moreover, using a small room or a sound booth can eliminate a lot of the noise.

Incorporating audio into the eLearning course is a science in itself. The most popular type of audio used in eLearning courses is known as voice-over narration. This type of narration is typically added to slides, interactions, or quizzes. Just like with any other media in the course, the length of the audio should be as short as possible. Otherwise, learners will not be able to maintain their concentration. It is best to describe each scene in less than 60 seconds, and whenever possible, keep the descriptions under 20 seconds in length.

Many instructional designers avoid adding audio to their courses because they are concerned that learners will not be able to read the text on the screen and listen to the narration at the same time. Not only that their concern is valid but it also has scientific proof behind it. Even though providing the same information in different modes may seem appealing as it addresses multiple learning styles, according to Ruth Clark, learning is actually suppressed when screens are explained by combining narration and text.

So, how can you accommodate visual learners without displaying text on the screen? First, unless it is a podcast, the screen should have some graphics on it. To add text, ISD specialists can simply summarize narration or add only key words to each screen. If the client wants to have both on-screen text and audio, the request can be accommodated by giving an option to turn the audio off. Offering the opportunity to take the course without audio is a good instructional practice in any situation as it allows learners to take the course in public places without disturbing other people.

Exercise 21

Now think about the audio for your course. Will you include voiceovers? If so, are you going to record your own narration or hire a professional narrator? Explain your decision.

Chapter 24:
Graphics in ELearning

This chapter will cover:

- Benefits of adding graphics to eLearning courses
- Types of visuals
- Seven types of graphics for eLearning
- Ruth Clark's visual design model
- Color theory basics
- Typography basics
- Types of image files

The main job of an instructional designer is to design instructionally sound courses. In most cases, ISD specialists are not expected to also be professional graphic artists. However, to make your lessons more visually appealing to learners, you should be aware of basic graphic design principles.

Without a doubt, graphics play a significant role in designing eLearning courses. Visually appealing courses draw learners' attention. No one wants to take training where they have to read page after page of text. Additionally, visual learners find graphics beneficial for understanding, analyzing, and processing information. However, simply adding images to your eLearning will not enhance it in any way. It is important that the graphic used in the course is relevant and appropriate to the topic. There are different types of visuals that can be included such as clip art, photographs, cartoons, animations, and 3D images. Consistency plays an important role when it comes to selecting visuals. For example, using cartoonish drawings when most other photos are realistic should be avoided. Otherwise, the overall course design will appear inconsistent.

According to Ruth Clark and Chopeta Lyons, there are seven types of graphics for eLearning:

Decorative graphics – Even though this type of graphic looks appealing, it does not add any instructional value. Instructional designers use these graphics on book and course covers. Overall, decorative visuals should be avoided as much as possible.

Mnemonic graphics – This type of graphic is used to represent factual information. You can use mnemonic graphics to help learners retrieve facts from memory by looking at images that represent these facts.

Representational graphics – This type of graphic is used to represent on-screen text. In other words, learners should be able to understand what the text is about just by looking at the graphics. You can use representational graphics to convey information to the learner.

Organizational graphics – This type of graphic is used to help learners organize the information provided in the eLearning course. Charts and graphs are the best examples of organizational graphics. You can use organizational graphics for comparing and contrasting information as well as for helping learners organize the knowledge they already have and the knowledge they are obtaining from the course.

Relational graphics – This type of graphic is used to show the quantitative relationship of variables. Two examples of relational graphics are pie charts and line graphs. You can use relational graphics when you want learners to see the relationship between the numbers presented in the content.

Transformational graphics – This type of graphic is used to show changes over time. Examples of transformational graphics include timelines and before and after images. You can use transformational graphics when you want to show how the objects are affected by a process.

Interpretative graphics – This type of graphic is used to illustrate abstract theories or principles. Examples of interpretative graphics are diagrams and animations. You can use interpretative graphics as simulations with series of animated images to show how something works.

Once the decision for the type of graphic is made, the next step is to choose the appropriate size and format. Even though high-resolution visuals look nice and crisp, they take a considerable amount of space. Furthermore, high-resolution graphics may take a long time to load, causing frustration for learners. By scaling small images up, graphics will appear pixilated. The best approach to resizing images is to start with the highest possible resolution and squeeze the graphic down as much as possible.

Types of Image Files

When it comes to visuals in eLearning, not only do they have to be appropriate, but they also have to be properly formatted to give your course a professional look. The most commonly used images on the web and in eLearning are PNGs, JPGs, and GIFs. The table below compares the three types.

Table 15 File Formats

Format	General Characteristics
PNG	<ul><li>Excellent quality</li><li>Can create transparent images</li><li>Large file size</li></ul>
JPG	<ul><li>Excellent quality</li><li>Cannot create transparent images</li><li>Smaller file size than PNGs</li></ul>
GIF	<ul><li>Lower quality than PNGs and JPGs</li><li>Can create transparent images, but they appear pixilated</li><li>Small file size</li></ul>

The file type chosen for images depends on client's needs and priorities. If the stakeholder wants the course to load quickly, then JPGs should be used as they are smaller in size and therefore load quicker than PNGs. If there is a need for transparent images, then PNGs should be used; if a patterned background is needed, then GIFs would be appropriate.

Graphics included in your eLearning course should be 508-compliant. There are several ways to ensure that visuals meet the accessibility requirements. First, whenever possible, they should be described with alternative text. The goal of alternative text is to convey the same information as the image. Visually impaired learners use screen readers to receive the same information as learners without disabilities. Not all graphics can be described with alternative text, however. For instance, alternative text cannot be added to charts and graphs. Therefore, providing a text version of the information included in these visuals should be considered to address Section 508 requirements.

Ruth Clark and Chopeta Lyons' Visual Design Model

Ruth Clark, together with Chopeta Lyons, developed a Visual Design model. The aim of this model is to help instructional designers without graphic experience envision the appropriate art for their courses. The model consists of five phases and focuses mainly on planning graphics, not on the design and development of visuals. The five phases of the Visual Design Model are to:

- *Define Goals*
- *Define Context*
- *Design Visual Approach*
- *Identify Communication Function Needed to Match Content Types*
- *Apply Principles of Psychological Instructional Events*

Define Goals Phase – During this phase, you should define the instructional goal for a given project. Which graphics you choose for the course will depend on your goal. According to Ruth Clark, there are three possible instructional goals. They are to

- inform or motivate learners;
- build procedural skills and teach content associated with these skills; and
- build problem-solving skills and teach content associated with these skills.

Define Context Phase – In this phase, you are responsible for identifying the target audience, delivery methods, the learning environment, and constraints. If learners are visually impaired or color blind, the message the graphic is trying to convey will be lost. Additionally, external factors such as poor lighting, low bandwidth, and a small budget can restrict the graphic design.

Design Visual Approach Phase – During this phase, you are responsible for assessing general requirements such as real estate, page orientation, and the colors of each graphic that will be included in the course.

Identify Communication Function Needed to Match Content Types Phase – In this phase, you identify graphics that will illustrate key instructional points. For example, if there are multiple types of content in the course, organizational visuals should be used. If your aim is to teach procedures, concepts, or facts, representational graphics should be considered. Transformational graphics, on the other hand, should help you teach processes and principles.

Apply Principles of Psychological Instructional Events – The final phase in planning graphics for your eLearning course. In this phase, you should review the graphics to ensure they meet the key instructional events, including gaining learners' attention, activating learners' prior knowledge, minimizing cognitive load, and maximizing learning transfer as well as building new mental models and supporting motivation.

Basics of Color Theory

Using colors appropriately is a science in itself. If the colors in the course do not appeal emotionally to learners, their interest will immediately drop. When selecting graphics, it is important to consider the overall look and feel of the course. The color, quality, and shapes of the graphics should be very similar to the shell of the course. Otherwise, they will look out of place and distract learners. Understanding the basics of color theory can help you create better graphics. The color wheel organizes the primary, secondary, and tertiary colors. The primary colors are red, blue, and yellow. From these colors, secondary colors originate. They are green, orange, and purple. Finally, by mixing both primary and secondary colors, tertiary colors emerge. In addition to primary, secondary, and tertiary colors, the color wheel consists of different shades, including dark and light values.

When creating an eLearning course, moods that different colors convey should be taken into consideration. It is generally recommended to use passive colors such as blues and greens for the background. If certain information in your course needs to be emphasized, using yellow, red, or even purple is advisable. These are active colors and help learners pay closer attention to details.

Contrast also plays an important role in the look and feel of the course. When deciding on the color of the background and font, it is necessary to establish good contrast between the two. For example, learners should have no problem reading black text on a white background. However, if yellow font appears on the white background, the text will most likely be illegible.

Typography

The font used in the eLearning course has direct impact on how learners react to your training. Therefore, having a basic understanding of typography is essential for evoking positive emotions about the course. While creating contrast is important, too much contrast can be distracting to learners. Type is broken into the following categories:

- *Serif fonts* – Have a small line attached to the end of a stroke in a letter. Serif fonts include Times New Roman and Courier.
- *Sans-serif fonts* – Do not have serifs and are typically associated with a more modern look. Popular sans-serif fonts are Arial and Helvetica.
- *Script fonts* – Resemble handwritten letters. Some examples are Script MT Bold and Kunstler Script.

When choosing fonts for eLearning courses, it is best to stay within the same family and limit the course to three fonts.

Exercise 22

Think again about the "look and feel" of your course. What will be the color scheme? Which fonts will you use? What type of visuals are you going to include? What is the purpose of your visuals?

Part IV - Advancing Your Skills

"You can't teach people everything they need to know. The best you can do is position them where they can find what they need to know when they need to know it."

Seymour Papert

Chapter 25:
Working with Subject Matter Experts (SMEs)

This chapter will cover:

- Roles and responsibilities of Subject Matter Experts (SMEs) in course design
- Process for selecting information for the course
- Repurposing classroom materials
- Communication with the SMEs
- Collecting content from the SMEs

Subject Matter Experts, or SMEs, are individuals who have knowledge about a specific area or topic. All people are Subject Matter Experts in one area or another. A teenager, for instance, can be an SME in social networking while a housewife can be an SME in raising children. SMEs play a vital role in course design and serve as knowledge sharers in the training world. Often, the success of the course depends on SMEs. To develop a good relationship with SMEs, you should understand their role in the design process. Since you will be working hand-in-hand with SMEs, developing a successful relationship is critical. SMEs will not only provide the content for the course but will also review the design documents and scripts as well as test media and assessments for accuracy.

Before you even begin gathering content from SMEs, you need to ensure that the SME is truly an expert in his or her field. Since most instructional designers are not familiar with the subject area for the eLearning course they are creating, the client is typically responsible for selecting the SMEs. During the project-planning phase, project managers will provide a description of what is expected from the SME in terms of expertise and experience. The project manager should describe in detail the SME's responsibilities, including expected meetings and document reviews. In the project plan, the project manager should document the risks associated with having an SME that does not meet the described requirements. This way, everything is documented on paper, and the client will take full responsibility for the quality of course content, missed deadlines, or any other consequences associated with the SME's poor performance.

Subject Matter Experts should be aware of all the expectations. All responsibilities should be clearly defined prior to the initial meeting. The role of an instructional designer is to design courses while the role of an SME is to provide expertise in a subject area. SMEs should not be expected to arrange content in order. Often, SMEs provide either too much or too little content, and it is your job, as an instructional designer, to include the right amount of material in the course. Some SMEs are so knowledgeable that they want to share everything they know, thinking that every piece of information is indispensable. To ensure that SMEs only provide relevant information, you should follow the two steps below:

1. Ensure the content provided by the SME meets the intended objectives.
2. If it does not, go back to the SME and ask relevant questions to get all the information needed to satisfy learning objectives. If the content covers all the objectives, break the information into the following three categories: *must know, need-to-know*, and *nice-to know*. The must-know information is what the learner absolutely needs to know to obtain knowledge or learn the skill. The need-to-know information is not as essential as must-know but may clarify certain concepts for learners. The nice-to-know information, on the other hand, is not needed at all. It may be helpful to the learner, but achieving objectives and learning new skills is possible without being exposed to the nice-to-know material.

When working with SMEs, you should always ask for examples of the content. Many SMEs use their knowledge and skills every day. The content is common sense to them; therefore, they may forget to share elements or steps crucial to your learners. You should catch situations where elaboration and examples may be needed and ask SMEs to fill the gaps. If SMEs have a tendency to provide too much content, reminding them that the course is not infinite and that they should only include the most important information from their content should help them identify the must-know material. If SMEs have a difficult time organizing all the content they want to share, a mind map or a graphic organizer will help them consolidate their thoughts.

Use the checklist below to collect content for each learning objective from your SMEs.

- What information do learners need to know to meet the objective?

- What skills do learners need to perform to meet the objective?
- What images can help learners understand the content?
- What activities can help learners understand the content?
- What are some examples or scenarios that illustrate the content?

Oftentimes, SMEs teach the classroom version of the same course; therefore, they already have training materials prepared. While these materials can be adapted to the eLearning lesson, they will have to be modified or even reformatted to meet the requirements of the eLearning environment. Keep in mind that the SME's training materials were created for classroom training where the instructor teaches the course; therefore, they are most likely missing the information needed to understand the content without the instructor's presence. SMEs can help you fill the gaps where necessary. Utilizing already existing materials and repurposing them for eLearning can save a lot of time for both instructional designers and SMEs.

Effective communication plays a crucial role when dealing with SMEs. Just like everyone else, Subject Matter Experts have busy schedules. Sometimes, they are not even part of your team and have many other on-the-job responsibilities. You should ensure the SME's time is not wasted with multiple meetings and meaningless questions. Prior to the meeting with the SME, some preparation work must be done. The goal is to get quality content, not to waste the SME's time by asking rudimentary questions. Researching the topic before the meeting to become acquainted with basic concepts and terminology can help instructional designers achieve that goal.

Meetings with your SMEs will be much more productive if you inform them of the goals and objectives ahead of time. You can also prepare your questions and send them electronically to the SME. Then, if there are additional questions or content that requires clarification, you can schedule a phone call or a live-conference call to address the issues. This approach works well as it allows SMEs to provide answers to questions at their convenience without attending any prescheduled meetings. Letting SMEs know how much their time and dedication to the project are appreciated is also a good practice. You may even consider sending a glowing thank you note to your SMEs' supervisor.

Recording meetings and conversations can be a major time saver. Oftentimes, instructional designers take written notes and then forget what they mean or cannot make sense out of their writing. The recorded version of the meeting will save both you and the SME a lot of time as multiple phone calls and meetings will be avoided. Before recording a meeting, however, always obtain permission.

Because learning theories is instructional designers' second nature, many tend to mention them when talking to their SMEs. However, most of the time, SMEs are not familiar with instructional design theories and terminology. To avoid miscommunication, you should consider explaining terminology in layman words. For example, instead of saying *WBT*, it is best to say *Web-Based Training*, and instead of saying *using Bloom's taxonomy to write objectives*, say, *using measurable action verbs such as develop and complete to write objectives*. Because most SMEs are not learning experts, they do not know much about creating instructionally sound courses. Therefore, in many instances, they want to include certain elements in their training that do not work from the instructional design standpoint. Providing reasons why SME's ideas are impractical may overcomplicate things. Instead, instructional designers should show examples of successful eLearning materials and use these examples to explain why the recommended approach works best.

While it is important to value the SME's time and efforts, it is equally important to stay on top of the deadlines. Even though the project may be important to you, it may be last on the SME's list. As an instructional designer, it is your responsibility to have the course ready on time; therefore, frequent reminders and follow up emails to your SMEs may be a necessary step to meet your deadlines.

Exercise 23

Think about the responsibilities of your SMEs. Will they solely be responsible for providing content, or will they also review the materials? Decide on the methods you will use to collect information from your SMEs. Then, make a list of questions you will ask your SMEs.

Chapter 26:
ELearning Project Management

This chapter will cover:

- Role of instructional designer as project manager
- IPECC model for project management
- Project management tools

Most instructional designers play many roles and wear multiple hats. Project management is often one of them. The key to successful project management is a well-managed process combined with supporting tools. Skilled project managers apply their knowledge, skills, tools, and techniques to meet project requirements. You should know how to manage eLearning projects to ensure on-time delivery and top quality outcomes. Moreover, effective project management will help you avoid communication problems with other team members and minimize other issues related to poor management.

All projects are unique and temporary in nature. One project may only consist of a few tasks and can be completed in less than a month, while another may have so many activities that project managers will easily lose track of them and take well over a year to complete. Regardless of the scope, all projects have a definite beginning and end. ELearning projects, however, are more difficult to manage than most other projects because they include both training and technology. Every project must plan for risks. Projects must be delivered on time, within cost and scope, and meet customer quality requirements. Because most eLearning projects are more complicated than traditional projects, there is more risk associated with them. Moreover, there are more time constraints as well as budget and communication problems.

The most commonly used model in project management is known as the IPECC model. It is used for all types of projects, not just eLearning ones. IPECC model stands for:

- *Initiating*
- *Planning*
- *Executing*

- *Controlling*
- *Closing*

Initiation Phase

During the *initiation* phase, project managers present their vision, state expectations, define goals and objectives, as well as the scope of the project. To fully understand the requirements and desired outcomes of the project, a business requirements analysis needs to be conducted. The following steps outline the scope of the analysis.

Step 1 – Identify the stakeholders and the target audience.

Step 2 – Gather requirements for the course from both stakeholders and your target audience.

Step 3 – Categorize requirements into the following four categories:

- *Functional Requirements* – Describe the end-user perspective
- *Operational Requirements* – Describe what needs to be done to keep the course functional over a period of time
- *Technical Requirements* – Describe the technical requirements needed to successfully implement the course
- *Transitional Requirements* – Describe the steps needed to be taken for the smooth implementation of the course

Step 4 – Analyze, prioritize, and record requirements.

Step 5 – Ensure that the requirements you collected reflect stakeholders' needs.

During the *initiation* phase, you will develop a project charter. The project charter is a document that serves as a contract between an eLearning project manager and the client. This document is the foundation of any project and should be written in the most comprehensive way possible. The project charter answers all questions associated with the project. The length usually depends on each project's complexity and scope. For example, a project charter intended for a twenty-minute linear course developed using a rapid eLearning tool can be as short as two pages. On the other hand, a project charter for a ten-hour non-linear course that consists of multiple interactions and serious games may take up to twenty pages. Most project charters include the following elements:

- Objectives
- Deliverables
- Success Metrics
- Major Risks
- Budget
- Project Team
- Timeline
- Key meetings
- Activities for the project

Another document created during the initiation phase is known as the preliminary project scope. Its purpose is to identify the project's objectives. Some of the elements included in this document are:

- Objectives
- Project requirements
- Boundaries
- Assumptions
- Constraints
- Milestones
- Project costs

Planning Phase

The *planning* phase is probably one of the most important phases in project management because it ensures that the project is delivered on time and within budget and scope. During this phase, project managers refine the scope, assemble their team, and identify specific tasks and activities that need to be completed. After gathering all the required information, they begin writing a project plan. A project plan is a living document. It reflects both changes and new additions. A detailed project plan includes the project charter and preliminary project scope documents. It also includes information about the stakeholders, project team, budget, and resources as well as milestones and deliverables.

Executing Phase

The *executing* phase deals with leading the team, solving problems that occur along the way, and doing all the other work required to deliver the eLearning project. In other words, this is the phase for carrying out the project plan. During the executing phase, project managers also ensure that all team members understand what is expected of them and produce quality work on time.

Controlling Phase

During the *controlling* phase, the project manager makes necessary corrections and adjustments to the schedule created earlier based on the problems that occurred in the previous three phases. During this time, the project manager monitors the scope, schedule, budget, and risks for the project.

Closing Phase

The fifth and final phase is known as *closing*. At this point, the project manager delivers the project to the client, ensuring that all deliverables meet the requirements. This is also the time to write an evaluation report documenting all the lessons learned during the project. Many project managers deliver their projects without ever evaluating them. Nonetheless, this step provides an opportunity to reflect on the project and learn from mistakes to avoid them in the future.

As instructional designers and eLearning project managers move through project management phases, they should remember to schedule frequent meetings with their stakeholders and regularly update them on the status of the project. This approach will not only help to build relationships with clients, but it will also catch problems early in the process, avoiding needless rework and saving valuable time for both project managers and their team members.

Project Management Tools

Example of a typical Gantt chart

		Task Name	Duration	Start
1		Project	19.47 days	5/6/2011
2		Start	0 day	5/6/2011
3		Task A	4 days	5/6/2011
4		Task B	5.3 days	5/6/2011
5		Task C	5.15 days	5/12/2011
6		Task D	6.32 days	5/12/2011
7		Task E	5.15 days	5/19/2011
8		Task F	4.5 days	5/20/2011
9		Task G	5.15 days	5/26/2011
10		Finish	0 day	6/2/2011

Example of a typical PERT chart

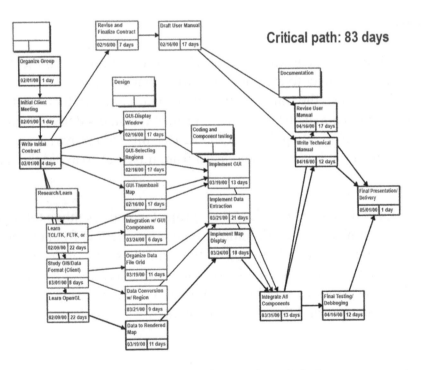

Critical path: 83 days

To successfully complete an eLearning project, it is important to stay on schedule. eLearning project managers have many responsibilities, so missing a deadline is easy. There are several tools that will help you deliver projects on time. The first one is a Gantt chart. A Gantt chart is a horizontal bar chart that enables project managers to organize the events identified during the planning phase. This chart allows project managers to visualize all the tasks as well as the costs associated with each event. On the Gantt chart, you can specify the time needed to complete each piece of the project by indicating the start and finish dates. Moreover, the chart summarizes the elements of the project. When project managers set up the Gantt chart for their project, they need to include the individuals responsible for each task, the amount of time they will need to complete each task, and the problems that may be encountered along the way. It is important to remember to update the Gantt chart whenever the deadline changes and as soon as each task is completed.

Even though the Gantt chart lists tasks, it does not provide an indication of the relationship between these tasks. This is where a PERT chart comes into play. A PERT chart is a project management tool used to schedule, organize, and coordinate tasks within the project. Many project managers prefer the PERT chart to the Gantt chart because it shows the relationship between tasks and therefore works better for more complex projects.

There are many different software programs that can be used to create both Gantt and PERT charts. However, the Microsoft Project is the most popular project management tool available on the market. This software program helps project managers develop a plan, assign resources to activities, track progress, manage the budget, and analyze workloads. If the project is relatively simple and does not have many activities, project managers may consider developing their charts in Excel.

Exercise 24

Think about each phase of project management. What tasks are you going
to complete in each phase to ensure the successful delivery of your project?
Which project management tools will you use and why?

Chapter 27:
Job Aids

This chapter will cover

- The role of job aids in eLearning courses
- Reasons to include job aids in your eLearning courses
- Types of job aids and appropriate use of each type
- Electronic Performance Support System (EPSS)

Even though the main role of an instructional designer is to design courses, what goes into the course is often a client's decision. Since most clients possess the content but do not know much about the learning theory, their content often includes a lot of unnecessary information. While stakeholders do not always want to hear an instructional designer's opinion about what should and should not be included in the course, ISD professionals can influence the presentation method of the content.

Typically, when teaching a process or practical skill, developing a job aid should be considered. Job aids are tools that allow individuals to access the information required to complete a task quickly and efficiently. They are also known as quick reference guides, checklists, and performance aids, which help individuals apply new skills to real-world problems without having to refer back to long training courses. This training tool covers only relevant information in the form of systematic instructions, worksheets, checklists, flowcharts, diagrams, and templates. Regardless of the format chosen for the job aid, it should

- include only the "must-know" content;
- utilize easy to understand short descriptive words; and
- incorporate simple, clear and illustrative graphics.

While it is not always possible to create job aids to meet all learning styles, the majority of learners benefit from visuals. You should consider including highlights, boxes, and arrows that emphasize the text. There is no standard size for a job aid – it can be just one page in length or fifty pages, depending on the content or procedure it is trying to convey.

There are many ways to make a job aid part of the eLearning course. It can be embedded into the lesson, added as a Word or PDF attachment, or made available as a mobile application. Each of these methods has its advantages and disadvantages, so just like with everything else in eLearning, the decision should be based on the content. For instance, if the information is related to the current video or activity in the course, embedding a job aid may be the best solution. If you want learners to be able to print a job aid and use it as a desk guide after the training, then adding it as a Word or PDF attachment may work best. If your goal is to provide learners with a reference they can access anytime and anywhere, your best bet is to create a mobile application. Sometimes, however, to accomplish the desired goal, you will have to select two or three options.

Most training courses contain so much information that it is impossible to retain all of it. In addition, people tend to forget information and lose skills when they do not use them on a regular basis. Job aids fill that gap while serving as reference, reminder, and refresher tools. When employees have a job aid in front of them, they can work faster as they do not have to stop and think of the next step. Job aids also work well in situations when certain tasks or skills are rarely used. They can help organizations keep the training costs down. If, for example, the organization has to train employees to follow a constantly changing procedure, it is better to create a job aid rather than a training course as it is much easier to replace a job aid than to rebuild the entire eLearning lesson.

You should consider adding a job aid as an attachment to eLearning courses if the intent is to

- provide a quick overview of job tasks to new employees;
- teach complex, difficult to remember tasks that involve multiple steps and lengthy decisions;
- decrease informational overload from the training;
- help individuals make accurate decisions;
- reduce on-the job accidents;
- improve work quality;
- increase retention;
- promote transfer of training to the job; or
- deliver just-in-time information.

Once the job aid is complete, you can find someone who does not know anything about the procedure or skill and ask that person to review it to reveal problems, ambiguities, and missing steps.

Determine the Format of a Job Aid

Use the table below to determine the type of job aid that suits your content's specific needs.

Table 16 Job Aids

Job Aid	Type of Task
Step-by-Step Instructions	• The task includes linear steps. • The task does not have any decisions associated with it.
Worksheets	• The task includes information that does not have an immediate application. • The task includes calculations.
Checklists	• The steps to complete the task do not have to be done in a linear order. • The task includes planning or inspecting something.
Flowcharts	• The task includes yes or no decisions that must be made in a specific order. • Each step in a task is associated with specific decision.
Diagrams	• The task illustrates a certain idea or concept. • The task explains how something works.

Templates	• The task includes creating a document, letter, or report. • The task requires standardization; e.g., same style and structure.

Use the questions below to ensure the effectiveness of the job aid.

- Did you gather the appropriate information such as sample documents, screenshots, and flow charts?
- What type of graphics would best illustrate the points/steps/procedures?
- What format would work best?
- What size and page layout are most appropriate?

Electronic Performance Support System

The Electronic Performance Support System, or EPSS, is any computer software program within a larger application that guides people through completing a task. It is an electronic job aid. The goal of EPSS is to provide the information or resources necessary to achieve performance requirements without training intervention or any other external support. Some of the reasons to consider EPSS include:

- a performance problem due to the lack of knowledge or skills;
- unavailable training for new employees;
- guidance to complete a complex task;
- infrequent performance of a task.

Whenever there is a performance issue related to knowledge or skill deficiency, consider developing a job aid. Even if the training is available, a job aid can increase retention, on-the-job learning transfer, and more importantly, improve performance.

Exercise 25

Think about your topic and objectives and decide whether including a job aid in your eLearning course will be beneficial. If you decide to include a job aid, which format would you choose, and why?

Chapter 28:
Web 2.0 and Mobile Learning

This chapter will cover:

- Web 2.0 technology and mobile learning solutions
- Incorporating social networking tools in eLearning
- Using podcasts and vodcasts in eLearning
- Designing courses and supplemental materials for social and mobile learning.

Web 2.0

According to a definition, Web 2.0 is a term used to describe the second generation of the World Wide Web, focused on collaboration and information sharing. Some of the key characteristics of Web 2.0 are:

- applications that can be accessed from anywhere; and
- tools that encourage people to create, exchange, and share information

Web 2.0 technologies are comprised of wikis, blogs, social networking tools, content hosting services, and podcasts. In today's world of electronic communication, Web 2.0 greatly influences how people learn.

Social learning is a subset of eLearning. It refers to learning from and with other people using social media tools such as

- Facebook
- Twitter
- YouTube
- LinkedIn
- Blogs, and
- Wikis

Social learning is often used for collaboration purposes. Many instructional designers consider social learning an informal learning. Social networking tools are ideal for people who live or work in a variety of locations. Perhaps the best aspect of these tools is that they are free; therefore, people use them to connect with others to share their knowledge.

Today, some organizations tend towards social learning tools more than others do. Additionally, many organizations run their own blogs and manage Facebook pages. The decision to incorporate these tools into the organization's learning environment mostly depends on their leaders' perspective and goes back to generational learning styles. Whereas younger generations tend to use social learning tools on a regular basis and even find them motivational because they allow to share knowledge with others who have similar interests, older generations remain wary of using these tools and may not see them as learning instruments.

Social learning tools allow learners to share the best practices and discuss solutions to problems with other professionals in their field. Some instructional designers incorporate social learning tools into their courses to establish a common ground among learners. For instance, they may post videos or blog articles with the information that they want their learners to be familiar with prior to the course. Instructional designers also use social learning tools to share links to additional resources either prior, during, or after the learning event. After watching a video or reading an article associated with the link, many people tend to comment and reflect on what they have seen or read. This often leads to multiple threads and knowledge sharing.

Wikis and Blogs

Wikis are collaboration websites on which anyone within the community of users can contribute to and edit the content. Most wikis are specific to the subject. Some companies use wikis to post their meeting notes or share valuable information about certain topics.

Blogs, on the other hand, are journals where people write their thoughts on a specific topic. As opposed to wikis, blogs are usually written and maintained by a single contributor and commented on by other visitors. Some instructional designers use blogs as part of their course design to post questions and assignments. When designing blended learning experiences, you can create wikis or blogs and have learners participate by contributing their opinions and reflecting on their learning.

In addition to wikis, blogs, and other social learning tools, instructional designers use YouTube to upload videos and have learners watch and comment on them prior to the learning event.

Mobile Learning

Mobile Learning, or mLearning, is another subset of eLearning that focuses on learning with mobile devices such as smartphones, tablets, and eBook readers. Mobile learning is convenient because people have instant access to mobile devices almost anywhere.

Mobile devices provide coaching, assessments, evaluations, on-the-job support, information, references, podcasts, forms, and checklists. In these ways, mLearning supports traditional learning modes as well as other eLearning modes and makes learning more portable and accessible. MLearning can reach a large number of people at the same time and provide them with just-in-time training. However, before delivering an eLearning course via mobile device, you should review learning objectives to ensure that the mLearning solution is truly needed.

Podcasting and Vodcasting

Podcasting and vodcasting are types of mobile learning. Podcasts are audio recordings of a training program. Vodcasts are video-based podcasts. Podcasts can be listened or downloaded to hand-held devices such as iPods or mp3 players. Vodcasts, on the other hand, require a digital video player such as QuickTime or Windows Media Player. You can simply make audio files of your course lectures available for learners to download. To be more creative, you can also turn your content into a radio show, play, or journalistic investigation using an informal style and various voices. This will excite learners and possibly increase their retention level. In order for podcasts and vodcasts to enhance the learning experience, they should not be a substitute to complete courses but rather an addition to them. Effective podcasts and vodcasts should not exceed 20 minutes and must follow the same ground rules for recording eLearning audio and video.

Convenience is the main benefit of podcasts and vodcasts. Learners can listen to the recordings when they work out in the gym, drive to work, or even cook dinner, and they do not have to be connected to the Internet. Podcasts are inexpensive and can be created with Audacity, a free software program for recording and editing audio.

Even though podcasts and vodcasts are convenient and can be a great enhancement to eLearning courses, they lack interactive elements and therefore do not appeal to all learning styles. For this reason, instructional designers should use podcasts as a supporting material that learners can explore on their own, not as a standalone course. If the content is not technical in nature, creating a podcast can be beneficial while more technical and difficult to understand content that requires visualization may need to be presented in a vodcast format. Before making the decision to add podcasts and vodcasts to the courses, ensuring that they align with learning goals and objectives is necessary. Otherwise, their instructional value will be lost.

Designing For Social and Mobile Learning

The ISD principles and best practices for developing eLearning materials may not always apply to the design and development of mobile and social learning experiences. Since mobile devices are significantly smaller in size than computer screens, instructional designers should

- keep the content short and simple of no more than five minutes in length;
- produce non-linear content;
- minimize interactivity whenever possible;
- use bullets to present information in a concise form; and
- avoid complex navigation.

Both social and mLearning are alternative delivery methods; therefore, it is best to use them as performance support tools that supplement training courses. For instance, social and mLearning activities can be incorporated into eLearning modules or become part of an instructor-led training. Moreover, these alternative solutions are an excellent blended learning approach to effective training.

In spite of its effectiveness, not all content is suitable for mobile learning. As a rule of thumb, whenever a course requires some type of a learning aid such as a glossary, an mLearning solution can be used. Pre-course presentations and reading materials, pre- and post-tests, and updated content can also be delivered via mLearning. For instance, if an eLearning module has already been created and after a few years all the information remains relevant but there are certain additions to the content, the mLearning solution will be a safe approach. Additionally, there are situations when something goes wrong and people need to learn how to solve a problem immediately. There is no time to go through the entire eLearning module, and there is certainly no time to attend a traditional learning session. In these cases, mobile and social learning are perfect ways to help people get what they need quickly and efficiently.

MLearning solutions work best for the following presentation methods:

- Job Aids
- Checklists
- Desk and Reference Guides
- Podcasts
- Vodcasts
- Updates
- Social Networking
- Coaching
- Assessments and Evaluations
- Surveys
- Games and Simulations
- EBooks

Mobile courses need to be created from scratch. You cannot simply convert your already existing eLearning course into a mobile one because, at the very least, it will not be displayed correctly on mobile devices. Instead, you will have to create two separate versions of the same course using the mobile first approach.

As you are creating mobile solutions for your eLearning courses, the questions below should guide you through the planning process.

- Why is a mobile solution needed for this course?
- Does your target audience use mobile devices?
- Does your target audience have access to mobile devices?
- What are the learning objectives?
- How will these objectives be evaluated?
- How often does the content change?
- Does the content already exist in any other format?

An instructional designer's job is to design learning experiences that help learners gain new knowledge and skills. Experienced instructional designers know what type of learning solution would best meet their learners' needs. The best way to get a feel of what works best for both social and mLearning is to try them yourself.

Exercise 26

Think about your topic and your objectives. Then, decide whether you need to create a mobile learning solution to supplement your eLearning course. If you decide that you do need an mLearning solution, how are you going to approach its design?

Will there be a social learning component to your course? If so, what type of social learning tools would you use and why?

Summary

There are many decisions involved in creating an effective eLearning course. As you plan your training, you need to decide how many modules or lessons to include and split the content accordingly, paying close attention to objectives. For optimum retention, you should keep each lesson no longer than 20 minutes in length. Creating a storyboard is probably one of the most effective methods for organizing the material. Not only will storyboards lay out the content, but they will also serve as guidelines for programmers, multimedia specialists, and graphic artists who will be working on the course. Successful storyboard design will allow for visualizing the course and identifying gaps that need to be filled. In addition to separating and organizing the content, instructional designers should create a consistent navigation and layout of the lesson.

Another important step in the ISD process is going through the content and analyzing it for possible games and interactivities. By varying presentation of information as much as possible, instructional designers will be able to address the needs of most learners. For example, they can show a video clip for visual learners, create voiceover slides for auditory learners, and design a game or role-play for kinesthetic learners.

Whenever you are tasked with designing an eLearning course, the first step should always be conducting a needs analysis and reviewing the existing content. Then, based on the information gathered from the analysis, you can develop measurable learning objectives, keeping in mind that if the problem is not related to lack of knowledge or skills, even the best eLearning course will not solve it. When the content and objectives are in place, the decision about the presentation methods should be made. Some of these methods include:

- Video
- Audio
- Coaching
- Scenarios
- Role-plays
- Case studies
- Demonstrators
- Simulations
- Games
- Charts and diagrams
- Puzzles

- Assignments
- Activities and exercises
- Reading materials

The table below suggests methods for presenting different types of information.

Table 17 Teaching Suggestions

Information Type	Methods
Facts, theories, procedures	<ul><li>Competition games</li><li>Simulations</li><li>Activities and exercises</li><li>Case studies</li><li>Scenarios</li></ul>
Cognitive skills	<ul><li>Demonstrations</li><li>Simulations</li><li>Coaching</li><li>Exercises</li><li>Role-play games</li><li>Adventure games</li></ul>
Making decisions or judgments	<ul><li>Case studies</li><li>Role plays</li><li>Adventure games</li><li>Detective games</li><li>Simulations</li><li>Scenarios</li></ul>
Reasoning and analyzing	<ul><li>Simulations</li><li>Games</li><li>Puzzles</li><li>Scenarios</li><li>Role-plays</li><li>Case studies</li></ul>

While ADDIE is the most commonly used ISD model, choosing the rapid eLearning approach may be wise as this method allows you to create training materials quickly and efficiently. As a result, clients will receive a quality product and spend significantly less money on it. Most of the time, if the course focuses on transmitting information, using a rapid eLearning tool is the best option. With rapid eLearning tools, you can save money by quickly adding audio, video, graphics, animations, and web objects without hiring expensive graphic artists, multimedia specialists, and computer programmers.

In addition to choosing the right development tools, you must consider technical issues such as the hosting of the course. You should also address SCORM and 508-compliance requirements.

When most people think of eLearning, they typically think of online courses; however, today's generation is so well versed in technology that eLearning is now available as podcasts and blogs. Educational software can be downloaded to mobile devices, iPods, and PDAs. This forces instructional designers to find ways to make their eLearning content available as mLearning. Nowadays, in addition to being able to learn from computers, the new generation wants to be able to download podcasts to smartphones and read blogs and forum postings pertinent to the topic. By incorporating social learning tools and making them part of the blended learning solution, you can add the collaboration element to lessons and address the needs of the younger generation at the same time.

The entire development process of the eLearning courses can be complex and overwhelming. By splitting the project into sections and putting check marks next to the already completed sections, you will ensure that all the important points are covered and the development of the course is moving in the right direction.

Conclusion

We have now come to the end of *Instructional Design for eLearning: Essential guide to creating successful eLearning courses*. However, as the fields of instructional design and eLearning continue to evolve, the learning journey will never end. You should always aim towards continuous professional development and constant acquisition of new knowledge and skills. In addition to introducing the major ISD theories and models, this book covered the basics of instructional design such as

- learning theories,
- learning styles,
- motivation,
- memory, and
- the six principles of effective eLearning courses.

The book has also walked you through the course creation enabling you to

- conduct needs analysis and gather data;
- design an effective eLearning lesson according to Gagné's Nine Events of Instruction;
- create design documents, storyboards, and scripts based on the instructional design best practices; as well as
- effectively implement and evaluate eLearning courses.

Moreover, after reading this book, you should be able to utilize your skills to

- identify an eLearning authoring tool that meets specific project's requirements;
- decide on the type of interactivity and presentation method to be included in the course;
- design effective simulations, games, and learning scenarios;
- incorporate audio, video, and graphics in eLearning courses;
- productively work with SMEs;
- utilize project management methods and techniques to successfully manage eLearning projects; and

- identify the situations when eLearning courses can benefit from job aids, social, and mobile learning solutions.

As we have already discussed in this book, there is no single, unique approach to course design. All instructional designers have their personal preference for certain methods and techniques. As they gain experience, they also develop their own best practices. However, I hope that you will transfer the skills you gained from reading the *Instructional Design for eLearning* to the job and enhance the courses you develop with the suggestions and tools presented in this book.

To your instructional design and eLearning success!

Self-Evaluation

Use the checklist below to self-evaluate knowledge and skills acquired from this text.

Table 18 Self-Evaluation Checklist

You should now be able to	Yes	No
Define the terms instructional systems design, eLearning, and blended learning		
Differentiate between CBT and WBT		
Explain advantages and disadvantages of eLearning		
Decide when eLearning is appropriate		
Name major contributors to the field of instructional design		
Describe most popular ISD models		
Describe the steps in the ADDIE model and apply them to the course design		
Apply the principles of major learning theories to your course design		
Define the concept of andragogy and describe Malcolm Knowles's six principles of adult learning		
Describe major learning style models and apply them to the training courses		
Apply models and principles of motivational design to your own courses		
Describe the role of memory in eLearning design		
Describe cognitive load theory and apply it to your course design		
Apply Ruth Clark's six principles of effective eLearning courses		
Conduct needs analysis using appropriate data collection methods		
Write SMART learning objectives using the A-B-C-D format and Bloom's taxonomy		
Name the three learning domains		
Identify the stages of revised Bloom's taxonomy		

Name the five stages of SOLO taxonomy and apply them to learning objectives		
Construct a lesson plan using Gagné's Nine Events of Instruction		
Create a design document		
Construct an eLearning storyboard and prototype		
Write voiceover scripts using plain language principles		
Create a style guide for your eLearning course		
Conduct alpha and pilot testing		
Name major LMSs and CMSs		
Design SCORM and Section 508-compliant eLearning courses		
Construct the five types of evaluations		
Create valid and reliable assessment items for your eLearning materials		
Construct intrinsic and extrinsic feedback statements		
Explain the levels of interactivity in eLearning		
Identify and apply interactive presentation methods to eLearning courses		
Apply the storytelling techniques to create games, simulations, and scenarios		
Describe the types of learning games		
Select the appropriate game type for the eLearning course		
Identify major eLearning authoring and development tools available on the market		
Select the appropriate software program for projects' needs		
Identify the types of videos in eLearning		
Provide reasons for including video and audio in eLearning courses		
Design screencasts for eLearning courses		
Explain the benefits of graphics in eLearning courses		
Identify and describe the types of graphics		
Apply Ruth Clark's visual design model to eLearning courses		
Explain the basics of color theory and typography		
Recognize most commonly used file sizes		

Explain the role and responsibilities of Subject Matter Experts in designing eLearning materials		
Communicate with Subject Matter Experts		
Collect information from Subject Matter Experts		
Use the IPECC model to manage eLearning projects		
Explain reasons for including job aids in eLearning courses		
Name the types of job aids and describe the appropriate use for each one		
Design learning experiences for Web 2.0 and mobile technology		

Instructional Design and eLearning Glossary

Abraham Maslow's Hierarchy of Needs – a theory that states there are five basic human needs that must be satisfied for internal motivation to occur. These needs are physiological, safety, belongingness, self-esteem, and self-actualization.

Accelerated Learning Rapid Instructional Design (RID) – a model for creating courses under tight deadlines with limited budget and constantly changing content.

ADDIE – the classic model that most instructional designers use. ADDIE stands for Analysis, Design, Development, Implementation and Evaluation.

Adobe ELearning Suite – a toolbox for creating eLearning courses, which includes Adobe Captivate, Adobe Flash, Adobe Dreamweaver, Adobe Photoshop, Adobe Acrobat, Adobe Presenter, and Adobe Audition.

Alpha testing – the initial quality assurance test that involves usability testing to confirm the course works the way it should.

Alternative text – also known as Alt-text. When users mouse over a visual, alternative text pops up and provides a description of that visual.

Andragogy – the term coined by Malcolm Knowles. It is an adult learning theory that believes that adults learn differently from children and describes assumptions about adult learners.

Animation – a simulation of movement created by showing a series of visuals.

ARCS Model – a model of motivational design pioneered by John Keller. It is a systematic approach to designing motivational learning. It consists of the following four steps for promoting motivation in the learning process: attention, relevance, confidence, and satisfaction.

Assessment – the evaluation of comprehension and ability of the learner to do something as a result of a training course.

ASSURE – a model that assumes the course design uses different types of media. The model is used for designing eLearning courses. ASSURE stands for Analyze Learners, State Objectives, Select Media and Materials, Utilize Media and Materials, Require Learner Participation, and Evaluate and Revise.

Asynchronous eLearning – a self-paced learning experience that allows learners to go through courses as quickly or as slowly as they desire.

Audience analysis – a process of collecting information about learners' background, experiences, and motivators.

Authoring tools – software programs used for developing, editing, testing, and arranging eLearning courses.

Avatars – a graphical representation of characters.

Behaviorism – a learning theory based on observable and measurable changes in behavior, which assumes that learner's behavior is shaped through positive or negative reinforcement.

Beta testing – the second phase of the quality assurance process, also known as Pilot testing. Beta testing requires a group of users who review the eLearning course for errors and ensure the course works the way it should.

Blended learning – a combination of several media such as eLearning and mobile learning in one course.

Blog – short for web log. It is a website where an individual writes entries on a regular basis.

Bloom's taxonomy – was pioneered by an educational psychologist, Benjamin Bloom. In his taxonomy, Bloom identified three learning domains: cognitive, affective, and psychomotor. Instructional designers use these domains for writing measurable and observable learning objectives.

Camtasia Studio – a video-based screen capturing software program.

CBT – an acronym that stands for computer-based training. It is a form of education where learners take training courses while on the computer.

Chunking – refers to breaking learning content into small manageable pieces.

Cognitive load theory – the scientific basis for efficiency in learning developed by John Sweller. It is a set of principles proven to result in better course design. There are three types of cognitive load: intrinsic load, germane load, and extraneous load.

Cognitivism – a learning theory that assumes an existing knowledge structure is used to process new information and believes the information is received, stored, and retrieved.

Complex Interactions – Level 3 interactions that include animations, complex simulations, and scenarios.

Constructivism – a learning theory that focuses on how learners construct knowledge based on their prior experience. Constructivists believe in experiential, self-directed learning.

Content Management System (CMS) – often the main function of a Learning Management System, which acts more like a database.

Corrective feedback – information provided to learners regarding their performance to help them progress toward their goal.

Data collection methods – methods used to gather information for different types of analysis. Some examples of data-collection methods include surveys, interviews, and focus groups.

David Kolb – an American educational theorist who developed the learning style inventory.

Delivery methods – a method of transferring a lesson to learners. Some of the delivery methods include CD-ROM, ILT, CBT, and WBT.

Design Document – documents the entire design process for a specific project. It provides all the necessary information about the course to instructional designers, graphic artists, multimedia specialists, programmers, project managers, and all other team members and stakeholders.

Desktop authoring tools – authoring tools installed on the desktop. Some of the most popular ones are Articulate Storyline, Captivate, and Lectora.

Diagnostic assessments – pre-tests used to determine learners' initial knowledge of the material prior to the training course.

Donald Kirkpatrick – a father of evaluation, who created the four levels of evaluation: reaction, learning, behavior, and results.

Dr. Sivasailam "Thiagi" Thiagarajan – internationally recognized expert in learning games for personal and company development.

EBook reader – a device used to read digital e-books.

eLearning – a form of learning conducted via Internet, intranet, network, or CD-ROM. eLearning gives people an opportunity to learn just about anything at any time and place.

Electronic Performance Support System (EPSS) – any computer software program within a larger application that guides people through completing a task. It is an electronic job aid.

Enabling Objectives – objectives that support the terminal objectives. They define the skills, knowledge, or attitudes learners must obtain to successfully complete terminal objectives. Enabling objectives are more specific than terminal ones.

Evaluation – a process that ensures that training meets the standards and expectations. Evaluation helps instructional designers identify strengths and weaknesses of the course, and confirms that all course objectives have been met and the business goal has been achieved.

Extrinsic feedback – a direct type of feedback that comments on the learner's performance in a straightforward way.

Extrinsic motivation – refers to performing activities with a goal to get something at the end such as monetary rewards, certificates, or good grades.

Face-to-face training – a method of delivering training in the classroom setting with live instructor.

Five Why technique – a way to gather information about performance gap and root causes. The essence of this technique is to repeatedly ask the Why questions until arriving at the root cause of the problem.

Flash player – a plug-in software that adds functionality to the web browser.

Formative evaluation – a process that occurs in all phases of the course design, and ensures that training stays on track while it is being developed.

Forum – an online message board where ideas on a particular topic can be shared.

Gagné's Nine Events – a nine-step process known as the events of instruction. These nine-steps are:

- Gain attention
- Inform learners of objectives
- Stimulate recall of prior learning
- Present the content
- Provide guidance
- Elicit performance
- Provide feedback
- Assess performance
- Enhance retention and learning transfer

Gantt chart – a horizontal bar chart that enables project managers to organize the events identified during the planning phase.

Generational learning styles – learning preferences based on generation. The four generational learning styles are traditionalists, baby boomers, generations X, and Y or millennials.

George Miller's magical number "seven, plus or minus two" – a rule that states that short-term memory is only able to hold about seven bits of information.

HTML – a Hypertext Markup Language used for creating websites.

ILT – an acronym for Instructor Led Training. It is a traditional learning experience conducted in a classroom setting and facilitated by a *live* instructor.

Implementation – delivery of a course.

Instructional Systems Design – also known as ISD. It is a systematic approach to creating effective training courses.

Interactivity – an exercise or activity that allows the learner to become more involved with the content by discovering information and checking knowledge through assessments, simulations, and games, as opposed to simply reading text on the screen.

Interface – refers to the "look and feel" of the course.

Intrinsic feedback – an indirect type of feedback. This type of feedback immediately lets learners know they made a mistake, and allows them to make adjustments based on that feedback.

Intrinsic motivation – refers to internal drives and desires such as gaining new knowledge and skills.

IPECC – the most commonly used model in project management. It is used for all types of projects, not just for eLearning projects. IPECC model stands for Initiating, Planning, Executing, Controlling, and Closing.

Jack Phillips – pioneered the fifth level of evaluation known as Return-of-Investment or ROI, which compares the monetary program benefits with the program costs.

Job aid – a tool that allows individuals to access the information required to complete a task quickly and efficiently.

Kolb's learning cycle – composed of four stages: concrete experience, reflective observation, abstract conceptualization, and active experimentation. Kolb developed learning styles based on his four-stage learning cycle. These styles are convergers, divergers, assimilators, and accommodators.

Learning – a process of gaining knowledge and skills.

Learning game – an activity inserted into any learning module with the goal to improve the learning process and motivate the learner to complete the course.

Learning goals – goals that provide information about the purpose of the course.

Learning Management System (LMS) – a software application used to plan, implement, and assess learning process. LMS allows instructors and administrators to create and deliver content to the maximum number of people, monitor participation, and assess performance.

Learning objectives – measurable and observable statements that define the scope of the course and help learners focus on specific outcomes. Learning objectives describe the knowledge, skills, or attitudes that learners should demonstrate after completing the course. Objectives should be written using the A-B-C-D format. The A-B-C-D format stands for Audience, Behavior, Condition, and Degree.

Limited interactions – Level 2 interactions that give learners more control over the sequence of a course.

Linear navigation – set up in a way where learners must go through the entire section until they can move to the next one. Linear navigation requires learners to complete the entire training.

Long-term memory – a location in the brain where the information is stored permanently.

Malcolm Knowles – a theorist of adult education who pioneered the concept of Andragogy and identified six principles of adult learning.

Media – refers to audio, video, animations, and graphics in an eLearning course.

Mobile learning – also known as mLearning is a subset of eLearning that focuses on learning with mobile devices such as smartphones, tablets, and eBook readers.

Multiple Intelligences theory – a theory pioneered by the psychologist, Howard Gardner. According to his theory, people are born with certain aptitudes used to learn new information and solve problems. Gardner's Nine Intelligences are:

- Linguistic Intelligence
- Logical/Mathematical Intelligence
- Musical Rhythmic Intelligence
- Bodily/Kinesthetic Intelligence
- Spatial/Visual Intelligence
- Naturalistic Intelligence
- Intrapersonal Intelligence

- Interpersonal Intelligence
- Existential Intelligence

Needs analysis – a process of collecting information to determine the needs that must be addressed in a training course.

Non-linear navigation – also known as branched navigation, allows learners to jump from one section to the next in any desired order.

Passive interactions – Level 1 interactions that involve very limited interactivity such as assessment at the end of the lesson or module.

Performance Analysis – a process of collecting information to identify and close the gap between the current and the desired performance.

PERT chart – a project management tool used to schedule, organize and coordinate tasks within the project.

Podcast – an audio recording of a training program.

PowerPoint plugin authoring tools – tools that use PowerPoint as the authoring environment such as Articulate Studio

Presentation methods – techniques used to present learning material such as video, audio, scenarios, and games.

Prototype – an interactive model of an eLearning course that contains the overall course layout including graphics and structural elements.

Quality assurance – refers to ensuring the quality of an eLearning course.

Raptivity – a rapid interactivity building tool.

Real-Time interactions – Level 4 interactions that involve all the elements of Levels 1, 2, and 3 plus very complex content, serious games and 3D simulations.

Reliability – refers to the ability of the same measurement to produce consistent results over a period of time.

Remediation – refers to providing specific performance feedback whenever necessary.

Repurposing – refers to restructure of the already existing content into a different format to accommodate a different delivery method.

Reusable Learning Objects (RLOs) – course pieces that can be reused in a different context such as another course.

Robert Gagné – an American educational psychologist best known for his conditions of learning for training applications. He developed a theory that states there are five major levels of learning including verbal information, intellectual skills, cognitive strategies, motor skills and attitudes.

Robert Mayer – one of the key contributors to the field of instructional design, who developed behavior learning objectives.

ROI model – Jack Phillips added a fifth step to the already existing four levels of evaluation. His fifth level is known as Return-of-Investment or ROI. It compares the monetary program benefits with the program costs and should be measured about three to twelve months after the training.

Root cause analysis – a process of collecting data used to address the real problem behind the performance gap.

Ruth Colvin Clark – an instructional design and workforce learning specialist who developed the six principles of effective eLearning courses and, together with Chopeta Lyons', created a Visual Design model.

Schema – also known as schemata, is a term used in cognitive psychology, which describes structures that organize knowledge about something for interpreting and processing of information.

SCORM – an acronym that stands for Shareable Content Object Reference Model. SCORM is a set of technical standards that ensure the course works well with other eLearning software.

Screen reader – software that reads the text on the computer screen.

Screencasts – the recording of a computer screen and converting this recording into a movie.

Script – a written text for audio narration.

Section 508 – part of the Rehabilitation Act of 1973, and amended in 1998, which mandates that all electronic and information technology must be accessible by people with disabilities.

Self-paced learning – refers to asynchronous learning environment and provides learners with complete control over the flow of the training course.

Server-based tools – tools that are hosted on the server and can be accessed through Internet. CourseBuilder is an example of a server-based authoring tool.

Short-term memory – refers to the temporary storage for manipulation and processing of information.

Simulations – scenarios that allow learners to go through real-life situations.

SMART objectives – focus on the result rather than activities and allow learners to measure their own success. SMART stands for Specific, Measurable, Attainable, Relevant, and Timely.

SnagIt – a screen-capturing tool that creates highly engaging images, presentation videos, tutorials, and training documents.

Social learning – a subset of eLearning, which refers to learning from and with other people using social media tools such as Facebook, Twitter, YouTube, LinkedIn, Blogs, and Wikis.

SOLO taxonomy – stands for the Structure of Observed Learning Outcomes. It is a hierarchical taxonomy developed by John Biggs and Kevin Collis that can help instructional designers and educators create objectives and evaluate learning outcomes.

Storyboards – visual organizers that instructional design and eLearning professionals use to illustrate ideas and communicate these ideas to other team members.

Storytelling – a learning tool that teaches, motivates, and entertains learners by telling a story.

Style guide – a standardized guide for writing eLearning documents or designing learning experiences.

Subject Matter Experts (SMEs) – individuals that have knowledge about a specific area or topic.

Successive Approximation Model (SAM) – an agile instructional design model created by Michael Allen, a recognized pioneer and leader in the design of interactive multimedia learning tools and applications. The model emphasizes collaboration, efficiency, and repetition. SAM assumes that mistakes will be made throughout the process and focuses on iterative design with frequent early evaluation.

Summative evaluation – a process of reviewing a course after implementation. Summative evaluation measures training outcomes in terms of learners' opinion about the course, assessments results, job performance, and return of investment (ROI) to the organization.

Synchronous eLearning – a type of eLearning that is done in real-time with a live instructor.

Task analysis –a process of collecting information to identify knowledge and skills needed to accomplish instructional goals.

Teaching – a process of transferring knowledge and skills to learners.

Template – a form that provides the structure of the document and used to populate information in appropriate fields.

Terminal objectives – describe what the learners are expected to be able to do by the end of the course. Terminal objectives focus on the results not processes.

The Dick and Carey Systems approach – a model based on theoretical principles of learning and Robert Gagné's conditions of learning and focus on selecting and organizing appropriate content for each module.

The Four-Door (4D) ELearning model – a simple model developed by Dr. Sivasailam "Thiagi" Thiagarajan that allows eLearning professionals to develop eLearning courses cheaply and rapidly while addressing different types of learners.

Usability – refers to the ease of use of a learning course.

VAK Model – a model that describes the three learning preferences-and how people learn. Some people learn best from lecture (audio), others learn best from visuals (visual), yet others prefer hands-on activities (kinesthetic).

Validity – refers to measuring what the assessment instruments intended to measure.

Virtual Worlds – immersive 3D online environments in which users can interact with any other users and characters.

Vodcast – a video-based podcast.

WBT – an acronym that stands for web-based training. WBT courses run off the Internet and are intended for synchronous and asynchronous delivery.

Web 2.0 – a term used to describe a second generation of the World Wide Web focused on collaboration and information sharing. Web 2.0 technologies are comprised of wikis, blogs, social networking tools, content hosting services, and podcasting.

WIIFM – an acronym that stands for "What's in it for me?" It is a technique used to design motivational courses that learners can relate to.

Wikis – collaboration websites to which anyone within the community of users can contribute to.

Working memory – location in the brain where information is temporarily stored and manipulated.

References

ASTD learning system. Alexandria, VA: ASTD Press, 2006.

Allen, Michael W., and Richard Sites. *Leaving ADDIE for SAM an agile model for developing the best learning experiences*. Alexandria, Va.: ASTD Press, 2012.

Clark, Donald. "Instructional System Design (ISD) Handbook (ADDIE)." Colocation | Broadband Wireless | Dedicated Servers | Web Design & Development | DSL | Web Hosting | Infinity Internet. http://www.nwlink.com/~donclark/hrd/sat.html (accessed April 11, 2013).

Clark, Donald . "Bloom's Taxonomy of Learning Domains." Colocation | Broadband Wireless | Dedicated Servers | Web Design & Development | DSL | Web Hosting | Infinity Internet. http://www.nwlink.com/~donclark/hrd/bloom.html (accessed June 12, 2013).

Clark, Ruth Colvin, and Richard E. Mayer. *E-learning and the science of instruction: proven guidelines for consumers and designers of multimedia learning*. 2nd ed. San Francisco, CA: Pfeiffer, 2008.

Clark, Ruth Colvin. *Evidence-based training methods: a guide for training professionals*. Alexandria, Va.: ASTD Press, 2010.

Clark, Ruth Colvin, and Chopeta C. Lyons. *Graphics for learning proven*

*guidelines for planning, designing, and evaluating visuals in training
materials*. 2nd ed. San Francisco: Pfeiffer, 2011.

Hodell, Chuck. *ISD from the ground up: a no-nonsense approach to instructional
design*. 2nd ed. Alexandria, VA: ASTD Press, 2006.

Hodell, Chuck. "The Subject Matter Expert's Role in Training and ISD." In
*SMEs from the ground up a no-nonsense approach to trainer-expert
collaboration*. Alexandria, VA: ASTD Press, 2013. 1-14.

Malamed, Connie. "The eLearning Coach - Instructional Design and eLearning:
The eLearning Coach." The eLearning Coach - Instructional Design and
eLearning: The eLearning Coach. http://theelearningcoach.com/
(accessed July 12, 2013).

"Mobile Learning Guide Part 1: Designing it right | Elearning Reports." Custom
E-learning Training & LMS Solutions Kineo.
http://www.kineo.com/elearning-reports/mobile-learning-guide-part-1-
designing-it-right.html (accessed September 10, 2013).

Moore, Cathy. "Instructional design: How to write motivational learning
objectives." Training design ideas from Cathy Moore. http://blog.cathy-
moore.com/2007/12/makeover-turn-objectives-into-motivators/ (accessed
October 1, 2013).

Quinn, Clark N., and Marcia L. Connor. *Engaging learning: designing e-learning simulation games*. San Francisco, CA: Jossey-Bass, 2005.

Ward, Desirée, and Diane Elkins. *E-learning uncovered: from concept to execution*. Jacksonville, FL: Alcorn Ward & Partners, 2010.

Index

CPSIA information can be obtained at www.ICGtesting.com
Printed in the USA
LVOW03s1743230614

391288LV00009B/167/P

SCOTLAND THE REAL DIVIDE

Poverty and Deprivation in Scotland

Edited by
Gordon Brown and Robin Cook

MAINSTREAM
PUBLISHING

This edition published by
MAINSTREAM PUBLISHING COMPANY (EDINBURGH) LTD.
25 South West Thistle Street Lane
Edinburgh EH2 1EW

The publishers gratefully acknowledge the financial assistance of the
Scottish Arts Council.

ISBN 0 906391 18 0 (casebound)
ISBN 0 906391 19 9 (paperback)

Cover design by Deborah Harvey

Printed by Billing & Sons Ltd., Worcester

CONTENTS

CONTRIBUTORS

GORDON BROWN is Labour Member of Parliament for Dunfermline East and currently the chairman of the Labour Party in Scotland. He edited *The Red Paper on Scotland*, published in 1975, and was co-author of *The Politics of Nationalism and Devolution*.

ROBIN COOK is Labour Member of Parliament for Livingston and is a Labour front bench spokesman on Treasury affairs. Until his election to Parliament, he was tutor/organiser for the Workers' Educational Association in Edinburgh and chairman of the City of Edinburgh Housing Committee.

WILLIAM McILVANNEY is author of *Docherty, Laidlaw, The Papers of Tony Veitch* and numerous other prize-winning novels.

GEOFF NORRIS is author of *Poverty in Scotland: The Facts* and is now employed in Newcastle.

STEPHEN KENDRICK is a research worker at Edinburgh University and is engaged on an investigation into the 1981 census and long-term social changes in Scotland.

IAN LEVITT is a lecturer at Plymouth Polytechnic. His doctorate thesis at Edinburgh University is a study of the development of Scottish social welfare in the first half of the twentieth century.

ADRIAN SINFIELD is Professor of Social Administration at Edinburgh University and author of *What Unemployment Means* and other major studies of unemployment.

TREVOR DAVIES is a freelance broadcaster and producer, and is a former councillor in Edinburgh.

FRED TWINE is lecturer in sociology at Aberdeen University and was, until recently, a councillor in Aberdeen.

GEOFF PAYNE is head of the Department of Social Studies at Plymouth Polytechnic and was leader of the Scottish Mobility Study.

GRAEME FORD is a research worker at Aberdeen University with the Medical Research Council and worked as a researcher on the Scottish Mobility Study.

ALISTAIR GRIMES is employed by Lothian Regional Council. Until recently he worked for the Scottish Council of Social Services and is secretary of the Scottish Fuel Poverty Action Group.

KAY CARMICHAEL was, until recently, Offenders Officer for Strathclyde Region. Before that she was deputy chairman of the Supplementary Benefits Commission and was a lecturer at Glasgow University.

EVELINE HUNTER is a freelance writer and is author of *Scottish Woman's Place*.

BILL CLARK is a training officer with Strathclyde Region.

JOHN CASSERLY is a senior social worker with Strathclyde Regional Council.

JOHN HUBLEY was, until recently, a research worker at Paisley College of Technology and is now at Leeds Polytechnic.

DAVID RAFFE is a lecturer in the Centre for Educational Sociology at Edinburgh University and is a co-author of the recently published *Reconstructions of Secondary Education*.

RONALD YOUNG is Secretary of the Strathclyde Regional Council Labour Group. He is a lecturer at Paisley College of Technology and has written widely on local government.

The assistance of David Donald, Peter Taylor and Allan Hutton, of Glasgow College of Technology, and of the Nuffield Trust, is much appreciated. Arising from the seminars organised by Glasgow College of Technology, there are a number of additional papers on "areas of deprivation" which, it is hoped, will be published at a later date in updated form.

Gordon Brown

INTRODUCTION

"EIGHTY-TWO years old and hardly a stick of furniture to call my own. I can't afford to heat my house and eat as well."

After five burglaries, a flooding and even a mugging, all in her eighty-third year, this is how Glasgow widow, Margaret P—, sums up her life. But her biggest headache, she says, is having to live on £32.75 a week, after rent. Margaret simply cannot afford the food, gas, electricity, and other essentials that a pensioner needs.

Margaret's predicament typifies the new face of mass poverty in Scotland, and Britain, today. She is not starving, but she is not properly fed. She is not homeless, but her house is damp and barely tolerable. She may not die of hypothermia, but she has inadequate heating. She is not a prisoner in her own home, but she does not have the resources to travel far. "Luxuries" such as fresh meat, a colour television, or new clothes, cannot feature in her household budget.

There are more than one million Scots as poor as Margaret, or poorer. As Table 1 shows, the number of Scots who now depend on means-tested supplementary benefits exceeds three-quarters of a million people, 300,000 more than four years ago, and nearly half a million more than in the 'forties when the welfare state was created. Add those who do not claim, and those who are in low-paid jobs, and the numbers on or below the government's own "poverty line" exceed one million. They live on incomes that give a married couple with two youngsters only £59.20 weekly, or £8.46 a day, a payment which is only 25% more generous, in real value, than Seebohm Rowntree's poverty line of 1936 which he considered "the minimum in which physical efficiency could be maintained". It was, he said, "a standard of bare subsistence rather than living", and yet the 1980s benefits level is designed by government regulations to cover the weekly costs of "food, household fuel, buying, cleaning, repairing and replacing clothing and shoes, normal travel costs, miscellaneous household expenses such as toilet articles, window cleaning, cleansing materials, and the replacement of small household goods (for example, crockery, cutlery, cooking utensils, light bulbs) and leisure and amenity items such as TV licence and rental, newspapers, confectionery and tobacco".[1]

Table 1.

NUMBERS DEPENDENT ON SUPPLEMENTARY BENEFIT

	May 15, 1979	Dec. 8, 1981	Feb. 28, 1983
Supplementary Allowance	69.079	80.849	103,164
Unemployment Allowance	76,223	160,864	205,304
Supplementary Pension	147,693	143,525	146,364
Total Claimants	293,005	385,238	454,832
Estimated[1] numbers of children in families on Supplementary Benefit	70.000	158,000	200,000
Estimated[1] numbers of married women in couples in receipt of Supplementary Benefit	45,000	76,000	96,000
Estimated total who depend on Supplementary Benefit	408,005	619,238	750,832

1   The estimates are extrapolations from government figures. In December 1981, the government estimated that 158,000 children were in families dependent on supplementary benefits, and 76,000 married women were in this position (*Hansard*, 16 March 1983).

For the first time since the war, not only are the numbers of poor rising dramatically but, also, government legislation is ensuring that the poor cannot enjoy the benefit of any increased prosperity that may come to the nation. As one confidential government document made clear, redistribution of income from the rich to the poor is "not among the government's objectives". The real incomes of the poor have simply been cut.

There can never, of course, be an exact definition of what constitutes the "poverty line". Today, most would reject a "starvation" standard for defining what it is to be poor. Simply, they would not accept that today's poor are only those who face starvation. Most would also reject a "destitution" standard whereby being poor is to be deprived of the basic necessities of life: food, clothing or accommodation. A Minister at the Department of Health and Social Security stated as much in September 1979:

> It is not sufficient to assess poverty by absolute standards. Nowadays it must be judged on relative criteria by comparison with the standard of living of other groups in the community . . . beneficiaries must have an income which enables them to participate in the life of the community.[2]

But what is it to be poor if we adopt that relative, rather than absolute, standard? Geoff Norris suggests that if a slightly more generous definition than the government's own "poverty line" was adopted — an income level at

140% of the supplementary benefit line — more than 1,600,000 Scots would be in poverty today, three hundred thousand more than three years ago. But at that level, single claimants would have only £31.50 weekly and married couples with two children only £74 after paying rent. It would be an income level less than half the average household income in Scotland. And would that allow families and individuals the opportunity to "participate in the life of the community"? In his book, *Poverty in the United Kingdom*, Professor Peter Townsend has suggested that poverty is more than simply low week-to-week money income. It is also "the lack of *resources* necessary to permit participation in the activities, customs and diets commonly approved by the community".

> Individuals, families and groups in the population can be said to be in poverty when they lack the resources to obtain the types of diet, participate in the activities and have the living conditions and amenities which are customary or at least widely encouraged or approved in the societies to which they belong.[3]

While no exact comparative information on household resources is available, the Family Expenditure Survey suggests that around one Scots household in every ten has a weekly income that is only 25% of the average household income in Britain. Two households in every ten have incomes that are only 33% of the average, or less, and three households in every ten have incomes that fall below 50% of the average household income.[4] It is of course those with lowest incomes that are most likely to occupy the 75,000 houses classified as "slums", the 45,000 houses without either inside toilet or bath, or the 75,000 homes suffering from severe problems of dampness, and which cost most to heat. In addition, 13% of Scots households have no washing machine; 20% no telephone; 47% no central heating; and 51% no car.[5] For most, this is the consequence of financial stringency, not personal choice. A significant minority have failed to derive any benefit from the mass consumption society. A measure of extreme deprivation has been attempted by the National Children's Bureau, whose recent "Children in Adversity" survey found one in every ten Scots children disadvantaged: in bad housing, on low incomes, in single-parent or large families, and suffering as a result significantly poorer health and worse educational achievements.[6] The results of the 1981 census confirm this picture. More than 80,000 children under eleven are either in single-parent or large families where the breadwinner has few, or no, employment skills and has therefore little opportunity to earn anything above a poverty wage.

The majority of the poorest do not live in areas that are classified as "multiply deprived". But even so, as the 1981 census reveals, there are pockets of extreme poverty and deprivation. As Ronald Young shows, in some communities perhaps as many as two-thirds of households are families where the male breadwinner is unemployed or where there are pensioners or single parent families facing poverty.

Explaining Scotland's poverty

Why the problem — and why, in particular, the severity of poverty with its attendant deprivation in Scotland? Kendrick, Payne and Levitt all emphasise the extent to which poverty is generated from the workplace, because of inadequate wage rates and, consequently, insufficient resources to cover periods of unemployment, sickness and old age. People are poor if, from their workplace earnings (or lack of them), they are unable to ensure security in retirement, to provide for the needs of their families, or to protect themselves adequately when sick, disabled, injured or unemployed.

Scotland's poor are therefore not poor because they are Scottish: they are poor because, if they are not unemployed, they are in the wrong job, generation, sex or class — and because our welfare state fails to compensate them for it. In other words, Scotland's high levels of poverty are not the result of fecklessness, incompetence, poor household budgeting, excessive drinking or smoking or personal deficiencies amongst "the poor": they are rooted in the industrial and occupational structure of the Scottish economy and, in particular, they arise from the highly uneven and uncontrolled character of Scotland's economic development.

Of course, many Scots have benefited from Scotland's free market economy — and still benefit today. Inequalities in wealth are greater in Scotland than in the rest of Britain and considerably more so than in Europe and America. The top 1% of Scots own one-quarter of personal wealth; the top 5% one-half and the top 10% four-fifths. Five hundred individuals or companies own half of Scotland's land, and shareholdings, also, are concentrated in fewer hands. Even after tax, the top 10% of income earners take home more than the bottom 50%.

There are two reasons why poverty is deep-seated. For the past fifty years and more, the heavy industries that ensured Scotland's industrial growth — coal, iron and steel, heavy engineering, textiles and ship-building — have undergone a protracted decline. Indeed, the highly skilled workforce, which was the backbone of these industries, has suffered as much from insecure employment and reduced living standards as any group. In twenty years 200,000 skilled jobs — one in every three skilled jobs — have been lost, an unparalleled fall in skilled opportunities. But, more than this, as skilled jobs have gone, Scotland's new occupational structure has evolved in a haphazard fashion. Perhaps one-quarter of a million Scots, the sons and daughters of fathers who held manual jobs, have graduated into white collar work. But, at the same time, there are more than 400,000 Scots, that is nearly one worker in every five, in the less prestigious or less rewarding, semi-skilled or unskilled occupations. Alone of modern European economies, Britain's and Scotland's, manual working class is self-recruiting — second, third and fourth generation manual workers, who are also the most vulnerable to unemployment. Manual workers' chances of being on the dole are six times higher than that for white collar workers. They are the losers from contemporary economic change and their plight is made worse by the advantaged status of their white collar counterparts.

Payne suggests that it would be wrong to speak simply of a "dual" labour market — the unskilled worker and the rest. The real divide, he implies, is between those who, for the most part, have security in white collar jobs, and those manual workers who suffer unacceptably high risks of unemployment and low pay. A recent measure of this is that in the last four years the real value of wages for manual work has fallen, while white collar wages have risen.

Scotland is, as Twine shows, one of the low pay economies of Britain, with an estimated 650,000 Scots earning below £85 weekly. This comprises nearly one in every three of the employed labour force, with 90% of the low-paid in manual work. Indeed, proportionately, the earning potential of the poorest tenth of workers is now no greater than it was one hundred years ago, and it has, in fact, declined significantly in the last four years. Without earnings from overtime, Twine shows, even more — 800,000 in all — would be on low pay, earning less than two-thirds of the average wage. Low pay, he shows, is concentrated among working women; but for both men and women the problem is almost certain to worsen, as not only is overtime restricted, but the wages "floor" is being lowered. Already, the "Fair Wages" clause of 1897 has been removed from the Statute Book. Now, the 1983 Conservative manifesto seeks to ensure that for more than a quarter of a million workers in Scotland covered by Wage Council agreements, "wages councils do not reduce job opportunities by forcing workers to charge unrealistic wage rates or employers to offer them". The "unrealistic" pay rates range from £75 per week to less than £40.

Opportunities and earnings at the workplace might not be so crucial to poverty, or prosperity, were it not for the inadequate "safety net" of the modern welfare state. Of course, the Beveridge Report of 1942 did not recommend a social security system that rectified the injustices of the market economy. Quite the opposite. Benefits, the report argued, should be lower than wages if in work; otherwise they might act as a disincentive to take on paid employment. But if the economy of 1983 cannot guarantee work at decent wages, the welfare state of 1945 has never guaranteed adequate family support, pension levels, or protection against sickness, disability, handicap or unemployment.

The largest group of today's poor are now the unemployed and their families. Pensioners are the second biggest single group, ensuring a profile of poverty in Scotland in 1983 that resembles that of 1933. As Sinfield and Davies show, the price of being out of work is very high. More than half the unemployed are on supplementary benefits, and only 90% of them receive the full benefits they are due. But, as a number of recent studies have confirmed, unemployment brings with it more ill-health, more psychological distress, more family break-ups and even more suicide attempts. 70% of children in Strathclyde Region who come into care are from families where the breadwinner is unemployed; in two-thirds of cases involving child abuse, the father is out of work. Suicide attempts among unemployed people have trebled in three years.

However, families and households have also changed in a way that adds to the problems of poverty. At the beginning of the century half our households contained five, six, seven or even more members. Today, less than one household in eight is so large. The "extended family" is a thing of the past, as declining birth rates, high emigration and family break-ups have altered the ways people live. In itself, this ought to have helped to reduce the concentration of poverty, but there have been associated changes which have made more people wholly dependent on state support.

For every hundred people able to work, there are now seventy dependent upon them; there were fifty half a century ago. First, there are more old people. Pensioners now comprise one in six of the Scottish population. One-quarter of a million of them live on their own — twice as many as twenty years ago. The number of old people living beyond seventy-five is now well over quarter of a million. The number will double again in twenty years. As Grimes shows, one-quarter of a million pensioners are on the breadline. But for the very old, poverty is to be measured as much by the quality of social service provision as it is by the quantity of financial incomes. As one government report, *Changing Patterns of Care for the Elderly*, has made clear, the numbers of home helps, health visitors, and even meals on wheels will need to double simply to keep pace with rising demands. The number of sheltered homes needs to treble, amenity homes to rise by a factor of six. Even with that increased emphasis on community care, places in old people's homes, and hospitals, will also need to be increased.

There is a second way in which the risks of poverty have been exacerbated by changing living patterns. Just under 100,000 households, with 150,000 young children, are now single-parent families. Most of them have a household head who is a separated or divorced mother, an indication of the fact that nearly one marriage in three fails. A significant number of women — 16,000 — are unmarried mothers living only with their children. Their numbers are now increasing at the rate of 2,000 every year. If one pensioner in every three is in poverty, the majority of single-parent families are also in that position.

There is a third, more extensive problem, almost as common to all families as it is to single-parent families. Government financial support for children is now significantly less than it was at its peak in the 1950s. To match the level of child support in 1955, child benefit today would have to be more than £9, instead of its current rate of £5.85 (or its November 1983 rate of £6.50). Families with children are therefore more likely to be poor.

As the birth rate has fallen — few couples now plan more than two or three children — large families are fewer in number. Although their hardship is probably the greatest, the 75,000 children under eleven years of age who are in large families are now a minority group of the children in poverty. It is the age at which couples have their first child that largely determines their standards of living. Professional couples are likely to marry later, and postpone the birth of their first child, while both continue to earn from work. Couples from semi-skilled or unskilled occupations tend to marry young and start families immediately so that, for many, poverty is a continuous experience in childhood, youth and adulthood.

As both Kay Carmichael and Eveline Hunter demonstrate, the stereotyped "nuclear family" is as much the exception of modern Scotland as is the "extended family". Two-parent families now comprise only a minority of Scottish households. The so-called "typical" worker — a married man with two children and a non-working wife at home — is so much the exception that he comprises only one in every twenty of the workforce. And neither is their much factual evidence to support Mrs Thatcher's view that mothers have neglected their children. Although one-quarter of today's labour force is comprised of married women, only 6% of married mothers with children under five work full time. It has been estimated that four times as many families would be in poverty without the addition of the wife's, mainly part-time, earnings.

As Kay Carmichael concludes, the one single measure that would help ease family poverty would be higher child benefits. It would be cheaper to raise child benefit than to riase the tax threshold or introduce a lower tax band of, say, 20% to 25%.

But, as Eveline Hunter suggests, much more needs to be done to eliminate the present discrimination against women in the labour market. The problem is particularly serious for single parents. If they find work, it will almost certainly be part time and badly paid. Nursery, playgroup and child-minding provision is much less widespread in Scotland than in the rest of Britain, and its absence deters mothers from seeking jobs. It means that most rely on inadequate single-parent benefits that fall far short of the guaranteed maintenance allowance that was recommended by the Finer Commission, but never implemented.

If the unemployed, low-paid, elderly and large or single-parent families comprise the majority of today's poor, there are significant minority groups whose case has often gone unrecognised or unheeded. As Clark and Casserly show, one household in twelve could have someone with a handicap that requires special attention and resources. Financial support for the disabled has never been adequate. Equally, community facilities are underdeveloped. Only 12% of the mentally handicapped who might benefit from them have places in day centres. The mentally ill have even fewer. Only 40% of the physically handicapped in need of residential accommodation actually get it. For the mentally handicapped the figure is 33%. 50% of the handicapped who would benefit from places in adult training centres go without them. A single disablement benefit is urgently needed, as is new investment in community and residential provision.

In the 1960s and 1970s much of the debate on poverty and deprivation was concentrated on "areas of need", with "positive discrimination" programmes to tackle "multiple deprivation". The evidence, as Ron Young suggests, is that where there has been public investment in problem areas, it has been inadequate, only a fraction of either local authority or central government social service spending. Public spending on education, housing, health and transport has always been, and is still, proportionately higher for the most advantaged social groups. High educational expenditure favours mainly middle-class students in higher and further education, as Raffe shows. Cook demonstrates that recent changes in housing finance have eliminated state subsidies to council housing, while increasing tax reliefs for owner occupiers. Even health service funds appear to be concentrated disproportionately on middle-class users of the service. The result is, as Hubley shows, that health inequalities are as glaring as ever. While the evidence contained in the much publicised Black Report is exclusively English, a similar study in areas of Glasgow has found that the prevalence of cancer is 80% higher in the poorer areas of the city than in the more prosperous communities. The incidence of heart disease is 50% higher, strokes 100% higher, and bronchitis and asthma 400% higher. As Hubley shows, social differences in infant mortality rates remain so great that the son or daughter of an unskilled worker is two-and-a-half times more likely to die than his or her professional counterpart. If programmes of public spending are to remove existing inequalities, then those areas and groups who need help most must have far greater financial support that has been offered until now, and their claims on public spending must take precedence. The most recent, and most widely publicised, of these experiments is the Glasgow Eastern Area Renewal Project.

The future under a Conservative government
The new problem for the poor is that the welfare services which were established from 1945 onwards are now, themselves, endangered by a new Tory social ideology which is doing to the legacy of Beveridge what "monetarist" dogma has done to the heritage of Keynes. In the past five years housing spending has fallen by 55%; spending on education by 6.5%; and although social security expenditure has risen by 21%, the numbers of claims upon it has increased much faster, as unemployment has more than doubled.

Social security benefits in Scotland would, in total, be £200 million higher every year were it not for the Conservative government's decisions not to link pensions, and other benefits, to earnings rises, to cut and then to tax unemployment benefit, and to reduce a variety of important benefits for the disabled and the sick.

That there are far more severe economies on the way is evident from recent government announcements that future spending on social security and health should be adjusted downwards. Spending on the National Health Service has already been cut by £16 million. From November 1983, the government is to return to the "historic" basis of calculating social benefits at the precise moment when, as prices begin to rise again, the poor will be penalised most. Pensioner couples are immediately £1.20 worse off than they had expected, and supplementary benefits are 95p less than they would have been. It is hardly much compensation that, having destroyed the link between benefits and rising earnings, the government has renewed its commitment to protect pensions, and long-term supplementary benefits, against inflation. The "minimum" standard of 1979 has become the "maximum" of 1983. No similar guarantees of price-protection have been made to recipients of child benefit, the sick or single parents on short-term supplementary benefits, or the unemployed.

It will in fact be the new benefit levels for the unemployed that will reveal the new "national minimum" of the late 1980s. Benefit scales, set against average earnings, are now lower than National Assistance rates in 1948. Next year, unemployment benefits (and supplementary benefits for the unemployed) are likely to be cut in a manner not so much reminiscent of the 1930s, when benefits were cut as prices fell, but the 1830s, when the harsh "less eligibility" principles of the Victorian poor law were first introduced. The new Minister for Social Security has in the past been associated with views that would demand not only benefits cut but the imposition of a "work-test" on the unemployed. One extreme view suggests that if unemployment were to rise to four million, and the supplementary benefits budget were to be cut by 4% in real terms, and if only benefits for pensioners and short-term claimants other than the out-of-work were protected against inflation, then benefits for the unemployed would have to be reduced by 25% by 1985.

The argument for cutting benefits owes little to any view of social justice. The new Chancellor of the Exchequer, Mr Nigel Lawson, has argued that the unemployed could easily price themselves back to work, by accepting lower wages, or be priced back to work, by having benefit cuts forced upon them. In other words, benefits should be set not at a level to permit the minimum degree of comfort or security, but lowered to a level which is some fraction or proportion of the lowest wages in the marketplace, whether these wages are sufficient for subsistence or not. But there is no evidence that supports any Conservative proposition that there are jobs for the unemployed to take up, or that the unemployed are work-shy because benefits are too high. Recent inquiries by the Institute of Fiscal Studies, and by the government's own investigators, have found almost no evidence that current levels of benefit deter the unemployed from seeking gainful employment.

It is almost inevitable, however, that the Government will argue for both lower wages and lower benefits as essential to ensure a British economic recovery. If wage councils cannot be abolished, as the government would like, then their activities will almost certainly be curtailed. In the public sector, one of the government's rationales for "privatisation" is to force employees away from national wage bargaining, which the government believes leads to excessive pay settlements, and so to make public sector workers dependent, in future, on smaller, more local private employers. The government have themselves admitted that one of the objects, if not the principal object, of trade union reform, is to erode the trade union movement's bargaining power and so to achieve low wage levels. The government's argument is likely to be that, as wages are lowered to ensure greater "competitiveness", benefit rates will have to be cut accordingly. This will be done, despite the evidence that it is low investment, rather than high wages, that is the cause of Britain's economic difficulties, and despite the fact that if no jobs exist for the out-of-work, no amount of poverty or enforced destitution will create jobs.

The Conservatives are in fact well on their way to redefining the "national minimum",, the "poverty line" and the "safety net" in a manner more reminiscent of the 1934 Poor Law Amendment Act than of more recent social welfare legislation. In a report entitled *Voluntary Unemployment Deductions*, hardship is defined as no more than "going without food or essential services", in other words, to be equated with absolute destitution.[7] This is to abandon the principles of the Beveridge report, which argued that even those men who made themselves voluntarily unemployed should receive a level of national assistance which gave them money "at the margin" for "things which though not necessary may appear|preferable to the individual".[8]

Three recent government initiatives have suggested that the government now propose a wholesale, root and branch, reform of social services. In July 1983, Mrs Thatcher announced that a long-term demographic study would be undertaken to ascertain what precisely the "burden" on the taxpaying community of an ever-increasing population of pensioners, unemployed, and single-parent families was likely to be in the 1990s. It is already clear that serious consideration is being given to the privatisation of "earnings related" pension schemes and to the future of child benefit.

Other versions of Scotland's and Britain's future have already surfaced in leaked documents from the government's "Think Tank" unit and from a policy-making group of Ministers entitled the Family Policy Group. In a set of proposals that would effectively dismantle the "safety net" of the post-war welfare state, Ministers have suggested that the poverty line should be redefined as a bare "minimum", that the wages councils should be abolished, and that the Equal Opportunities Commission which is designed to protect women's rights should be "reviewed". Financial support for single parents should be reconsidered because it does not "strike the right balance . . . in encouraging responsible and self-reliant behaviour by parents".[9]

The "Think Tank" proposals, leaked in October 1982, would introduce vouchers and loans in place of free education as of right, substantially reduce all state social security benefits, and compel all individuals to take out private medical insurance, with charges for visits to the doctor and to hospitals. Under the "family group" proposals, the "privatising" of the personal social services would be on the agenda, with the likely rundown of the state home-help service, the selling-off of both old people's homes and sheltered houses for the elderly and disabled, and even the contracting out of the meals-on-wheels services to food manufacturing companies. Under even more radical versions of privatisation proposals, from the Adam Smith Institute, hospital and school administration, hospital portering, and even the ambulance service, fire-fighting and much of police work, would be placed with private contractors, with fees-for-service in place of the current policy that health should be free, or virtually free, at the time of need.

Integral to all these proposals is a coherent strategy to minimise the "social wage", and so, expenditure on housing, health, education and the social work services. Under the guise of reinforcing the "family unit", the financial burden of community support for the disabled, the elderly, out-of-work teenagers and young children would fall exclusively on families, and especially women, who are to be encouraged with measures to direct them back to the home, or the kitchen sink. In the most extreme version of the new Right's proposals, those of Professors Hayek and Friedman, the only recipients of state aid would be the destitute and the deranged—and only then because, otherwise, they would become a costly nuisance. Elsewhere in their unrealised state, market forces will shape such social services as there are. Schooling, medical care, and all social provision outwith a grimly deterrent "poorhouse" must be bought and sold. The market would determine their price. It is liberty, and not social justice, say Professors Hayek and Friedman, which is the proper goal of "government".

The problem is that both the detailed proposals of the family policy group and "Think Tank", and the Friedman-Hayek analysis that underlines them, are as much at odds with the facts of life in a complex society and the climate of social values as is Mrs Thatcher's incantation of Victorian bliss. Neither the Friedman dreams of human improvement by unrelieved competition nor the Hayek nightmare of degradation by the "nanny" state have ever come true, at least on this planet. That the welfare state has overreached itself is a myth: that the family has abrogated its responsibilities is another. Only one old person in twenty is in any form of institutional care. Only one in fourteen has a home-help. Although there are more old people than ever before, no respectable study has yet shown a diminution of family care for them, where families exist. Equally, all the evidence suggests that the problem is unemployment — and not the unemployed. Indeed, although Mrs Thatcher and prominent Tories argue for the "free market" economy on the grounds that it rewards the ambitious, the determined and the inventive (the poor unemployed therefore being feckless, lazy or incompetent), her most prominent philosophical supporters admit that, while the free market sponsors liberty, its results are unfair and unjust to many people.

The starting point of a new strategy

Making the case for social justice is not the same as solving the problem of poverty. If life is more complex than it seems to the ideologists of the new Right, changing circumstances force the Left to reassess its social strategy. In the past it was argued that, as the British economy expanded, there would be sufficient resources to fuel rising public expenditure needs, an expanding welfare state, and increased measures to help the poor. The state would compensate those who would otherwise be the victims of a relatively successful market economy. The experience in periods of economic growth has hardly supported this view. Wealth and income inequalities in Scotland have remained as pervasive as ever. Nor have public expenditure policies necessarily benefited those most in need. In their articles in this collection, Raffe, Cook and Hubley show clearly that, person for person, the top income groups benefit far more than the low income groups from public spending on health and social services, education and housing.

The era of automatic growth is not only over but unlikely to return in the near future. New principles for social security in a low-growth economy are badly needed. The first prerequisite for eradicating poverty is the redistribution of income and wealth from rich to poor. If there is to be no consensus for equality, then there should at least be one in favour of minimising those inequalities which are the result of inherited privilege or private power, and are grounded neither in need or merit, or contribution to the community.

Yet, as the need for redistributive policies has grown, any consensus that would achieve them has withered. Indeed, the social solidarity, the sense of common feeling and community that would support such intervention, has given way to a new ideology that favours more inequality. It is not simply that Mrs Thatcher has popularised a view that the poor are largely undeserving, feckless, incompetent or reckless, but that the new Right have consistently won the argument that further moves towards equality are absurd, impossible and undesirable. For the Right, inequality is inevitable because talent, merit and ability are, to them, largely innate characteristics. They believe differential and unequal rewards are in any case essential to the running of a modern, complex society. Quite simply they say that certain positions are "more important" than others, talents are scarce, those with talent must be persuaded to train, take jobs, and perform them adequately, and therefore must have very different incentives.

It is time for the Left to argue the case for equality. Most inequalities are based neither on merit nor on any contribution to community welfare. Today, it is still inheritance that is responsible for the vast inequalities in wealth that distort society, and income inequalities result as much from shareholdings, and other unearned rewards, as from individual choices, about jobs, training, or spending. Class is not directly determined by merit, educational attainment is influenced more by family background than by IQ, and educational qualifications, in any case, are not the sole determinants of economic or social success.

How much support is there for an egalitarian ideology that argues people are, by nature, more co-operative than they are appetitive, and suggests people's aspirations are shaped less by the desire for wealth, status or power, than by a desire to gain job satisfaction, to serve the community, or to develop their own potential? The answer is that, if public spending and intervention are currently equated with queues, waiting lists and bureaucratic bungling and therefore unpopular, opinion polls have consistently found a majority in support of measures that redistribute income and wealth from rich to poor and give working people a more equal say in the running of industry and society. In circumstances where eradicating inequality would be a precondition of greater personal liberty, as well as re-establishing a sense of community, the goal would not simply be the minimalist one of equalising opportunities, a strategy akin to what Tawney described as "the impertinent courtesy of an invitation to unwelcome guests in the certainty that circumstances would prevent them from accepting it". Nor would the goal be simply to equalise incomes in the form of arithmetical equality. Rather, the aim would be to movilise our social resources, and government agencies, in what Tawney called a plan "to narrow the space between valley and peak".

What are the measures a government might take? As the contributors to this volume suggest, five initiatives that radically reform the existing tax, social security and welfare systems are of paramount importance. The first is an end to mass unemployment and an end to the poverty that is its consequence. At a minimum, benefits for the unemployed must be no different from those of other groups who depend on state help. The second is a legal minimum wage. Twine suggests that a legal minimum wage is preferable to alternative proposals based on negative income tax, tax credits or social dividend schemes. Third, most authors argue explicitly for a more generous definition of the state's minimum "safety net". At whatever level it is set, it should be designed to guarantee a living standard that enables today's victims of poverty to participate more fully in their communities. Fourth, more public spending is needed. It should be concentrated on the areas and groups most in need. Rising levels of public expenditure are not only socially desirable but economically justifiable as a means of reducing unemployment.

Finally, the need for redistribution of income and wealth is stressed by almost every author. This would mean restoring to the centre of the tax system two basic principles: the first, that those who cannot afford to pay tax should not have to pay it; and the second, that taxation should rise progressively with income. Programmes that merely redistribute poverty from families to single persons, from the old to the young, from the sick to the healthy, are not a solution. What is needed is a programme of reform that ends the current situation where the top 10% own 80% of our wealth and 30% of income, even after tax. As Tawney remarked, "What some people call the problem of poverty, others call the problems of riches".

References
1   Regulation 4(1), Supplementary Benefit (Requirements) Regulations, as cited in Child Poverty Action Group, *National Welfare Benefits Handbook* (London, 1983), p. 18.
2   House of Commons, *Hansard*, Vol. 793, 7 September 1979.
3   Peter Townsend, *Poverty in the United Kingdom* (Harmondsworth, 1979), p. 31.
4   Regional Abstract of Statistics (HMSO, 1983), p. 100.
5   Ibid., p. 98.
6   Peter Wedge and Juliet Essen, *Children in Adversity* (London, 1982), p. 30.
7   *Voluntary Unemployment Deductions*, Report of Social Security Policy Inspectorate (London, 1983).
8   *Social Insurance and Allied Services*, Cmnd. 6404 (HMSO, 1942), pp. 83, 142.
9   *The Guardian*, 17 February 1983.
10 For a fuller discussion of the views of Professors Hayek and Friedman, see, for example, Vic George and Paul Wilding, *Ideology and Social Welfare* (London, 1976), pp. 21-41.

William McIlvanney

BEING POOR

I BELIEVE one of the highly developed national skills the Scots have is the ability to deny the reality of their own circumstances. In my more fanciful moments, I wonder if it doesn't relate to a central psychic need to hide from the painful truth of their own history, from the fact that they sold their independence and did it — clichés of Scottish tight-fistedness notwithstanding — very cheaply. Whatever the causes, the results can have a certain grand absurdity when expressed in unimportant areas, like football. In areas of importance, the results can be damaging to the development of a realistic sense of how we live.

One such damaging result is for me the Nelsonian attitude of many Scots to the deprivation around them. Putting to their eye a telescope with a ben and loch painted on the lens, they say, "I see no poverty". They have for long been aided in their illusion by the poor themselves. Scots pride, that formidable quality, has always tended to rebound upon itself. For generations the poor of this country have equated poverty with shame and have consequently hallucinated adequacy in a desert of deprivation.

When the sick man refuses to moan, the healthy are grateful. But their gratitude is a balm applied to themselves. It allows them, first of all, not to share the other's pain and soon to imagine that it isn't there. In the 1930s Edwin Muir was amazed at how effectively well-off Glaswegians failed to notice the city's destitution. But that comfortable blindness was never a Glasgow monopoly. And it has in recent years developed thicker cataracts of complacency, thanks to repeated applications of the phrase "The Welfare State".

Ours is a caring society, people think vaguely. Steps are being taken. Provision has been made. Such bromide thoughts minister as effectively to the conditions of our society as an aspirin would to cancer. The truth is that the Welfare State is often less panacea for the poor than valium for the rich, more concept than reality, more psychic palliative than physical cure.

Scotland is still a society of chronic injustice. In some ways its condition has worsened precisely because the more superficial manifestations of poverty have been cosmetically treated while its root effects remain. We do not see children barefoot in winter now. But the disease of poverty is still rife enough among us in its subtler forms. Its effects aren't always dramatic but they are always destructive. Numerous statistics testify to its presence. For example, it has been estimated that 800,000 Scots live below the government's own poverty guideline (that is, a family of four on less than £56 per week).

The statistics are there. Unfortunately, they're not all that's there. For being poor is never merely statistical. It is specific and individual and sore enough, even in its milder forms.

Take as an example a woman living in Livingston new town, to whom I was directed by a social worker as representing an ordinary kind of hardship. I'll call her Kathy, because it isn't her name. Her circumstances are hardly exceptional. Stated baldly, they have a dull familiarity to them in the present epidemic of dissolving families, as arresting as a hyphen in a graveyard.

She is forty-one. Six years ago her husband, who was twenty-nine at that time, left her, ironically, for an older woman. Their daughter was seven at the time, their son six. There followed one of those periods of social disorientation that tend to be experienced by such an amputated half of a couple, when you're living by braille. The nerve-ends seem to be on the outside of the skin and the hurts home in. Paranoia hovers near and the insensitivity of others feels like a plot.

Her own incredulity at the behaviour of others had its justifications. She remembers a couple of them with special clarity. During her first Hogmanay alone, her estranged husband and the woman he was living with arrived at the door at 2 a.m. on New Year's Day to wish her a Happy New Year. At another time her father-in-law turned up with a tenner to help her out. Wrapped in the note she found a durex, which he had apparently thought was a tasteful way of suggesting what he had in mind.

After almost a year of emotional confusion she moved to Livingston with the children, having come to the admission that she had to work out her problems for herself. She's still trying to do that. Central to the difficulty of doing so is simply lack of money.

Her ex-husband pays her nothing. But every week she receives £46.12 supplementary allowance, £13.80 child benefit and she is allowed to make £12 per week from part-time work. It's hardly the stuff of which a tear-provoking Victorian print might be made. There are hundreds of thousands far worse off than she is. It's all the more significant then that her life shows a lot of the corrosive effects of being even mildly poor.

One of these is the sense of defeat, of being trapped in a self-perpetuating set of circumstances. Her part-time work earns her £21.13 a week. She is allowed to make £4 clear. Beyond that, up to £20, she is allowed to keep a half of her earnings. Above £20, anything she earns is taken back. In other words, no matter how much part-time work she does, she can't earn more than £12 from it in any given week.

That sense of helplessness is exacerbated by some of the attitudes of others and by a conscience about as tractable as a piece of heavy engineering. A friend has remarked to her, "You're nothing but a sponger". ("If that's what a friend thinks of me, what are other people thinking?") Feelings of amorphous guilt grow like a fungus in the secretiveness the dread of such reactions promotes, choking off her natural sociability. Her only apparent indulgence, smoking, is something she's not keen to let other people see her doing.

The guilt that waits in ambush in some of the simplest actions has promoted in her a hypersensitivity to the complex and largely incomprehensible rules she feels governing her life. She mentions the thought of the police coming to her door, for a reason she can't and doesn't want to imagine, and the moment is like a child trying to contemplate the bogeyman.

Even the obeying of the rules can lead to guilt. When the family was moving to Livingston, she consulted with the housing authority to make sure it would be all right to bring the family pet, a golden labrador called Tanya. She was informed dogs were forbidden in the type of housing she was moving into. Advised by the vet that the dog would pine in another house, she had it put down and told the children, who had an extravagant affection for it, that it had been taken by other people. Arriving at Livingston, she found that several neighbours living in the same type of housing kept dogs. "I can still cry for it."

Breaking the rules certainly leads to guilt. About three years ago, she started doing extra shifts at her part-time job as a kitchen-assistant. The additional money she was making became addictive. "It's not as if I was spending the money on drink and bingo," she says, watching for a reaction. "It was to get things we needed." But she knew the money was more than she was allowed to make and the guilt grew like compound interest.

At the end of the year, she could cope with it no longer. Having confessed, she was greatly relieved not to be prosecuted. Instead, she agreed to pay back £327.13 at the rate of £6 per week. It took her just more than a year. Talking about it now, she has no self-justifying analogies to make with other people's financial fiddles, just an immense thankfulness that it's over and a determination not to do it again.

That determination seems to imply her acceptance of being immured indefinitely in her present circumstances. She can see no significant alleviation of them in the foreseeable future. The children, at thirteen and twelve, are at that stage when the young grow like the Incredible Hulk in a bad mood, with a corresponding need for new clothes, unfortunately not supplied magically by the props department. She says she gets no clothing grant. It looks as if they'll be outgrowing their mother's purse for a long time yet. Paradoxically her ambitions for them threaten to lengthen that time. She is determined that if anything thwarts her daughter's desire to be a teacher or her son's desire to be a civil engineer, it won't be their financial situation.

Such long-term ambition by proxy seems to be the only kind Kathy can

afford to indulge. Talking of herself, she gives the impression she has a
horizon of about six inches. She hopes to hold on to her part-time job. She
hopes, by scrupulous managing of money, to be able to let the children go on
such school trips as are on offer. Asked what her greatest ambition is for
herself, she claims it is to have the house redecorated, "To get it the way I want
it". She admits how badly the paint and the furniture need renewing, but she's
too used to them for her embarrassment to be more than token.

She has had a long education in learning by daily rote the acceptance of
diminished dreams. Her father died when she was thirteen and she can
remember her partially blind mother going to collect her 13/6d. a week to
keep them both. She expresses no bitterness about her circumstances, as if
even that were something the rules perhaps don't entitle her to.

She simply stays at home except for the few hours she works each day and
one night a week when the local amateur dramatic society is preparing its
pantomime. On those nights she and the children go along to help in the
rehearsals and perhaps get a small part. It's an economical activity, involving
only the bus fares and the price of coffees.

Kathy's case is unremarkable. It is at least partly the result of personal
experiences no one could have legislated for, but its most definitive element
remains insufficient money to live anything like a reasonably fulfilling life and
no apparent possibility of getting more. She is one of very many trying to fight
a rearguard action of personal decency against the economic odds in a society
where the principles behind the distribution of the available wealth have
developed, it should be acknowledged, beyond the logic of the fruit-machine
and the morality of a Monopoly board, but not far enough beyond them.

She and others like her are able to maintain a superficial appearance of
sufficiency and to do it successfully enough, in many cases, to convince not
only others but themselves. They may live in different types of areas. They will
have little sense of sharing a common condition with one another. They will
assuredly have no sense of a common voice. They're rather like a reservist
army of the poor, uniform only in a kind of discreet malnutrition of the spirit,
not yet mobilised into an open acknowledgment of their shared state. For
many of them perhaps their greatest pride is that they have not yet had to
make such open acknowledgment. In a truly caring society it would be made
for them.

G. M. Norris

POVERTY IN SCOTLAND, 1979-83

Introduction: Defining poverty

T HIS article is concerned purely with the problems of families with low or
inadequate incomes. Whilst any full discussion of poverty would
normally take into account not only monetary incomes but also income in
kind as well as access to services such as housing, health care and educational
resources these latter topics are covered to some extent elsewhere in this
volume.[1] Lack of money is the key characteristic shared by a variety of groups
whom we shall call the poor. The measures used to identify these groups and
their relative sizes will be measures of income. A low income level may of
course be balanced by a high level of monetary assets but given the extremely
unequal distribution of wealth in Scotland[2] the possibility that the country's
low income families possess significant wealth can be discounted.

The only satisfactory way of measuring the extent of money poverty in
Scotland is to examine the distribution of disposable incomes for families of a
similar size and type. The main difficulty then becomes deciding what point
on these income distributions, when account is taken of family size and type,
constitutes an appropriate cut-off point for identifying the poor. A lengthy
discussion about the appropriateness of different cut-off points would
however be largely academic because we do not possess adequate information
about the distribution of disposable incomes in Scotland for different family
types to enable us to assess the effects of using different poverty lines.
Information does exist, however, about the numbers and types of families
whose incomes are at or below one particular poverty line and this permits us
to make reasonably accurate estimates of the extent of poverty in Scotland on
the basis of that definition of poverty. This definition is based on what may be
termed the "official" poverty line; it is the level of incomes approved by
Parliament for claimants dependent on supplementary benefit.[3] Estimates of
the numbers of people living in families with incomes at or below this level
have a number of advantages:

(1) This poverty line takes into account the needs of families of different type
    and size so that small and large families can be treated in the same way.

(2) The income levels represented by the supplementary benefit scale rates have maintained a reasonably stable relationship with average gross earnings in the post-war period so that comparisons over time can be made.

(3) No one using this measure of poverty can be accused of over-generosity. It provides an absolute minimum measure of real poverty. The supplementary benefit rates are set by Parliament as a minimum living standard below which no family in the country, no matter how dependent, should fall.

The scale rates currently provide an income which is below 40% of median household incomes for similar families.[4] Moreover, there is an abundance of evidence to suggest that long-term dependency on these income levels can produce chronic hardship.[5]

The remainder of this article is in five parts. The first gives an estimate of the extent of poverty in Scotland at the moment and notes its growth over time. The second looks more closely at the different groups who make up the poor, whilst the third attempts to examine briefly the relationship between money poverty and the broader notion of deprivation. Some of the more general causes of poverty are briefly discussed in the fourth section, before the final part examines some of the relevant policy issues.

How many poor in Scotland?

It is possible to provide reasonably accurate estimates of the numbers of poor people living in Scotland from official statistics published by the Department of Health and Social Security. The latest published figures relate to a week in December 1981. Table 1, however, shown at the end of this section, gives estimates for earlier years as well as a projection for the end of 1982. The precise way in which these figures have been calculated is described in footnote 6.

The first problem is to identify those groups whose incomes are at or below supplementary benefit level. The estimates in the table are made up of:

(1) those people living in families actually dependent on supplementary benefit;

(2) those people living in families which are eligible for supplementary benefit but who are not receiving benefit because they do not claim it, known as eligible non-claimants;

(3) others living in families with incomes below supplementary benefit level who are not eligible to receive this benefit: these are mainly families with heads in full-time employment, the working poor.

The numbers in families in receipt of benefit at the end of 1979, 450,000, is one-and-a-half times the numbers provided for by the old National Assistance Board in 1961, around 300,000. This increase in numbers is a consequence of an increase in pensioners dependent on supplementary pension, from about

120,000 in 1961 to 173,000 in 1979, a massive increase on the numbers of those dependent on the supplementary allowance as a result of unemployment, from 66,000 to 156,000, and a further increase in the population in single-parent families claiming an allowance, from 30,000 to 89,000. The increase in poverty in Scotland which occurred between 1961 and 1979 pales into insignificance when compared to the dramatic increase which has occurred in the three short years between the end of 1979 and the end of 1982. The numbers of people dependent on supplementary benefit has gone up from 450,000 to 770,000 in this period, an increase of over 70%. Whilst the number of pensioners has stayed about the same, major increases can be seen in:

—the numbers of unemployed and their families, an increase of
  two-and-a-half times from 156,000 to 388,000;
—the number of single parents and their families, an increase of
  60% from 89,000 to 142,000;
—the numbers of other groups (mainly the sick and disabled),
  an increase of double from 32,000 to 68,000.

There is little doubt that the major cause of this change is the remarkable increase in unemployment in Scotland over this period from about 7.5% in 1979 to over 15% at the end of 1982. An additional factor, however, is probably the reduction in the real value of the national insurance benefits, which for many dependent groups used to keep their income above the supplementary benefit level. The main elements of this attack on the national insurance system have been the abolition of the earnings related supplement, the 5% cut in the uprating of short-term NI benefits "in lieu" of taxation in 1980, and the failure to maintain the value of the children's element of national insurance benefits. All these changes have had the result of pushing greater numbers of people into dependence on supplementary benefit.

When eligible non-claimants and the working poor are taken into account the number of people living in families whose incomes are at or below the supplementary benefit level at the end of 1979 was 656,000, 13% of the Scottish population. By the end of 1982 this total had risen to around 1,014,000, a rise of over 50% in only three years. This means that now one in five of Scottish people are living in poverty.

Many families in receipt of supplementary benefit actually have an income which is marginally above this level as a result of both weekly and lump sum additions to the basic scale rates for special circumstances and the extent to which some incomes are disregarded totally or in part when eligibility for supplementary benefit is determined. As a consequence of this some families whose income is marginally above supplementary benefit but who do not receive the benefit have similar total disposable incomes to supplementary benefit recipients. The existence of these families is taken into account by adding to the basic estimate of the poor an estimate of the numbers of people in these families which are on the margin of poverty. An income of up to 40%

above the supplementary benefit line is taken as the upper limit for such families.[7] The working poor will form the largest single group within this category along with pensioners, whilst the remainder will consist of the unemployed and the sick and disabled who are dependent on national insurance benefits which, with marginal additional incomes from other sources such as occupational pensions, part-time earnings, take their total incomes just above the supplementary benefit level. It is estimated that the numbers of people living on the margins of poverty in Scotland is around 650,000. Thus our total estimate for the numbers of people in Scotland who were in poverty or who were on the margins of poverty in 1982 is 1,664,000, almost one-third of the population.

Table 1.

NUMBERS OF PEOPLE IN POVERTY AND ON THE MARGINS
OF POVERTY, SCOTLAND, 1973, 1979, 1982

| | Date | | |
| | November | December | December |
Category	1973	1979	1982
1. Persons in families in receipt of supplementary benefit:			
(a) Pensioners	208,000	173,000	172,000
(b) Family head unemployed	91,000	156,000	388,000
(c) Single-parent families	61,000	89,000	142,000
(d) All other families	48,000	32,000	68,000
Total provided for by SB	408,000	450,000	770,000
2. Persons in families which are eligible non-claimants of SB:			
Total	135,000	136,000	196,000
3. Total in poverty	622,000	656,000	1,014,000
4. Persons in families whose income is above SB level but below 140% of SB level:			
Total on margins of poverty	697,000	662,000	650,000
5. Total in poverty or on margins	1,319,000	1,318,000	1,664,000

Who are the poor?
An analysis of the main groups in poverty in Scotland is restricted to a breakdown of those whose incomes fall below or at the supplementary benefit line because the available information does not permit detailed examination of those who are on the margins of poverty.

Pensioners, one of the two largest groups, constitute 22% of those who are in receipt of supplementary benefit and, when an estimate of pensioners who are eligible for this benefit but do not claim it is added the total number of pensioners living at or below the poverty line comes to about 260,000, 25% of all those who are in poverty. This figure represents approximately 30% of the population of pensionable age. In the majority of cases pensioners are poor as defined here because of the inadequacy of their basic national insurance pension, the current level of which is close to the long-term supplementary benefit scale rate. All pensioners whose only source of income is this national insurance basic pension will be eligible for a supplementary pension unless they have negligible housing costs, whilst a large number will be only just above the qualifying level as a result of a small occupational pension.

In 1982, for the first time, half of those in receipt of supplementary benefit were the unemployed and their families. When an estimate of eligible non-claimants are added the total of people in families dependent on unemployed men and women whose income is at or below supplementary benefit level rises to 455,000, 45% of all those in poverty. In spite of national insurance flat rate unemployment benefits usually over half of the Scottish unemployed are dependent on supplementary benefit to some extent. This high level of poverty amongst the unemployed is the result of the number of men and women whose entitlement to the national insurance benefit is either reduced or exhausted as a result of the inadequacy of their record of national insurance contributions or the length of time they have been out of work.[8] Recurrent unemployment, which affects a claimant's contribution record, and long-term unemployment, which exhausts his or her entitlement, are by no means uncommon amongst the Scottish unemployed. Normally up to 40% of the currently registered out-of-work in the country have been unemployed at least once in the previous year. In Scotland over one-third of the unemployed had been out of work for over a year and 54% had been unemployed for over six months in January 1983.

The unemployed are a particularly important group for they are numerically the most volatile element within the poor. The rise in the numbers of poor families documented in Table 1 is almost entirely due to changes in the level of the unemployment rate in recent years. A one percentage point change in the unemployment rate in Scotland currently adds or substracts almost 30,000 people to the poverty count. Given the rise in unemployment in Scotland in recent years it is clear that the nature of poverty has undergone a significant change. Up to the early 'sixties the poor consisted of a large group of pensioners plus a number of smaller other groups, single-parent families, the sick and the disabled and the unemployed. In recent years the significance of the unemployed has increased so that by now the unemployed and their families form by far the largest single group amongst the poor. In 1973 half the poor were pensioners. In 1983 70% of the poor will be the families of unemployed people and single parents. A major consequence of these changes therefore is that there will have been a substantial increase in the proportion of the poor who are children.

The most important of the other smaller groups within the poor is the single-parent family group which, including eligible non-claimants, now accounts for over 150,000 people in Scotland living at incomes at or below the supplementary benefit line. The remaining group, about 80,000 people in poverty in total, will consist of families with sick or disabled heads under retirement age and people staying at home to look after dependent relatives, usually pensioners, who are not children.

It is difficult to accurately assess the numbers of working poor in Scotland and the estimates have had to be made on the assumption that the working poor represent a similar proportion of the working population in Scotland as they do in Great Britain as a whole. This is probably an underestimate as Scotland contains a higher proportion of men with low earnings than the country as a whole. Department of Health and Social Security figures for the end of 1981 suggest that there are around 50,000 people living below supplementary benefit level in families supported by a full-time worker on the basis of this assumption. The significance of the working poor is, however, much increased when those on the margins of poverty are analysed. Using similar assumptions and evidence it is indicated that about 200,000 people in families supported by full-time employment live on the margins of poverty in Scotland, about one-third of all those with incomes at this level. Although a significant minority of these families may consist of men earning around average wages whilst having to support a large family it is probable that the bulk of their numbers are made up of younger men with low earnings with only a small number of young children where the wife is unable to work. The significance of women's earnings, in spite of their low level, in enabling a family to raise itself above the poverty line, cannot be understated at this point. The figures suggest that the number of working poor has declined in recent years in Scotland as increasing unemployment has moved lower paid workers into unemployment.

Poverty and deprivation

The rather narrow view taken in this article in concentrating on money poverty has to be placed in the context of the more widely based approach which underlies the overall content of this volume. Deprivation is understood by this author to draw attention to not just the problem of low incomes and the absence of control it implies over goods sold in the market but also to the relative lack of access to goods and services made available through non-market processes. Of key importance here are access to adequate housing, jobs, health care, and educational facilities. There is very little evidence available to throw light on the relationship at the individual level between money poverty and access to these other resources. Information does exist at the area level covering a small number of topics indicating that in Scotland particularly areas containing high proportions of the unemployed, for example, tend to be poor housing areas.[9] Of impressionistic evidence there is an abundance. Anyone who has worked and lived in such areas knows that the poorer, more desperately hard-up members of the community do often tend to concentrate through the logic of housing allocation policies[10] in poorer housing areas where schools and health facilities are often also of lower quality. The problem of inner city areas with their rundown and outdated physical and social infrastructure offers a particularly good example of this phenomenon.

On one issue there can be no doubt, however. Throughout our welfare state there run two parallel sets of facilities; one freely provided (or almost freely provided) set of public facilities and a set of privately provided services accessible only to those with sufficient money to pay for them. There are private schools, private medical facilities, private pension and sickness insurance schemes and a private housing market. Two points need to be made. First, in order to persuade people to purchase goods and services which they could obtain free through public provision, private provision has to offer a superior service to that offered by the welfare state. These private institutions could not otherwise survive. Second, the notion of consumer choice posited by those who support the extension of this private welfare sector is a palpable nonsense when applied to the poor. People who have difficulty feeding their children adequately can hardly be expected to make "sacrifices" to pay what are to them unbelievable sums for the education of these same children. The poor are restricted totally to a dependence on state-provided facilities and any attack on the quality of service or the level of provision in this sector is a direct attack upon the overall living standards of the poor. For the one-third of the Scottish population on or around the poverty line, private sector provision is an irrelevance.

The causes of poverty

An explanation of poverty in Scotland in terms of a descriptive categorisation of the poor themselves scratches only the surface of the problem. We know that one quarter of the poor are old, almost one half are unemployed and the remainder are a mixture of low-wage earners, single-parent families and the sick and disabled. What these facts reveal, however, are certain underlying basic social features and assumptions. Ours is a society based on a belief in the fundamental rationality of a free market for the exchange of commodities and in particular of labour. The poor are a consequence of the operation of that belief. A free market for labour implies a structure of incentives in which some skills, supposedly more scarce or more valuable, attract higher rewards than others. Furthermore, the logic of this market dictates that in order to persuade people to work at all, entering paid employment has to be more highly rewarded than not working. The structure of incentives within the market rests on the maintenance of the division between the non-working, who make up the bulk of the poor, and those who work. The poor are penalised for their inability, very rarely their unwillingness, to enter paid employment. This free market theology has dominated the thinking of the present government and these principles lie behind its attack on the poor.

A number of problems remain however. Around one-half of the poor — the old, single-parent families and the sick and disabled — consists of people who not only cannot work but for whom there is no suggestion that they should be forced to do so. The incentive argument is not relevant to them. The poverty of these groups is a reflection of the government's unwillingness to devote sufficient resources to providing adequately for those people whom society does not wish to work and indeed whom we often positively encourage not to work. The second major group, again in Scotland about half the poor, are the unemployed and the working poor. These people are poor because of the failure of the market itself to function adequately. They are the victims of an economy in recession. To be more accurate they are the real victims of inflation, for it is in pursuit of the goal of reducing inflation that our economic system has been permitted for several years now to run at, in post-war terms, historically unparalleled unemployment levels. The unemployed and the low paid have not been the cause of inflation nor have they benefitted from it; they are nevertheless paying the price.

Poverty and policy
Poverty and inequality are one of the unavoidable costs of a doctrinaire allegiance to the dominance of free market forces. It is clear, however, that both problems can at least be alleviated whilst not destroying the fabric of a society based on such an economic system. There are three general areas in which action can and should be taken.

As far as the unemployed and the low paid are concerned there is no substitute for a reasonably secure job offering a living wage. The provision of such jobs is of paramount importance in any attempt to reduce poverty in Scotland. As has already been noted, a reduction in the unemployment rate of one percentage point will take about 30,000 people out of poverty. A policy for poverty therefore has to start with a policy for jobs.

It will take several years for even an aggressive jobs policy to reverse the trends of recent years and consequently the social security system will be the main source of income not only for those who are outside the working population (i.e. the retired, the sick and disabled) but for those who are unemployed for some time to come. The trend in recent years has been for supplementary benefit to become increasingly important and for the incomes of groups dependent on this and related benefits to fall relative to the incomes of the working population. Considerable reform of the system, including the restoration of the value of benefits which have declined, is required. One glaring problem for example can be seen in the situation of the long-term unemployed. This group, which is increasing in size, will only benefit slowly from an upturn in the economy and yet the group is probably the poorest amongst the poor. Unlike all other people dependent on supplementary benefit the unemployed continue to remain eligible only for the short-term supplementary benefit rate even after one year on benefit. The scandal of the continuance of this policy can best be illustrated by the fact that the difference between the short-term rate and the long-term rate to which all other long-term supplementary benefit recipients are entitled is now worth £10.60 per week to a married couple. The long-term aim of reforms should be to ensure that the supplementary means-tested system returns to the role of a safety net for a small number which was always the original intention.

As has already been pointed out, the importance of an adequate level of public services provided by the state cannot be underestimated for the maintenance of reasonable living standards, in the broadest sense of that term, for the poor. It is unfortunately the case that in the current economic and political climate the issue here is likely to be more the question of maintaining existing standards rather than the possibility of extending welfare provision into new areas or expanding existing services. Of necessity, defending a position which has already been attained in this field may well be the most significant contribution which can be made to preventing further erosion of the life-chances of the poorest and weakest members of our society.

Four years of the Conservative administration have already shown, however, that policies which meet these needs are unlikely to be adopted. There is no doubt that the result of the present government's policies has been a substantial increase in the number of people in poverty and a reduction in the living standards of the poor relative to the rest of the population; as the poor increase in number the gap between them and the rest of society will widen. These tendencies are not just the inevitable or accidental results of the impact of the world recession on the Scottish economy but are a central element of the government's strategy. The government is committed to a long-term strategy of increasing growth in the private sector of the economy by increasing incentives, particularly for the higher paid, financing such incentives out of reductions in public expenditure on which the poor are dependent for their income and services.

The increase in the number of poor people in Scotland since the election of the current government has already been noted above and derives directly from the redundancies and recruitment cutbacks in both the public and the private sectors of the economy which have increased Scottish unemployment by over 180,000 since the beginning of 1979. These increases of unemployed have "achieved" an addition to the numbers in poverty of around 270,000 in just over three years.

It is not just the increase in the numbers of the poor which is important, however, what is far more crucial, because it reveals the nature of the government's long-term philosophy, is the series of changes to legislation and regulations concerning national insurance benefits, supplementary benefits and other benefits. The significance of these changes is that they will effect a reduction in the living standards of the poor relative to the population as a whole. It is sometimes suggested that a short-term increase in unemployment, for example, and hence an increase in poverty, is an unfortunate but necessary price which has to be paid in order to secure future higher levels of growth for the economy. The long-term interests of the poor, it is argued, are likely to be best served by the ultimately higher level of real economic growth which will be the result of a policy based on short-term sacrifices. Whilst it would be possible to question the rationality of this policy in terms of its probable actual effects on real growth in the future a far more important criticism is that it is of course not necessarily the case that the poor will benefit in the same way as the rest of the population from any increased growth which may occur. For this to happen the government in power actually has to take particular steps to ensure that any increases in real wealth are in fact redistributed towards the poor. The argument of the remainder of this section is that the current government is extremely unlikely to take such steps and that in fact the general message from the changes which have been made so far in social security regulations is that in fact the very opposite is more likely to occur.

The most important of the recent changes involves the severing of the link between increases in earnings and increases in the retirement pensions and long-term supplementary benefits. Under the previous government, increases in the retirement pension were determined by the increase in average earnings or the increase in prices whichever was the greater. Long-term supplementary benefit rates were tied to the retirement pension as a matter of custom. The current administration has removed the link to earnings of the pension, and hence long-term supplementary benefit rates, thereby ensuring that whilst recipients of these benefits will be protected from the effects of inflation they will not necessarily share in any increase in general prosperity which would be reflected in a rise in real earnings levels. The effect of this change in any single year is not particularly important, what is far more significant is the principle it sets up for the level of social security benefits in the long term, namely that these benefits cannot be expected to rise at the same rate as real increases in the standard of living of the working, i.e. non-poor, population. Whilst short-term supplementary benefits formerly rose at the same rate as prices the recent increases of these and most non-taxable national insurance benefits (e.g. unemployment benefit, sick benefit) were held back to a level 5% lower than the increase in prices. This reduction in the real value of these benefits was carried out in the anticipation that in future years these benefits would become taxable, bringing into the taxation net a whole range of the poorest people in the country who had hitherto not had to pay income tax. The decision to cut the increase in these benefits by 5% represents, of course, rough and arbitrary justice as it is by no means the case that all those in receipt of these benefits will actually end up paying tax when the taxation of such benefits is introduced.

As well as implementing such changes which, at a time when the level of taxation for higher income groups was being significantly reduced, have effected a significant redistribution of income from the poor as a whole to the rich, the government have also introduced a number of changes which have particularly affected those on the margins of poverty. Three changes in particular may be cited. These are the proposal to abolish the earnings related supplement for the unemployed and those on sick benefit, the reduction in the scope of the fuel discount schemes and the removal of price controls and the statutory means test for free school meals. The point about all these changes is that they affect those people who are not in receipt of supplementary benefit but who are usually receiving income just above the required level. Effectively these changes will be pushing many members of the group on the margins of poverty close to the poverty line itself. The changes themselves will have, of course, no effect on the incomes and living standards of those who are well above the poverty line.

The abolition of the earnings related supplement to unemployment and sickness benefit will remove an important cushion which softens the impact of job loss on the unemployed for example. From the date of abolition, January 1982, it is highly probable that large numbers of the unemployed have become eligible for a supplementary allowance as soon as they have lost a job. This means a much higher proportion of the unemployed as well as the sick and disabled are now in poverty than was the case in the past. Table 1 figures bear this out. Large numbers of families on the margins of poverty were previously protected to some extent from the high cost of winter fuel bills by the fuel discount scheme. The scope of this scheme has now been drastically reduced to cover only those in receipt of supplementary benefit where there is a child under five or someone over seventy-five in the household. Finally, changes introduced in the Education Act concerning charging for school meals and the eligibility criteria for free school meals will have the effect of both reducing the numbers of children who are likely to be receiving free school meals whilst increasing significantly the cost of such meals to those who have to pay for them.

The total effect therefore of four years of the Conservative administration on poverty in Scotland can be summarised in four trends:

(1) The numbers of people in poverty has increased dramatically and will continue to do so as unemployment continues to rise.

(2) The poor will not share in any real increase in living standards which are experienced by the remainder of the population.

(3) Many of those who were on the margins of poverty have now become poor themselves.

(4) The living standards of many who remain on the margins of poverty will be reduced.

In conclusion Scottish society will become characterised by increasing polarisation as the poor become greater in number and relatively poorer.

References
1   For a full discussion of the relationship between money income and other aspects of deprivation see *Poverty in the United Kingdom*, P. Townsend (Penguin, 1979).
2   See *The Distribution of Personal Wealth in Scotland*, A. Warrison, Fraser of Allander Institute, Research Monograph No. 1.
3   For any one family the "poverty line" using this method is defined as the appropriate scale rate for that family plus the rent allowance that the family would receive if they were in receipt of supplementary benefit. There are separate scale rates for single persons, married couples and for children of different ages. Thus at rates operative in November 1982 a married couple on their own would be entitled to benefit which took their total income up to £41.70 (at the short-term rate) plus the rent allowance. The level for a man and his wife and two children aged twelve would be £68.00 plus rent allowance per week.
4   For example the November 1979 short-term scale rates for married couples with one or two children aged twelve were under 40% of the median disposable income of households of a similar type.
5   See, for example, *Poverty: the Facts*, Poverty Pamphlet No. 17, Child Poverty Action Group, and P. Townsend, op. cit., chapter 8.
6   The sole published source used for the construction of these estimates is *Social Security Statistics*, Department of Health and Social Security. This source is published annually, the latest available edition being published in 1982, providing figures for the end of 1981. The publication usually includes the following tables.
    (i)   A table showing number of recipients of regular weekly payments of supplementary benefit in a week in Scotland in December (Table 34.34).
    (ii)   Table showing number of recipients of benefit and number of persons provided for by benefit, analysed by type of benefit nationally (Table 34.31).
    (iii) Table showing numbers of low income families plus persons in those families by status of family head (e.g. working, sick and disabled) distinguishing those in receipt of supplementary benefit and those with incomes up to 140% above SB entitlement. This table is again only a national table (Tables 47.07 and 47.08).
    (iv)   Tables or information relating to level of take-up of benefits or various kinds (Table 34.28).
    Figures for the end of 1982 relating to number of benefit recipients in Scotland by type of benefit were provided by the Department of Health and Social Security prior to publication.
    The table in the text was constructed by taking the DHSS figures for the number of benefit recipients in Scotland for the year in question and multiplying the figure for each benefit type by:
    (i)   a factor to determine the number of people provided for;
    (ii)   a further factor to provide an estimate of eligible non-claimants;
    (iii) a third factor to obtain the numbers of people in families with incomes above SB level but below 140% of that level.

Because the multiplying factors were usually derived from the tables listed above they are effectively *national* multiplying factors. Where available multiplying factors specific to Scotland were used. In fact differences between national factors and Scottish specific factors are negligible.

The least satisfactory estimates are those of the numbers of working poor in Scotland. Here it had to be assumed that Scotland had the same proportion of the working poor as the UK as a whole. The DHSS has changed the way in which it provides the estimates used to generate the figure of the working poor in recent years so that more recent figures are lower than in previous years.

7   The importance of the introduction of those on the margins of poverty into any discussion of the poor is first discussed in detail in *The Poor and the Poorest*, B. Abel-Smith and P. Townsend (Bell, 1965).

8   Receipt of full flat rate unemployment benefit is dependent on the national insurance contribution record in a previous year. Previously there was an earnings related supplement which ceased after six months unemployment. Now only the flat rate benefit is paid and this continues until the recipient has been out of work for twelve months, after which the unemployed man or woman is only eligible to receive a supplementary allowance.

9   See *Census Indicators of Urban Deprivation*, Working Note No. 10, Department of the Environment, 1975.

10   See "Housing Allocation and a Deprived Scottish Estate", *Urban Studies*, J. English, 1976.

Stephen Kendrick

SOCIAL CHANGE IN SCOTLAND

Introduction

UNLIKE the rest of this book, this chapter does not focus explicitly on patterns of poverty and social inequality in Scotland. Rather it is an attempt to briefly survey some of the main directions of social change in Scotland.[1] Changes in industrial and occupational structure work to determine the number and types of jobs available. Demographic trends operate to determine the types of family and household circumstances in which people live. Everyone in Scotland has a position with respect to the employment structure — inside it, with a particular type of job, or outside it. Similarly everyone in Scotland has their own family or household circumstances. A person's simultaneous position in terms of the employment and household structures — an unemployed man with children, the child of a working single parent, a retired person living alone — largely determines his or her positioning in the overall pattern of inequality. The cross-cutting of the employment and household structures then largely defines the shape of inequality. More importantly it is the complex cross-meshing of changes in the two structures which work to produce equally complex changes in the structure of inequality. The last fifteen to twenty years have seen massive changes in both structures.

The first part of the analysis will follow through from change in the industrial structure to change in the occupational structure and women's employment patterns. This will be followed by a briefer account of some recent trends in marriage and fertility patterns. Equally important topics such as the rise in the number of single-parent families and the unemployed are treated elsewhere in the volume and will be treated only in passing in the present chapter. These groups of course define the three most vulnerable groups in society and it is the growth in their numbers in the last few years which need not have, but in fact has, led to a quantum jump in levels of poverty in Scotland. However, the full import of these changes cannot be assessed unless we step back a little. Scotland is an old and complex industrial society. The purpose of the present chapter is to move us closer to grasping the historical uniqueness of what is happening in and to Scotland today.

It is important to stress that while one can partition social change into aspects such as industrial change, occupational change and demographic change, they are all tightly interwoven and mutually determining. Most importantly this is because they are lived simultaneously by the people who, although in a capitalist society are primarily their victims, are also, in ways ranging from the factory sit-in to planning a family, their creators.

Perhaps the best illustration of such interweaving is the complex of social changes surrounding the increase in the number of married women in employment since the war. The main enabling factor was the expansion of employment in the service sector while two necessitating factors were the fall in the age of marriage and the extension of full-time education which meant that the pool of single women was greatly reduced. Partly because of the household situation of this new married labour force and partly because of the cheapness and flexibility, due to a weak bargaining position, of part-time labour, such part-time employment was the form which the entire expansion of female employment since the war has taken. This expansion of employment opportunities, however restricted and low paid, for married women since the war was itself one of the main determinants of the massive fall in the birth rate from the early 1960s to the late 1970s.[2] This should illustrate how soon we can find ourselves in the middle of a complex system of cause and effect between demographic and economic processes — a system which makes the isolation of one or the other highly counterproductive.

The kinds of macro-structural change upon which we focus no doubt appear highly impersonal and perhaps over-deterministic. In a capitalist society, however, most social change is of this impersonal, structural nature — it does happen behind people's backs. It is the very illusion of individual choice in capitalist society which makes it so. It is no coincidence that a government which has wittingly or unwittingly intensified the impact of the most devastating set of social changes in Scotland's history, clings so tightly to the illusion of individual choice and denies vehemently that unemployment, for example, has anything to do with depression, divorce, riots, alcoholism or crime. Such macro-structural connections are also concealed by the cult of academic or bureaucratic specialisation, and although this treatment of many individual topic areas will no doubt appear gauche or superficial to the specialist, it is to be hoped that this will be compensated in terms of a sense of the whole.

Industrial change

The fundamental driving force behind changing employment patterns is industrial change. Both in terms of internal regional specialisation and industrial diversity Scotland's pattern of industrial change over the last hundred and fifty years or so has been particularly complex for such a small country. Despite this complexity, however, the fundamental causal principle behind the pattern of industrial change in Scotland for most of its history has been extremely simple — the capitalist drive for profit. We make this point here because the necessity of introducing any other mechanisms, such as national oppression, internal colonialism, dependence or whatever, has never yet been established — despite the fact that such assumptions often structure accounts of Scottish society.

The year 1851 provides a convenient benchmark, close to the high watermark of Scotland's first phase of industrialisation, based over-whelmingly on the production of textiles. By 1851, 43% of Scotland's workforce was employed in manufacturing.[4] What is perhaps surprising is that this figure has never since been surpassed by more than a couple of percentage points. By 1911, for example, the same series shows a figure of 44% of total employment in manufacturing (Table 1). Making due allowance for a change in the basis of classification in 1911 (whose effect can be assessed on the basis of the two distributions given for 1911) we can summarise the long-term trend in the share of manufacturing as follows. There was a basic stability throughout the century from 1851 to 1951, interrupted only by the pre-war depression (as there had been smaller dips reflecting previous downturns). Even by 1971 the share of manufacturing was down only 3 percentage points from the 1951 figure. Even taking 1921 as a peak, the fifty years between then and 1971 saw a sustained fall of only 5.4 percentage points.

Table 1.

SCOTLAND, EMPLOYMENT BY SECTORS, 1851 TO 1981

	Agri-culture	Mining & quarrying	Manufac-turing	Construc-tion	Inter-mediate	Service
Series A						
1851	26.0	4.4	43.2	5.5	5.0	15.9
1871	23.6	5.6	40.9	6.6	6.5	16.8
1891	15.3	6.3	43.2	6.4	9.3	19.6
1911	11.4	8.7	43.9	6.0	10.3	19.8
Series B						
1911	11.8	8.0	36.5	5.9	18.5	19.3
1931	10.1	6.0	30.3	4.2	25.4	24.0
1951	7.4	4.5	35.1	6.9	21.9	24.1
1961	5.8	3.9	32.5	7.9	23.7	26.2
1971A	4.1	1.7	32.2	8.2	21.0	32.8
June 1971	2.7	1.9	33.4	7.9	20.6	33.4
June 1981	2.3	1.9	25.4	7.5	19.8	43.1

From June 1971 to June 1981, however, according to Department of Employment figures constructed on a slightly different basis, manufacturing's share of total employment fell by 8 percentage points from 33.4% to 25.4%, with a further fall to 24.3% as the current recession has gathered steam. It would seem then that the decade 1971 to 1981 saw the largest ever decadal drop in the share of employment in manufacturing. While it might be argued that at least some of this recent fall has been cyclical and that a recovery similar to that which occurred after 1931 will take place again, it is much more plausible that whatever recovery there may be in the overall level of employment in the next twenty years, it is unlikely to involve an increase in the share of manufacturing. Internal forces, such as the impact of electronics on labour requirements and external ones such as the move towards a new international division of labour whereby labour-intensive production is tending to migrate towards peripheral or semi-peripheral zones with supplies of cheap labour, are much more powerful than they were in 1931.

As is true in general of patterns of social change in Scotland compared with those in England in particular or in Britain as a whole, this pattern of change in the sectoral structure of employment was in no way unique to Scotland. Throughout the period covered in Table 1 Scotland, of the ten Standard Regions of Britain, was the one with the sectoral employment structure closest to that of Britain as a whole. Within this general pattern of parallel development, however, one relative shift is perhaps worth noting. From 1851 to 1911, the proportion of the total workforce employed in manufacturing was around 2 percentage points higher in Scotland than was the case in Britain as a whole. By 1931, however, the depression had pushed Scotland's figure to 2 percentage points below that for Britain and ever since Scotland has had relatively fewer workers in manufacturing than in Britain as a whole. In June 1981, the proportion for Britain as a whole was 28.6% — the region with the lowest share being the South-East at 23.1% and the region with the highest the West Midlands at 39.7%. The figure for Scotland was 25.4%.

Conversely, Scotland historically had a lower proportion of its workforce in the service sector. During the 1970s, however, Scotland moved above the British figure for the first time and by June 1981, 43% of Scottish workers were in the service sector compared with 41.9% in Britain as a whole. Only the South-East (47%) and the South-West (44%) of England had higher proportions in services than did Scotland. At an aggregate level then the move towards a "service economy" has been occurring marginally faster in Scotland than in the rest of Britain.

The long-term relative stability of the share of manufacturing employment in Scotland hid some massive shifts in the industrial composition of this manufacturing activity.

As was noted above, Scotland's first wave of industrialisation was based overwhelmingly on the development of the textile and the clothing and footwear industries. In 1851, 44% of the industrial (see Note 4) workforce was in the textile industry and 18% in clothing and footwear. Moreover this specialisation was shared by all the industrial areas of Scotland. From this common specialisation in the production of textiles in 1851, the general pattern was for the regions to fan out into specialisation in one or more of the growth industries of the late nineteenth century — coal, steel, shipbuilding and engineering.

This specialisation occurred along two main axes. The first was exemplified by Clydeside with its concentration on shipbuilding and heavy engineering. The second main wing of specialisation was into coal-mining — particularly in West Lothian (57% of industrial employment in coal in 1911), Fife (44%), Stirlingshire (34%) and Ayrshire(28%). There was a partially parallel concentration of steel-making into Lanarkshire and Stirlingshire. In addition there were two regions which stayed with the earlier specialisation in textiles — Dundee and the Borders. The degree of regional specialisation occurring in the period 1851 to 1911 is indexed by the fact that the mean percentage difference between the industrial structures of the twelve main industrial regions of Scotland increased from 26 to 43. These patterns of regional specialisation may appear to be purely historical interest but it is worth stressing that despite their being overlain by a twentieth-century pattern of regional specialisation in industries such as chemicals and electronics, this pattern laid down in the second half of the nineteenth century still accounts for much of the industrial structure of modern Scotland.

The accepted image of Scotland's industrial structure in the late nineteenth century is one of marked specialisation compared with the rest of Britain. In fact in this period Scotland as a whole was one of the least specialised regions of Britain (if we take the positive percentage difference between Scotland's industrial employment structure and that of Britain as a whole and do the same for the other nine Standard Regions, Scotland turns out to be much the closest in industrial structure) and in many respects its industrial structure was the most diversified of them all. It was individual regions, counties and towns *within* Scotland which were fatally dependent on individual industries.

However, it was true that the industries which were relatively (but not enormously) over-represented in Scotland were precisely those which depended for their exports on Britain's dominant position in a world economic order of a particular structure — that strange Victorian amalgam of Empire and free trade. In terms of adaptation to this environment, Scotland could be said to have been the most successfully imperialist part of Britain — excepting of course the home of finance capital in the South-East of England. Scotland was ultra-imperialist in another sense. The seeds of Scotland's industrial decline were sown in the years of its greatest industrial success, years when Scotland did have an institutionally separate system of industrial and financial capital. It was this "Scottish capitalism" which achieved a rate of export of capital far beyond that which obtained south of the border — the export of capital to dependent areas in which a higher rate of profit could be achieved being a classically imperialist and of course capitalist pattern. If capital was being exported it obviously wasn't being invested at home. It was Scottish capitalism's industrial overintegration and subsequent financial over-integration into the imperial economic structure which together produced Scotland's vulnerability to the harsher economic climate after World War I. Finance capitalism's insistence on the maintenance of the Gold Standard and a grossly overvalued pound hardly helped matters.

In Britain as a whole in the course of the twentieth century there was a degree of convergence between regional industrial structures as areas such as

Table 2.

SCOTLAND, PRINCIPAL INDUSTRIAL AREAS. SELECTED INDUSTRIES AS PROPORTION OF TOTAL INDUSTRIAL EMPLOYMENT.

Industrial Order	2	3	4,5	6	7	9	10	11	13
	Mining	*Food/Drink/ Tobacco*	*Chem. manuf.*	*Metal eng.*	*Mech. eng.*	*Elect.*	*Ships*	*Vehicles*	*Textiles*
1911									
Ayrshire	29.4	4.6	3.4	8.1	8.8	0.5	10.0	1.3	17.6
Dunbartonshire	6.7	2.4	0.8	4.1	18.4	0.4	47.3	1.4	10.3
Lanarkshire	17.8	7.7	1.7	15.2	14.8	1.2	11.8	2.1	5.9
Renfrewshire	1.0	6.0	1.4	3.5	17.9	0.6	30.2	1.2	26.8
Midlothian	18.6	12.8	2.9	2.0	6.8	2.2	7.7	1.9	4.6
West Lothian	63.0	4.1	6.0	9.8	1.8	0.3	1.2	0.4	2.5
Clackmannanshire	17.9	12.6	0.1	1.3	2.5	2.8	14.4	0.2	33.5
Stirlingshire	36.6	3.5	3.8	29.4	2.0	0.5	3.0	1.0	5.0
Fife	48.6	3.6	0.4	1.8	3.0	0.4	0.9	0.8	13.0
Angus	0.7	5.7	0.6	1.2	9.1	0.5	7.1	0.9	60.1
Aberdeenshire	1.6	19.0	2.8	0.9	7.4	0.8	8.9	2.6	12.1
Borders	1.1	6.4	0.3	0.8	3.1	0.4	0.9	1.9	65.1
SCOTLAND	18.1	6.0	1.5	7.3	9.1	0.8	5.9	1.2	19.9
1971									
Ayrshire	12.2	7.2	12.0	5.2	13.3	1.9	1.1	5.7	20.1
Dunbartonshire	0.4	12.3	2.3	4.2	39.2	3.9	13.9	1.7	2.4
Lanarkshire	1.7	13.0	2.5	12.5	15.7	9.6	5.6	4.3	3.8
Renfrewshire	0.1	8.9	4.2	2.4	15.6	6.7	13.3	19.5	12.2
Midlothian	12.0	22.2	4.4	1.7	6.2	11.5	3.0	1.9	3.2
West Lothian	19.0	10.1	0.6	9.5	4.6	14.0	0.1	22.4	2.4
Clackmannanshire	10.8	15.8	0.4	0.0	17.2	0.7	0.0	0.0	30.1
Stirlingshire	5.1	5.9	22.2	19.7	4.0	2.0	1.5	3.0	1.5
Fife	17.3	7.8	1.4	2.6	9.5	12.7	10.3	1.0	8.0
Angus	0.2	8.9	1.9	1.7	23.0	5.2	2.3	0.3	27.8
Aberdeenshire	0.9	34.8	2.2	0.2	10.9	1.0	6.3	1.1	9.2
Borders	1.4	3.4	1.0	0.3	4.2	4.9	0.3	0.4	67.0
SCOTLAND	5.0	13.7	4.5	6.8	14.0	7.2	5.6	5.1	10.4

Wales and the North-East moved back from their extreme specialisations of the nineteenth century. Within Scotland no such convergence took place. Although there was a move away from some of the unevenly distributed traditional industries — coal and textiles in particular — much of the new industrial development — chemicals, electronics and cars — was highly unevenly distributed and in the case of cars equally vulnerable (see Table 2). Oil development added the final tilt to the crazy paving of industrial development in Scotland.

Table 3 gives the pattern of change in the structure of industrial employment in Scotland from 1911, a date close to the zenith of Scotland's industrial might, to 1971, the eve of the last chapter of Scotland's industrial decline.

Table 3.

SCOTLAND, INDUSTRIAL EMPLOYMENT AS PERCENTAGE OF
TOTAL EMPLOYMENT, 1911 TO 1971

2. Mining and quarrying	18.1	16.4	11.4	10.8	5.0
3. Food, drink and tobacco	6.0	11.6	11.1	10.4	13.7
4,5 Chemicals and coal prods.	1.5	2.7	4.4	4.4	4.6
6. Metal manufacture	7.3	7.2	7.2	7.9	6.8
8. Instrument engineering	0.4	0.5	1.0	1.4	2.5
9. Electrical engineering	0.8	1.2	2.1	4.0	7.2
10. Ships and marine eng.	5.9	4.9	8.8	7.9	5.6
11. Vehicles	1.2	3.3	4.2	4.0	5.1
12. Other metal goods	5.0	2.2	3.4	2.8	4.1
13. Textiles	19.9	17.8	13.5	12.3	10.4
14. Leather etc.	0.7	0.7	0.7	0.5	0.5
15. Clothing and footwear	11.8	6.3	4.6	3.5	4.5
16. Bricks, pottery, glass	1.8	2.0	2.5	2.6	3.0
17. Timber and furniture	4.1	5.5	4.5	3.5	3.8
18. Paper, printing, publish.	4.9	6.8	6.0	7.1	7.3
19. Other manufacturing	1.4	2.7	2.4	2.4	2.2
	100%	100%	100%	100%	100%
Industrial employment (thousands)	862	670	870	798	731

The pattern is in general a familiar one. The traditional industries which showed the heaviest decline in employment were coal-mining, textiles and clothing and footwear, which in 1911 together accounted for almost half of all industrial employment compared with only 20% in 1971. Rather more surprising is the fact that both metal manufacture and shipbuilding and marine engineering employed roughly the same share of the industrial labour force in 1971 as they had in 1911. Their nemesis was yet to come. If any one industry represented the heart of Scottish manufacturing in the post-war years it was mechanical engineering which was the largest single employer from the mid-1950s. Even in 1971 it employed almost as many people as the three twentieth-century "growth industries" — chemicals, electrical engineering and vehicles — put together.

The course of industrial collapse since 1971 is charted in Table 4. 1974 represented a peak in both total employment and in employment in manufacturing. The pacing of long-term manufacturing decline in the 1970s and the early 1980s probably reflects the combined impact of several levels of factors.

Table 4.

EMPLOYEES IN EMPLOYMENT BY INDUSTRY,
JUNE 1971 TO JUNE 1982

Industry						
1. Agriculture, forestry, fishing	55	50	47	45	44	-12%
2. Mining and quarrying	39	34	38	41	42	+24%
4,5. Coal, petroleum and chem. prods.	31	31	34	30	29	-6%
6. Metal manufacture	46	43	32	28	26	-39%
7-12. Engineering and allied industries	276	287	226	199	185	-36%
13-15. Textiles, leather and clothing	106	106	82	71	66	-38%
16-19. Other manufacturing	113	111	90	79	75	-32%
20. Construction	159	179	161	144	130	-24%
21. Gas, electric, water	31	28	29	28	28	N.C.
22. Transport and comm.	143	139	133	127	123	-12%
23. Distribution	238	242	234	225	220	-9%
24-26. Financial, prof. & misc. services	538	599	696	682	679	+13%
27. Public admin. and defence	131	145	148	149	150	+3%
Total manufacturing	669	676	550	489	457	-32%
Manufacturing as percent of total	33.4	32.4	27.4	25.3	24.3	
Total employees	2003	2084	2036	1931	1872	-10%

Most general are factors common to advanced industrial societies, usually discussed in terms of "the occupational transition" or "the shift to a service economy" involving primarily a shift in employment from the manufacturing to the service sector. Also common to the older industrial societies are factors associated with a changing international division of labour whereby labour-intensive industries tend to migrate to areas where labour is cheaper. This last process has of course been intensified by a mechanism which is specific to Britain but the irony of which is particularly cruel in Scotland's case. The major effect of the discovery of oil off Scotland's shores has been to boost the value of the pound and make the generally hostile environment of a world in slump even more crippling to the competitiveness of Scottish manufacturing industry.

Industrial change and occupational change
The best source of data on long-term trends in occupational structure in Scotland this century is Geoff Payne's[5] reclassification of occupations of the *economically active* (working or looking for work) population to the modern socio-economic groups from 1921 to 1971.[6] We will use this series as a basis for a brief survey of trends from 1921 to 1961 and then move over to census data on the socio-economic group structure of the *employed* population for the period 1961 to 1981.

The pattern of change from 1921 to 1961 is relatively complex but three broad trends stand out clearly.

The first and most obvious is the long-term decline of the agricultural occupations from 9% of the economically active population in 1921 to 4% in 1961. This quite simply parallels the decline in employment in the agricultural sector. Second is the rise in the share of white-collar employment (s.e.g.s 1 to 6) from 23% in 1921 to 35% in 1961. The biggest contributor to this growth was socio-economic group six — junior non-manual occupations. The group is dominated by the clerical occupations with the next largest component being shop assistants and suchlike. S.e.g. 6 as a whole increase from 13% of the economically active population in 1921 to 20% in 1961. The next biggest contribution was from s.e.g. 5 — intermediate non-manual occupations which rose from 3% to 6% of the total. Again this group was dominated by two occupations — teachers and nurses. Both s.e.g.s 5 and 6 had a strong — and in the case of s.e.g. 6 increasingly — female component and it is probable that these groups accounted for most of the rise in total female employment before 1961. The rise in employment in the four "higher" non-manual groups — s.e.g.s 1 to 4, employers, managers and professionals — was rather more modest from 7% to 9% of the economically active population. As will be seen, patterns of change in white collar employment have been quite different since 1961.

The one strong trend among the manual group was the long-term decline in skilled manual workers — from 31.2% in 1921 to 26.3% in 1961. Half of this decline was concentrated into the decade 1921 to 1931, clearly reflecting the decline of Scotland's traditional heavy industries. The number in mining and quarrying occupations was down 18% to 124,000 and the number of metal workers down 23% to 189,000 — this being a count of those economically active rather than employed, the decline in the number of the latter being certainly more steep. Again industrial trends probably underlay the maintenance of skilled manual workers after 1931, especially from 1951 to 1961 when they remained relatively unchanged as a share of the e.a., this largely reflecting the maintenance especially of the engineering industry in these decades. In the forty years from 1921 to 1961 there was very little change in either semi-skilled occupations (14% in 1921 and 15% in 1961) or unskilled occupations (9% in both 1921 and 1961).

The story of occupational change in Scotland from 1961 to 1981 is told in Tables 5A to 5C. The shape of change in white-collar employment since 1961 is quite different from that in the previous period. The size of the junior non-manual group (s.e.g. 6) stayed remarkably constant from 1961 to 1981 in sharp contrast to its earlier expansion. We can surmise some kind of equilibrium resulting from the growth in the amount of information to be routinely handled and a reduction in the amount of labour required to handle each unit of information. The shift in the sex balance in this group continued apace however. In 1961, 60% of junior non-manual workers were women and in 1981, 74%.

Table 5.

MARRIED WOMEN, PER CENT ECONOMICALLY ACTIVE BY
AGE GROUP, SCOTLAND, 1921 TO 1981

Age group	1921	1931	1951	1961	1971	1981
16 to 19			27.3	34.9	40.6	45.0
20 to 24	7.4	11.4	24.9	32.2	41.7	54.1
25 to 29	4.8	7.8	17.8	22.5	31.9	46.5
30 to 34	4.3	6.9	15.4	22.4	37.7	49.0
35 to 44	4.7	6.5	16.7	27.8	52.0	63.9
45 to 54	5.1	6.0	14.0	27.0	54.5	65.8
55 to 59		5.3	8.5	18.6	42.2	50.5
60 to 64	4.4	4.2	4.0	8.7	22.7	22.2
65 to 69	3.1	2.7	2.1	3.4	8.7	6.2
70 plus	1.5	1.2	0.9	0.8	2.1	2.0
All aged 16 and over	4.8	6.4	14.2	22.8	40.2	48.5

The intermediate non-manual group (s.e.g. 5) grew by around 35% in each decade. In the 1960s, the major driving force behind this increase — especially for women — was the expansion of the health and education establishments, boosting in particular the numbers of teachers and nurses.

The "higher" non-manual groups (s.e.g.s 1 to 4) made a much greater contribution to the overall growth in non-manual employment than had been the case before 1961. All of this growth was of a "bureaucratic" nature in that the numbers both of self-employed professionals (s.e.g. 3) and employers and managers in small establishments (s.e.g. 2) fell between 1961 and 1981. In the 1960s, this was especially true of small employers, the number of whom declined by 26% between 1961 and 1971. Around three-quarters of the increase in the number of professional employees (s.e.g. 4) took place in the 1960s and they only grew by 15% after 1971. Conversely, the growth in the numbers of employers and managers in large establishments (s.e.g. 1) —

employers making up only a tiny proportion of this group — was fastest after 1971, when they increased by 72% compared with 33% in the previous decade. In general, this growth in the number of "higher" non-manual occupations was due to occupational change itself. The only exception was the contribution made by the expansion of the industrial order "professional and scientific services" to the growth in the numbers of professional employees in the 1960s.

Another occupational symptom of the shift to a "service economy" was the growth in, overwhelmingly female, employment in s.e.g. 7, personal service workers. The bulk of this group consists of occupations such as bar staff, canteen assistants and, most numerous, maids and related workers. So although the group cannot be unambiguously classified as manual, its growth is yet another aspect of the general expansion of low-paid work for women.

Turning to the truly manual occupations, by far the most significant shift is the loss of over 200,000 skilled manual jobs or over a third of the 1961 number. In 1981 they made up 19.2% of total employment compared with 27.6% in 1961. Although less significant numerically, the decline was sharpest for women skilled manual workers — almost half of these jobs disappearing. For both sexes the decline was evenly balanced between the two decades — a decline of around 18% per decade for men and 27% per decade for women.

From 1961 to 1971, the pattern of industrial change was more important than occupational decline within industries in producing the decline in male skilled manual jobs — the decline of the mining and shipbuilding industries making the main single contributions. Since 1971, however, it is almost certain that the fall in employment in the steel and engineering industries (with a continuing contribution from shipbuilding) took over as the main determinant of the loss of skilled manual jobs in Scotland (cf. Table 4).

Skilled manual women workers have historically been concentrated in the textile industry. In the 1960s, textiles accounted for half the loss of skilled manual jobs for women, both because of its general decline and because of deskilling within the industry. It is probable that the continued decline of this industry was the main factor again in the 1970s.

Patterns of change in semi- and unskilled manual employment are more difficult to summarise and, as always, different jobs are involved for men and women.

Only a relatively small proportion of men categorised as belonging to the semi-skilled manual group (s.e.g. 10) conform to the stereotype of a man standing at a production line — the largest occupational group being warehousemen and storemen although it should be noted that the number of machine tool operators doubled in the 1960s. The one point to be made is that all the decline in male semi-skilled manual workers took place in between 1961 and 1971, their numbers stabilising thereafter. In contrast, two-thirds of the rather steeper decline in women semi-skilled workers — who do consist largely of factory workers — took place after 1971 and by far the most likely candidates in accounting for this loss are the textile and clothing industries.

Finally we come to the unskilled manual group and the greatest contrast in trend between men and women — primarily because there is the greatest contrast in the nature of the jobs involved. As far as men are concerned, s.e.g. 11 is made up primarily of occupation codes 107 to 114 which designate labourers and unskilled workers not elsewhere specified and is concentrated in the manufacturing and construction sectors. Most women classified as unskilled manual workers are in the occupations of chars and office cleaners — mostly part time, see below — and about two-thirds of the group as a whole was employed in the service sector in 1971.

Male unskilled workers stayed steady as a share of total male employment from 1961 to 1971. Thereafter one only needs to recognise that the collapse in employment in manufacturing hit the unskilled the hardest to account for the 37% fall in their numbers from 1971 to 1981. All the expansion in female unskilled jobs, however, took place between 1961 and 1971 and their numbers actually fell between 1971 and 1981.

Obviously this has only been a very superficial survey of a complex set of trends and for the period since 1971 much more work is needed. The point which needs making in conclusion, however, is that dealing with intercensal periods can be misleading — they do not necessarily match the rhythms of industrial change. On the one hand, one major trend underlying many of these occupational shifts — the expansion of employment in the service sector — appeared to be grinding to a halt by the end of the 1970s. The other major trend behind much of the occupational change of the 1970s — the collapse in manufacturing employment — was still in full flood at the time of the 1981 census.

Women in employment
Only in the last couple of years has the growth in employment in the service sector come to an end (cf. Tables 1 and 4). The steady growth of the service sector as a proportion of total employment from 24% in 1951 to 43% in 1981 provided the underlying dynamic behind the greatest single change in employment patterns since the war — the massive entry of married women into paid employment.

Over the last one hundred and fifty years, the aggregate level of women's participation in the labour market has described a gentle U-curve. Both the decline in women's employment in the second half of the nineteenth century and the rise in the middle years of this century were associated with long-term patterns of industrial change. As we have seen, industrial change in Scotland from 1851 to 1911 took the form of a diversification away from a general specialisation in the textiles and clothing and footwear industries. Throughout Scotland's industrial experience these industries have been the principal manufacturing employers of female labour. In 1851 they accounted for 92% of female employment in manufacturing and almost half of total female employment. As the textile and clothing industries lost their dominant position to the "second wave" industries of coal, steel, ships and engineering which employed overwhelmingly male labour, women as a proportion of total employment fell from around 34% in 1851 to around 29% in 1911.

The other main category of female employment was domestic service which accounted for just under 30% of total female employment throughout the second half of the nineteenth century.

For much of the first half of the twentieth century, two counterposing tendencies worked to keep the proportion of vital employment which was female at around 30%. On the one hand there was a general tendency for the proportion of female employment within industries to increase but this was counteracted by the changes in the industrial mix and in particular by the relative contraction of the textile and clothing industries. By the time the number of women employed in domestic service began to contract rapidly in the 1930s this was balanced to some extent by the expansion of women's employment in other service sectors. This level of 30% of the workforce was, of course, exceeded in the two world wars and to a lesser extent in the depression when there was a tendency for the male-dominated occupations to be hit harder by unemployment.

It was only after 1951, however, that the sustained rise in the employment of women began to take off. According to the census, women made up 30.4% of total employment in 1951, 32.3% in 1961 and 39.3% in 1971. Switching to Department of Employment figures, relating solely to employees, the figure rose from 39% in 1971 to 42% in 1976 to 43% in 1981.

Looking at the process from another direction, the economic activity rate for women (i.e. the proportion of women in employment or classified as seeking employment) rose from 33.6% in 1951, to 35.9% in 1961, 42.4% in 1971 and to 46.6% in 1981.

There are three main points to be made about this increase in the employment of women in the post-war years.

The first is that it occurred entirely outside the manufacturing sector. The proportion of women in the manufacturing workforce has remained remarkably stable since the war at around 30%. As total employment in manufacturing has dwindled so has the employment of women in manufacturing dwindled. The increase in the employment of women can be entirely accounted for in terms of the expansion of the services sector. Both an increase in total employment in the service sector and an increase in the proportion of this employment which is female have contributed. In 1951, only slightly more women worked in the service sector (252,000) than in manufacturing (232,000). By 1976 there were almost three times as many women in services (475,000) as there were in manufacturing (189,000). This is the only reason we need to explain why the recent collapse in the level of employment has hit the number of male jobs much more drastically than the number of female.

The second point about the increase in women's employment since the war is that it has consisted entirely of increase in the number of married women going out to work. This has produced the major contrast between the post-war pattern of female employment and that of the century before the war. One important factor was the decline in the average age of marriage in the twenty-five years after World War II. In addition the last century has seen a dramatic decline in the number of women never marrying. If we add in the fact that the post-war years, in particular from the 'sixties onwards, saw an increase in the length of time women were staying on in full-time education, it becomes clear that the pool of single women available for full-time employment dwindled significantly after the war and that this in itself explains much of the change in employment patterns.

During the 1960s, when the overall rise in the number of married women working was at its steepest, it was concentrated in particular among women in the age groups immediately after the child-raising years. During the 1970s, the increase in economic activity among these age groups was matched by that among younger age groups (see Table 6).

The final point to be made with respect to the overall increase in female employment is that it can be accounted for entirely in terms of an increase in the number of part-time jobs. Using the standard definition of part-time employment as involving a working week of less than 30 hours, a very low proportion of women's jobs were part time in 1951. By 1961 the proportion was 17% and in 1971, 33% (census data). By 1981, according to Department of Employment figures, 41% of female employees worked part time. Between 1961 and 1971 in fact, while the total number of women in employment increased by 80,000, the number of women part-time workers went up by 145,000. (N.B. these figures include c.24,000 teachers, or 73% of all women teachers, who were classified as part time presumably because many school hours clock up to less than 30 hours). Apart from this anomaly with respect to teachers, part-time employment in 1971 was overwhelmingly concentrated into a few low-paid occupations. 41% (37,000) of shop assistants, 68% (29,000) of "maids and related workers" and 85% (43,000) of chars and office cleaners were part time. These three occupational categories alone accounted for half of all women part-time workers in 1971. There were around 35,000 clerical part-time jobs for women although the number of part-time factory production jobs is unlikely to have exceeded 20,000. 13,000 part-time nurses constituted the only category any distance up the occupational hierarchy, although this is hardly reflected in terms of pay.

We are fairly safe in saying, however, that the expansion of female employment in the last twenty years or so has consisted overwhelmingly of married women taking part-time jobs in the service sector, jobs which are even more firmly biased towards the bottom of the occupational hierarchy by whatever criterion you care to choose than are women's jobs as a whole.

Table 6.

PEOPLE OF PENSIONABLE AGE. BY AGE GROUP, MARITAL STATUS AND SEX, 1911 TO 1981. THOUSANDS.

MEN

	Aged 65 to 74		Aged 75-plus	
	S,W,D.	Married	S,W,D.	Married
1911	31	47	16	11
1931	43	71	22	16
1951	52	96	37	29
1961	42	101	38	33
1971	47	128	35	35
1981	49	140	38	46
Change 1951-81	-7%	+44%	+3%	+62%

WOMEN

	Aged 60 to 64		Aged 65 to 74		Aged 75-plus	
1911	36	33	72	34	40	6
1931	48	52	90	51	52	9
1951	62	64	121	73	81	16
1961	69	77	136	79	101	19
1971	68	92	155	97	126	22
1981	52	85	146	110	153	29
Change 1951-81	-16%	+32%	+20%	+51%	+89%	+83%

Trends in marriage and fertility

Quantitatively, the single most massive social change in Scotland, as in the rest of the industrialised world, in the last twenty years has been the fall in the birth rate — from a value of 20 births per 1,000 population in 1964 to a historic low of 12 per 1,000 in 1977.[7]

Reliable birth records based on registration go back to 1856. From then until the mid-1870s, the Scottish birth rate stayed fairly steady at around 35 births per 1,000 of the population. Then followed a long and steady decline over the next sixty years, interrupted only by fluctuations during and after World War I, to a level of 18 per 1,000 by the mid-1930s. This low level was maintained during World War II, in contrast to the marked drop in the birth rate during World War I, then followed the brief post-war baby boom of the late 1940s, taking the birth rate up briefly to the low twenties. By the early 1950s, the rate was back down to around 18 per 1,000. The subsequent and more celebrated baby boom of the late 1950s and early 1960s was quantitatively a matter of a mere two births per 1,000 population, taking the rate up to a peak of around 20 per 1,000 in the early 1960s, and was soon dwarfed by the massive decline in the birth rate which followed. The birth rate dropped below the previous lowest sustained level, that of the 1930s, by 1971, and continued to decline to a low point of 12 per 1,000 in 1977. Since then there has been a marginal and extremely tentative turnaround which levelled off at a rate of 13.4 births per 1,000 in 1981 and looks to have turned down again in 1982 (a birth rate of 12.8) and 1983.[8]

In broad terms, these post-World War II trends have been typical of much of Western Europe. If anything, Scotland's baby bulge of the early 1960s was somewhat more marked than was the norm for Western Europe as a whole and the subsequent decline was rather steeper. This can be seen in terms of Scotland's ranking with respect to the major Western European countries (i.e. excluding Luxembourg and anything smaller, and taking Northern Ireland, on the one hand, and England and Wales together, on the other, as separate units). At the height of the baby bulge in the early 1960s, Scotland's birth rate was exceeded only by those of Eire, Northern Ireland, Spain, Portugal and the Netherlands. By the time the birth rate touched bottom in 1977, Scotland had moved well into the bottom half of the ranking. The subsequent recovery took Scotland's birth rate by 1981 to a level which was exceeded only by those of France, Spain, Portugal and the two Irelands. So although Scotland belongs firmly within a middle band of West European nations, it could be said that its birth rate has fluctuated more than most within those bands.

Historically, the trend of Scotland's crude birth rate paralleled that for England and Wales for most of the second half of the nineteenth century, then diverged until it was 3 to 4 births per 1,000 above that of England and Wales in the 1940s since when there has been a gradual convergence so that by 1980, Scotland's birth rate was only 0.1 above that for England and Wales. The convergence has probably in part been a reflection of declining religious and social class fertility differences. The second half of the 1960s and the early 1970s saw a diminution of the Catholic fertility differential within Scotland (this can be seen in ecological terms in the convergence down towards the norm in the marital fertility rates of those areas of Scotland with the highest proportions of Catholics). In addition the social class fertility patterns showed a rapid convergence in the 1970s (see below). Thus the bias in Scotland towards higher fertility caused by its differential religious and social class make-up has probably been of decreasing significance in recent years.

Changes in the birth rate can be seen as determined by changes in the age structure of the female population and by changes in the fertility of women.

The latter in turn, either in general or for a specified age range, can be broken down into three components. The fertility rate of a specified group of women is composed by definition of:

1. the marital fertility rate multiplied by the proportion of women who are married; plus
2. the illegitimate fertility rate multiplied by the proportion of women who are unmarried.

This boils down to taking note of the movement of three components if one is interested in accounting for changes in total fertility:

(a) the proportion of women who are married;
(b) the marital fertility rate;
(c) the illegitimate fertility rate.

Marriage patterns
The one trend in marriage patterns which has overshadowed all others in Scotland as in much of the developed world over the last fifty years has been a marked increase in the proportion of the population of marriageable age who are married, this being particularly true of younger age groups. This has been due both to a lowering of the average age at first marriage and a decrease in the proportion of people never marrying. Only in the 1970s have there been signs of the trend coming to an end with a stabilisation of the average of first marriage and a decrease in the numbers of marriages and the proportion married in the younger age groups (Table 7).

The mean age of first marriage for women in Scotland hovered around the 25 years old mark throughout the second half of the nineteenth century. By the second decade of the twentieth century it had risen to around 26 years old where it remained until the 1930s. Then followed the long decline to a level of 22.4 years old in 1971 since when it has varied only marginally (22.5 in 1977, 22.6 in 1978). The age of first marriage for men has moved fairly closely in parallel, the smallest gap being in the 1870s when men were on average 1.8 years older than women at first marriage and the largest in the 1940s and '50s when men were on average 2.4 years older.

It is likely that the main factors underlying the fall in the average age of marriage after the Second World War were economic. First, rising living standards and full employment made it feasible to set up a household at a younger age and, second, the supply of houses in which to set up these households was greatly improved in the post-war years. Likewise, the decline in marriage rates since the early 1970s is likely to have a good deal to do with tightened economic circumstances, especially for younger age groups, since then.

Table 7.

MARRIED WOMEN PER 1,000 WOMEN

Year	All Ages	16-19	20-24	25-29	30-34	35-39	40-44	45-49
1851	279	21	247	512	634	673	650	624
1901	300	21	234	515	657	695	696	671
1931	353	28	228	498	657	697	699	683
1951	427	44	396	698	784	793	765	720
1961	677	73	516	803	842	835	820	783
1966	684	93	574	820	849	842	825	796
1971	703	100	575	837	882	880	852	813
1976	685	93	524	796	875	879	867	829
1978	669	80	495	765	858	875	866	833
1980	650	70	465	732	834	868	861	837
1981	594	62	461	769	853	863	858	835

(Source: Table Q1.4 R.G.A.R. 1981)

The proportion of women in the 40 to 44 age group who have ever been married gets fairly close to being equivalent to the proportion who ever marry. In Scotland, the proportion of women aged 40 to 44 who had ever been married rose from 779 per 1,000 in 1861 to 794 per 1,000 in 1881 and then declined gradually to 769 in 1931 before shooting up to 898 in 1971. This proportion will have continued to rise in the 'seventies as the effect of the marriage boom of the 'fifties and 'sixties continues to work through. The rise in the proportion ever married was somewhat faster in Scotland than in England and Wales as Scotland has caught up from the position in 1861 when the Scottish proportion ever married at age 40 to 44 was 10% below that in England and Wales. Some of this difference, but not all, was due to the extremely high numbers of unmarried women in the peripheral regions of Scotland — the Highlands, the Far North and the Borders.

Although all of the Registrar General's Social Classes[9] have experienced the decline in the average age of marriage, this average is much lower for the manual groups and in particular the unskilled manual group. Table 8 gives an idea of the quite remarkable class variation involved.

It seems likely that up until 1971 at least, the average age of marriage had moved down very much in parallel for the social classes. Although very little work has been done on these differentials, the main factors involved are fairly obvious. Probably most important is the fact that for those moving on to non-manual jobs, the educational process is relatively prolonged compared with those moving into manual, and particularly unskilled manual jobs. Also important, particularly in Scotland, will be the different housing patterns of the different social classes, with middle-class groups much more committed to home-ownership as a corollary of marriage.

Table 8.

CURRENTLY MARRIED WOMEN UNDER 45 WHO HAD MARRIED IN
THE TWO YEARS BEFORE (1971) CENSUS

	Per cent who had married at age of			
Social Class	Under 20	20-24	25 or over	N
I	6.9%	70.0%	22.1%	407
II	14.4%	62.9%	22.7%	749
III Non-manual	20.2%	64.5%	15.3%	678
III Manual	32.9%	54.4%	12.7%	2,371
IV	38.9%	47.5%	13.6%	887
V	44.2%	43.0%	12.8%	486
All	28.9%	56.1%	15.0%	5,966

(Source: 1971 Census of Scotland Fertility Tables, Pt. II, Table 1.)

Marital fertility

Details of age specific marital fertility rates have been published by the
Registrar General for Scotland from mid-1938 with 1939 being the first full
year. Comparison of the 1939 figures with whose for 1931 presented in
Scottish Population History[10] shows that there had been a moderate decline in
the marital fertility rate for all ages during the 1930s, e.g. from 588 births per
1,000 married women to 526 for the 15 to 19 year old age group and from 257
to 220 for 25 to 29 year olds. The only earlier figures available are for 1855.
The largest proportional declines between 1855 and 1931 were experienced by
the older age groups, e.g. the marital fertility rate for women aged 40 to 45 in
1855 was 113 births per 1,000 women, compared with 36 per 1,000 in 1931 and
26 in 1939. This decline in the fertility of older age groups of women has thus
been in progress at least from the beginning of registration right up to the
present day.

Only the two youngest age groups, particularly the 16 to 19 year olds,
suffered a marked dip in marital fertility during the Second World War. The
immediate post-war peak in fertility did little more than restore pre-war levels
of marital fertility for these 16 to 24 year olds whereas for the older age groups,
it was more of a genuine peak.

As we have seen, the second post-war baby boom lasted from the mid-1950s
to the early 1960s. The total and marital fertility rates for women aged 15 (16)
to 44 bottomed in 1952 and peaked in 1962. In this period the total fertility rate
rose by 24% from 80 to 99 while the marital fertility rate rose from 131.3 to
148.8 or around 11%. On the basis of these figures and allowing for some
contribution from the rise in the illegitimate fertility rate over the same period,
the increase in the proportion of women who were married appears to have
accounted for around half of the rise in the total fertility rate, the increase in
fertility within marriage for much of the rest.

In general, the effect on the total fertility rate of the fall in the marital fertility rate after the mid-1960s was somewhat mitigated until the early 1970s by the continued increase in the proportion of women who were married. Since then, the moderate decline in the proportion married compounded the decrease in marital fertility until 1977 and has offset the increase since then.

In parallel with the birth rate, the marital fertility rate touched its historic low point in 1977 but its subsequent rise was even more short-lived than that of the birth rate — the latter being marginally prolonged by the increase in the number of potential mothers due to the high birth rates of the late 1950s and early 1960s.

Perhaps the most puzzling feature of the dip in the marital fertility rate at the beginning of the 1980s was that it was primarily a matter of a fall in the marital fertility rate of women aged 25 to 29; the fertility of younger women continuing to increase.

It seems likely that the most important single factor behind the fall in marital fertility since the early 1960s was the increase in employment opportunities for married women. This makes sense, however, only in the context that the couples who were having smaller families in the late 1960s and 1970s had developed their definitions of a satisfactory standard of life for themselves and, most important, for their children, on the basis of having grown up in a period of rising living standards. These relatively high consumption motivations created the motivation both for restricting the number of children and in part, and in cases where it wasn't more a matter of necessity, for married women going out to work. It would be wrong to pin the fall in the birth rate entirely on such economic factors however. Both the well-documented fall in social class fertility differentials and the rather more tentatively identified fall in the Catholic fertility differential suggest that other factors, and in particular an increase in the effectiveness and availability of contraception as well as changes in attitudes towards contraception, played a part.

Illegitimate fertility

After a peak of 12.3 births per 1,000 married women in 1945, the illegitimate fertility rate declined to a low of 8.2 per 1,000 in the early 1950s. Then followed a steady climb to a new post-war peak of 18.5 births per 1,000 unmarried women in 1971. After a decline to a trough of 14.2 in 1977 the rate climbed to a new high of 18.6 in 1981. 1981 also represented a peak in the proportion of all births which were illegitimate at 14%.

Taking the three main contributing age groups — 15 to 19; 20 to 24 and 25 to 29 — the increase from 1977 to 1981 was fastest among the older age groups. Among 25 to 29 year olds the illegitimate fertility rate climbed from 23.6 to 37.6; among 20 to 24 year olds from 21.8 to 29.2 and among 15 to 19 year olds from 10.9 to 12.7, so that by 1981 teenage mothers accounted for a smaller proportion of illegitimate births than at any time since the late 1960s — although the numbers involved were at an all-time high. The forces underlying these trends are probably even more complex than those underlying trends in marital fertility. However, the simple fact that both illegitimate and marital fertility rates for all three age groups between 15 and 30 touched bottom in the same year — 1977 — suggests that at least some common factors are involved — and of course, as cohabitation becomes more common an increasing proportion of illegitimate births will consist of children born to stable relationships only legally separated from marriage.

Class differentials in fertility

The most detailed information on social class differentials in fertility has been contained in the census fertility tables. Table 9 is a very brutal boiling down of the information in the Social Class fertility table of 1971.

Table 9.

MEAN FAMILY SIZE BY DURATION OF MARRIAGE & SOCIAL CLASS 1971

Year	Length of marriage	All	I	II	IIINM	IIIMan	IV	V
All		2.18	1.82	2.01	1.81	2.22	2.33	2.68
1966-71	0- 4 yrs	0.80	0.65	0.70	0.64	0.84	0.90	1.06
1961-66	5- 9 yrs	1.98	1.89	1.87	1.76	1.99	2.03	2.41
1956-61	10-14 yrs	2.47	2.29	2.25	2.17	2.55	2.49	2.97
1951-56	15-19 yrs	2.61	2.33	2.37	2.21	2.66	2.70	3.19
1946-51	20-24 yrs	2.53	2.32	2.23	2.11	2.61	2.60	3.04
1941-46	25-29 yrs	2.52	2.19	2.21	2.15	2.54	2.67	3.07
1936-41	30-34 yrs	2.57	2.15	2.24	2.20	2.56	2.76	3.00

(Source: as Table 8.)

The impression given by Table 9 and one which is confirmed by more detailed analysis (e.g. breaking down by age at marriage) is that fertility differentials between the Social Classes changed very little in the period from World War I to the early 1960s.

The period of the falling birth rate from 1964 onwards was also a period of convergence in fertility patterns between the Social Classes, a convergence which does not appear to have been affected by the recent tentative upturn in the birth rate.

Convergence can be seen most clearly in terms of the parameter which has historically displayed the greatest Social Class differential, the existence of very large families. In terms of the Registrar General's data the trend away from large families can best be seen in terms of trends in the proportion of births in the Class which are of parity five or greater. In the early 1960s, fifth and further births accounted for between 18 and 20% of births to Social Class V mothers, 13-14% in Social Class IV, 10% in SC III, 7-8% in SC II and finally 3-4% of all births to Social Class I mothers. These proportions all dropped rapidly in subsequent years as the birth rate in general fell. By the years 1979 to 1981, the proportion of births to mothers in Social Class V which were of parity five or greater had fallen to below 5%. For social classes III and IV the figure was down to below 3% and for social classes I and II to below 2%. In other words, there would seem to remain only relatively small differences in mean family size across the social classes and this is a historically unprecedented situation.

In terms of the parity distribution of births, the small upturn in the birth rate since 1977 has consisted almost entirely of an increase in the proportion of births which are third births — from between 13 and 14% of all births in 1977 to between 15 and 17% in 1981, a rise which has been shared by all the social classes. Apart from this very recent and tentative increase in third children, however, what the longer term trends unequivocally show is a sustained move shared by all the social classes — but most dramatic in the case of Social Class V because it had the furthest to go — towards the two-child family.

Differences in family formation patterns between the social classes then are no longer primarily a matter of the number of children. Impressive differences do remain, however, in the ages of mothers across the classes. This is, of course, largely a reflection of continuing differences in age of marriage across the classes. We can follow trends in the age distribution of mothers by the same means as we followed trends in the parity distribution of births.

The figure which shows the overall trends most clearly is the proportion of legitimate *first* births to mothers in each class where the mother is aged under twenty. In 1955, 15% of legitimate first births in Social Class V were to mothers aged under twenty. In the same year the proportion fell off towards Social Class I: 14% in SC IV; 10% in SC III; 3% in SC II and 2% in SC I. The proportion moved up steadily throughout the 1960s for all classes, particularly the manual groups and most dramatically for Social Class V. In the years 1975 to 1977, when paradoxically enough the birth rate as a whole was approaching its all-time low, 45% of first-time married mothers in Social Class V were under twenty. In complete contrast the proportion had only moved slowly up to a peak of 6 to 7% around 1970 for Social Classes I and II. Since the mid-1970s, the proportion of first births to mothers under twenty has moved down again for all classes — again most sharply for Social Class V. In 1980 the figure for Social Class V was 40% and in 1981 36%.

Most of these trends in the ages of first-time mothers were paralleled in terms of trends in the ages of all mothers. For example, in the mid-1970s, 23% of *all* births to Social Class V mothers were to mothers aged under twenty, and this proportion too began to fall off rapidly as we entered the 1980s.

At the other end of the age and class spectrum, the most dramatic recent development has been an increase in the proportion of births to mothers aged 30 or more in social classes I and II. After a long decline, this proportion reached a low of 30% in 1975, since when it moved up to a level of 40% in 1981.

This brief discussion has only touched upon the complexities evident in trends in the parity distributions and age of mother distributions of births across the social classes. Demographers have only recently begun to come to terms with the mechanisms underlying the general fall in the birth rate over the last twenty years. The mechanisms underlying differential fertility trends across the social classes are even less well understood.

At the risk of over-simplification it could be said that we are now at a position in which there are no longer any great differences between social groups in their degree of access to and use of efficient contraceptive methods. Decision-making about the conscious control over having children — family-planning in short — has spread to all social groups. In this situation, the changes in economic environment which determine the immediate costs and benefits of having children will have a relatively rapid impact on fertility. We can see the recent downturn in fertility as a reflection of the impact of the current recession. Fertility differentials between social classes then become less a result of differences in the ability or motivation to plan families but rather a result of differences in the kinds of economic factors which impinge on the family-planning decisions of the different social groups. In such a situation, fertility levels become almost impossible to predict and highly contingent on economic trends.

Conclusion

There is very little, if any, exaggeration involved in saying that in each of the four areas of social change we have been looking at — industrial structure, occupational structure, women's employment patterns and demography — the last twenty years have seen aggregate changes unprecedented in a similar time span in Scotland's historical experience.

In terms of industrial structure, a third of all manufacturing jobs lost since 1974. In occupational terms, a third of all skilled manual jobs lost since 1961. In terms of women working an increase from 23% to 49% in the proportion of women in work or actively seeking work. Finally, from 1964 to 1977, the most rapid and sustained fall in the birth rate ever. As we have seen these processes have been tightly bound together. To caricature (somewhat), industrial change was one of the main driving forces behind occupational change, the nature of these industrial and occupational changes provided a need for increased employment of married women and this increase in employment opportunities for married women was probably a major factor behind the fall in the birth rate.

Moving along this "causal chain", there is a change in the kind of social mechanisms which are involved. Changes in industrial and occupational structure are primarily the expression of structural, market forces over which individuals have very little control but which serve to define the structures of opportunity or non-opportunity with which individuals are faced. Trends in marriage and fertility reflect the responses of individuals, or more precisely couples, to changes in these opportunity structures. Quite naturally, people struggle to control their own lives in the only sphere in which they have at least some chance of shaping their own destinies — the family — in the form of decisions about marriage and having children. Demographic trends in Britain are more and more an aggregate reflection of such struggles for control in family circumstances which provide an increasingly fragile haven from the macro-economic forces which are battering at their defences.

This should remind us that although the changes which have been documented, especially if we include the rise in the number of old people living alone, amount to a massive and unprecedented shift in the shape of Scotland's social structure, in an even more important sense, nothing has changed. Whether we look at inequalities in wealth and income, in educational attainment or in relative chances of achieving high status jobs, the extent of class inequality and the mechanisms underlying this inequality have remained relatively untouched.

For twenty-five to thirty years after the war, this fact was camouflaged by generally rising living standards and such factors as a high level of upward social mobility. Poverty never went away of course but it had to be "rediscovered" in the 1960s so powerful had been the effect of the rhetoric of reform and egalitarianism. Now that the good times are over, this veil created by relative prosperity has been stripped away and the mechanisms of class oppression are being revealed with Victorian savagery.

It must be remembered that when we speak of the old, of single-parent families and of the unemployed as the groups most vulnerable to poverty in our society, it is not a random selection from these groups which defines those who are hardest hit but those among them who have been unable to build up resources and are entirely dependent on State benefits. The primary determinant of this lack of resources — and of unemployment itself — is still social class, with manual workers in general more vulnerable and those directly or indirectly dependent on unskilled manual employment being especially likely to be the victims of poverty at every stage in their life from childhood to old age.

References

1   Much of the empirical analysis in this chapter was carried out as part of the project "A Socio-graphic account of the modern Scottish social structure", financed by the Social Science Research Council at the Department of Sociology, University of Edinburgh, under the direction of Frank Bechhofer and David McCrone. Fuller, but now two years out of date, accounts of many of the long-term processes discussed are contained in the project working paper on "Population" and "Industrial and Occupational Structure". The same team are currently engaged in analysing patterns of social change in Scotland since 1971 under a grant from the Nuffield Foundation and highly preliminary results of this analysis also appear in the chapter.

2   The fullest statement of this case in a British context is made by John Ermisch. See especially, John Ermisch, "Investigations into the causes of post-war fertility swings" in D. Eversley and W. Kollmann (eds.), *Population Change and Social Planning*, 1982, Edward Arnold.

3   All the industrial and sectoral distributions from 1851 to 1971 in this chapter are derived from Clive Lee's reclassification of census occupational and industrial tables to conform as closely as possible to the 1968 Standard Industrial Classification. The data are published in C. H. Lees, *British Regional Employment Statistics, 1841-1971*, 1979, Cambridge University Press, and we are grateful to him for supplying unpublished Scottish county data.

4   The sectors used throughout and their composition in terms of Industrial Orders are as follows:
Agriculture, forestry and fisheries, I.O. 1. Same name.
Mining and quarrying, I.O. 2. Same name.
Manufacturing, I.O. 3 — Food, drink and tobacco; 4 and 5 — coal and petroleum products and chemicals and allied industries; 6 — metal manufacture; 7, 8 and 9 — mechanical, instrument and electrical engineering; 10 — shipbuilding and marine engineering; 11—vehicles; 12—metal goods n.e.s.; 13—textiles; 14—leather etc.; 15—clothing and footwear; 16 — bricks, pottery and glass; 17 — timber, furniture etc.; 18 — paper, printing and publishing; 19 — other manufacturing industries.
Industrial employment refers to manufacturing plus mining and quarrying.
Construction, I.O. 20. Same name.
Intermediate, I.O.s 21 — Gas, electricity and water; 22 — transport and communication; 23 — distribution.
Services, I.O.s 24 — Insurance, banking, finance and business services; 25 — professional and scientific services; 26 — miscellaneous services; 27 — public administration and defence.

5   G. Payne, "Occupational Transition in Advanced Industrial Societies", *Sociological Review*, Vol. 25, No. 1, 1977.

6   Brief definitions of the socio-economic groups:
1 and 2. Employers and managers in central and local government, industry, commerce etc. in non-agricultural enterprises employing 25 or more (s.e.g. 1) or fewer than 25 (s.e.g. 2) persons.
3 and 4. Professional workers. Self-employed (3) and employees (4).
5. Intermediate non-manual workers.
6. Junior non-manual workers. Employees, not exercising planning or supervisory powers.
7. Personal service workers. Engaged in service occupations caring for food, drink, clothing and other personal needs.
8. Foremen and supervisors—manual.
9, 10, 11. Skilled, semi-skilled and unskilled manual workers.
12. Own account workers (other than professional)—no employees other than family.
13 and 14. Farmers—employers and managers (13)/or own account (14).
15. Agricultural workers.

16. Armed forces.
17. Inadequately described.
6   Sources of Tables 5A to 5C.
    1961: Census of Scotland, 1961, Vol. 6, Occupation, Industry and Workplace, Table V,
    Industry by Socio-economic group.
    1971: Unpublished version for Scotland of Great Britain, Economic Activity Tables,
    Table No. 33, Industry by social class, socio-economic class and sex.
    1981: Small Area Statistics for Scotland, Regional Summaries, Table 50.
7   Most of the demographic data in this section is drawn from the Annual Reports of the
    Registrar General for Scotland. When no specific reference is given this source can be
    assumed.
8   Registrar General for Scotland, Weekly Return, March 12, 1983.
9   Registrar General's Social Classes:
    I.   Professional Occupations.
    II.   Intermediate Occupations.
    III. Skilled Occupations. (Primarily consists of skilled manual but also includes rough
          equivalent to "junior non-manual".)
    IV.   Semi-skilled Occupations.
    V.   Unskilled Occupations.
    N.B. All data refers to Social Class of husband.
10 The incomparable source for the demography of Scotland prior to 1939 is *Scottish
    Population History*, M. W. Flinn (ed.), 1977, Cambridge University Press.

Ian Levitt

SCOTTISH POVERTY:
THE HISTORICAL BACKGROUND

THE words "deprivation", "poverty" and "social inequality" have, over the last fifty years, come into such common usage that it is hard to imagine a time when there was a totally different conception of poverty and the poor.[1] Eighty to a hundred years ago the fact that many Scots were poor would have been regarded as inevitable and even acceptable. Unequal distribution of income, wealth, status and power was justified by the principles of liberal-capitalist advancement: without inequality there could be no incentive to work and no social progress.

Apart from the Highland fringe, Scotland had prospered with the development of capitalism. Her population had doubled in the last fifty years of the nineteenth century, cities had mushroomed and many new towns, like Motherwell and Clydebank, had grown out of small villages. Scottish entrepreneurs moved rapidly to use the indigenous resources of coal, iron and water to create an industrial structure dominated by West Central Scotland and based on coal-mining, iron and steel smelting, shipbuilding and engineering. All the evidence suggests that Scottish wage levels rose sharply during that period and that Scottish workers' wages were roughly comparable to those earned across the border.

General economic progress has ensured that the Scots of the 1980s are better housed, fed, paid and are healthier than the Scots of the 1870s. But over the last hundred years Scotland, despite being one of the first industrialised countries, has lost its relatively advantageous position in the league table of economic progress. This decline can be related to three factors: speed of industrialisation which led to over-dependence on the traditional industries and caused the rapid building of slum working-class housing; the general economic malaise of the inter-war period; and the failure to push through radical social and economic changes in the decades after 1945.

The aim of this chapter is to indicate the effect this decline had on poverty and inequality. The absence of a fast-growing economy blunted arguments that the economic and social distribution of goods, services and benefits need not be a major concern of the government, and made irrelevant the belief that economic growth would raise the general standard of living enough to quell social discontent. Mass unemployment compounded social problems and created a crisis of expectations and a renewed interest in the distributional aspects of the social and economic system. The fear of a "two nation Scotland" — a Scotland split between rich and poor — that so worried Conservative politicians, like Noel Skelton, in the 1920s, might become a reality. The social and economic system therefore came under review at the turn of the century, and this concern gathered pace in the inter-war period. Scotland moved from a highly aggressive form of liberal-capitalism to flirtation with corporate social planning.

The fundamental question, once this concept became accepted, was its extent and its effect on changing the distributional aspects of the system. We suggest that intervention served not to reduce inequalities to any great extent, but rather prevented any further deterioration in the relative minimum living standards of the poor. In the nineteenth century poverty was accepted as unalterable: to judge from the present system of social and economic rewards, one might conclude that the perspective was an honest one.

The inter-war depression began when the factory gates started to close in the last weeks of 1920, but the clouds had been gathering for the preceding three decades. That period had seen a steady increase in the number of unskilled and relatively unhealthy men unable to find anything but the most irregular of jobs; the failure of the market to provide improved working-class housing; and the slowing down of improvement in the infant mortality rate.[2] The confidence of the Scottish welfare authorities was so badly shaken that by 1914 a number of commissions had been set up to report on related topics such as housing, the poor law, local welfare services and hospitals.

Table 1.

THE INFANT MORTALITY RATE
(Number of deaths under 1 year of age per ,000 live births)

1891/5	126
1911/5	113
1931/5	81
1951	37
1961	26

Source: Annual Reports, Department of Health.

If Scotland's economy had been based upon different industries the calamities of the years after 1918 might not have occurred. With a confident, growing economy and a spirit of innovation, funds, both taxable and charitable, might have been there to counteract the morass of social problems looming on the horizon. This, though, is historical speculation. Throughout the 1920s emigration and low wages were seen as the only basis for a return to economic sanity. Without burdensome social costs, capitalists could seize the advantages of a low-wage economy to amass profits and hence stimulate a general recovery. This belief stood in contra-distinction to the results of a number of official and unofficial surveys showing that the industrial decline entailed some deep-rooted structural changes in the Scottish economy and its social environment.

One such report, made in secret by the Scottish Office in August 1921, reported a picture of "unrelieved blackness". It remarked:

> The main belt of severe unemployment and accompanying distress runs through the mining, steel and shipbuilding areas of Fife, Edinburgh, Stirling, Linlithgow, Lanark, Dumbarton, Renfrew, and Ayr . . . it is difficult to pick out any industrial occupation as being principally affected by unemployment: almost all are in bad condition . . . those engaged in export trade and the means of export are worse than those engaged in home trade . . . certain luxury services, such as sweet manufacture, pastry-baking, and amusement catering, are remarkably vigorous . . . it is estimated that round about 25,000 men employed recently in coal-mining are in excess of capacity of the mines to absorb them for years to come.[3]

The officials did not recommend that Scotland should become a nation of sweet manufacturers, but they gloomily recognised that the Scottish economy was based on a narrow range of industries. They warned their political masters that the diminished level of local and personal resources demanded national policy of, if nothing else, subsistence doles, because

> . . . there are very inflammable elements which, while subjected during ordinary times to damping down by the saner and much larger section of the community, will not improbably be fanned into activity as the endurance of that more sober section is broken by the continued tightening of waistbelts around empty bellies.

Any plans to leave the plight of the unemployed to the vagaries of charitable effort were quickly abandoned and legislation was passed to allow the Poor Law to assist the unemployed, whose needs were not covered by the insurance schemes. Riots in Dundee, Port Glasgow, Greenock, the Vale of Leven and Motherwell merely emphasised the necessity of providing some statutory minimum dole.

It was another ten years before a statutory minimum dole, the Public Assistance means test, was introduced, but it is possible to compare the benefit rates that were officially advised (and hence an unofficial minimum) by the Scottish Office from 1921, with those that operated in later years. Table 2 shows clearly that once the maximum percentage of the 1920s became the minimum of the 1930s, very little relative improvement occurred in the position of those on welfare benefits for the next thirty years. Only if the family means test was operated (and it seems that less than 40% of recipients had anything deducted) would the post-1940 relative levels be said to be superior. Of course the real level of benefits did increase, in fact they more than doubled, but so too did wages.

Table 2.

BENEFIT RATES AND AVERAGE WAGES 1923-63

1923	37-50%
1933	50-60%
1963	55-65%

assumes man, wife and three children on Poor Law relief 1923 and 1933, and National Assistance 1963. Benefits as average of male manual earnings. For UK comparisons see G. Feigehen (et al), *Poverty and Progress in Britain* (1977).

Source: Annual Reports, Department of Health.

It would be misleading to discuss the real and relative changes in benefit levels within this period without considering the numbers who actually received them. The remarkable feature of the inter-war period is the emergence of a profile of recipients similar to the 1980s. A typical Poor Law recipient, pre-1914, was a woman, widowed or otherwise single, and sick and disabled. By 1938 about half those on the Poor Law who were not unemployed were men. The immediate post-1945 boom certainly reduced these numbers, but with each successive slump in the 1950s and 1960s this profile re-emerged. Other groups which increased their reliance on means-tested benefits included the elderly, seeking to supplement their pension, and divorced or otherwise separated women. Once the long-term unemployed are included in the comparison, the profile of the 1960s onwards begins to resemble that of the pre-1939 period, with means-tested rolls consisting of the long-term unemployed, the sick and disabled, the pensioner and those from broken homes.

There is, however, another dimension to the changes in the composition of welfare rolls. Before 1914, many areas and districts could be designated poor and poverty-stricken, but few had more than 5% of their population on Poor Relief. Some of the highest percentages could be found in rural areas, particularly the Highlands. But after 1920, with whole streets, villages and even districts out of work in the industrial areas, welfare rolls began to bulge. In Glasgow the Poor Law disabled roll alone accounted for around 40% of the population in areas such as Bridgeton, the Gorbals and Cowcaddens. This area-based pattern of welfare rolls remains an important aspect of social "deprivation" today.

These structural changes in the profile of welfare rolls did not go without contemporary comment, especially in the survey work that was increasingly undertaken. Despite a general improvement in social well-being — real wages for the employed did after all rise — never had so much consideration been given to the relative changes in the material position of the poor.

Early survey work in the 1920s revealed that although the skilled manual worker's family position continued to improve, the families of the unskilled were increasingly at risk in contracting disease, debt and poverty. During this period Jimmy Maxton made his notorious House of Commons speech calling the government and its supporters "murderers". In response the government became much more sensitive to criticism and when, in 1923, the West Highland crops failed, it moved quickly to avoid any starvation. But this represented the outer limit of public welfare policy — the prevention of mass physical deterioration. Holding this limit certainly seems to have worked, because Scottish Office officials reported to Labour's Secretary of State in 1930 that although young children were the most vulnerable group to suffer from lack of family income, the welfare services were coping within reasonable bounds.

The policy of limited intervention was soon shattered with the advent of mass unemployment in the 1930s. Further surveys revealed how deep a scar the depression had left on many working-class households. Although the skilled worker had a spirit and willingness to see the depression through to the better times ahead, the same was not true of the groups below the skilled. Years of squalor and intermittent employment had sapped their ability to face life on the dole and on low wages. A Scottish Office official felt so strongly about these conditions that he thought they might "be a prelude to a more serious organic breakdown if the conditions prevail over a long period".[4]

Surveys reinforced growing pressure from political and administrative sources for more statutory assistance for welfare recipients, better health services and some degree of economic reconstruction without emigration. Indeed a 1934 Court of Inquiry into alleged excessive welfare benefits by the new Labour administration at Greenock was easily turned into a propaganda exercise. The Scottish Secretary of State, Sir Godfrey Collins (Nat. Lib.), subsequently approved of the increased benefits. He believed that the Scottish population with its high proportion of long-term unemployed had fewer resources to withstand further privation.

The economic conditions had obvious consequences for the population's eating habits. Pre-1914 surveys revealed that the poor were likely to be susbsisting on a few staple items like potatoes, bread, oatmeal, cheap cuts of meat, and tea. Even if they had enough to eat, it was unlikely that they had a balanced diet.

Post-war surveys showed a steady improvement in general dietary intake of all groups as real wages and benefits rose. But there still remained a remarkable differential in eating habits, with the poor continuing to rely on carbohydrates and other "stodgy" foods to overcome their insufficiencies.

In the inter-war period Scotland had twice the proportion of its population in poverty as England. Because of Scotland's historically high birth-rate there were more mouths to feed on less income. This was not just confined to the urban industrial areas, because the farm labourers in the north-east were equally poor.

With greater poverty amongst its population, it is hardly surprising that Scotland's health "indicators" lagged behind England's. The infant and overall mortality rates were considerably higher. The incidence of TB was higher. When these figures were broken down into class and housing areas they showed how far the poor were behind everyone else. Their health "indicators" remained consistently similar to those of the middle class some twenty to thirty years previously.

Table 3.

NUMBER OF HOSPITAL IN-PATIENTS PER ANNUM 1890-1960

1890	75,000
1913	162,000
1936	306,000
1960	571,000

Source: I. Levitt, "Inter-War Scottish Medical Policy" (1977); unpublished paper.

In a society which prided itself on its medical schools and fine voluntary hospitals, this proved very difficult to rationalise. Table 3 shows a steady increase in the use of hospital services after 1913, so it could not be said that the existing services were not being utilised. But what could be and was increasingly said was that far more resources needed to be provided to counteract the lack of improvement of the general level of Scottish health compared with other countries.

In the 1920s it was obvious that demand had outstripped the capacity of the existing system to supply the necessary medical facilities. With the advent of the 1929 Local Government Act which allowed local authorities to build and maintain general hospitals it was felt that these shortages would be overcome. This was not to be. On the one hand the existing charitable institutions, like Greenock Royal Infirmary, objected to their traditional territory being encroached upon and, on the other, it proved very difficult to get the many small local authorities, like those in Lanarkshire, to agree to co-operate on a single viable project.

It was with these considerations in mind that Walter Elliot, the Scottish Secretary, sent a memorandum to the Cabinet in 1937 pleading for more resources to mitigate poverty in Scotland. He stated that:

> . . . The social condition of Scotland is indicated by the fact that 23% of its population live in conditions of gross overcrowding compared with 4% in

England . . . as evidence of the extent of the problem it may be estimated that about one-third of the families in Scotland live in houses without separate water-closet accommodation. The results of these conditions are evident in the vital statistics. Until 25 years ago the infant mortality rate in Scotland was lower than in England, but since then the Scottish rate has fallen more slowly than in England which it now exceeds by 35%. Maternal mortality is half as high again as in England. In proportion to the population twice as many cases of pneumonia and of scarlet fever were notified . . . while the diphtheria figure was higher by a third; and in each case the disparity had worsened as compared with ten years earlier. . . . It is the consciousness (of the problem's) existence which is reflected, not in the small and unimportant Nationalist Party, but in the dissatisfaction and uneasiness amongst moderate and reasonable people of every view and rank. . . . This uneasiness is reflected, for instance, in the reluctance of private enterprise to embark on new development in Scotland, a reluctance which is very clearly seen in the field of housing. Whereas in England private enterprise has built 2,500,000 houses as against 1,000,000 by local authorities, private enterprise in Scotland has built 90,000 against 180,000 by local authorities. If the trend continues the local authorities will eventually have as its tenants a third of the population of Scotland, which will produce repercussions which have certainly never been deliberately sought.[5]

This memorandum, the culmination of five to ten years' radical rethinking of Scotland's position relative to its economic decline, marks the decisive turning point in measures designed to alleviate poverty. It was now acknowledged that Scotland suffered from lack of employment opportunities, from poor housing and diet, ill-health, a fragmented social security system and a lack of central and local government control. Moreover, all of these factors interacted to multiply the problems. The fear of a "two nation" Scotland was a reality. If capitalist enterprise could not provide an answer by itself, there remained only the State. The initiative in pursuing social and economic development had now passed to central government, and between 1937 and 1948 it slowly asserted the right to determine to others what kind of ameliorative measures were necessary.

The new Welfare State finally wrested the social security system from the local authorities. Hospitals and medical care were almost completely nationalised. New Towns were created which enabled an executive rather than local democratic action to attract employment and build houses. Only social work services, still in their infancy,were left with the local authority. The question after 1948 was how far the new measures actually reduced the existing spectrum of inequalities. The answer was soon apparent, but, in an age of increasing affluence for the average Scot, it became obscured behind the slogans of the "never had it so good" era.

The position of those on means-tested welfare benefits has already been examined, showing not only that the gap between wages and benefits had hardly narrowed, but that the pre-war profile of recipients had re-emerged.

What of medical services and Bevan's dream of an improvement in everyone's health? As before, the poor barely kept pace with everyone else in the race for a fit nation. As Table 3 indicates there was no abatement in the use of hospital facilities. But what struck Health Service administrators most in the years following 1948 was that there was a subtle shift in the class composition of patients. The majority of pre-war patients had come from the working classes, but now more and more middle-class patients sought admission. On the one hand it certainly made it a truly "national" service, but on the other the newer patients began to demand a different form of service. They were less prepared to accept the queues and the waiting lists, the strict and cost-conscious diets, poor decoration and other non-medical aspects of hospitals. In consequence, most of the expenditure allocated for the rise in "unmet need" went to satisfy this group's desires. Large capital projects which might have alleviated the pre-war shortages in areas like Greenock and Ayrshire were shelved. Only in the early 1960s were large-scale projects re-examined. And it was not only large-scale hospital extensions that bore the brunt of stunted growth. Maternity care also suffered — a serious matter, as the infant mortality rate for the unskilled remained at twice the level for the middle classes. Other more specialised areas, such as geriatric care, where residential accommodation was vital in prolonging the lives of so many otherwise condemned to remain in urban tenements, suffered a similar fate. From the mid-fifties, Scottish Office officials continued to lambast the local authorities for their unwillingness to embark upon new medico-welfare projects for groups such as the handicapped, and complained bitterly that it proved impossible to get agreement amongst the many small authorities to initiate worthwhile schemes.

Thus although there was an improvement in the general health of Scotland, there was a switch from the old-time infectious diseases, the last major one being TB, to newer illnesses associated with "mental, degenerational and functional failures linked to age and neurosis associated with the conflicts and stresses of modern life".[6] Illnesses in this category, such as lung cancer, were much more common among those on low incomes.

Walter Elliot's concern for the development of public housing proved justified in the years immediately following the war. Table 4 indicates the phenomenal growth in public housing, surpassing the levels obtained before 1939. Of course this was all part of the wartime pledge to build homes for the returning servicemen and their families and further alleviate gross overcrowding. It also enabled TB to be brought under more effective medical control, by stopping the spread of infection through overcrowded households.

But the Conservative administrations in the 1950s and early 1960s still shared both Elliot's and Skelton's desire for a property-owning democracy and, as soon as building controls were abolished in 1954, new policies emerged to encourage home ownership. The end of cheap land for local authority

Table 4a.

NUMBER OF HOUSES BUILT 1919-60

	Local Authority	Private	
1919-39	232,000	105,000	337,000
1940-60	389,000	49,000	438,000
Total	621,000	154,000	775,000

Table 4b.

HOUSING STOCK 1960

Local Authority	Private Rent	Owner/Occupier
39%	43%	18%

Source: Annual Reports, Department of Health.

development was accompanied by new policies encouraging town centre development on old demolished sites, and multi-storey flats, which were certain to emphasise the social divisions within Scotland. As the more affluent moved to peripheral ribbon developments associated with detached or semi-detached housing, the remainder had to make do with high-rise developments and/or live in areas poorly provided with more modern amenities. On top of this, local authorities were unable to provide sufficient homes quickly enough in expanding areas. The SSHA had to be given additional powers to build where necessary. Despite their phenomenal growth even the new towns had their critics, because they wrenched long-standing industries from urban centres like central Glasgow and Leith, leaving them to decay, with above-average numbers of the elderly and the unskilled left behind in the flight to the new towns.

The yawning gap between the better-off and the poor was further widened in the 1950s and early 1960s by the crisis of Scotland's traditional industries. The post-war revival in these industries had finally spluttered to a halt, with a massive outflow of labour in prospect and no alternative domestic employment in sight. This was coupled with the knowledge that the Scottish economy's ability to provide jobs had not narrowed the pay differentials with England which had emerged in the inter-war period. The prospects for the 1960s and 1970s were those of an economy beset by low wages and high unemployment, in which poverty and inequality would be rife. The only alternative was to go beyond the level of intervention agreed in the previous generation and devise a whole new series of measures to combat the predicament. Other chapters in this collection examine the success or failure of these new policies.

References
1   This paper is largely drawn from contemporary sources including: the Annual Reports of the Board of Health and the Department of Health; Scottish Record Office files HH, LD, ED; D. N. Paton, "Poverty, Growth and Nutrition", *MRC* (1926); Dunfermline Carnegie Trust, *Family Diet and Health in Britain* (1955); *Report on the Hospital Services (Scotland)* (1926); *Report of the Committee on the Scottish Health Services*, Cmnd. 5206 (1936); *Report on Infant Mortality* (1943); *Report of the Scottish Hospital Survey* (1946); Glasgow Public Assistance Committee Minutes and Records; *The Clyde Regional Plan* (1946); G. McCrone, *Scotland's Economic Progress 1951-60* (1965); A. K. Cairncross, *The Scottish Economy* (1954); *Housing Overcrowding Survey (Scotland)*, Cmnd. 5171 (1936); A. K. Skelton, *Constructive Conservatism* (1924). For an account of the changes of the numbers on social security between 1945 and 1961, see the author's "Poverty in Scotland" in *The Red Paper on Scotland*, ed. G. Brown (1975). For a description of nineteenth-century attitudes to poverty see I. Levitt and T. C.Smout, *The State of the Scottish Working Class in 1843* (1979).
2   See Table 1.
3   SRO HH 31/36: "Reports and Memorandum by the Board of Health into Industrial Unemployment and Distress 1921". See also the author's "The Scottish Poor Law and Unemployment" in B. Saul and T. C. Smout, *Wealth and Stability* (1979).
4   SRO HH 64/151: "Inquiry into the Physical Condition of Children in Scotland 1930-7".
5   SRO DD 10/292: "The State of Scotland".
6   *Department of Health Annual Report*, Cmnd. 9742 (1955).

Geoff Payne and Graeme Ford

INEQUALITY AND THE OCCUPATIONAL STRUCTURE

Scotland's Economic Base

S COTLAND's occupational structure is a product of two main factors. First, the industrial character of Scotland has, throughout this century, been more dependent on primary and heavy manufacturing industry than has that of England and Wales. The old "staples" — agriculture and fishing, iron and steel, coal, shipbuilding and textiles — required particular skills which are quite different from those now required by, say, modern electronics manufacture or an expanded local government service:

> In insurance, banking, finance and business services, some 87% of the employees fall into social classes (Registrar-General's) I, II and IIIN. Conversely, in mining and quarrying, 91% fall into social classes IIIM,IV and V.[1]

But between 1921 and 1971 the male labour force in these industries had fallen from 654,500 to 238,660 (and was still falling).[2] During this period, any new employment was created by technological innovations which resulted in new factories and offices around London and in the Midlands, rather than in Scotland (whose fate was shared by the North-East of England, South Wales and in varying degrees by the whole of the English North and South-West). The "early cradles of the Industrial Revolution", which are also geographically peripheral, have been collectively disadvantaged for most of this century.[3]

Clearly not every Scot, Geordie or Welshman is disadvantaged. Just as some industries were hardest hit, so too were certain towns and certain occupational groups. But the effect of declining employment opportunities is a progressive run-down of the regional economy: low collective income results in reduced consumer demand, depressed commercial activity and smaller rating returns. This in turn leads to poorer public services, older and more decrepit buildings, fewer social amenities, less able public servants. The general impact goes beyond the crisis of the individual, and lasts beyond a single generation.

The second feature of Scotland's industrial base to affect her occupational structure is the internal organisation of "Scottish" industry. Relatively few of the companies operating in Scotland (or on Tyneside, or in South Wales) have their head offices or technical departments there. Many Scottish firms are branches of large national and multinational operations based in London or New York and increasingly now in Europe. This is no accident: Scotland has plenty of unemployed to man production lines. Governmental financial incentives to industry have helped to direct new branch plants to Scotland in times of expansion, plants which can be, and have been, most effectively closed down in a recession without great harm to the parent company. This system creates few non-manual jobs north of the border, because the technical and administrative units of the parent company are located elsewhere.

Scotland's Occupational Structure

The net result of the type and organisation of Scottish industry is that Scotland has fewer non-manual jobs than England or Wales. According to the 1971 census (SEG's 9-11 and 15), 57.8% of men in Scotland were in manual jobs, compared with 51.3% in England and Wales. Two national sample surveys (1972, 1975), using the Hope-Goldthorpe occupational grading scale, show a figure of 61% adult males against 53.9% in England and Wales.[4]

There are several ways in which the occupational structure is important as a determinant of disadvantage. First, the occupational order is "the backbone of the reward structure".[5] In providing an income, the occupation works both at an individual (or family) level and also at a local economy level to produce specific patterns of consumption and public services. Second, some jobs are better than others, quite apart from income. Numerous studies have shown that most people rate jobs as being more or less worth while, affording more status, giving greater satisfaction or being generally more desirable than others. If the supply of desirable jobs in a region is small, the inhabitants are at a disadvantage because they have a smaller chance of getting a good job without migrating. And third, some jobs have positive disadvantages, such as probability of periods of unemployment, or the risk of injury or death.

Furthermore, the supply of such jobs — the structure of occupational opportunity — is constantly changing. The pattern for the lifetimes of present-day Scots is shown in Table 1. Two trends can be discerned in these figures. In the first place, Scotland, England and Wales have all become more non-manual in character since the First World War. However, Scotland has benefited less from this change than England and Wales, so not only has there always been a relatively higher proportion of Scots who are manual workers, but that difference is increasing.

Within the manual sector, the proportion of skilled workers has dropped most sharply, while unskilled work in the 1970s still occupies 9.9% of the adult population compared with 9.4% in 1921 — an absolute increase of over 26,700 workers. This is not true of England and Wales, where the proportions of *all* types of manual work have declined. That is to say, the shrinkage of

Table 1.

CHANGES IN OCCUPATIONAL STRUCTURE, MALE AND FEMALES

Scotland	1921	1931	1951	1961	1971
Non-manual	31.1	31.9	36.6	41.6	45.8
Manual	68.9	68.1	63.4	58.4	54.2
Total	2,116,799	2,176,250	2,221,603	2,281,870	2,266,230
England & Wales	1921	1931	1951	1961	1971
Non-manual	31.6	32.5	38.8	45.0	50.8
Manual	68.4	67.5	61.2	55.0	49.2
Total	16,776,419	18,483,961	19,642,941	21,442,011	21,875,970

Figures recalculated from Census Data for the "economically-active" population. Non-manual consists of SEGs 1-6, 8, 12-14; manual consists of 7, 9-11 and 15; Armed Forces and Unclassified are excluded.

manual work in Scotland has eaten away at the most skilled and, of course, best-paid type of manual employment in a way that is quite different from south of the border.[6]

This leaves us with a slightly complicated pattern of occupational change. While fewer Scots now do manual work, the type of manual work done is more likely to be unskilled. What we have is a kind of polarisation of the occupational order in which the opportunities for jobs with good pay and working conditions, security, job satisfaction, longer holidays, etc. (i.e. the non-manual jobs) have increased, but at the expense of the better manual jobs. The middle of the occupational structure has been squeezed, the bottom has remained the same. Some idea of this can be gained from Figure 1, which shows the three bands of "non-manual", "skilled and semi-skilled manual" and "unskilled manual" occupations. The width of each band represents the proportion of the workforce in the category at that date. In the first case, which shows male and female workers combined, the lower band remains stable, the middle band contracts, while the upper (non-manual) band expands, showing a near balance of non-manual and "skilled and semi-skilled" manual sectors.

In the second case, which shows male workers (men having been the main breadwinners for much of the last fifty years), the balance between the two upper occupational strata is not so close, but the same trend can be identified.

The outcome of these structural changes is twofold. First, about 10% of all Scots (and an even greater proportion of the adult male labour force) end up as unskilled manual workers, and this shows no sign of diminishing. Second, the number of Scots who received relatively good incomes from non-manual

Fig. 1.   OCCUPATIONAL STRUCTURES, 1921 and 1971

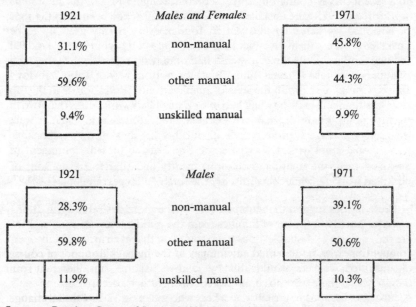

1921	Males and Females	1971
31.1%	non-manual	45.8%
59.6%	other manual	44.3%
9.4%	unskilled manual	9.9%

1921	Males	1971
28.3%	non-manual	39.1%
59.8%	other manual	50.6%
11.9%	unskilled manual	10.3%

Source: Based on Census of Scotland 1921, Occupations Report, Table 2, p. 12, and 1971
Census Scotland, 10% Sample Advance Figures Pamphlet.

Non-manual = SEGs 1-6, 8; 12-14
Manual   = SEGs 7; 9; 10; 15
Unskilled = SEGs 11
Excluded   = SEGs 16, 17

employment increased. Thus those at the bottom of the job hierarchy are *more* deprived in comparison with the "average Scot" whose level of income has moved up. While many have been improving their lot, the unskilled workers have not, and as a result they are becoming increasingly isolated from the opportunities enjoyed by the rest of society. Not all unskilled workers are deprived, nor is it the case that all the deprived are unskilled manual workers; but the overlap is considerable.[7]

This then is the structure of occupations in which a Scot must operate. The rates of unemployment and the range of types of employment vary from area to area. Glasgow has a higher proportion of manual employment than the national average; Edinburgh's proportion is lower. In talking about the unskilled male worker, we do not mean that he is necessarily in employment: even out of work, a man carries around an occupational identity and the knowledge that he is likely to compete for jobs in a very limited sector of the job market.

Inheriting Disadvantage
In a recent survey of adult males in Scotland, roughly 14% of the adult male workforce in 1975 were unskilled workers, while 17% had been born the sons of unskilled workers.[8] Of these latter, four in every twenty grew up to be unskilled workers themselves, and eight in twenty had become other kinds of manual workers. Only three in twenty had obtained professional, managerial or supervisory jobs (Classes 1 and 2), as the bottom row of Table 2 (below) shows. Compare this with the sons of managers and professionals in the top row: less than one in twenty had become an unskilled worker, less than two in twenty other kinds of manual workers, and fourteen in twenty were themselves managers, professionals or in other highly skilled or responsible non-manual employment. At the same time, of the present contingent of unskilled men (the right-hand column), nearly one-quarter are the sons of unskilled workers, while four-fifths are the sons of all types of manual worker.

These figures suggest that competition for the more desirable occupations operates heavily in favour of families from the middle class. Of course, there are only so many "desirable" jobs to go round, so that even in a perfectly open competition, with no inherited advantages of family background, some sons of unskilled workers would still by chance become unskilled workers themselves. If there were no connection between father's occupation and son's occupation, the sons of unskilled workers who make up 17% of the sons from all family backgrounds would be expected to contribute 17% of the men now doing unskilled work. In fact they contribute 24%. The sons of managers and professionals make up 6% of all sons, so their expected contribution to the ranks of the unskilled would also be 6%: instead it is 2%.

These statistics are relevant to the argument about the "cycle of deprivation", which for unskilled manual workers is largely determined by the limited opportunity for superior employment and by the competition from other occupational groups. If twenty-four in every hundred sons of unskilled families themselves become unskilled workers, this is not automatically evidence of a cycle of deprivation, because seventeen out of those twenty-four would "inherit" that destiny even in a perfectly fair and equitable (in terms of opportunity) society. The problematic cases are the seven extra men in every hundred who get trapped with the "normal" seventeen at the bottom. Even without regarding the unskilled as disadvantaged by definition, we can argue that any group suffering successive generations of inequality is disadvantaged. What is more, unless that structure of inequality is known for both generations, there is no way of evaluating what proportion of the inheritance was "inevitable". In the case of unskilled manual workers, where the proportion of poor jobs has remained more or less constant while other types of jobs have changed (Figure 1 above), how has that affected the life

Table 2.

OCCUPATIONAL MOBILITY BETWEEN GENERATIONS: ADULT MALES

Father's occupation when respondent was 14 years old	Respondent's Occupation at Interview							Totals
	Professional, Managers, etc.	Semi-Professionals, Senior Staff	Foreman self-employed artisans	Routine white collar	Skilled Manual Workers	Semi-skilled manual	Unskilled manual	
Professionals, managers, proprietors, etc.	128	71	18	29	14	14	12	286
Semi-professionals, senior supervisory staff	108	193	62	45	54	72	35	569
Foremen, self-employed artisans	76	95	121	26	91	110	75	594
Routine white collar	41	35	16	15	21	14	11	153
Skilled manual workers	91	128	172	63	400	265	217	1836
Semi-skilled manual workers	51	92	131	47	193	257	152	923
Unskilled manual workers	55	75	124	42	166	167	158	787
Totals	550	689	644	267	939	899	660	4648

chances of men born the sons of unskilled workers in the past fifty or sixty years?

To explore this, we can compare the experiences of such men born in four 10-year periods since the first decade of this century. In the first place the chance of "inheriting" unskilled employment has tended to fall a little, the figures being 23%, 20.2%, 17.3% and 18.5%.[9] But this chance is determined both by changes in the number of sons and in the number of jobs in the unskilled category: as we noted earlier the difference between those observed in the relevant category and the number one might expect by chance tells us something about the strength of the connection between one generation and the next. The ratio of the "expected" number to the actual observed number provides a simple way of making the comparison over time. For the oldest men, this ration is 1.18 (in other words, we actually have six men "inheriting" unskilled employment for every five we would expect on the basis of a random chance). For successive cohorts, the ratio is 1.28, 1.35 and 1.72. The ratio shows that the number of "extra" sons being trapped is increasing, with nearly nine men observed for every five expected in the youngest cohort.

What seems to be happening is that while the structural change enables more of the unskilled sons to escape unskilled work, those who are trapped form a large part of the present unskilled workforce because the changing structure gives greater help to the sons from other family backgrounds to avoid unskilled employment. The paradox is that more sons of the unskilled are now getting better jobs, but relatively, the sons of the unskilled are not doing as well as sons from other backgrounds: their share of the benefits of a changing society is slipping back.

Here we must sound a note of caution. We have assumed that as the occupational structure changes, new entrants to the job market respond more directly to fill the new job-slots. Men already part-way through their careers find it almost impossible to change: a labourer cannot become a doctor, and even the reverse is almost as true — why employ a drop-out professional with no labouring experience if there are plenty of labourers available? Certainly the proportion of all sons starting non-manual work has almost caught up the proportion of non-manual fathers who have a generation's start on their offspring.[10] But there is always some upward social mobility for men during their careers, so that the 1909-1918 cohort have probably reached their peak, while the 1939-1948 men may still have some way to go. The rate of progress also varies: there is more movement between generations in some periods than others. It may be that the figures for the younger men exaggerate the picture of what will eventually happen. This caveat applies more to movement into the non-manual sector than into the skilled trades, as the latter are normally entered through apprenticeships completed by the age of 21.

Scotland's Labour Market

This kind of movement has an important bearing on the "dual labour market" thesis, which argues that there is a primary labour market with high wages, good conditions, stability of employment, and a secondary labour market where the reverse is true, with higher turnover, worse rates of lateness and absenteeism, poor work relationships, etc.[11] The particular attraction of this thesis is the attempt to connect manpower levels, employers' needs and pay levels, but in Britain there is very little information about how that connection actually works. Bosanquet and Deoringer have indicated that unskilled workers (plus women and young workers) are most likely to be poorly paid, to change jobs most frequently, and to be most prone to unemployment,[12] but we cannot be certain that this stems from the surplus availability of such unqualified manpower.

If there is a dual labour market in Scotland, one requirement would be that the primary and secondary sectors are clearly different. In the first place, it would be necessary to establish the extent to which there is more unemployment, higher rates of job turnover, and lower wages for unskilled men. And secondly, there would have to be very little exchange between them: that is, there would be virtually no career movement or movement between generations from one to the other. Without these preconditions, there is no dichotomy in the labour market to be explained.

Dealing first with the question of unemployment, Table 3 clearly shows the greater insecurity of unskilled employment. The share of unemployment borne by the unskilled is far greater than the group's proportion in the labour force.

Table 3.

RELATIVE UNEMPLOYMENT RATES*

	% of those unemployed	% of workforce
Non-manual	28.9	45.9
Skilled and semi-skilled	41.6	40.3
Unskilled manual	29.5	14.2
	100.0	100.0
	n=346	n=4060

*Not registered unemployed, but those saying they were not working in reply to a question about earnings.

At the time of the interview, less than one in three of those found to be unemployed were from the non-manual sector, which makes up about 46% of the population. Among skilled and semi-skilled, the proportions were about equal. But the unskilled had 29.5% of the unemployed, despite being only 14.2% of the workforce. To put it another way, the unskilled sector had more of its members out of work than the non-manual sector, which is three times bigger. Almost one in five of the unskilled men in the sample were out of a job.

However, this insecurity is not so clearly reflected in the number of jobs making up the employment histories of unskilled workers. These findings support the usual view that job turnover is higher for unskilled workers, but not to the extent that one might have expected. Perhaps it is only the female and youth part of the sector that shows the sharper contrast with non-manual adult males.

Income Patterns

Turning to levels of income, the Scottish data match the information generally available through official statistical reports, such as the *New Earnings Survey*. However, the SMS survey was a protracted one, undertaken during a period of rapid inflation, so there are some obvious drawbacks about discussing its income data. The absolute values are already largely irrelevant, while even the relative position can only be a very crude indicator of the state of earnings over one part of a period of considerable change.

The ratio of average gross earnings for unskilled, skilled and non-manual workers, in 1975 pounds, showed a difference of about £7 per week between unskilled and other manual workers, and £18 per week between the unskilled and average non-manual worker. These are, of course, only average earnings, and there was some overlap between the highest incomes in one category and the lowest incomes in the next. Perhaps the best way of thinking about the income pattern is to look at the cumulative percentages in Table 4, which show that unskilled work is not synonymous with low pay, but does carry a much higher chance of a low wage. Even within the unskilled category, some are at more disadvantages than others.

Table 4.

CUMULATIVE PERCENTAGES FOR GROSS WEEKLY EARNINGS,
SEPTEMBER 1975

	£38 or less	*£48 or less*	*£58 or less*	*£77 or less*	*£78 or more*	*n*
Non-manual	8.0	20.0	38.2	71.2	100.0	1863
Skilled and semi-skilled	8.7	30.7	60.3	88.0	100.0	1637
Unskilled manual	17.1	33.2	78.9	97.0	100.0	560

Movements between jobs

On the questions of unemployment, job turnover and earnings, it would therefore seem that the unskilled are relatively disadvantaged, but it remains unclear whether their world of work is fundamentally different from the other sector or sectors. The SMS evidence is at best a weak support for the predicted characteristics of a secondary sector. If attention is focused on the other manual workers as shown in Tables 3 and 4, one might equally well argue for a *triadic* labour market model.

This brings us to the second major prerequisite of the dual labour market thesis, the requirement that the two sectors are relatively closed, so that movement from one to the other is not common. We can examine this by seeing if people change their employment from one sector to another during their careers, for example between their first and last jobs. The results of this analysis are given in Table 5, in which "first" is taken to be the first "real" job, excluding any temporary or part-time work taken to fill in before, say, starting an apprenticeship at 16.

Table 5.

MOBILITY BETWEEN FIRST AND PRESENT JOB FOR MALES AGED 20-64

| Respondent's First Job | Respondent's Job Now | | | |
	Non-Manual	Skilled and semi-skilled	Unskilled Manual	Totals
Non-Manual	83.8 (49.2)	11.0 (7.4)	5.2 (9.7)	1289 (26.8)
Skilled and Semi-skilled	32.6 (42.9)	52.0 (78.3)	15.4 (64.0)	2887 (60.0)
Unskilled	27.6 (8.0)	43.4 (14.3)	28.9 (26.4)·	633 (13.2)·
Totals	2196 (45.7)	1919 (39.9)	694 (14.4)	4809 (100)

First figure is row percentage; figure in brackets is column percentage.

Most strikingly, the third row of this table shows that, of those who started work as unskilled manual workers, 27.6% are now non-manual workers and 43.4% are doing manual work requiring some degree of skill. Only 29.0% are still in the same sector as they started, so that nearly three in every four have moved out of the unskilled manual sector during their careers. Again, as the right-hand column shows, those presently in unskilled employment come from a range of occupational origins. Nearly two-thirds are from the skilled and semi-skilled category and only just one-quarter started their working lives as unskilled workers. Part of this exchange may be an artefact of the categorisation of jobs to "semi-skilled" as opposed to "unskilled", but the levels of exchange are so high that it seems implausible to explain them away as mere products of occupational classification.

These results do not support the thesis of a dual labour market, because such large numbers of workers are moving between the major sectors during their working lives, and therefore are selling their labour in what are supposed to be two exclusive markets. The only area where some degree of closure is evident is in the top row, which shows that 83.8% of men starting in non-manual work were still doing the same type of work at the time of interview. But even here, more men move into non-manual work than start in it, so the non-manual sector cannot be regarded as "closed". What is true, however, is that the movements are chiefly in one direction: into the non-manual sector but not out of it.

We leave it to the reader to consider whether the results in Table 5 support a triadic labour market model, and even if they do, whether such a model is useful. The importance of these data, and those in Table 2, is that they challenge many of our more treasured assumptions about the rigidity of the class structure. We can no longer treat the stratified order as a neat, tidy and fixed pattern, but this in turn must not be allowed to divert our attention from those who do remain trapped and disadvantaged at the bottom of the social structure, despite changes in occupational opportunity.

Who are the "Deprived"?
For the purposes of this chapter, we have treated all unskilled workers as being relatively disadvantaged, and so they are. But other groups of people, particularly the old, or single-parent families where the parent is female, are completely missing from the data that have been presented here. This does not matter much where one compares like with like — adult male with adult male with respect to occupation — but it is more important when one needs to fill out the picture by looking at the total labour market. The same applies to other aspects of lifestyle, such as possession of basic consumer durables, or living in decent housing. Because it was not primarily designed to look at such problems, the SMS sample must necessarily under-report housing deprivation. Furthermore, small groups do not show up well in a national sample: 50,000 deprived people would be no mean group, but they count as a single percentage of the Scottish population, and would only show up as less than fifty "cases" in our data.

In discussing housing deprivation below, therefore, it must be emphasised that only part of the total picture is being presented. Its usefulness is to complement information about special groups, in order to throw into relief the extent to which such groups are disadvantaged. Furthermore, housing deprivation among the adult working population is deprivation indeed, for who is better equipped to escape it than those able to work?

In the 1975 sample, 42.3% had experienced some kind of lack in basic household amenity: no piped hot water; no fixed bath or shower; no inside lavatory; sharing a kitchen with another family; or sharing a bathroom with another family.[13] Most of this bad experience had been at an earlier time rather than now. Only just over 8% reported having these disadvantages at the time of interview, with about two-thirds of these having more than one disadvantage.

Are these disadvantages inherited in a cycle of deprivation? Treating all of the five items as equal, it was possible to compare two generations as in Table 6.

Table 6.

EXPERIENCING HOUSING DEPRIVATION

Number of deprivations experienced at the age of 14 years	Number of deprivations currently experienced*				
	0	1	2 or 3	4 or 5	Total
0	2777	27	52	49	2905
	57.7	0.6	1.1	1.0	60.4
1	128	36	19	5	188
	2.7	0.7	0.4	0.1	3.9
2 or 3	549	23	38	9	619
	11.4	0.5	0.8	0.2	12.9
4 or 5	988	34	43	32	1097
	20.5	0.7	0.9	0.7	22.8
Total	4442	120	152	95	4809
	92.4	2.5	3.2	2.0	100

* See text for definition of deprivations.

If there were a cycle of deprivation, we would expect to find most people in the same degree of deprivation now as when they were fourteen. In the table, this would mean those cells on the diagonal that runs from top left to bottom right. In the cell for "no deprivation at 14" and "no deprivation now", there are 57.7% of the sample, but in the other diagonal cells there are only 0.7%, 0.8% and 0.7% respectively. In other words, there may be a cycle of *advantage* which keeps those who group up in good housing, out of bad housing in their adult lives (57.7%), but there is little support for the more conventional view of inherited disadvantage. This remains true even if we add in the cells immediately adjacent to the diagonal (so that, say, lack of one type of amenity might lead to two or three being lacking, or two or three might be associated with only one disadvantage later in life). In this manner, one would still produce only 3.5% of the sample whose deprivation could in any way be said to be inherited.

Table 5 can be used to test the value of the cycle theory in predicting (i.e. in one sense, explaining) the distribution of deprivation. Each person in a given level of deprivation in childhood should, according to the theory, be in the same level in adulthood. Following this maxim, 2,833 (2,777 + 36 + 38 + 32) would be "correct" predictions: that is, 60%. But 2,777 of these would not really come into it. This leaves correct prediction in 106 cases out of 1,904 people "at risk", or 5%.

A more generous view would be to treat any level of deprivation as being just "deprivation": in this case, of 1,904 people who started in housing deprivation, 1,665 have escaped from it, and 239 have "inherited" it. Similarly, of 2,905 who did not suffer deprivation in childhood, 128 have fallen into it in adult life. That gives 3,016 "correct" predictions (62.7%), against 1,793 incorrect ones (37.3%) overall. If we leave out those who escaped childhood housing deprivation, that gives 239 correct — or 12.6% of the remainder — and 1,665 incorrect — 87.4%. A theory which predicts accurately only three times in every twenty (assuming that we can apply it to these data) is not acceptable, even by sociological standards.

Conclusion

Any analysis of disadvantage which is based on occupation must be limited. As we have noted, the old, the single-parent families, the chronically sick do not show up in this kind of data. However, if one does detect fundamental differences between occupational groups, then that evidence is all the more important. What is there to say for a system which penalises a substantial part of its *working*, healthy, productive population?

It is true that this chapter has largely concentrated on that least competitive sector of the workforce, the unskilled manual workers, those general labourers, porters and cleaners who have nothing to sell but their simple and often inexpert muscle power. Various definitions have put these workers at anything from 10-15% of men, so that whatever their limitations, they are an integral part of society. What is more, it has been shown that they have persisted as an element in the Scottish economy to a greater extent than in England. Indeed, the growth of better-paid non-manual jobs has left them relatively more disadvantaged than ever before.

What is particularly disturbing is that, paradoxically, at a time when Scottish society as a whole has become more middle class and thereby "open", there are clear signs that there is an increasing rigidity in the inter-generational recruitment pattern of the unskilled. Although there are more openings in non-manual work, each new generation of unskilled manual workers seems to be successively more composed of men who are themselves the sons of other unskilled men. Nor is it easy to see what governmental policy can realistically be expected to bring about a solution to this worsening problem.

It is a problem which, as other chapters in this book show, extends beyond work itself. Disadvantage in the occupational field is frequently associated with other kinds of deprivation which are also spatially concentrated. If this state of general disadvantage is becoming the fate of family following family, then it is the state of disadvantage *per se* which assumes a new importance, rather than as a mechanism of transfer of misfortune. By placing deprivation in the context of structural occupational opportunity (or rather, lack of it), we can see it as an inherent problem of industrial capitalism, instead of just a peripheral dysfunction.

This chapter has attempted to balance the plight of the unskilled against other categories of disadvantage. It is not sufficient to identify the unskilled worker, thereby implying that the remainder of society forms one wholistic mass which is uniformly advantaged. There exist considerable differences within the other occupational groups.

It was this point that prompted the critique of the dual labour market approach. In terms of unemployment, job turnover and low wages, not only are the unskilled disadvantaged, but, relative to the non-manual sector, so are the skilled and semi-skilled manual workers. However, the data on career movements show clearly that there has been a considerable amount of change between these occupational levels, contrary to the dual labour market model. In some respects, particularly this last one of career movements, the important distinction is between non-manual and manual.

Where, then, does the "real divide" lie? A great deal of conventional sociological analysis has used the familiar manual/non-manual dichotomy, but this is not adequate, because it hides the plight of the less skilled. Equally, to dichotomise at a lower level would blur the differences between non-manual and skilled manual groups by combining them. In one sense, the divide is an illusion: its usefulness in polemic is undoubted, but its utility in social analysis is limited.

This does not mean that one is forced back onto some vague continuum of advantage or disadvantage. Each categorisation scheme is valuable if it helps to identify differences of condition. This is particularly so when these can be related to some causal explanation, such as the labour requirement of a capitalist society. There is no single divide which is equally applicable to all problems: instead, there are a variety of divides which can be employed to highlight different facets of the essential inequality of contemporary society. By the same token, identifying two contrasting groups of haves and have-nots is not enough, unless we recognise the complexity of the system which binds them together.

References
1   I. Reid, *Social Class Differences in Britain*, Open Books, London, 1977, p. 74.
2   G. Payne, G. Ford and C. Petrie, "Occupational Mobility in the Scottish Context", SSRC International Seminar on Social Mobility, Aberdeen University, Sept. 1975, (mimeo) Table 1.
3   S. Glynn and J. Oxborrow, *Inter-War Britain* (Allen & Unwin, London, 1976), pp. 87-115; E. J. Hobsbaum, *Industry and Empire* (Penguin, Harmondsworth, 1969), pp. 207-224.
4   Based on J. Goldthorpe and C. Llewellyn, "Class Mobility in Modern Britain", *Sociology*, vol. 11, no. 2, p. 262 (the 1972 Oxford Mobility Study of England and Wales) and unpublished data from the 1975 Scottish Mobility Study.
5   F. Parkin, *Class Inequality and Political Order* (MacGibbon and Kee, London, 1971), p. 24.
6   A more detailed account can be found in G. Payne, "Occupational Transition in Advanced Industrial Societies", *Sociological Review*, Vol. 25, no. 1, Feb. 1977, p. 5.
7   See N. Bosanquet and P. Deoringer, "Is There a Dual Labour Market in Great Britain", *Economic Journal*, Vol. 83, 1973, p. 421, and J. Askam, "Delineation of the Lowest Social Class", *Journal of Biosocial Science*, Vol. 1, 1969, p. 327.
8   The definition of unskilled workers is slightly different from that used in the census data quoted above. The Scottish Mobility Study was carried out by the Department of Sociology at Aberdeen University, and financed by SSRC Grant No. HR/2173/1.
9   The "fit" between structure and mobility cannot be a neat one, partly because the definition and ages of "unskilled manual workers" in the census (which gives us the evidence on structure) are not the same as those used in the survey (which provides the evidence on mobility). Again, the youngest cohort born in 1939 to 1948 is probably affected by the relative youth of its younger members, whose careers have had less time to stabilise.
10   G. Payne, G. Ford and C. Robertson, "Changes in Occupational Mobility in Scotland", *Scottish Journal of Sociology*, Vol. no. 1, Nov. 1976, p. 75.
11   P. Doeringer and M. Piore, *Internal Labour Markets and Manpower Analysis* (D. C. Heath, New York, 1970).
12   Bosanquet and Doeringer, op cit.
13   The "inside lavatory" concept is taken from the census (as are all the amenity indices). But how do tenement-dwellers describe the lavatory on the landing, which is outside their own flat, but inside the tenement? We suspect that the census data on inside lavatories (presumably implying privacy, control of cleanliness and comfort?) under-estimates the Scottish dimension of this problem.

Trevor Davies and Adrian Sinfield

THE UNEMPLOYED

"In the coming years my purpose is to see that private enterprise can start
to earn the returns that it needs.... Nothing must be done to imperil your
chances. This is why the Government must keep *public* spending down...
We owe it to the unemployed."

—Prime Minister Margaret Thatcher's final words in
speech to the Confederation of British Industry on
16 June 1981.

How many unemployed?

ONE week after this speech a new post-war record was announced for
Scotland. Unemployment had passed 300,000, exactly one year after
200,000 had been achieved, in itself an occasion for much gloom and despair.[1]
Two years later, at the start of Mrs Thatcher's second term of office, the
number of people to whom the Prime Minister "owed" that debt had
increased even further. However, the talk about "the light at the end of the
tunnel", "the up-turn round the corner" and "the recession bottoming out"
and other inelegant and mangled metaphors continued to appear in
ministerial statements. Yet in her first four years in office the dole queues in
the United Kingdom lengthened from 1.2 million to 3 million, or one in eight
members of the labour force. In Scotland more than one worker in seven is
among those officially counted as unemployed compared with one in eighteen
in May 1979.

These figures, however, only take account of those who are officially
recognised as unemployed. There are many more who would work, if they
had the chance, who do not appear in the official count — the vast "silent
reserve" of married women, the young people on all the various Manpower
Services Commission schemes for "training" or "work experience" and the
early retired workers who do not have to sign on. Adjustments to the British
definition and measurement of unemployment to bring them into line with
agreed ILO practices[2] also indicate that the total number out of work is higher
than the official figures would indicate. The full number affected by
unemployment is even greater. A poll for *The Scotsman* newspaper revealed

that three out of ten families in Scotland fear that one of their number will be unemployed. Even those who detect signs of a return of business confidence and a recovery in the British economy do not predict that there will be more jobs as a result; they do not even hold out hope that the steady increase in the numbers of those without work will be halted.

Why has there been no public uproar?

"Unemployment" now tops the list as the most urgent political question in the minds of the electorate, according to the polls, but there has been no vast and sustained public uproar, let alone a revolution, over the rising numbers out of work. Indeed one in four of those out of work and three out of ten trade unionists voting supported the Conservatives who had been in office during the 150% increase in the total unemployed (according to the ITN Exit Poll). While even the more stolid newspapers and weeklies of fifteen, ten or even five years ago predicted a collapse of the social and economic fabric of our society, the protest and upheaval expected never materialised as unemployment reached such "intolerable" or "unacceptable" levels as half a million, one million or one and a half million.

There are perhaps four main reasons why there has not been greater uproar — what might be described as four "myths" of public perception.[3] The first of these is that our suffering is simply part of a world recession. Certainly, all economies have had to face common problems like the dramatic rise in energy costs in 1973, but the evidence shows that the increases in unemployment have varied greatly (see Table 1).

Table 1.

UNEMPLOYMENT RATES IN EIGHT COUNTRIES
(Approximating US concepts, seasonally adjusted)

	Great Britain	United States	Canada	Japan	France	Germany	Italy	Sweden
	%	%	%	%	%	%	%	%
1960	2.2	5.5	7.0	1.7	1.8	1.1	3.8	1.4 (1961)
1965	2.2	4.5	3.9	1.2	1.6	0.3	3.5	1.2
1970	3.1	4.9	5.7	1.2	2.6	0.8	3.1	1.5
1975	4.1	8.5	6.9	1.9	4.3	3.6	3.2	1.6
1979 April	5.7	5.7	7.6	2.1	6.2	3.3	3.9	2.2
1983 April	13.8	10.2	12.5	2.7	8.2	7.2	5.1	3.1

Source: Constance Sorrentino, p. 171 (see note 3), and more recent data supplied by her.

When the Conservatives took office in 1979 unemployment in Britain was in line with that in the United States and Canada, which had been the "unemployment leaders" of the major market economics for many years before. Within four years the picture changed with Britain overtaking Canada and increasing at nearly twice the rate of the United States. The long-term trend shows that Britain's position has been slipping for many years, and successive governments have failed to give enough attention to tackling the problem of unemployment. This has led some commentators to observe that, when the Western world catches cold, the United Kingdom catches pneumonia. More recently, however, British policies have made the recession deeper, not only for us but for the rest of the world too.[4]

A second myth has been that the growing number of school leavers is the main cause of rising unemployment. Certainly young people — and especially those who have just left school — are particularly vulnerable to unemployment, but regarding those in search of their first job as responsible for their plight is a good example of what an American psychologist has called "blaming the victim".[5] This is almost to reverse cause and effect. Over ten years ago we knew enough about the effect of the birth rate and the demographic structure throughout the labour force as a whole to realise that the British labour force would be increasing in the late 1970s and into the 1980s. We were also aware that the increasing rate of technological change meant that industrial training and further and technical education were critically important for a country that wished to take advantage of the new technologies. Except for those who argued, as did Sir Keith Joseph in a television interview in November 1980, that "jobs must be allowed to create themselves", most commentators have recognised a need to plan ahead and to exploit the opportunities provided by meeting the new technology with much better educated and trained labour force entrants. Instead, unemployment amongst youth in Britain is now much higher than the average rate of unemployment — quite disproportionately higher than it was when total unemployment was around 2% to 3%.

The third myth has been that our high unemployment is inevitable because of the impact of "the micro-electronics revolution" and other technical changes. Again a more detailed examination of the evidence so far seems to suggest the opposite. Many countries already making use of the "micro-chip" and other developments have had more success than Britain has had in keeping unemployment down or even reducing it: Japan is by no means the only example. Although the micro-chip can both destroy and create employment, the real danger facing Britain is a continuing decline in our economy together with a continuing failure to invest in training and retraining, which will leave us totally unable to take advantage of any of the benefits of the new technology. We will be unable to compete in world markets and will stand to lose even more jobs.

The fourth and final myth is that benefits are so many and so generous that unemployment "has lost its sting". But while welfare benefits may be a reasonable cushion for those who are out of work once and only briefly, for any substantial period of unemployment they are quite inadequate. This myth, however, dies very hard and deserves longer discussion, which it is given in the second half of this chapter. First, however, it is necessary to examine the characteristics of the unemployed.

Who are the unemployed?

"Economists and public policy-makers," wrote an American anthropologist, "debate the question: how much unemployment can the country stand? Strictly speaking, it is not 'the country' that is being asked to 'stand unemployment'. Unemployment . . . strikes from underneath, and it strikes particularly at those at the bottom of our society."[6]

The inequality in the impact of unemployment is even greater in Britain.[7] The most vulnerable are the low paid, the unskilled, the older worker, the disabled, the young and the less fit. They, of course, tend to be the least articulate and the least well educated — in short, those least able to press their own plight upon a remote government and an ill-informed press. While media attention has been focused on higher paid executives and others experiencing unemployment for the first time, the risk of unemployment for the higher occupational groups has only recently risen to the earlier post-war levels for the unskilled, which were about a sixth of present levels. The great majority of the unemployed receive little attention and come from the lower paid sectors of the labour force. Among men becoming unemployed in autumn 1978, one-half had earnings in the bottom fifth of the earnings distribution.[8] The unskilled tend to be the lowest paid and the most vulnerable to unemployment, and they formed two-fifths of the Scottish out-of-work in September 1982.[9] Those without a skill are also particularly liable to prolonged unemployment and repeated spells out of work.

The high risk of unemployment for young people has already been stressed. In April 1983 over one-half of the women and one-third of the men officially out of work in Scotland were under twenty-five years of age, and an increasing number were suffering prolonged unemployment. Older people continue to be particularly vulnerable to prolonged unemployment. Once they become unemployed, those in their fifties or older find it very difficult to get a job, especially if they are disabled or their health is deteriorating. Indeed, those suffering any form of handicap, whether physical, mental or social, have much higher rates of unemployment.

Where do the unemployed live?

The risk of being unemployed has long been greater for the people of Scotland than for those living in many other parts of the United Kingdom. Scotland suffered terribly during the years of prolonged high unemployment between the wars. After the Second World War and into the 'sixties, unemployment in Scotland tended to be twice the average rate for the United Kingdom as a whole. As unemployment everywhere has climbed, the further deterioration in the Scottish economy has been relatively slower, and the gap between Scotland and the rest of the United Kingdom has now fallen to between 15 and 20%. The development of North Sea oil and gas has provided some protection and stimulation to the Scottish economy during this period, but no silver lining, however bright, should distract attention from the clóud itself — the long-term social and economic costs of prolonged high unemployment.

The exploitation of the North Sea has been a major factor in increasing the differences between the regions of Scotland. Table 2 shows the contrast in the experience of different regions by examining the change for selected years since 1967. This might be described as the first of the bad years when British unemployment began to rise. Apart from a brief period at the end of 1973, the figure has not fallen below half a million since then.

Table 2.

SCOTTISH UNEMPLOYMENT RATES BY REGIONS,
RANKED BY LEVEL IN MAY 1983

	May 1967	May 1971	May 1976	May 1979	May 1983	May 1983
	% rate	1967 = 100 as index of change				% rate
Western Isles	22.9	79	59	57	90	20.6
Strathclyde	4.3	156	177	205	393	16.9
Central	3.1	155	184	200	487	15.1
Tayside	3.2	175	191	225	443	14.2
Highland	5.2	119	106	161	252	13.1
Dumfries and Galloway ·	5.4	100	131	142	239	12.9
Fife	4.2	131	143	162	300	12.6
Lothian	2.1	224	248	286	562	11.8
Orkney	4.6	89	56	126	254	11.7
Borders	1.3	231	277	269	731	9.5
Grampian	3.0	127	100	147	287	8.6
Shetland	8.3	58	35	32	87	7.2
Scotland	3.6	153	178	203	405	14.6

Source: *Scottish Abstract of Statistics*, No. 9, 1980, p. 95, and May 1983 from Department of Employment press release.

In percentage terms Scottish unemployment doubled in the twelve years between May 1967 and May 1979, and then doubled again in the next four years to May 1983. This national pattern, however, conceals wide regional variations over the sixteen years with unemployment in the Western Isles and

Shetland actually dropping a little. While the rest of the country experienced changes more in line with the national picture, the speed and time of the changes varied considerably. Unemployment increased four-fold in Strathclyde and Tayside and even more in Central, Lothian and the Borders. This largely reflects the differences in the industrial and occupational structure of the regions.

The official number of registered unemployed in rural areas, particularly the more remote ones, is not an accurate measure of the utilisation of a region's labour resources. Self-employment and close-to-subsistence farming in the Highlands, the Western Isles, Shetland and Orkney understate the problems of these areas, particularly as the figures take no account of substantial emigration. One in five of the Western Isles labour force are still registered unemployed in 1983 — one in four among men.

The great variation in unemployment across Scotland is underlined by a UK survey that identified Grampian as having the highest growth potential for the 1980s in the whole of the United Kingdom and Strathclyde the worst.[10] In November 1980 the regional planners in Grampian forecast "a period of unparalleled economic vitality" with the creation of over 16,000 new jobs during the 1980s.[11] But even in Grampian the national industrial decline has had its effects and, six months after that report, the first quarterly economic review of the Region's Department of Physical Planning reported that unemployment in Grampian was then increasing faster, albeit from a lower base, than it was for Scotland as a whole — 24% compared with 13%. The loss of development area status may have deprived many of the longer established industries, such as fishing, of much needed protection against the present recession.[12]

The risk of being out of work has been about twice as high in Strathclyde as in Grampian and in 1980 that Region suffered two-thirds of all the Scottish redundancies in manufacturing. Although the proportion has dropped since, present developments give very few signs of encouragement. The contrast is brought out by comparing the Scottish constituencies most and least badly hit by unemployment at the time of the last census in April 1981. Table 3 shows the wide difference between Gordon and Provan in Glasgow. The four worst constituencies for men and for women are included: the next four were also Glasgow constituencies.

Since the census unemployment has risen by about a third nationally so the rate for the constituency of Provan is likely to be nearer 50% than 40%. Within some districts, such as the worst council housing estates in Glasgow, the rate is probably well above 50%. In some households two or three wage-earners may be out of work, and among many families there may be two or three generations out of work. While the younger school-leavers are still looking for their first job, both parents may be also unemployed, with one or both the grandparents having to accept "early retirement".

Table 3.

UNEMPLOYMENT RATES FOR SELECTED CONSTITUENCIES
IN SCOTLAND AT 1981 CENSUS

	Men (aged 16-69) %	Women (aged 16-59) %
Glasgow, Provan	35.0	19.5
Glasgow, Garscadden	27.3	13.2
Glasgow, Springburn	27.2	15.3
Glasgow, Central	27.0	13.6
Motherwell, North	19.8	17.8
Monklands, East	21.5	15.2
Gordon	3.8	4.1
Kincardine and Deeside	5.1	4.9
Scotland	14.4	9.9
Great Britain	11.6	7.7

Source: *Parliamentary Constituency Monitor*, Census Scotland 1981, Central Register
Office Scotland, Edinburgh, 1983, CEN 81 PCM 24, Tables E and F—"out of
employment" calculated as percentage of "economically active of usually resident
population".

The problems facing unemployed people in these areas are considerable,
and are increased by the stigma which often attaches to the estates of poorest
housing. Research and other work in Ferguslie Park, Paisley, and similar
areas, has shown not only how few jobs and job opportunities there have long
been in such areas, but also how the residents' difficulties in finding work can
become compounded over time by employers consciously or unconsciously
discriminating against applicants from particularly "notorious" areas.

The unemployed are not only the redundant
Redundant workers are usually regarded as the most deserving of the
unemployed, for it is clearly a significant loss to be deprived of a job and the
seniority and status that has built up with it over the years. Major closures
such as the Talbot car plant at Linwood and the aluminium smelter at
Invergordon catch public attention and sympathy for those affected. But the
impact of a major closure reaches much further than those who are paid off.
The plight of those already out of work, those looking for their first job or
those hoping to move to better jobs, is made far worse.

A study of two major redundancies in Dundee showed very clearly that the
newly redundant tend to win out in competition for new jobs with those
already unemployed and looking for work. Over eight hundred employees
were paid off by National Cash Register Manufacturing Ltd. in the twelve
months from December 1976. Another seven hundred were made redundant

by Sidlaw Industries, Britain's largest jute manufacturer, when they closed three manufacturing units between April and October 1977. Enquiries of the employers taking on redundant workers from these two companies showed that all but 5% of the jobs they took could have been filled by those who were already unemployed or seeking to change their jobs. Living in the neighbourhood of a major redundancy means that, if you are already unemployed, you stay unemployed longer — by an average of four months in this particular instance.[13] The redundant workers may well be more skilled than the average unemployed or may simply have a more stable employment record. It is, however, increasingly acknowledged that employers often tend to discriminate against the unemployed, many using the length of time since the last job as a crude yardstick in recruitment.

The state employment service could do more to protect the most vulnerable in the labour market. Official evidence, however, confirms the general impression that the longer a person is out of work the less likely he is to have his name submitted to potential employers. In this way therefore the Employment Service reinforces the disadvantages already faced by those out of work for a long time. A special programme to place the hard-to-employ was shut down in its pilot stage — despite considerable initial success — when the MSC budget was cut back by the government. Informal complaints from DHSS staff allege that they have not been given access to job vacancies notified to the job centres on the grounds, apparently, that sending their clientele to these employers would threaten good relations with them. Unofficially, the DHSS staff complain that the Employment Service sees its first duty to the employer and puts the unemployed, especially those long out of work, a very poor second: where these difficulties have been overcome and job vacancies passed on, they claim that they have been able to achieve some significant successes.

Most unemployed are still poor

Over the years we have all learned to become increasingly sceptical, if not downright suspicious, of dazzling displays of statistical revelation. So what do the cold statistics of unemployment mean in real, human terms? Briefly, they mean that many people in this country are forced to live in poverty and often for many years.

The link between unemployment and poverty was very evident in the 1930s and has still not been broken, despite the persistence of beliefs to the contrary. There are two main reasons. First, as we have already shown, unemployment remains disproportionately concentrated among those whose earnings from work have been low or relatively brief and, second, the benefits and support services are by no means as generous nor as comprehensive as it is widely believed. Both points have now been supported in a substantial amount of research.

Study after study has shown that the standard of living of the unemployed is very low indeed.[14] The extent of the poverty and hardship has been confirmed not simply by independent studies but also by the government's own studies undertaken by the Manpower Services Commission, the Department of Health and Social Security and the Department of Employment as well as by the now defunct Supplementary Benefits Commission. Families are most vulnerable, particularly those where the main wage-earner has been out of work for a long time. On virtually every measure of disadvantage and deprivation that one might choose, families with children have been shown to be worst off. They had, for example, most "unmet needs" in terms of bedding, clothing and household equipment that the Supplementary Benefits Commission itself set out in its guidelines.[15]

The risk of poverty is all the greater for many of those becoming unemployed, who have few resources built up to protect themselves and their families because of previously low wages or recent unemployment. Poverty is all the more likely when unemployment becomes prolonged. Between the mid-1970s and the start of this decade the average time spent on the dole increased from one month to three months.[16] By April 1983 the number of people in the UK registered unemployed for at least six months was approaching two million — more than the total number out of work only two-and-a-half years before. The number out of work for one year or longer had risen over 1.1 million. It is hard to realise that this exceeds the total number out of work which shook the Heath government into its U-turn ten years ago.

Scotland has long suffered from above average unemployment and consequently more from prlonged unemployment. In April 1983 there were some 236,000 men registered out of work. More than three out of five had been unemployed for at least six months, more than two out of five a year or longer and more than one out of five two years or longer.

The extent of poverty during unemployment, and particularly prolonged unemployment, would of course be much less if we had an efficient benefits system. Redundancy payments take the sting out of unemployment for some although they are meant to compensate for loss of security and are paid whether or not the redundant worker remains unemployed. Despite the attention given to the occasional "golden" pay-offs and references to "three-month millionaires", the average payment under the state scheme is still only £1,000 and this is determined by length of service, previous earnings and age. There is no entitlement for those under eighteen or with less than two years' service with the same company. But redundancy payments are only paid to a minority of those out of work for a significant length of time. In autumn 1978 only one in ten men becoming unemployed had received redundancy payments:[17] and this proportion may well have dropped.

The great majority of unemployed are entirely dependent upon their state benefits — the flat-rate national insurance unemployment benefit or the means-tested supplementary benefit. If they have recently been unemployed and have drawn insurance benefit, the twelve-month payment period for the flat-rate benefit is reduced. The inadequacy of the national insurance scheme is shown by the fact that one in three of the men officially registered as unemployed in Scotland in May 1983 were drawing any unemployment benefit (31% according to unpublished data supplied by the DHSS). The main failing of the insurance benefit is its limited duration at a time when prolonged unemployment has been sharply increasing. More than two out of five men out of work had drawn all the twelve-month benefit to which they were entitled; they could only requalify after they have got another job and worked for some months.

Seven in every ten men out of work in Scotland have been forced to apply for supplementary benefit, or "social security" as it is still more generally known. However long they remain out of work they do not qualify for the higher long-term rate which is paid to all retired people as soon as they apply for supplementary benefit and to all other recipients after one year. The unemployed can only receive the short-term rate, which is £41.70 for a married couple and £25.70 for a person living alone, and rent and rates are generally paid in addition to this. The long-term rate would mean an increase of 25% for a married couple.

The government has acknowledged the inadequacy cf supplementary benefits. "The provision for children under the Supplementary Benefits Scheme," said the Minister for Social Security to the House of Commons in February 1980, "is not good enough, has never been good enough and will not be good enough following the Review changes."[18] This public admission may make it even harder to understand how it is that the unemployed have subsequently suffered further cuts in their standard of living as a result of specific government decisions including the abolition of the earnings-related supplement in 1982. The basic insurance benefit was cut by 5% in November 1980 as a forerunner to the taxation of benefit. This saving in public spending at the expense of the unemployed will not be restored until November 1983 after much intensive lobbying, including some backbench Tory MPs, won a concession in the pre-election Budget.

The changes introduced in supplementary benefits by the 1980 Social Security Act meant a significant cutback on single payments, especially for items such as clothing, which official as well as independent research has shown that the unemployed and their families particularly lack. It is true that the exercise of discretion in giving out these "exceptional needs payments" in the past was somewhat arbitrary and very often the unemployed seemed to be the least likely to receive sympathetic treatment. Nevertheless, the proposal of the DHSS Review team was that the general level of benefits should be raised and that single payments should be made on a regular basis once or twice a year to those on supplementary benefit for a long time. Unwittingly perhaps, the Review team played into the hands of a government that was convinced that public expenditure was far too large and that benefits went to many who did not need them. With surprisingly little reaction from the trade union movement and many others on the Left (in contrast to the 1930s), the government chose to implement the recommended cuts and to ignore most of the suggested improvements which would have created additional cost.

At the same time there has been a major cutback in government services to help the unemployed, again as part of the public expenditure saving. Despite the expenditure on special programmes for youth, and now the Youth Training Scheme, there have been major cuts in programmes and in the basic services in job centres, training and elsewhere. The reductions in Employment Service staff combined with the increase in unemployed "customers" has meant that the ratio between unemployed and staff has more than doubled since the Conservatives came to office. While the great majority of all the special programmes have been concentrated on the unemployed under the age of twenty-five or even younger, and most on sixteen-year-olds, the main help for other unemployed now comes from the Unemployment Review Officers of the DHSS whose numbers were doubled by the government as part of their "crackdown on fraud and abuse" at the beginning of 1980.

The wider impact of unemployment
Lack of opportunity to work brings many other disadvantages and problems besides financial hardship — as if that were not enough. There is increasing evidence of the strain that unemployment and poverty impose on families and individuals, and this is particularly severe in high-unemployment districts. In Clydebank, according to a special enquiry by the Strathclyde Social Work Department, "during the past year unemployment rose by 27% largely as a result of the Singer closure . . . rent arrears increased by 21%, households on Fuel Direct increased by 18%, Rent Direct by 14% (households on supplementary benefits already in arrears on these payments now made direct to the agency, the DHSS) and Education Department clothing grants increased by 23%, casework with families increased by 21% and reports to the Children's Hearings by 38%".[19]

In the second quarter of 1981 the Citizens' Advice Bureaux in Edinburgh received nearly twice as many queries relating to redundancy and employment problems in general as a year before; social security questions increased almost threefold. Only a minority of those with difficulties actually consult any agencies. People whose incomes have dropped are, understandably, particularly likely to fall into debt and become subject to warrant sales, the harsh system of debt-collecting in Scotland.[20] Increasing and prolonged unemployment will mean many more financial problems that will affect people's standard of living and create anxiety and suffering. In Strathclyde in 1980 "70% of all children received into care are from families where the head of household is unemployed".[21] Strathclyde's policy to reduce the numbers of children coming into care has been seriously impeded by the increase in unemployment and the financial and other pressures and hardships that accompany it.

While the reports of increased family violence and breakdown are themselves disturbing evidence of greater unhappiness, misery and suffering, the courage and determination with which many workers and their families endure hardship and destruction of their hopes and ambitions is remarkable. Ironically, perhaps, it is the very isolating nature of the experience of unemployment and its poverty forcing people back into themselves that has so far helped to protect this government and the wider society from more sustained and violent protest.

Up to now there has been widespread neglect of the tremendous costs, both social and economic, resulting from continuing high and prolonged unemployment. In 1981 the Manpower Services Commission put the loss of revenue from the drop in income tax and national insurance contributions and the increased spending on benefits at some £8.5 billion, adjusting for inflation.[22] More recently, the government has rejected these estimates but the House of Lords Select Committee on Unemployment produced a cost to the Exchequer of "over £15 billion" in 1982. "Some recent estimates put the total unemployment bill at £19-£20 billion."[23]

At local level the loss in revenue has also been considerable. In 1980-81 Strathclyde lost £4.25 million a year from the rates as a result of the main closures including Talbot Linwood (1980-81 estimates including metered water income, Strathclyde 1981).

These economic costs alone mean a tremendous cutback in a whole range of "welfare state" services. These are particularly important to those on lower incomes, with no access to the growing range of private and occupational benefits — often largely subsidised by the taxpayer — which are available to an increasing number of better-paid, higher-status employees.

But the cost of increased unemployment is not simply economic. There is disturbing evidence on the impact of high levels of unemployment on people's health. Poor health and disability are clearly associated with unemployment, in part because people with these difficulties are more vulnerable to being out of work, in part probably because of hardships due to inadequate benefits and services. There is more controversy over claims of increased mortality but the risk of attempted suicide at least appears to grow as unemployment lasts longer. The pressure of prolonged unemployment and a reduced standard of living may also compound existing health problems. In addition, the stress of redundancy may lead to a deterioration of health not only among those who have lost their jobs but among those who remain but fear that they may be next to be displaced: and the families of both groups may also suffer.[24]

With increased unemployment the security of workers is diminished and many lose any opportunity of moving to better and more rewarding jobs as they grow older. The freedom of not only the unemployed but many of those in work becomes substantially diminished — and this of course is why some businessmen still talk about unemployment as allowing them to shake out "dead wood". When workers are scarce, many of the more marginal groups in the labour force become "essential manpower", wooed by employers with a whole range of measures, adjustments and adaptations. With increasing unemployment, not only are these people seen as "surplus labour", but married women, for example, are accused of taking "men's jobs" and the National Front whips up racial hatred by suggesting that repatriation would do much to solve the unemployment problem among "whites". As the Full Employment Action Council in the United States has emphasised, unemployment "makes us compromise with the quality of life".

What then should be done?
If there is no significant change in economic strategy, current predictions suggest that by the time this book is published the official UK total of unemployed is more likely to be heading for four million than coming back down towards two million. Even the lower figure will be six times the level of the first twenty years after the war, and about three times what the very cautious Manpower Services Commission estimates would be a reasonable target for "full employment" given the changes in the employment structure and elsewhere since then.

It is easier to sit back, analyse present problems and criticise present policies than it is to take responsibility for more effective action, or to see that these policies are carried through successfully. In our view, however, any attempt to tackle the social and economic costs of unemployment must include a proper acknowledgement of the burden borne by those left out of work and their families.

Unemployment has long been recognised as a weapon which may be used to control the unions, to impose industrial discipline, to bring down the cost of labour or reduce the rate of inflation. If once accepts (which we do not) the creation of short-term increases in unemployment in the war against inflation, then the obligation to help those who have to bear the costs of the policy imposed upon them is even greater than if the cause of their misfortune is entirely outside governmental control. Yet the present government has rejected this responsibility by phasing out the earnings-related supplement and letting the value of benefits fall. Even the most conservative of politicians should recognise the force of John Stuart Mill's declaration that "there cannot be a more legitimate object of the legislator's care than the interests of those who are thus sacrificed to the gains of their fellow citizens and to posterity".

Adequate compensation is needed for those left out of work. Benefits must be available by right and not dependent upon a means test to those who have already become poor. When the numbers who want to work far exceed the jobs available, there is even less justification for limiting the duration of benefits, and so forcing those most affected by prolonged unemployment on to means-tested assistance. The link between unemployment and poverty must be broken, and this can only be done by a range of measures including the ensuring of sufficient take-home pay and benefits to those in work. Adequate child benefits and the raising of the tax threshold are both essential in removing the pressure of the "poverty trap" on the poorly paid as well as the unemployed.

A decent income for those out of work is crucial, but it must be accompanied by improved services — not an employment and training service that is sacrificed to the immediate demands of emergency "special programmes" to reduce the politically sensitive "body-count" of the unemployment statistics. The Manpower Services Commission has been forced to abandon the development of a comprehensive service, aimed to meet the needs of the labour force and changing technologies, and now provides "make-work" schemes, offering little chance of a secure and satisfying job, let alone any form of career. An effective service is especially important in protecting those who are the most vulnerable in the labour market and is an essential implement to any genuine training initiative.

In the long term these and other activities need to be co-ordinated as one part of a socialist policy on work that is also concerned with the quality, rewards and conditions of economic activity in an industrial society. It is not enough to fight unemployment. We "ought to be planning for productive employment. But one cannot do that unless there is something that one desires passionately to see accomplished. Employment is wanted not for its own sake but as a means to an objective."[25] Today we need to look beyond employment and consider any contribution to the work of society, whether waged or not.

People want to take part in this work: they do not have to be driven to it as those concerned with the need for a "work ethic" seem to believe. It is people's contribution to the society in which they live and their means of participating in the rewards that society offers. And there is plenty of work that needs to be done. "We have oversized classes when thousands of teachers are unemployed, old people dying of cold when engineers and electricians are rotting in the dole queues, the biggest slump ever in the construction industry when seven million people live in slum or semi-slum conditions."[26] Other examples can easily be added, including the appalling state of disrepair of the sewage system of many of our cities, and the need to modernise the railways and invest in energy conservation measures.

Work of this kind needs public expenditure and, despite today's many publicity campaigns, we believe this to be neither wrong nor undesirable. Indeed, if there is "no more legitimate object of the legislator's care" than those "sacrificed to the gains of their fellow citizens and to posterity", we ought to provide work for those we allow to be unemployed — and, incidentally, the work will be of benefit to us all.

But we do not believe in the virtuous necessity of work in itself. If it were possible for all of us to have more leisure, we would all benefit; we would all have more freedom to seek enjoyment and fulfilment as we wish. Adequate leisure is essential to civilisation and culture, but the requirement for a socialist society is that all, and not just the better-off, should have the opportunity and the resources to take part. At the moment the organisation of employment prevents the fairer sharing of more leisure time. Some, like the unemployed, have more spare time than they want; others are trapped in full-time jobs with many hours of overtime, and no time or energy to spend on themselves and their families. The enforced "leisure" of unemployment is not leisure at all in the way that we normally use the term. The sense of not being wanted and the lack of resources means that unoccupied days are far from being "free time". It is only through the proper distribution of work, not the increase of unemployment, that we can all share in the fruits of leisure as well as the fruits of work.

It would be good to think that a combination of science and sane organisation could change this. Both the desirability and the practicality of doing so were demonstrated by two world wars, when observers commented that the general level of physical well-being was greater during the war than either before or after. In 1935 Bertrand Russell wrote, "If, at the end of the war, the scientific organisation, which had been created in order to liberate men for fighting and munition work, had been preserved, and the hours of work had been cut down to four, all would have been well. Instead of that the old chaos was restored, those whose work was demanded were made to work long hours, and the rest were left to starve as unemployed."[27]

The last decade's retreat from full employment as a societal goal, "passionately desired", once again underlines the fact that the distribution of work and its rewards is a central political issue. "Whether we can get full employment in any country depends on whether those who, in the last resort, control the money power — the spending on which employment depends — wish sufficiently to get things done. We shall not get full employment by trusting to self-interest."[28] A fairer and better distribution has to be fought for as a basic part of any campaign to reduce inequalities, extend freedom for the great majority of the population and create a better society. In the 1980s this is a challenge to all who profess to be socialists.

References
1   Except where specified, data on unemployment are taken from the official *Employment Gazette* or Department of Employment press notices. In October 1982 the count was transferred from job centres to unemployment benefit offices. This and subsequent changes mean that the number of people available for work but omitted from the official statistics is increased, and women are particularly likely to be under counted.

2   Constance Sorrentino, "Unemployment in International Perspective", in *The Workless State*, ed. Brian Showler and Adrian Sinfield (Martin Robertson, Oxford, 1981).

3   See Stephen Maxwell, "The Politics of Unemployment in Scotland", in *Political Quarterly*, January 1981.

4   D.I.H. Jones, "How Britain's Unemployment Compares with Other Major Industrial Countries", *Unemployment Unit Briefing* No. 7, April 1983.

5   William Ryan, *Blaming the Victim* (Orbach and Chambers, London, 1971).

6   Elliot Liebow, "No Man Can Live with the Terrible Knowledge that he is Not Needed", *New York Times Magazine*, 5 April 1970.

7   Clive Smee, "Unemployment and poverty: some comparisons with Canada and the United States", SSRC Research Workshop on Employment and Unemployment, June 1980.

8   *Employment Gazette*, August 1980: see also *The Economist*, 4 December 1982, pp. 23-24.

9   Ibid., November 1982, Table 2.12.

10 Ian Dey and Neil Fraser, "Scotland at Sea — the Government, the Recession, and Scottish Unemployment", in *The Scottish Government Yearbook*, ed. Henry and Nancy Drucker (Paul Harris, Edinburgh, 1981).

11 *The Guardian*, 17 November 1980.

12 *Press and Journal*, Aberdeen, 21 May 1981.

13 *Redundancies in Dundee*, Summary and Report of the Scottish Economic Planning Department, Edinburgh 1980.

14 For a brief review of the evidence, see chapters 2.4 and 4.2 of Sinfield, *What Unemployment Means* (Martin Robertson, Oxford, 1981); and *The Economist*, op. cit.

15 Marjory Clark, "The Unemployed on Supplementary Benefit", in *Journal of Social Policy*, vol. 7, no. 4, October 1978.

16 W.W.Daniel, "Why is high unemployment still somehow acceptable?", in *New Society*, 10 March 1981, pp. 495-7.

17 *Employment Gazette*, August 1980.

18 Supplementary Benefits Commission, *Annual Report 1979*, Cmnd. 8033 (HMSO, 1980).

19 Strathclyde Regional Council, "Cost and Impact of Unemployment" and "Redundancies in Strathclyde in 1980", Reports by Chief Executive to Policy and Resources Committee; Strathclyde (duplicated), 1981.

20 Michael Adler and Edward Wozniak, "The Origins and Consequences of Default — an Examination of the Impact of Diligence (summary)", in Central Research Unit Papers, Report for the Scottish Law Commission, no. 5; Scottish Office, Edinburgh, February 1981.

21 Strathclyde Regional Council, op. cit.

22 *The Times*, 22 April 1981.

23 *Observer Business*, 24 July 1983.

24 Jennie Popay, "Ill Health and Unemployment", *Unemployment Alliance Briefing Paper* no. 2, November 1981; and Stephen Platt, "Unemployment and Suicide: is there a causal link?", *Unemployment Unit Bulletin*, no. 6, December 1982.

25 William H. Beveridge, *Full Employment in a Free Society* (Allen & Unwin, London, 1944).

26 *Life Without Wages*, TUSTU (North-East Trade Union Studies Information Unit), Newcastle 1980.

27 Bertrand Russell, *In Praise of Idleness* (Allen & Unwin, London, 1935), p. 16.

28 Beveridge, foreword to Max Cohen, *I was one of the Unemployed* (Left Book Club, London, 1945); see also Adrian Sinfield, "The Necessity for Full Employment", in *The Future of the Welfare State*, ed. Howard Glennerster (Fabian Society, London, 1983).

Fred Twine

THE LOW PAID

Who are the low paid?

THE annual New Earnings Survey[1] (NES) presents what is essentially a "snapshot" of the low paid and we still know little of those who remain low paid year after year, or who fall in and out of low pay during the course of a year. The survey probably underestimates the scale and frequency of low pay in Britain, especially in the context of over three million unemployed; perhaps a third or more of the unemployed would have been in, and are likely to return to, low paid jobs.

The persistence of low pay highlights certain contradictions of welfare capitalism in post-war Britain. Reward from the labour market is still full of inequalities, and many have insufficient income to raise themselves and their families above the "official poverty line", once income tax and other deductions are made. However, simply to focus on low pay in terms of failure to meet family needs tends to concentrate attention on heads of households, who are conventionally taken as male, implying that low pay among women is of secondary importance, despite significant numbers of female-headed households. As labour market reward for men has never taken account of their families' needs, we must beware of inadvertently justifying low pay among women by argument that they are not heads of households.

To give men and women equal attention we must consider low pay in terms of the general inequality of labour market reward rather than family need. Like unemployment, low pay is a problem of industry, not the family. Thus, the perspective taken here is one that focuses on the reward attached to particular positions in the labour market, rather than the characteristics of individuals who may occupy those positions at a moment in time. We are concerned with the extent to which pay at the bottom of the earnings distribution falls below that of the average earner. This is close to the definition suggested by Peter Townsend in his mammoth study, *Poverty in the United Kingdom*, where he argues for a definition of low pay in terms of 60% of mean weekly earnings during the year.[2]

In April 1981 the average or mean gross weekly earnings of all men in Britain was £140.5 per week, thus 60% gives a figure of £84.3. (A similar approach taking the gross weekly earnings of all male workers at the lowest decile of earnings provides a figure of £82.9 per week. In recent years these two calculations have resulted in closely comparable figures, but this is less so in April 1981, suggesting that the bottom decile have fallen further below the level of average earnings.) The figure used in this study as a measure of low pay is £85 per week for workers working full time whose pay was not affected by absence. It should be noted that most definitions of low pay have their strengths and weaknesses and these matters have been well discussed in Townsend,[2] in the *Royal Commission in the Distribution of Income and Wealth*,[3] and in *DHSS*.[4]

Low pay in Britain: the Scottish dimension

In April 1981, Scotland contained 10.6% of all male, and 11.5% of all female low paid workers in Britain. Only the South East and North West regions had larger percentages of Britain's low paid workers (Tables 1 and 2). Within Scotland, 16.4% of manual and 8.1% of non-manual men were paid less than £85 per week. Only the South West and East Anglia had more of their manual men low paid.

Significant numbers of women are low paid in every region of Britain, ranging from 42.1% in the South East to 62.0% in the East Midlands and Yorks/Humberside. Within Scotland 60.7% of all women received less than £85 per week in April 1981; 76.6% of manual and 54.5% of non-manual women workers.

These comparisons tell only a partial story as the regional distribution of the low paid must be compared with the regional distribution of all employees. A region may have a large proportion of all those low paid simply because it has a large proportion of all employees. The ratios in Table 3 identify those regions having a disproportionate share of the low paid.

Scotland was the worst region in Britain for its disproportionate share of all low paid workers. The South West and East Anglia had a higher disproportionate share of low paid males, and the East Midlands and Yorks/Humberside of low paid females, but overall Scotland came out worst. Only the South East had less than its proportionate share of the low paid.

Low pay: inequality in Scotland

Scotland's low paid workers were heavily concentrated in Strathclyde, the concentration being greater among female (46.0%) than male workers (37.8%). The four regions with major urban concentration, Strathclyde, Lothian, Tayside and Grampian, together contained more than three-quarters of all Scotland's low paid (Table 4).

But again, some regions had more than their proportionate share of Scotland's low paid, compared to their share of employees. The Borders had dramatically more than its share of low paid males, and Tayside, Dumfries/

Table 1.

DISTRIBUTION OF LOW PAY IN GREAT BRITAIN (APRIL 1981): MALES
(Full-time male workers aged 21 and over with gross weekly earnings (inc. overtime) below £85)

REGION	MANUAL		NON-MANUAL		ALL	
	% below £85 in each region	Regional distribution of those below £85	% below £85 in each region	Regional distribution of those below £85	% below £85 in each region	Regional distribution of those below £85
South West	21.0	9.9	8.3	9.0	15.0	9.6
East Anglia	18.8	4.6	8.2	3.7	14.4	4.4
Scotland	16.4	10.9	8.1	9.8	13.0	10.6
Yorks/Humberside	15.8	10.5	8.5	9.5	13.0	10.3
Wales	15.6	5.2	9.1	5.0	13.1	5.1
East Midlands	14.9	7.6	8.5	7.1	12.5	7.5
North West	14.4	11.5	7.5	12.2	11.4	11.7
West Midlands	14.3	9.8	7.8	9.5	11.6	9.7
Northern	13.1	5.8	7.5	4.9	11.1	5.6
South East	13.0	24.1	5.3	30.5	8.8	25.9
Great Britain	15.0	99.9	6.9	101.2	11.3	100.4

Source: NES 1981 unpublished tabulations.

Table 2.

DISTRIBUTION OF LOW PAY IN GREAT BRITAIN (APRIL 1981): FEMALES
(Full-time female workers aged 18 and over with gross weekly earnings (inc. overtime) below £85)

REGION	MANUAL		NON-MANUAL		ALL	
	% below £85 in each region	Regional distribution of those below £85	%below £85 in each region	Regional distribution of those below £85	% below £85 in each region	Regional distribution of those below £85
South West	79.2	6.7	53.1	8.0	58.7	7.6
Yorks/Humberside	78.8	9.5	56.2	9.3	62.0	9.3
East Anglia	77.6	3.2	51.8	3.1	58.2	3.1
East Midlands	76.9	8.9	55.2	6.7	62.0	7.5
Scotland	76.6	12.7	54.5	11.0	60.7	11.5
West Midlands	76.2	10.4	54.6	9.9	60.3	10.1
Wales	75.9	4.4	51.9	4.2	58.0	4.3
Northern	75.6	5.8	55.8	6.1	60.8	6.0
North West	75.0	13.4	51.4	12.5	57.5	12.8
South East	64.8	25.1	36.8	29.1	42.1	27.8
Great Britain	73.3	100.1	47.5	99.9	53.6	100.0

Source: NES 1981 unpublished tabulations.

Table 3.

REGIONAL DISTRIBUTION OF THE LOW PAID COMPARED WITH THE DISTRIBUTION OF EMPLOYEES: GREAT BRITAIN 1981

REGION	(1) Regional distribution of all workers with gross weekly earnings below £85 p.w. (%)[1]			(2) Regional distribution employees (April 1981)[4]			(3) Ratio of (1) to (2)		
	Male[2]	Female[3]	All	Male[2]	Female[3]	All	Male	Female	All
Scotland	10.6	11.5	11.2	9.2	10.2	9.5	115	113	118
South West	9.6	7.6	8.2	7.3	6.9	7.2	132	110	114
Yorks/Humberside	10.3	9.3	9.6	8.9	8.1	8.6	116	115	112
East Midlands	7.5	7.5	7.5	6.8	6.4	6.7	110	117	112
North West	11.7	12.8	12.5	11.6	11.9	11.7	101	108	107
East Anglia	4.4	3.1	3.5	3.4	2.9	3.3	129	107	106
West Midlands	9.7	10.1	9.9	9.4	8.9	9.3	103	113	106
Wales	5.1	4.3	4.5	4.4	3.9	4.3	116	110	105
North	5.6	6.0	5.8	5.6	5.3	5.5	100	113	105
South East	25.9	27.8	27.2	33.2	35.4	33.9	78	79	80
Great Britain	100.4	100.0	99.9	99.8	99.9	100.0	—	—	—

Source: 1 NES April 1981 unpublished tabulations.
  2 Full-time male workers aged 21 and over.
  3 Full-time female workers aged 18 and over.
  4 NES April 1981 employees sampled in each region.

Galloway and the Highlands had markedly more. These are the four key regions for Scotland's low paid males. In contrast, the Islands had dramatically less, and Central region markedly less than their proportionate share of Scotland's low paid males. Only Dumfries/Galloway had a markedly larger share of Scotland's low paid females, and to a slight extent the Borders and Central region.

Quite different shares of male and female low pay occur in particular regions. Though the Borders had only slightly more than its share of low paid females, its dramatically high share of low paid males made it overall the worst region in Scotland for low pay. Both Tayside and Dumfries/Galloway had markedly high shares of all the low paid; but Tayside had near its proportionate share of low paid females, whereas Dumfries/Galloway had the highest disproportionate share of low paid females. In contrast Central region, whilst having markedly less than its proportionate share of low paid males, had rather more than its fair share of low paid females.

These contrasting regional patterns of labour market inequality for men and women require further study and analysis if we are to have a better understanding of the nature of low pay in Scotland.

It will be recalled (Table 3) that Scotland's disproportionately high share of Britain's low paid men was indicated by a ratio of 115, and that within Britain the ratio ranged from a low of 78 to a high of 132. Within Scotland the ratio for low paid males ranged from 40 up to 185. This indicates that there was greater inequality in the distribution of low paid men within Scotland than between Scotland and the other regions of Britain.

With regard to low paid women in Britain, Scotland's ratio was 113 within a range from 79 to 117. Within Scotland the female ratio ranged from 90 to 121. This suggests that inequalities in the distribution of low paid women within Scotland was quite similar to that within Britain. Thus, inequality was less among women than among men, but this is because such a large percentage of all women are low paid compared to men in every region of Britain *and* every part of Scotland.

Low pay and long hours

For some workers the financial impact of low pay may be softened by overtime working, but many keep above the low pay level only by regular periods of overtime, with consequent strain on themselves and their families. In Scotland (Table 5), the 16.4% of male manual workers low paid would have risen to 27.1% but for overtime working. Average weekly overtime was 5.0 hours, though this figure would have been higher for the 48.1% actually working overtime (NES Table 117).

Within Scotland, it is again the poverty wages of the Borders that stand out with 30.4% of male manual workers low paid, rising to 42.2% but for overtime working. This is probably related to the concentration of male employment in

Table 4.

REGIONAL DISTRIBUTION OF THE LOW PAID COMPARED WITH THE DISTRIBUTION OF EMPLOYEES IN SCOTLAND

REGION	(1) Regional distribution of all workers with gross weekly earnings below £85 p.w. (April 1981)[1]			(2) Regional distribution of employees (April 1981)[4]			(3) Ratio of (1) to (2)		
	Male[2]	Female[3]	All	Male[2]	Female[3]	All	Male[1]	Female[2]	All
Borders	3.7	2.7	2.0	2.5	2.1	1.8	108	143	121
Tayside	10.7	8.7	9.3	7.2	8.5	7.7	149	102	119
Dumfries/Galloway	4.1	2.9	3.2	2.9	2.4	2.7	141	121	111
Highlands	5.1	3.6	4.0	3.7	3.4	3.6	138	106	103
Fife	5.6	6.1	6.0	5.7	5.9	5.8	98	103	103
Strathclyde	37.8	46.0	43.6	43.5	44.8	43.9	87	103	99
Lothian	18.5	15.8	16.6	17.2	17.3	17.2	108	91	97
Central	4.0	5.4	5.0	5.8	5.0	5.5	69	108	91
Grampian	10.3	8.1	8.7	10.7	9.0	10.1	96	90	86
Islands	0.6	*	0.8*[5]	1.5	1.1	1.4	40	*	57*[5]
SCOTLAND	100.4	99.3	100.2	100.2	99.9	100.0			

Source: 1 Unpublished tabulations NES 1981.
2 Full-time males aged 21 and over.
3 Full-time females aged 18 and over.
4 NES 1981 employees sampled in each region.
5 Estimated.
* Insufficient sample size.

the low pay industries of Textiles, Agriculture and Forestry. Tayside and Dumfries/Galloway had about one in four, and the Highlands and Lothian one in five male manual workers low paid, rising to about two in five in Tayside and Dumfries/Galloway, and three in ten in the Highlands and Lothian but for overtime working.

In these regions the economies of whole towns, rural communities, families and individuals have a precarious existence built on low paying jobs and long hours of overtime. Even in the best of times, when employment has been high, family life for many manual workers takes place against a background of continuous economic stringency and uncertainty over the weekly wage. Now, with unemployment at record levels, many of these vulnerable workers will have been reduced to living on the short-term supplementary benefit rate for more than a year.

Even the relatively prosperous Grampian region had 15.5% of its male manual workers low paid, and is heavily dependent on overtime working in preventing this figure rising to 29.8%.

Of all male workers in Scotland in April 1981, 13.0% had earnings (including overtime) below £85 per week representing approximately 140,000 men, and but for the opportunity to work overtime this figure would have been approximately 215,000 or 19.7%.

This should alert us to the danger of fashionably simple policies to ease unemployment by ending overtime. Ending overtime working, without a statutory minimum wage, will dramatically increase the numbers of low paid. Already the low paid have a higher risk of unemployment and it would be quite unfair if we were to ease unemployment by increasing low pay. Such a policy would simply enlarge the whole area of labour market inequality and insecurity.

Extensive low pay among women is little reduced by overtime working. Of these regions for which data was available for female manual workers, Fife had the highest percentage low paid (82.8%) followed by the supposedly prosperous Grampian region (79.8%). Clearly, even in relatively prosperous areas there are limits to the prosperity distributed by the labour market, especially to female workers (Table 6).

Throughout Scotland over three-quarters (76.6%) of female manual workers were low paid, and this would have reached eight in ten (80.7%) but for some element of overtime working. The problem extends on a significant scale to female non-manual workers, with 54.5% low paid. Of *all* female workers in Scotland in April 1981, 60.7% had earnings (including overtime) below £85 per week, representing approximately 500,000 women. About 150,000 of these women actually had earnings (including overtime) below £60 per week.

Table 5.

THE INCIDENCE OF LOW PAY AND THE IMPACT OF OVERTIME IN SCOTLAND (APRIL 1981)
(Full-time *male* workers, 21 and over, with gross weekly earnings below £85. Pay not affected by absence.)

REGION	MANUAL		NON-MANUAL		ALL	
	% below £85 in each region (including overtime)	% below £85 in each region (excluding overtime)	% below £85 in each region (including overtime)	% below £85 in each region (excluding overtime)	% below £85 in each region (including overtime)	% below £85 in each region (excluding overtime)
	(1)	(2)	(3)	(4)	(5)	(6)
Borders	30.4	42.2	*		24.3	32.4
Tayside	25.2	39.6	10.4	11.3	19.3	28.4
Dumfries/Galloway	24.2	39.6	6.3	7.8	18.8	30.0
Highlands	20.8	29.5	13.9	14.9	18.2	24.1
Lothian	19.0	29.2	8.1	8.9	14.2	19.8
Fife	17.7	33.5	4.9	4.9	12.8	22.5
Grampian	15.5	29.8	8.0	9.3	12.5	21.5
Strathclyde	13.5	22.3	8.2	9.2	11.3	16.8
Central	11.0	18.6	5.9	7.1	9.0	14.1
Islands	7.5	13.8	*	*	5.3	9.7
SCOTLAND	16.4	27.1	8.1	9.0	13.0	19.7

Source: Unpublished tabulations NES 1981.
   * Insufficient sample size.

Table 6.

THE INCIDENCE OF LOW PAY AND THE IMPACT OF OVERTIME IN SCOTLAND (APRIL 1981)
(Full-time *female* workers, 18 and over, with gross weekly earnings below £85. Pay not affected by absence.)

REGION	MANUAL		NON-MANUAL		ALL	
	% below £85 in each region (including overtime)	% below £85 in each region (excluding overtime)	% below £85 in each region (including overtime)	% below £85 in each region (excluding overtime)	% below £85 in each region (including overtime)	% below £85 in each region (excluding overtime)
	(1)	(2)	(3)	(4)	(5)	(6)
Dumfries/Galloway	*	*	58.6	58.6	69.1	71.3
Borders	*	*	63.3	65.0	67.4	70.5
Central	76.7	76.7	59.7	60.4	64.9	65.5
Highland	*	*	59.0	59.0	63.8	63.8
Fife	82.8	85.1	50.4	51.1	62.7	64.0
Strathclyde	75.2	80.1	56.8	58.8	62.3	65.2
Tayside	79.8	83.7	53.1	54.0	61.6	63.4
Lothian	71.4	74.8	51.8	53.1	55.3	57.0
Grampian	79.8	84.3	45.7	45.7	54.5	55.7
Islands	*	*	*	*	*	*
SCOTLAND	76.6	80.7	54.5	55.8	60.7	62.8

Source: Unpublished tabulations NES 1981.
   * Insufficient sample size.

Industrial structure and low pay

As an aid to understanding the industrial structure of low pay, industrial groups may be initially divided into three main classifications related to their pattern of low pay, and their impact on the structure of low pay in Britain. Firstly, those industries which combine a high incidence of low pay with providing a high percentage of all those low paid may be classified as "Comprehensive" low paid industries; secondly, those industries which whilst having a high incidence of low pay provide only a small percentage of all those low paid may be classified as "Incidence" low paid industries; and thirdly, those industries which, though having a low incidence of low pay nevertheless provide a high percentage of all those low paid (because they contain a high proportion of all employees) may be classified as "Composition" low paid industries.

Thus, for Britain at the level of *all* male and *all* female workers certain industries may be classified as follows:

Table 7.

LOW PAY CLASSIFICATION OF INDUSTRIES: BRITISH

Low Pay Classification of Industry	All Male Workers	All Female Workers
"Comprehensive"	Distributive Trades Miscellaneous Services	Distributive Trades Miscellaneous Services
"Incidence"	Agriculture, Forestry and Fishing Textiles Clothing and Footwear Timber and Furniture	Agriculture, Forestry and Fishing Textiles Clothing and Footwear Timber and Furniture Construction
"Composition"	Professional and Scientific Services Construction	Professional and Scientific Services Public Administration Insurance and Banking

Where the classification applies to both male and female workers one may develop the classification to "Gender-Comprehensive" low paid, e.g. Distributive Trades; "Gender-Incidence" low paid, e.g. Professional and Scientific Services. And where only male *or* female workers are involved, "Female Incidence" low paid, e.g. Construction; "Male-Composition" low paid, e.g. Construction. These two may be combined so that Construction would be classified as a "Female-Incidence/Male-Composition" low paid industry whilst Public Administration would be simply a "Female-Composition" low paid industry.

Table 8.

LOW PAY AND GENDER CLASSIFICATION OF INDUSTRIES: BRITAIN

Low Pay Classification of Industry	Industrial Group
"Gender-Comprehensive"	Distributive Trades Miscellaneous Services
"Gender-Incidence"	Agriculture, Forestry and Fishing Textiles Clothing and Footwear Timber and Furniture
"Gender-Composition"	Professional and Scientific Services
"Female-Incidence"	Construction
"Male-Composition"	Contruction
"Female-Composition"	Public Administration Insurance and Banking

The classification in Table 8 is intended to encapsulate the *major* industrial patterns of low pay, and will be referred to later in discussion of regional variations in low pay.

Low pay by industry—Scotland
This section attempts to explain the pattern of low pay and its distribution between local government regions within Scotland, by an examination of the regional distribution of low paying industries within Scotland. Unfortunately, data specific to Scotland on the industrial distribution of low pay is not available due to the inadequacy of the NES sample within Scotland. Consequently, what is attempted is an identification of those local government regions within Scotland that had a disproportionate share of their employees in those industries which had a disproportionate share of the low paid in Britain.

If those regions within Scotland which had a disproportionate share of Scotland's low paid (Table 4) also had a disproportionate share of employees in low paying industries, then one pattern may help to explain the other.

A number of difficulties are involved in this exercise. Firstly, the data for Scotland is for "employees in employment" in 1978,[5] whereas we have used "prime earners" in 1981 for Britain. Thus differences in: age structure; those working part time; increases in unemployment since 1978, especially in Construction, may detract from the accuracy of any comparisons. Secondly, the 1978 data for Scotland excluded establishments which had less than three employees in 1976 — this will tend to undercount the low paid who are disproportionately located in small establishments. Thirdly, the industrial categories made available by the Department of Employment for "employees in employment" in Scotland in 1978 are in a more condensed form than those of the New Earnings Survey — and the latter have had to be accommodated to the former. This presents particular difficulty for our purposes for Agriculture, Forestry and Fishing subsumed within Primary Industries; Professional and Scientific Services subsumed within Other Service Industries; and Textiles and Clothing subsumed within Manufacturing Industries. Estimates are made for these industries based on data for "employees in employment" in Scotland in 1976.

These limitations must be borne in mind when considering subsequent analysis. However, as we shall be comparing distributions some of these factors may not have too much influence on the relative distribution of employees between particular industries in each region.

A comparison of industrial structure and low pay for males in Britain (column 4 of Table 9) shows that Miscellaneous Services, Distributive Trades, Primary Industries and Construction had more than their proportionate share of Britain's low paid males, and that three of these groups were disproportionately represented in Scotland (column 6). Scotland had slightly less than its proportionate share of males employed in Distribution. Conversely, Scotland had less than its proportionate share of males employed in those industrial groups which in Britain had less than their proportionate share of low paid males.

Of the four disproportionately low paid industrial groups for females in Britain (column 4, Table 10), Distributive Trades, Construction, Miscellaneous Services and Manufacturing Industry, only two — Distributive Trades and Miscellaneous Services — are disproportionately represented in Scotland's industrial structure. Scotland's share was proportionate in Construction, and slightly less so in Manufacturing Industry. Also, Scotland had a disproportionate share of females in Primary Industry, though this was not a disproportionately low paid industry for females in Britain, and Scotland had less than its proportionate share of the remaining industries with less than a proportionate share of Britain's low paid females.

Because such a high proportion of females in all industries in Britain are low paid, differences in industrial structure whilst important may be less significant than in the case of males, in explaining Scotland's disproportionate share of Britain's low paid females (Table 3).

These two processes, more workers in low paying industries, and fewer in

Table 9.

INDUSTRIAL STRUCTURE AND LOW PAY: MALES

Industrial Grouping	Percentage within each group earning below £85 p.w.	Distribution between each group of those earning below £85 p.w.	Distribution of 'prime earners' between each group*1 (Britain 1981)	Ration of (2) to (3)	Distribution of 'Employees in Employment' (Scotland 1978)	Ratio of (3) to (5)
	(1)	(2)	(3)	(4)	(5)	(6)
Miscellaneous Services	25.9	14.4	6.3	229	7.9	125
Distributive Trades	24.1	18.1	8.5	213	7.8	92
Primary Industries	17.0	6.3	4.2	150	6.6	157
Construction	12.3	9.4	8.7	108	12.3	141
Public Administration	9.2	6.4	7.9	81	7.7	97
Other Service Industries	8.6	19.8	26.1	76	21.2	81
Manufacturing Industry	8.1	25.4	35.6	71	34.7	97
Gas, Electricity and Water	1.1	0.3	2.8	11	1.9	68
Total: All Industries and Services	11.3	100.1	100.1	—	100.1	—

Source: Unpublished tabulations NES 1981, Dept. of Employment.
Unpublished tabulations "Employees in Employment" Scotland 1978, Dept. of Employment.
*1 'Prime earners' —those aged 21 and over, working full time, whose earnings were not affected by absence, NES 1981.

Table 10.

INDUSTRIAL STRUCTURE AND LOW PAY: FEMALES

Industrial Grouping	Percentage within each group earning below £85 p.w.	Distribution between each group of those earning below £85 p.w.	Distribution of 'prime earners' between each group*[1]	Ration of (2) to (3)	Distribution of 'Employees in Employment' (Scotland 1978)	Ration of (3) to (5)
	(1)	(2)	(3)	(4)	(5)	(6)
Distributive Trades	79.8	19.3	13.0	148	16.6	128
Construction	69.7	1.6	1.3	123	1.3	100
Miscellaneous Services	63.3	10.8	9.1	119	16.7	184
Manufacturing Industry	63.2	26.9	22.8	118	21.6	95
Public Administration	45.5	8.1	9.5	85	5.9	62
Primary Industries	47.6	0.5	0.6	83	1.0	166
Other Service Industries	40.3	32.0	42.5	75	36.2	85
Gas, Electricity and Water	25.0	0.6	1.3	46	0.7	54
All Industries and Services	53.0	100.0	100.1	—	100.0	—

Table compiled from unpublished data NES 1981 and unpublished data "Employees in Employment" Scotland, 1978.
*: "Prime earners"—those aged 18 and over, working full time, whose earnings were not affected by absence. NES 1981.

higher paying industries, combine to give Scotland more than its proportionate share of Britain's low paid workers (Table 3).

Low pay by industry—the Regions of Scotland

We turn now to a consideration of the industrial structure of the regions within Scotland, and its relationship to the regional distribution of low pay within Scotland.

The industrial structure of the Scottish regions is compared to that of Scotland as a whole by means of ratios of comparative structure (Table 12 and 14). A figure of 100 indicates the same share of employees in the industry in the region as in Scotland; a higher figure indicates a higher share, and a lower figure a lower share. Discussion commences with the four key regions that have a disproportionate share of Scotland's low paid workers, the Borders, Tayside, Dumfries/Galloway and Highland regions (Table 4).

In explaining the pattern of low pay within Scotland we can identify the importance of two industrial groups, Distributive Trades and Miscellaneous Services. These two "Gender-Comprehensive" low paid industries provide the "general base" for low pay in Britain — 32.5% of low paid males, and 30.1% of low paid females (Tables 9 and 10). Apart from males in Distribution, these two industrial groupings employ a disproportionate number of workers throughout Scotland, and provide a larger "general base" for low pay than in Britain. This "general base" may vary in size for particular regions, and for males compared to female, but remains of basic importance, especially Miscellaneous Services.

From this "general base" variations in proportions of low paid between Scotland's regions may be explained by disproportionate shares of other low paying industries. For males within Primary Industries, low paying Agriculture, Forestry and Fishing is disproportionately represented in all regions of Scotland except Strathclyde, Lothian and Central. However, it is particularly important in Dumfries and Galloway, the Borders and Grampian (Tables 11 and 13).

Borders Region

Although Agriculture, Forestry and Fishing is a "Gender-Incidence" low paid industry, and does not generally have a major impact on the composition of the low paid within Scotland, in some regions, its impact is quite dramatic. In Dumfries/Galloway 18.0% (E),[5] and in the Borders, 16.0% (E) of males are employed in Agriculture, Forestry and Fishing. For males in these two regions the industry has the impact of a "Gender-Comprehensive" low paid industry rather than a "Gender-Incidence" industry, in topping up the "general base" of low pay.

Generally in Britain, and in Scotland, Agriculture, Forestry and Fishing is an even less important source of employment for females than for males, and

Table 11.

INDUSTRIAL DISTRIBUTION OF MALE EMPLOYEES IN EMPLOYMENT: REGIONS OF SCOTLAND (1978)

Industrial Grouping	Scotland	Borders	Tayside	Dumfries & Galloway	Highland	Fife	Strathclyde	Lothian	Central	Grampian	Islands
Miscellaneous Services	7.9	7.9	9.5	7.4	11.4	5.7	6.9	9.4	6.3	10.2	8.2
Distributive Trades	7.8	7.0	8.0	7.4	7.1	5.7	7.7	7.9	5.7	10.7	8.9
Primary Industries*1	6.6	16.7	6.9	19.1	8.2	12.4	2.8	6.1	6.6	15.3	8.9
Construction	12.3	10.6	12.1	12.4	16.0	12.6	11.7	10.5	13.4	13.4	33.5
Public Administration	7.7	5.7	8.3	6.4	8.2	8.1	7.4	9.6	8.2	5.9	7.6
Other Service Industries*2	21.2	14.1	20.6	18.7	22.7	15.2	20.5	28.2	16.1	19.4	15.2
Manufacturing Industries*3	34.7	35.2	32.1	25.4	24.5	37.8	40.8	26.1	40.5	23.6	10.8
Gas, Electricity and Water	1.9	1.8	1.8	3.7	1.8	1.4	1.7	2.3	3.1	1.5	1.9

Source: Calculated from unpublished tabulations of "Employees in Employment", Scotland 1978. Dept. of Employment estimates used in
the text for sub-categories within these groups based on 1976 Dept. of Employment figures:
*1 Agriculture, Forestry and Fisheries.
*2 Professional and Scientific Services.
*3 Textiles and Clothing.

Table 12.

SCOTTISH REGIONAL RATIOS OF INDUSTRIAL STRUCTURE: MALES 1978

Industrial Grouping	Scotland	Borders	Tayside	Dumfries & Galloway	Highland	Fife	Strathclyde	Lothian	Central	Grampian	Islands
Miscellaneous Services	100	100	120	94	144	72	85	120	80	129	104
Distributive Trades	100	90	103	95	91	73	99	101	73	137	114
Primary Industries	100	253	105	289	124	188	42	92	100	232	134
Construction	100	86	98	101	130	102	95	85	109	109	272
Public Administration	100	74	108	83	106	105	96	125	106	77	99
Other Service Industries	100	67	97	88	107	72	97	133	76	92	72
Manufacturing Industries	100	101	93	73	71	109	118	75	118	68	31
Gas, Electricity and Water	100	95	95	195	95	74	89	121	163	79	100

Source: Calculated from unpublished tabulations of "Employees in Employment" Scotland 1978. Dept. of Employment.

Table 13.

INDUSTRIAL DISTRIBUTION OF FEMALE EMPLOYEES IN EMPLOYMENT: REGIONS OF SCOTLAND

Industrial Grouping	Scotland	Dumfries & Galloway	Borders	Central	Highland	Fife	Strathclyde	Tayside	Lothian	Grampian	Islands
Distributive Trades	16.6	15.9	14.0	16.2	17.1	16.3	16.8	17.5	15.0	18.6	13.6
Construction	1.3	1.0	1.3	1.4	1.1	1.1	1.4	1.3	1.2	1.3	—
Miscellaneous Services	16.7	20.4	17.2	17.1	29.8	15.6	15.1	14.3	17.0	20.3	31.8
Manufacturing Industries*3	21.6	20.4	39.5	24.6	6.9	29.1	24.2	22.9	14.5	16.3	8.0
Public Administration	5.9	4.5	3.2	5.4	6.2	4.8	5.0	9.5	7.9	5.1	4.5
Primary Industries*1	1.0	3.5	2.5	0.9	1.5	1.9	0.4	1.8	0.8	2.4	3.4
Other Service Industries*2	36.2	34.3	21.7	34.2	37.1	30.6	36.5	32.1	42.5	35.1	33.0
Gas, Electricity and Water	0.7	1.0	0.6	0.5	0.4	0.4	0.6	0.7	1.1	0.7	—

Source: Calculated from unpublished tabulations of "Employees in Employment", Scotland 1978, Dept. of Employment.
Estimates used in the text for sub-categories within these groups based on 1976 Dept. of Employment figures:
   *1 Agriculture, Forestry and Fishing.
   *2 Professional and Scientific Services.
   *3 Textiles and Clothing.

Table 14.

SCOTTISH REGIONAL RATIOS OF INDUSTRIAL STRUCTURE: FEMALES 1978

Industrial Grouping	Scotland	Dumfries & Galloway	Borders	Central	Highland	Fife	Strathclyde	Tayside	Lothian	Grampian	Islands
Distributive Trades	100	96	84	98	103	98	101	105	90	112	82
Construction	100	77	100	108	85	85	108	100	92	100	—
Miscellaneous Services	100	122	103	102	178	93	90	86	102	122	190
Manufacturing Industries	100	94	183	114	32	135	112	106	67	75	37
Public Administration	100	76	54	92	105	81	85	161	134	86	76
Primary Industries	100	350	250	90	150	190	40	180	80	240	340
Other Service Industries	100	95	60	94	102	85	101	89	117	97	91
Gas, Electricity and Water	100	143	86	71	57	57	86	100	157	100	—

Source: Calculated from unpublished tabulations of "Employees in Employment" Scotland 1978. Dept. of Employment.

with so many women low paid in most industries, it does not contain a disproportionate number of low paid females. However, in Dumfries/Galloway, the Borders and the Islands, and to a lesser extent in Fife, Highlands and Grampian, it may provide a rather larger share, than in other regions, of low paid females.

Textiles and Clothing, hidden within the condensed category of Manufacturing Industries, is another "Gender-Incidence" low paid industry of importance in certain regions of Scotland, though its impact on the composition of the low paid is small in Britain and in Scotland as a whole. The Borders had nearly 20.0% (E), and Tayside nearly 8.0% (E) of males employed in Textiles and Clothing; and the Borders had over 25.0% (E), Dumfries/Galloway around 10.0% (E), Central nearly 9.0% (E) of female workers in this industrial group. And whilst at the national level (Britain and Scotland) it is in a "Gender-Incidence" low paid industry, again, in the Borders it has the characteristics of a "Gender-Comprehensive" low paid industry.

Thus, in the Borders region both Agriculture, Forestry and Fishing and Textiles and Clothing are "Gender-Comprehensive" in impact — and this, on top of the "general base" of low pay in Distributive Trades and Miscellaneous Services, may help to explain why the Borders had such a disproportionate share of Scotland's low paid workers (Table 4).

Tayside Region
For males in Tayside region the "general base" of low pay in Distributive Trades and Miscellaneous Services seems slightly larger than in other regions. To this "general base" must be added, though on a lesser scale than in the Borders, a disproportionate number of employees in Agriculture, Forestry and Fishing, and in Textiles and Clothing (especially men) 8.0% (E) and, unlike the Borders, Tayside has slightly more than a proportionate share of employees (10.0% of males (E), 29.0% of females (E)) in the "Gender-Composition" low paid industry of Professional and Scientific Services — hidden within the condensed category of Other Service Industries.

These factors combine to make Tayside the second ranking region in Scotland for its disproportionate share of all low paid workers (Table 4).

Dumfries and Galloway Region
Dumfries and Galloway had a slightly lower male and a slightly higher female "general base" of low pay in Distributive Trades and Miscellaneous Services. To this must be added a disproportionate share of males (18% (E)) and females (3.8% (E)) employed in Agriculture, Forestry and Fishing. These factors· probably explain the region's third ranking in Scotland for its disproportionate share of Scotland's low paid males. However, to explain why Dumfries and Galloway ranks first for its disproportionate share of

Scotland's low paid females, we must add to its slightly higher "general base" not only Agriculture, Forestry and Fishing, but also a disproportionate share of females employed in Textiles and Clothing — 10.0% (E) and in Professional and Scientific Services — 30.0% (E).

Highland Region

The last of the four key regions for low pay in Scotland is the Highland region.

In the Highland region the "general base" of low pay in Distributive Trades and Miscellaneous Services is higher for males and females than in most Scottish regions, due to the larger numbers (especially females) employed in Miscellaneous Services. As with the other key regions this is topped up by a disproportionate number of males (7.0% (E)) and females (1.5%) employed in Agriculture, Forestry and Fishing. But, a further and major boost to low pay among males in the Highland region arises from the disproportionate numbers employed in Professional and Scientific Services — 16.0% (E), and Construction — 16.0% (E), though a fair proportion of the latter may be higher paid than elsewhere in Britain due to oil-related construction work, as in the Islands (Shetland). These seem to be the crucial factors affecting the disproportionate share of low paid workers in the Highland Region.

It may be observed from Tables 12 and 14 that some of the factors of industrial structure used to explain the disproportionate share of low pay experienced by the four key regions are evident in other regions.

Some of the factors relate to the "general base" of low pay in Distributive Trades and Miscellaneous Services which affects all regions in Scotland.

Grampian Region

However, Grampian region has not only an exceptionally high "general base" for both males and females, but also a disproportionate share of employees in Agriculture, Forestry and Fishing, and males in Construction. Two processes may offset the low pay implications of this industrial structure: firstly, it was shown earlier how important the opportunity to work overtime was in reducing low pay among male manual workers in Grampian. Low pay would have risen from 15.5% to 29.8% but for overtime (Table 5). Secondly, and related to the first point, is the higher level of economic activity in Grampian region — it still has the lowest unemployment rate in Scotland. This, along with higher wages in oil-related employment, will tend to maintain demand for goods and services in Distributive Trades and Miscellaneous Services — helping to maintain income levels and overtime working compared to other regions. These seem to be the counter influences keeping Grampian region only *just below* its proportionate share of Scotland low paid — a situation not without future problems if oil-related activity declines.

Islands Region

In the Islands, the disproportionate numbers of males employed in Construction — 33.5% (nearly three times the Scottish figure) is related to unusually high-paying oil-related construction work (though this may soon be coming to an end). This seems the major reason for its low share of Scotland's low paid males.

Problems of sample size make it more difficult to comment on female workers in the Islands. However, there is a general problem with the category of "Islands", as this combines Orkney and Shetland with the Western Isles. It is probable that problems of low pay are of greater significance in the Western Isles, where unemployment is currently around 30.0%, than in Shetland which has had the benefit of oil-related economic activity.

Fife Region

In Fife, as with Grampian, overtime working is important in keeping down levels of low pay among male manual workers — 17.7% as against 35.5% if overtime earnings are excluded (Table 5). Fife also has a lower "general base" of low pay in Distributive Trades and Miscellaneous Services. Furthermore, a significant number of males in Primary Industry are in higher paid Coal Mining rather than Agriculture, Forestry and Fishing, though females are disproportionately represented in Agriculture, Forestry and Fishing, and possibly in Electrical Engineering (routine assembly work).

Strathclyde Region

Strathclyde has less than its proportionate share of low paid males largely because it has less than its proportionate share of males in those industries which are disproportionately low paid.

However, Strathclyde does have slightly more than its proportionate share of low paid females, probably due to a slightly larger number employed in Construction and Manufacturing Industries (Textiles and Clothing, nearly 8.0% (E)) and possibly in Electrical Engineering (routine assembly work).

Lothian Region

Lothian is the only region other than the four key regions with more than its proportionate share of low paid males; though only slightly so. This is probably explained by its "general base" of low pay in Distributive Trades and Miscellaneous Services being higher than the Scottish average for males, and this is topped by a disproportionate share of males in Professional and Scientific Services — over 10.0% (E).

In general, Lothian had less than its proportionate share of females employed in those industries with a disproportionate share of low paid females.

Central Region

Finally, Central region had markedly less than its proportionate share of low paid males, compared with more than its proportionate share of low paid females.

Central region had the lowest "general base" for low pay among males in Scotland, together with a disproportionate share of industries with higher pay. Even its disproportionate share of low paying Primary Industries is made up of high-paying Coal Mining rather than Agriculture, Forestry and Fishing.

For women, Central has a "general base" of low pay among females comparable to the Scottish average, but a disproportionate share employed in Manufacturing Industry, particularly in Textiles and Clothing — about 9.0% (E), and Professional and Scientific Services — 25.0% (E).

This discussion of the relationship of industrial structure to low pay has demonstrated the centrality of those industries classified in Table 8 in explaining the regional patterns of low pay within Scotland. Of central importance are those "Gender-Comprehensive" low paid industries of Distributive Trades and Miscellaneous Services which, to varying degrees, provide the "general base" of low pay in all regions. Next in importance, especially for females, was the "Gender-Composition" low paid industry of Professional and Scientific Services, and then the "Gender-Incidence" low paid industries of Agriculture, Forestry and Fishing, and Textiles and Clothing. In the Borders region these two industries had the impact of "Gender-Comprehensive" low paid industries. Of less general importance, but of significance in certain regions, was the "Female-Incidence/Male-Composition" low paid industry of Construction.

From this description of the low paid we now turn to a consideration of policies to assist the low paid worker.

Policies for the low paid

The present economic climate in Britain seems the least favourable since the last war for a serious consideration of policies to assist the low paid. The traditional emphasis of many economists on economic growth as the pathway to raising low pay seems even more improbable than it did in the 1950s; it also tends to ignore the need for income redistribution. Seemingly radical strategies, involving varieties of Negative Income Tax, Tax Credit or Social Dividend schemes,[6] seem impossibly expensive to implement, even if doubts could be removed as to their effectiveness. The economists' traditional warnings of the negative and possibly self-defeating consequences of a statutory minimum wage may incline us away from intervening in the labour market distribution of rewards.

This gloomy outlook may appear to justify inaction. It seems doubtful that low pay can be tackled without intervening in the present labour market distribution of income. It might be argued that with three million-plus unemployed this is not the time to be concerned with the low paid: a job — any job — for the unemployed should be our central concern. Yet problems of low pay and unemployment are intimately related. Not only do the low paid have a higher-than-average risk of unemployment, but significant numbers of the unemployed can only look forward to jobs with low pay. Smith[7] concluded "that the unemployed tend strongly to be people who had low pay from their previous jobs; that they generally expect to command low pay in the future; and that when they do find jobs their earnings are again low — often lower than before".

Consequently, a crucial first step in assisting both the low paid and the unemployed is a policy for full employment.[8] This will not be enough if the jobs pay poverty wages: a full employment policy must be linked to a minimum wage policy, and a minimum income policy which can reflect family circumstances. In effect this is a "New Beveridge" strategy,[9] but this time including a minimum wage.

In essence this new strategy involves first setting a "minimum living standard" for everyone, probably based on the long-term supplementary benefit scale. To achieve this tax thresholds would be raised and tax allowances recast, whilst child benefits would be significantly increased. A Statutory Minimum Wage would underpin this by providing a minimum equality of labour market reward. Whilst a "New Beveridge" strategy is concerned to relieve the poverty that may arise for families as a consequence of low pay, a Statutory Minimum Wage is directed at reducing labour market inequality.

It is particularly important not to take statutory minimum wage policy in isolation; it must be securely placed within the complex of inter-relationships involving the taxation and social security systems. The effect of this inter-relationship is well illustrated by the withdrawal, in the 1981 Budget, of the so-called Rooker-Wise Amendment, which required Chancellors of the Exchequer to update the real value of the income tax thresholds in line with inflation. As a result the low paid (and everyone else) started to pay income tax at a lower real level of income, so that, in effect, they paid increased tax on their income and thereby its spending power was reduced. If, as low paid workers, they also draw Family Income Supplement and other means tested benefits, they will have found that the effect of the "poverty trap" has been accentuated. It will now be that much more difficult to effect a real increase in spending power as their income from work rises, as it will increasingly be accompanied by a fall in means-tested benefits, often equivalent in value to their rise in pay. In these circumstances pay increases to the low paid get swallowed up in the "poverty trap".[9] A minimum wage strategy related to tax thresholds and child benefit levels may enable them to burst free from this trap.

A strategy for a minimum wage

Earlier sections have shown that a significant proportion of the workforce are still poor; the proportion would be even larger but for overtime working. If their situation is to be relieved with the introduction of a minimum wage policy, the basis for this must be carefully considered.

Past discussions of a minimum wage policy have been attended by a conceptual confusion which has seriously limited the possibility of assisting the low paid. Previous considerations (by the Interdepartmental Working Party[10] and the National Board for Prices and Incomes[11]) have taken the gross weekly earnings of individuals, however earned, as their unit of analysis for the measurement of "low pay". Thus, a working week of forty hours, and one of forty hours plus five hours overtime, were both included within the boundary of their unit of analysis. No distinction was made concerning the variation in hours that might be worked to obtain a given gross wage, thus making it impossible to distinguish hours worked and rates paid. The unit of analysis embraced two interrelated structures and processes, that of rates of pay and patterns of working hours. As a result people might be "low paid" under their definition, either because they worked long or short hours for a low rate of pay, or because they worked short hours for a high rate of pay. It also excluded many who worked for long hours on low rates, but who obtained high gross wages (the "long hours" problem). In reality the concern was not "low pay" but "low earnings" — a quite different problem, with different possible solutions. With "low earnings" overtime working is seen as one possible solution to the problem, whereas with "low pay" the need to work overtime is part of the problem of inadequate income.

If this confusion is to be avoided, the number of hours worked must be made part of the boundary of the unit of analysis for "low pay". "Low pay" should be examined in terms of what a person is paid for, say, a forty-hour week, and this could be translated into a basic hourly rate to establish a minimum wage policy. Within this notion of "basic rates" is embedded a concept of "normal and fair" working circumstances, closely related to the time of day and week on which the work is carried out. This belief is embodied in the values of the wider society where it is expected that if people are required to work otherwise they are compensated for losing the opportunity to take part in society's normal non-work activities — engaging in hobbies, watching television, attending football matches, sharing evenings and weekends with family and friends, or just plain taking it easy having fairly contributed to the common wealth.

There is evidence that low paid workers will, because of their low rate of pay, tend to work longer than normal hours when they have the opportunity. This was well documented by Whybrew in his study of *Overtime Working in Britain*.[12] He found "that there is much evidence that overtime growth is influenced by relative pay factors, so that it is highest in industries and groups that have low average hourly earnings".

Intervention to establish a statutory minimum wage will result in some labour market reaction. Can a strategy be devised to implement a statutory minimum wage, while minimising possible negative repercussions?

The National Union of Public Employees "are convinced that the first step in the construction of a policy to eliminate low pay must be the acceptance of the principle that there is a level of wages below which nobody should be expected to work".[13] A commitment to redistribute income in favour of the low paid does seem to be the key. For the low paid to gain, especially in the context of limited economic growth, others who are better off would be required to lose something of what they already have, or might expect to have in the near future.

Of importance here is the indiscriminate assistance to those with higher incomes that results from the open-ended system of "tax expenditures". These require urgent reconsideration, especially in the context of current cuts in public expenditure where Treasury conventions of accountancy ignore this revenue foregone by the Exchequer.[14] The crucial context which would limit effects on the unemployment situation is the implementation of the minimum wage legislation during a period of high labour demand, with a government committed to a full employment policy. Even in this scenario, it would need to be introduced with the agreement and co-operation of the government, the Trades Union Congress and the Confederation of British Industry: indeed, it may be appropriate to establish a tripartite Low Incomes Commission.

A tripartite Low Incomes Commission could only operate sensibly in the context of a wider policy commitment by the government to full employment and a statutory minimum wage related to a more redistributive tax and social security system to produce a minimum income relfecting family needs. Within this context a Low Incomes Commission would be concerned, during the initial transitional period (five years), with issues of productivity, capital modernisation, retraining, labour utilisation, and industry wage structures, related to annual minimum wage targets in each industry. Concern with wage structures would need to distinguish between differentials (within bargaining groups) and relativities (between groups). As Pond observes: "Since the low paid tend to be concentrated in industries where earnings generally are relatively low, raising their earnings involves not so much a collapse of differentials as the disturbance of relativities between groups."[15]

It would be especially important for the Commission to establish whether its transitional strategy, working towards a national minimum wage, would be based upon "equal percentage" or "equal money" increases in wage rates, or some combination of the two. And whether differentials and relativities would be maintained in percentage or money terms.

Alternative strategies to a statutory minimum wage
The principal alternatives proposed to a statutory minimum wage and a "New

Beveridge" strategy have been various Negative Income Tax, Tax Credit and Social Dividend schemes. The first two of these are relatively simple extensions of the income tax structure, though there can be complex variations (see A. B. Atkinson).[16] They tend to be relatively conservative in their impact on the redistribution of income; indeed the Green Paper[17] gave most of the projected increase in pay to those above the poverty line.

In contrast, Social Dividend schemes involve a more radical change in the distribution of income in providing a guaranteed minimum income for all regardless of need. These are not without their anomalies, in that in both schemes both the low and high income groups do rather better than those in the middle. As Marshall observes: "the social dividend approach is universal in contrast to the more 'selective' approach of negative rates of taxation (and Tax Credits)".[18] Under a Social Dividend scheme everyone is entitled to a universal payment. All income is then taxed usually at a proportional rate, though this may vary; final income therefore comes in two parts, the social dividend and other post-tax income.

The choice of break-even income level is critical to the success or failure of all these schemes. As Marshall notes: "If the aim of policy is to remove poverty, then the guaranteed minimum allowance must equal the poverty line. But this might mean marginal rates of tax so high that the incentive to seek alternative forms of income from, say, market earnings, might be extremely weak for the low income groups. Yet the alternative of lower rates means a guaranteed minimum less than the poverty line."[18] An extra safety net might still be required, thus perpetuating existing difficulties of means testing and the "poverty trap".

It does not seem possible for these schemes to provide an adequate guaranteed minimum income for all, without also involving high marginal rates of taxation, though some variations may be possible (see Atkinson). Social Dividend schemes have a stronger claim to provide an adequate minimum income guarantee, but as Marshall concludes: "the Social Dividend redistribution (of income) requires a degree of benevolence in terms of both monetary contributions and in attitudes towards defining real income . . . not yet evidenced by a majority of the British electorate".[18] It may be that the same conclusions should be drawn concerning support for a statutory minimum wage, but as was recognised earlier the first step to helping the low paid is an act of political commitment.

We have considered only some of the issues here: what is required is a Special Committee, with broad terms of reference, to draw up a "New Beveridge" Report. It would examine the whole "social division of welfare"[19] involved in the interaction of our tax, social security and occupational welfare systems, as well as the role of a statutory minimum wage.

Just as the original Beveridge Report grew out of concern with the unemployment of the 1930s, and the need for social cohesion based on redistribution, so may the present economic crisis and its growing social unrest provide the context for planning for a future redistribution of income and a more equal society. There was vision and political commitment in 1945, we need fresh resolution and new political commitment for the 1980s.

References
1   Department of Employment, *New Earnings Survey 1981* (HMSO, 1982).
2   Peter Townsend, *Poverty in the United Kingdom*, Chap. 18, "The Low Paid" (Pelican, 1979).
3   Royal Commission on the Distribution of Income and Wealth, *Report No. 6: Lower Incomes*, Cmnd. 7175 (HMSO, 1978); and *Selected Evidence Submitted to the Royal Commission for Report No. 6: Lower Incomes* (HMSO, 1978).
4   Department of Health and Social Security, *Social Security Research*, "The Definition of Poverty" (HMSO, 1979).
5   Department of Employment, *Employees in Employment 1976 and 1978 in Scotland* (unpublished).
6   C. Sandford, C. Pond and R. Walker (eds.), *Taxation and Social Policy* (Heinemann, 1980).
7   D. J. Smith, "How Unemployment Makes the Poor Poorer", in *Policy Studies*, July 1980.
8   A. Sinfield, *What Unemployment Means* (Martin Robertson, 1981).
9   Alan Walker (ed.), *The Poverty of Taxation*; reforming the tax and social security systems, Poverty Pamphlet 56, Child Poverty Action Group, August 1982.
10   Department of Employment and Productivity, *A National Minimum Wage: An Inquiry*, Interdepartmental Working Party (HMSO, 1969).
11   National Board for Prices and Incomes, *General Problems of Low Pay*, Report No. 169, Cmnd. 4648 (HMSO, 1971).
12   E. G. Whybrew, *Overtime Working in Britain*, Research Paper No. 9, Royal Commission on Trade Unions and Employment Associations (HMSO, 1968).
13   A. Fisher and Bernard Dix, *Low Pay and How to End It: A Union View* (Pitman, 1974).
14   Alan Walker (ed.), *Public Expenditure and Social Policy;* an examination of social spending and social priorities (Heinemann, 1982).
15   C. Pond (ed.), *Low Pay Review No. 2*, Low Pay and Unemployment, August 1980.
16   A. B. Atkinson, *Poverty in Britain and the Reform of Social Security* (Cambridge University Press, 1970); and *The Tax Credit Scheme and the Redistribution of Income*, Institute of Fiscal Studies, 1973.
17   Conservative Government Green Paper, *Proposals for a Tax Credit System*, Cmnd. 5116 (HMSO, 1972).
18   G. P. Marshall, *Social Goals and Economic Perspectives* (Penguin, 1980).
19   A. Sinfield, "Analysis in the Social Division of Welfare", in *Journal of Social Policy*, April 1978.

Alistair Grimes

PENSIONERS IN POVERTY

A^T present there are 846,000 people over retirement age in Scotland,[1] a figure that represents nearly 17% of the population. Of these, some 267,000 are over the age of 75 (within which category are an estimated 43,000 over the age of 85).[2] These figures represent a remarkable change from the turn of the century. In 1901 there were only 215,000 people over pensionable age in Scotland, and in the UK as a whole there were 2.4 million pensioners[3] out of a total population of 38 million. In contrast, there were over 12 million people under the age of 16. The 1981 census reveals that there are now 1.16 million under 16s in Scotland (or 23% of the population) and that in the UK the number of under 16s has remained virtually at the 1901 level, whilst the number of pensioners has quadrupled. It is estimated that female pensioners now outnumber girls under 16.[4] Looking ahead to 1991, it is estimated that 18% of the population will be pensioners, compared with 6% in 1901. The present century has seen the average lifespan increase from 40 to 68 for men and from 44 to 74 for women.

These rather crude estimates hide a considerable variation *within* the general pensioner population. For example, though the total number of people over retirement age in Scotland is expected to rise by 5% in the next ten years, there will be a decline of about 29,000 in the number of people aged between 65 and 74. This will be more than offset by dramatic increases in the over 75s. The number of people aged between 75 and 84 will increase by 44,000 (or over 20%) and the number of over 85s will increase by 20,000 (or 49%).

Moreover, these projections hide wide variations within Scotland itself. Thus, within the general 5% increase we find that the Lanark Health Board expects an increase of 21%, whereas the Western Isles expects a decrease of 20%. In a similar way, increases of 39% and 37% in the number of over 75s in the Forth Valley and Lanark respectively will be accompanied by increases of only 10% in Highland and 8% in Shetland.[5]

A final point to be remembered is that in all of these categories women outnumber men; in the over 75s by 2:1 and in the over 85s by 3:1.

Every investigation into the condition of the elderly has concluded that old age brings not only increased physical frailty, but also poverty. Though pensioners form a sixth of the population, they provide more than a third of those who live at or below the official poverty line.[6] According to the figures produced by the Department of Health and Social Security (DHSS) there were 145,000 Scottish pensioners receiving supplementary pension in 1982. To this should be added dependants who are themselves pensioners and those who are eligible for supplementary pension but who do not claim it. Using an extrapolation from UK figures, the former may be estimated at anything between 15,000 and 30,000 people. The most recent estimate given for the latter, that of the Social Security Advisory Committee in its first report (1981),[7] was of over one million claimants — of whom two-thirds are pensioners. This would give a figure of 60,000 or so for Scotland. Put together, these figures would suggest that between 220,000 and 240,000 Scottish pensioners are on the poverty line.

One major reason for this scandalous state of affairs is the failure of the State pension to reach the target set for it on the Beveridge Report. Put simply, Beveridge believed that:

> Any plan of Social Security worthy of its name . . . means providing as an essential part of the plan, a pension on retirement from work which is enough for subsistence, even though the pensioner has no other resources whatsoever.[8]

But the level of pension is still *below* that of the long-term rate for Supplementary Benefit. Thus any household that is solely dependent upon a State pension will be automatically entitled to Supplementary Benefit (or a rent/rate rebate).

Along with other groups of people dependent upon State benefits alone, pensioners have suffered due to the decision of the government to uprate those benefits in line with prices, rather than in line with prices *or* incomes, *whichever was the greater*, as had been the practice under the previous administration. The real, but largely unspoken, justification for this, is that if differentials are to be maintained between those in and out of work, and real income is not rising, then the only alternative is to cut the living standards of those who are unable to work. The *public* justification for this is that benefits can only increase at a rate that is in keeping with present economic performance, or, as Lord Mansfield put it:

> No one stands to gain more from (the government's determination to put the country on the right (sic) economic road) than the elderly. . . .[9]

The good Lord is, however, mistaken, since if the economy does recover and real standards rise (in terms of wages outstripping prices), then pensioners will fall *further behind* those who are wage earners. This marks something of a conceptual breakthrough as far as the word "gain" is concerned. The issue is made slightly more complex by the failure of the ordinary Retail Price Index to reflect pensioners' actual expenditure. As the 1981 edition of *Social Trends* makes clear, inflation for "pensioner households" has, from 1966-79, been at a higher rate than the RPI.

Certainly, radical measures would need to be taken in order to alleviate the poverty of those pensioners who are dependent upon the State. Even the new pension scheme, introduced in April 1978, will not entirely solve the problem, for it is tied to the level of earnings (and will not help the low paid), and will do nothing to help those who are due to retire over the next twenty years.

The inadequacy of the present level of supplementary pension is shown by the large number of pensioners who currently receive either weekly additions or single payments from the DHSS. The 1979 report from the Supplementary Benefits Commission showed that over 80% of pensioners on supplementary pension were getting a weekly addition, mainly for help with heating.[10] In 1977 Scottish pensioners also received over 40,000 single payments (averaging £27) or about a quarter of all such payments in Scotland.[11]

It is, perhaps, worth ending our comments on the value of pensions by repeating that in the UK the retirement pension is still around a *third* of the average male manual wage, a figure that has remained the same since 1948. This figure compares unfavourably with other countries in the EEC. For example, the French pension is 50% (more for couples) of average earnings, the West German pension is 52.5% of average earnings, the Dutch pension ranges between 42% and 61% of average earnings and the Belgian pension ranges from 60% to 65% of average earnings.[12]

In some cases, the State pension is supplemented by an occupational pension. Though there has indeed been a growth in such pension schemes, their importance should not be overstated. By 1979 something like half the current workforce was covered by such schemes, but this, of course, is of little relevance to those already in retirement. Furthermore, the level of such a pension can differ substantially depending on age, class and former occupation. Elderly women, for example, are likely to be excluded from such schemes because of their poor paid employment record. In 1978 the average amount received by those with occupational pensions was still less than £10 per week.[13] Low though these amounts are, they can be sufficient to move the person just above the Supplementary Benefit level and thus disqualify them from getting other benefits that are conferred by that scheme.

One well-known problem associated with poverty and the elderly is the reluctance to claim supplementary, or other, benefits on the grounds that they constitute "charity". This reluctance has already been mentioned in connection with the 60,000 or so Scottish pensioners who are entitled to Supplementary Benefit, but who do not claim it. It is also hinted at in the low take-up of rent and rate rebates or allowances in those sectors where the elderly predominate — such as the private rented sector. Here the take-up rate is only half that of the public sector.[14] An example of this attitude is illustrated in an Age Concern report from 1974, where an interviewee stated: "I'm not down to a brass tack yet — I can still hold my head above water. I just have the pension. I don't want to take the Social Security if I can help it — it's just like taking charity."[15]

But what of those pensioners with incomes above the level of Supplementary Benefit? The first point to be made is that retirement brings about a dramatic fall in income. According to the Family Expenditure Survey for 1979, the average income for the elderly was about half of that for those aged between 50 and 64 even after tax and National Insurance had been taken into account — £56 as opposed to £108.[16] Weekly expenditure per head was also lower amongst the elderly at £31 compared with £42.[17] This general figure tends to hide the wide differences within the elderly population itself. According to *Profiles of the Elderly*[18] in 1977 the median income for the 50-59 age group was £102 per week and for the 60-64 age group £72 per week. But for the 65-69s it had already fallen to £42 and for the 70-74s it was down to £33. Right at the bottom, the over 75s had a median income of only £29 per week. This contrast of lifestyles within the elderly has been examined by Mark Abrams,[19] who has found that a one-person pensioner household, mainly dependent upon State benefits, will spend only 60% of the amount consumed by a similar pensioner household which has other sources of income. The former group will spend as little as £3 per week on leisure goods and services, including newspapers, alcohol and tobacco, holidays, transport, the cinema and the theatre, compared with £9 for the latter group. The story is virtually the same for households containing two retired persons. Put another way, the bottom quarter of income groups contains 60% of all adults over 65. Women emerge from this picture in a far worse position than men. Over 80% of single pensioner households are women and over 80% of the lowest income groups are also women.

The battle for survival endured by many pensioners can be seen by looking at the proportion of income that is spent on three essential commodities — food, fuel and housing. Where the head of the household is retired, 57% of the weekly income is spent on these three commodities. In the poorest elderly households, 70% of the income is taken up in this way.[30] The poorest, who as we have seen tend to be over 75, are also less likely to have consumer durables than even their fellow pensioners. For example, a study by A. Hunt found that whilst over half elderly households had a washing machine and three-quarters had a fridge, the figures for over 75s were 33% and 53% respectively.[21]

The comparatively low incomes of many elderly people are not the result of disaster or misfortune, but are directly related to their loss of employment and the status and level of reward they enjoyed whilst in work. Thus those who have had low-paid jobs, or have been subject to periods of illness and unemployment, are unlikely to have been able to put away considerable savings, to join an occupational pension scheme or to invest their earnings in capital assets (such as a house). Estimates on the level of assets amongst the elderly vary. Though it is true that a number of pensioners can live a comfortable life supported by their investments, for many more such a cushion does not exist. Peter Townsend in his *Poverty in the United Kingdom* has claimed that a quarter of pensioners had no assets. An Age Concern study also found that what assets there were could often be explained as money put aside to cover the cost of burial — even if this entailed cutting back on essentials.[22]

Lack of assets coupled with low income means that the elderly are crucially dependent upon access to other resources, including those resources provided by the "social wage" and public expenditure in general. There is a common, if unanalysed, assumption that it is quite acceptable for the elderly to have lower incomes and fewer resources on the grounds that they have fewer (and smaller) needs. There is little reason to accept this view of the matter; for it is just as plausible to suggest that the elderly would benefit greatly from being able to spend more on, or make greater use of, public transport, heating, holidays, furniture and even more suitable clothes. Retirement is, after all, a comparatively recent invention, and it seems hard to both cut older people off from their main source of income and assume that because you have done this that their needs are, therefore, fewer! Thus it is arguable that the elderly benefit greatly from public expenditure on such resources as libraries, museums, subsidised public transport and other public amenities; conversely, of course, they suffer when such expenditure is cut.

I shall end this brief survey by looking in slightly more detail at three areas that affect pensioners in particular: heating, housing and residential/community care.

The only national survey of temperature levels in the households of the elderly was carried out by Malcolm Wicks in 1972.[23] Even though this was a fairly mild winter, he found that nearly 10% of his sample were "at risk"—that is to say, within 0.5°C of the medical definition of hypothermia. This would mean 70,000-80,000 Scottish pensioners are at risk each winter. Though hypothermia is rarely the sole cause of death, it is an important contributory factor in some 3,000-5,000 deaths each year. Furthermore, Professor Markus of Strathclyde University has argued that a spell of cold weather will be followed by an increase in hospital admissions for cold-related illnesses, especially in the very young and very old.[24] Wicks found that half his sample had morning living room temperatures below that specified as a minimum for shops and offices and that only 10% had temperatures at or above the DHSS recommended level. On a more subjective note, even where the pensioner claimed to be warm enough, the interviewer often found the room "uncomfortably cold". The most common reason given for not having more heating was the high cost of fuel. The findings of Wicks and others have been confirmed by many smaller scale studies. Primrose and Smith[25] found that a selection of elderly people in Glasgow had few cases of hypothermia, but many cases living at temperatures below their "comfort zone".

Scotland, of course, already has a number of climatic disadvantages here. The work of Professor Markus has suggested that it can take 20% more fuel to heat a house in Glasgow to the same temperature as an identical house in Bristol, and 30% more in Aberdeen.[26] The other side of the equation is that fuel prices have increased very rapidly over the last ten years, and are expected to continue to do so for the foreseeable future. The Department of Energy, for example, expects fuel prices to *double in real terms* by the year 2000. Thus the elderly find themselves having to spend a large *proportion* of their income on fuel in order to stay warm. Evidence suggests that whilst an average family spends $5\frac{1}{2}\%$ of its income on fuel, pensioner households spend anything between 11% and 14% — twice as much.[27] But despite this fact, they are still able to spend less in *absolute* terms — pensioners spend only 77% of the average amount on fuel.[28]

Present measures to help the elderly, either by giving them more money, or by helping them to make better use of the money they are using, are the culmination of a series of panic-induced *ad hoc* schemes rather than a well-thought out attempt to come to grips with either end of the problem. Extra money has tended to go to those who are over 70 and receiving Supplementary Benefit, a move which has tended to work against those who are just above the Supplementary Benefit level, who are not claiming, or who are on other benefits such as rent/rate rebate. There is also no particular justification, either medical or social, for drawing a line at 70 for automatic heating additions. The various discount schemes used in the past have suffered from similar faults, and none of the measures presented has ever looked like an adequate substitute for a realistic increase in the basic pension itself.

Though some pensioners do live in modern, well-insulated houses, there is a substantial section that lives in old, poorly insulated housing, especially in the private rented sector. Some 75p in every pound spent on heating is wasted in a badly insulated house, so the importance of improvements here is obvious. Scottish local authorities have started on a ten-year programme to bring all of their houses up to a set standard, with a theoretical commitment to giving priority to the elderly. The actual state of affairs is patchy to say the least,[29] given the special severity of cuts in housing and the difficulty of identifying pensioner households outside of special categories such as amenity or sheltered housing. In the private sector, only £800,000 out of the £3 million allocated for Scotland was spent last year[30] and there is evidence from the success of local insulation projects, aimed at the elderly and low paid, that such groups have not been particularly forward in using this money. It would, perhaps, be unfair to suggest that although sympathetic noises are made about pensioners in legislation on insulation, they are of minor importance, since the main purpose of such legislation is to save energy. Since, as we have seen, pensioners are low energy users and would probably benefit from using more rather than less energy, they are not of central concern.

Over 90% of pensioners still live in "mainstream" housing as ordinary members of the community. Nevertheless they may need housing adapted in special ways to cope with particular difficulties. This is likely to become an increasing need in the 1980s as the number of frail elderly in the population grows. The ideal situation would be one in which there was flexibility of response within transfer and allocation policies, enabling the elderly to move closer to their younger relatives, or enabling groups of unrelated elderly people to share accommodation. Unfortunately, there is a current shortage of 1/2-apartment council housing which will make it more difficult for older people to move into more suitable accommodation. Some authorities, such as Dumbarton, recognise that there is a high "under occupancy" rate in houses inhabited by the elderly, but do not have the resources to do anything about it. The classic example of a stock "mis-match" in Scotland is in Glasgow, where it is expected that by 1984 there will be an overall surplus of 30,000 council houses and an almost identical shortage of 1/2-apartment houses.[31]

A second area of importance within housing is the provision of sheltered and amenity housing. The former type has the support of a warden service and, more importantly perhaps, is where the frail elderly can be helped by their fitter contemporaries. In this sense, sheltered housing is not an alternative to, say, residential care in a home, but part of a wider spectrum of care that is suitable for those at risk but not in need of full-time nursing or supervision.

The present position is that there is less than 35% of the estimated need for sheltered housing catered for in Scotland.[32] Only two Districts (Shetland, Cumbernauld and Kilsyth) have the required level of provision and there is little cause for believing that this position will change in the next few years. Even on the most optimistic assumptions[33] there will be less than two-thirds of the necessary places by 1984 and there is every reason to believe that such optimism is unjustified. Glasgow, for example, will need to create 4,000 places by 1984, a task complicated by the fact that its present stock of sheltered housing is badly distributed — a mere 1% being in those peripheral schemes that contain 13% of its houses. Likewise, Edinburgh provided under half of the required places in 1980 and will still be well short of the target by 1984.[34] These shortages are especially frustrating given the apparent popularity of such housing and long waiting lists; such facts may make current guidelines *underestimates* of need. A further factor worthy of comment is that some District Councils seem to wish to put the provision of sheltered housing more and more into the hands of housing associations. This has a number of implications. Not only may councils be seen to be passing the buck at a time when central government is exhorting them to pay more attention to those with special housing needs, but there is also the question of access to sheltered housing run by housing associations. The procedures here are too often little known and understood.

Finally, there is the issue of community and residential care. With the expected increases in the number of frail elderly, the development of such services are of vital importance. Yet there have been and will continue to be, cutbacks in domiciliary service and day services such as home helps and meals on wheels. Community care is of special importance to those who are alone and without family support — one-third of women over 75 have never had any children (more than 60,000 in Scotland). Whilst not wishing to underestimate the role that can (and should) be played by voluntary agencies, neighbourhood groups and community organisations, it needs to be stressed that such groups operate best when they are supported by strong statutory services, rather than being seen as replacements for such services. Likewise with residential care; though increased sheltered and amenity housing should help remove those cases where hospital or residential care is inappropriate back into the community, there will still be the need for increased spending in some areas of residential care, such as mental health. It is estimated that there are 45,000 Scottish pensioners suffering from dementia, 23,000 in a severe form.[35] A report by the Programme Planning Group of the Scottish Health Service in 1979 recommended expenditure of £44 million in this area over the next five years.

Increasing the living standards of the elderly is something that we all too easily support and yet consistently fail to act upon. It ought not to be beyond the power of any future government to increase that basic level of pensions above the poverty line by relating them more realistically to average earnings. The elderly do not want charity, but they have a right to expect a fair deal at the end of their working lives. Ours can be a dark and selfish culture — one that finds a perfect reflection in the Thatcher government — cold, unfeeling, utilitarian and unwilling to hear the calls of any except the powerful. It is no accident that unlike so-called "underdeveloped" countries we do not value the old for their wisdom or for their unquantifiable but unique contribution to the life of the community. And as we cheat the elderly out of a decent standard of living and their place in the decisions of the community, so we cheat ourselves and our children.

References

1 1981 Census.
2 1981 Census and Registrar General's 1976 based population projection.
3 *Social Trends* No. 11, 1981 (HMSO, London), Table 1.2.
4 Ibid.
5 *Report on Services for the Elderly with Mental Disability in Scotland*, Programme Planning Group of the Scottish Health Service Planning Council (HMSO, London, 1979), Appendix B.
6 The "poverty line" is understood here as the level of Supplementary Benefit. Those with incomes up to 40% above that level are on "the margins of poverty".
7 *First Report of the Social Security Advisory Committee* (HMSO, London, 1981), 7.
8 *Social Insurance and Allied Services* (HMSO, London, 1942), para. 239.
9 Speech to the AGM of Age Concern Scotland, 15th September 1979.
10 *Supplementary Benefits Commission Annual Report, 1979* (HMSO, London, 1980), Table 16.2.
11 "Note by the DHSS on some Scottish aspects of the (Supplementary Benefits) review" Planning Exchange meeting in Dundee, 6th November 1978.
12 Information supplied by Age Concern England.
13 S. Lloyd, "Poverty and Income Maintenance", in *Research Highlights No. 3;* Developing Services for the Elderly (Aberdeen University, 1982), 80.
14 D. Jordan, "Poverty and the Elderly", in *An Ageing Population*, ed. Carver & Liddiard (Hodder and Staughton, London, 1978), 172.
15 *The Attitudes of the Elderly and Retired*, Age Concern, 1974, 64.
16 *Family Expenditure Survey, 1979* (HMSO, London, 1980), Table 46.
17 Ibid, Tables 41 and 42.
18 *Profiles of the Elderly—Their Standards of Living* (Revised Edition), Age Concern, 1979, 8-9.
19 In *Research Highlights*, op. cit., 60-1.
20 *Family Expenditure Survey*, 1979, op. cit., Table 43.
21 Quoted in Lloyd, op. cot., 76.
22 op. cit., 82.
23 M. Wicks, *Old and Cold: hypothermia and social policy* (Heinemann, London, 1978).
24 BBC TV "Current Account", 15th January 1981.
25 W. Primrose and L. Smith, "Oral and Environmental Temperatures in a Scottish Urban Geriatric Population, *Journal of Clinical Experimental Gerontology*, 4(2), 1982, 151-65.
26 T. Markus, "Fuel Poverty and Scottish Homes", *Architect's Journal*, 3rd May 1979, 1077-82.
27 *Family Expenditure Survey on|Fuel*, Department of Energy, 1977.
28 Ibid.
29 See P. Taylor and A. Grimes, *Lagging Behind: an investigation into public sector insulation programmes*, Scottish Consumer Council/Scottish Fuel Poverty Action Group (forthcoming).
30 *Scottish Housing Statistics*, 1981/2.
31 See Glasgow District Council, *Housing Plan* 1979-84.
32 Need is based upon the assessment of 50 places per 1,000 elderly population for sheltered housing and 100 places for amenity housing. These targets were based upon surveys carried out over 20 years ago and may, therefore, not reflect the current situation. They are certainly not overestimates!
33 A full survey of the position in Scotland up to March 1980 and projections for 1983 can be found in D. Clark, *Sheltered Housing for the Elderly in Scotland*, Scottish Federation of Housing Associations, 1981.
34 Ibid.
35 *Services for the Elderly*, op. cit., 11.

Kay Carmichael

FAMILY POVERTY

EVERYONE carries in their head an idea of a family. This idea is usually based on a stereotype, pushed at us by advertising agencies, of a father, a mother and two children. The same advertising gives us an image of the couple in their early thirties with two healthy children in the pre-teen years living in a modern well-furnished house. There is no anxiety except on the part of the mother deciding which soap powder or convenience food she should use to preserve health and happiness. The only poverty demonstrated is spiritual.

What is the reality?

First, there are many families where there are no children. We call these households but they are nevertheless families: two elderly folk whose children have left or who may never have had children, an old lady and her daughter on whom she is dependent who may indeed have given up work to care for her, a woman and her severely handicapped adult son, a mentally handicapped brother and sister living together — these are families. The family is any group which is bound together, not only by blood, but by emotional and economic ties and part of whose function is to sustain and support its members in face of the stresses of the wider society.

Even if we concentrate on families with children our sterotype immediately breaks down. Many of these families have only one parent — at least 10%. In some areas of Scotland as many as 25% of the children have experienced the break-up of their parents' marriage. The total number of children in one-parent families is around 150,000. Of the children in Scottish families, many have parents who are sick or unemployed or they themselves are handicapped. 31% of single-parent families live below the poverty line.

Family poverty is a major problem, which will increase with rising unemployment and as marriages with children continue to break down. While these numbers grow, more and more children will be living at supplementary benefit levels. All unemployed families where the parents continue to be out of work, and about half of all one-parent families, end up on supplementary benefit. One recent study, *The Cost of a Child*, by David Piachaud, attempted to work out the minimum costs of raising a child in Britain today.[1] His conclusion was that "supplementary benefit scale rates for children need to be increased by about one half if they are to provide genuinely for even the minimum requirements of a child".

Families on supplementary benefit have particular difficulties. Because their basic income is so low, they spend a substantially higher proportion of their budget on such basic necessities as housing, fuel and food. This means that they are able to spend less than the average family on durable goods, transport and services. Supplementary benefit families have fewer durable goods than any other group of families. This means there are fewer telephones, washing machines, fridges, cars available to them. They travel less, make less use of restaurants, cinemas, hairdressers or clubs. Families with children are less likely to have savings and are more frequently in debt.

But the families who have most economic difficulties are the unemployed who have exhausted their contributory benefit and move on to supplementary benefit. They are financially worse off than the single-parent family or the family of the chronic sick. This is because they are never allowed to qualify for the long-term benefit rate which all other groups get after being on SB for two years. Their weekly income can be as much as 25% lower than the other groups although their needs are the same. It is as if every government is determined to punish the unemployed: the goal is to drive them back to work; the fear is that they will settle down to being unemployed. The irony is that there are no jobs for them to take. In Dundee in July 1981 there were 15,168 people for 304 vacancies. Underlying all this is the fact that the scale rates are too low for anyone on benefit to live a tolerable life.

David Piachaud has updated the Rowntree enquiry (1937), which attempted to assess "the cost of the various items necessary for the maintenance of Physical Efficiency" for a family of a man, woman and three children.[2] Rowntree presented a most basic estimate even at the modest expectations of living standards of the 1930s. His figures would translate at £44.50 per week. The SB provision for an unemployed family of that size was £56.50 per week. So the dole now provides about one-quarter more than Rowntree's minimum requirements for the maintenance of physical efficiency. But since the mid-1930s average earnings have risen forty times and retail prices by twenty times. In real terms average material standards have doubled since the 1930s. Even with the most careful budgeting, life at SB levels is described by Piachaud as "basic and bleak".

Studies on the standard of living of the unemployed show that those with greatest difficulty managing were those with children. A study by Burghes of sixty-five families living on supplementary benefit concluded: "Life on supplementary benefit is by no means the comfortable life that too many people believe it to be. Indeed, it is a bleak life."[3] The Supplementary Benefits Commission reported in 1977: "The supplementary benefits scheme provides, particularly for families with children, incomes which are barely adequate to meet their needs at a level which is consistent with normal participation in the life of the relatively Wealthy Society in which we live."[4]

In recent years all families with children, including those with a wage earner, have fallen behind all other households in financial terms, because of changes in prices, taxation and child benefits. From 1965 to 1979, the tax burden of a single person increased by 36%, while for a married couple with two children the increase was 144%. In the years since 1948, pensions and other main benefits have increased twenty-two times; child benefits have increased only ten times.

The average weekly wage of full-time adult male manual workers in Scotland can no longer be specifically indentified as a cause of family poverty. The differences between regions has been declining and manual workers in Scotland now earn on average slightly more than their English counterparts. The distinctive factors which give us higher incidences of family poverty in certain areas are higher unemployment, higher numbers of children in families, and the failure to take up a bewildering range of benefits. The most important of these are Family Income Supplement (FIS), free school meals, rent and rate rebates: claiming these can add several pounds to a weekly budget. Others — free prescriptions, dental and optical care, educational allowances — can affect the family's quality of life.

Many families suffer unnecessary hardship by not claiming benefits they are entitled to. The reasons are complex. Some do not have the necessary information; some are ashamed or too proud to claim, believing that if they are working they shouldn't be asking for charity; some are embarrassed or lack the skills to fill in complicated forms.

Another problem is that an increase in wages can lift the worker out of the benefit range so although his pay is higher he is no better off. This is known as the "poverty trap".

It would be bad enough if financial difficulty was the only result of poverty, but it can sometimes bring crippling, physical, emotional and psychological handicaps. The primary purpose of the family, as well as satisfying the sexual, emotional and social needs of the partners, has been to produce and socialise the children who will take over the organisation and ordering of our society from us. We live with the assumption that the human race has to continue.

The first difficulty poor families face is the production of healthy living children. Even in the journey from conception to birth the odds are too great for too many children in Scotland: pre-natal and infant mortality rates are still distressingly high in relation to the rest of Europe. This reflects the poor health of poor women as well as inadequate medical care during pregnancy and around the period of childbirth, and factors such as overcrowding, unemployment, inadequate services in the local area and the poverty of the families involved — most of whom will be living in the poverty ghettoes of our cities — can clearly be identified as influencing the mortality rate. Some infant deaths may still be inevitable for genetic or other factors, but deaths from poverty can be avoided.

If a child survives, it will learn about the world into which it has been born. First of all about comfort or the lack of it. This can be about food and warmth (young babies need warmer houses than the rest of us and that costs money) or it can be about the less definable but equally real communications of anxiety and security. Poor parents tend to be more anxious and less relaxed for obvious reasons: every day is a struggle. Babies living in poverty are at greater risk than other groups of children of being admitted to hospital in the first year of their lives; mothers in poverty are more susceptible to depressive illness. Children living in poverty are at greater risk of violence at the hands of their parents, since they can become the scapegoats for frustration and anger. Men and, increasingly, women can seek release and escape from the dreariness of their lives in drink, and in that state their aggression is turned on those closest to them. Wives and children are the most common victims. Such violence is common where groups of families live together in poverty, is a direct result of that state, and lays the base of later violence in that community which takes the form of mugging and vandalism. It is a language learned in childhood and which will in many cases be repeated by those children when they become parents. While it is not only poor parents who abuse their children (many middle-class parents do the same), the stresses of the poverty life are a significant factor in the high numbers of children at risk.

Lack of money deprives people, more than anything else, of choice. It's easy buying second-hand clothes if you know you *can* go to Marks & Spencer, walking if you have the money in your purse to take a bus, saying "no" to a request from children for sweets if you know you can afford to buy them. What is difficult is when the opportunities for choice are absent from all areas of life: no new clothes, no nights out, no room for manoeuvre if the budget is to balance. All this with a constant sense of failure at not having what other people seem to have, the necessities defined by Adam Smith: "By necessities I understand not only the commodities which are indispensably necessary for the support of life, but whatever the custom of the country renders it indecent for creditable people even in the lowest order to be without."[5]

Commercial television provides an image of what our society considers to be necessities: new clothes, new furniture, new everything. The constant sense of failure is, of course, communicated to the children, who in turn carry it onto the streets and into the schools. Ultimately they find some way of getting self-esteem through an alternative set of values.

No one can feel a failure indefinitely without ending up in a mental hospital. Many poor people do. There is a high correlation between poverty and mental hospital admissions, just as there is with poor health, low life expectation and bad teeth. Income partly determines where we live, which in turn determines the quality and quantity of available services. In an overworked slum practice, patients do not have the information middle-class people would assume was their right. The same applied to dental and optical services — notoriously inadequate for children of the poor. Most poor people live without a car, and services for their children need to be within pram-pushing distance.

Since there is a correlation between poverty and unskilled and semi-skilled status, children of the poor have had less access to choice in jobs. They tend not to have been given the opportunity to develop the social skills which would get them jobs in shops or offices, nor do they have the contacts and tradition which would help them to become tradesmen. They are unlikely to have had holidays, even to have been out of their own city, never mind abroad, and are therefore quite constricted in their view of the world and the possibility of alternative life styles.

Professor Donnison has shown that in Scottish industrial cities there are greater gulfs between the social classes than in similar English cities. The well-off middle class do much better than the well-off working class, who do much better than the poor, comparatively. For children the gulf between the classes is mostly too great to cross. Boyle describes how even in the same street the gulf between children in posh and poor closes was too wide for communication.[6] Scotland's cities are more deeply divided and the working class is more deeply divided than in either England or Wales.

The crippling effects of poverty are most evident in situations of crisis. In a family with some spare money, the death of a parent, an illness, or desertion of a parent can be handled in a variety of ways. For the poor the solution too often has to be to place the children into the care of the local authority. Lack of confidence in the parents distorts their relationship with authority figures and reduces their capacity to take responsibility for their lives and the lives of their children. It can then be difficult to reunite the family.

A distinction is made between the "respectable" and the "non-respectable" families of the poor. It derives from the Poor Law separation of "deserving" and "non-deserving" poor which still dominates our thinking. It is rooted in the work ethic: those who work and pay their own bills are clean and respectable even though they are poor. Those who do not work are not normally respectable unless they are old or convincingly sick. Healthy families with children but not work are thought to deserve no respect. These views are embedded in our social values and it is not surprising to see them reflected in the views and behaviour of authority figures from the health and social security services, from education and social security and even from the Church. They can also be found among landlords, shopkeepers, some politicians and sections of the media.

The poor are, as a result, constantly on the defensive, learn to expect little and trust no one until they have proved themselves. Identified by some as the "Lumpen proletariat" they rarely vote, are sceptical about political promises and retreat into apathy. They see what happens to their children is what happened to them. The children see what has happened to their parents and assume that will be their own future. Sporadic outbursts of anger on the streets are effectively put down. No one wants to hear the message.

What is the answer? There are two possibilities. One is ameliorative but important and possible, the second is radical, difficult and unlikely unless we have a great deal of courage.

The ameliorative possibility is simply to direct more money to families with children. This can be done by taxation policies, pricing policies for necessities like fuel, but most of all by directing specific income into the family through the instrument of child benefits. The amounts need to be significantly larger than any we pay currently: our child support for larger families in particular is lower than any country in Europe other than the Republic of Ireland. The Labour and trade union movements would have to abandon their long-held view that the standard of living for the children in a family should be centrally dependent on the breadwinner's wage, and that child benefits hold down wages. At least they should examine the facts. The child of an unemployed labourer has exactly the same needs as the child of a skilled tradesman or a bank manager. Fiscal policies and child benefit can be used to achieve a more egalitarian situation than exists at present. At the same time compensatory services for poor families with children have to be encouraged: they should have better than the average service from health and other services. We need to create an environment in which poor families would at least be treated with respect, courtesy and politeness. That is possible if we have the will.

A radical solution is also possible: we could attempt to abolish poverty. It is made by the organisation of our resources and could be unmade: it is not an act of God but an act of human beings. From the time of the Industrial Revolution we have used families of the poor as a stagnant pool of cheap unskilled labour which could flow into industry in periods of high activity and be sacked in times of recession. They produced children who could move into the dead-end jobs for school leavers and women for casual cleaning. No one has had any sense of responsibility to them; no union was interested in organising their casual labour: the nature of their jobs did not encourage the development of a political consciousness.

We now live in a post-industrial society and modern capitalism has no need for that reserve army. Its members were kept reasonably malleable in the past by occasional spells of work which relieved the poverty and monotony and kept some hope alive in the young. That time has passed. These men, women and children will not disappear: they are our responsibility. If we do not do something, when the message ultimately gets through that there is no future for them, they will try to make one for themselves, and their methods may be more destructive than constructive.

The poor need the opportunity to participate in a society whose clear aims are to abolish wealth and privilege and to redistribute income and jobs, resources, opportunities and power. This can only happen if the people reading this are willing to share their income, jobs, resources, opportunities and power. The poor have a great deal to teach us: they may be trapped in poverty but we are often caught in traps of bureaucracies, achievement, patronage and outmoded values.

We can no longer accept the poor as a permanent feature of urban societies. We can make a new world with new values. It is already struggling to be born out of technological changes and the resulting chaos. Changes will be painful for those of us who have been privileged in the old order and who have held views and assumptions that now need to be questioned.

To achieve any measure of equality and justice, an alternative society would need to make the income range for our population much narrower, which would require a new definition of an incomes policy. The redistribution of resources through free transport or subsidised holidays would have to be seen as a part of that incomes policy. Access to these would be part of the social wage along with health, housing and other social services. Creation of new jobs, job sharing and voluntary unemployment would require radical alternations in trade union structures and attitudes to make them relevant to work styles of the future rather than to those of the nineteenth century. The financial distinction between the employed and the unemployed will largely have to disappear. When all unpleasant tasks can be handled by machines it may well be a privilege to work for its own sake and satisfaction.

Personal dignity has to be separated from the paid-work experience. In order to achieve a more just society our overall standard of living might have to fall and we should not be afraid to face that possibility. The important reservation would be that we should share burdens equally among us and that we should protect the weak rather than the powerful.

References
1 *The Cost of a Child.* Child Poverty Action Group (London, 1979).
2 *Living from Hand to Mouth*, Child Poverty Action Group (London, 1980).
3 Ibid.
4 *Report of the Supplementary Benefit Commission*, 1977.
5 Adam Smith, *The Wealth of Nations* (Edinburgh, 1776).
6 Jimmy Boyle, *A Sense of Freedom* (Edinburgh, 1977).

Eveline Hunter

WOMEN AND POVERTY

The changing family

WOMEN are more likely to be living in poverty than men. That may sound bald but this essay will, hopefully, illustrate that women tend to earn less money, are entitled to fewer social security benefits, still have more restricted access to childcare and other social services and still are expected to carry the main burden of family care. Under present Conservative government policies even the small gains women have made in recent decades are being undermined.

One of the most striking aspects of poverty among women is the extent to which it is disguised in official statistics. The census allocates women's social class according to the occupation of their husbands. Poverty is usually defined in terms of low income male heads of households, employment in terms of economically active males. The Equal Opportunities Commission in their evidence to the Royal Commission on the Distribution of Income and Wealth put it this way.‡ "The married woman especially disappears from view within such categories as 'household' or 'head of household'. The whole question of economic disadvantage among women members of the labour force could be more clearly displayed if women always appeared as a category in the statistical studies."

Why has so little work been done until recently on women's economic disadvantages? The answer is obvious — women have always been, and still are, primarily considered as wives and mothers.

The notion that each woman has, or ought to have, a man to provide for her has shaped not only our legal system but also the provision of social services. It is well summed up in the words of the Beveridge Report which in 1942 laid the basis of Britain's social security system. "The attitude of the housewife to gainful employment outside the home is not and should not be the same as that of the single woman. She has other duties."[2]

Even in 1942 that narrow view of women's role in the family and in the economy was unrealistic. In the changing social and economic patterns of the 1980s it is absurd and extremely detrimental to those households not fitting the "traditional" mould. Yet now we are witnessing a government, led paradoxically by a woman, which is actually promoting the values of the last century, a government which is advocating the return of women to the home and family hearth. Mrs Thatcher makes no bones about the role she believes women should be taking in this beleaguered economy. On women are to fall the main burdens of caring for the sick, the elderly and the young.

Ten years ago in the height of the campaign for equal pay legislation it would have been unthinkable for a major party leader to publicly voice these views. Labour and Conservative politicians alike supported the idea of equality legislation, although the Conservative proposals for reform were more "conservative" than the legislation finally passed. This does not mean, however, that ten years ago politicians of both parties fully accepted women's changing role. There has always been on both sides a claim to support the traditional family as the cornerstone of British life.

Often these were no more than worthy statements, such as James Callaghan's statement in 1977 that "The family is the most important unit of our community. . . . Our aim is straightforward: it is to strengthen the stability and the quality of family life in Britain . . .". Or Patrick Jenkin's words that same year that "The family . . . has been the foundation for virtually every free society known to history".

These apparently inoffensive words had deeper roots than were immediately obvious. Only two years later Patrick Jenkin, the new Conservative Secretary for Health and Social Services at the time, felt able to say on television, "If the Good Lord intended us to have equal rights and to go out to work and to behave equally, He really wouldn't have created man and woman".[3] Similarly, Lynda Chalker, then Conservative Under-Secretary for Social Security, said, "Maybe in years to come, the country will look at the labour market and decide that perhaps it would be better for women with children to stay at home". That was in 1979 shortly after the Conservatives took power. Her words were prophetic. The "years to come" may be with us already, under a much stronger and more aggressive Conservative government in 1983.

It is not hard to see why Mrs Thatcher is now promoting a return to Victorian values. With massive cuts in spending on social services, health and housing, someone has to be left with the burden of caring that was once partly done by the state. At the same time the rising unemployment figures leave a weakened, frightened workforce vulnerable to the suggestion that women should give up work to help the unemployed young, male breadwinners and redundant middle-aged male workers who cannot find other jobs.

I am not arguing against the traditional family unit where the father earns a living and the mother stays at home to look after the house and children. For some people that arrangement can be a source of comfort and support. But the growing number of households which do not conform to the expected mould suffer severely because of social and economic policies which are geared towards an increasingly outdated form of family life.

According to the General Household Survey, married couples (with or without children) form only 67% of British households and only 5% of workers are married men with two children and a wife at home. There are about one million single-parent households in Britain, according to an estimate by the National Council for One Parent Families.[4] 82% of these families are headed by a woman.

These single-parent figures relate to 1979 and would probably be much higher now. The divorce rate in Scotland is now running at about 10,000 a year[5] and is likely to rise because of the recent liberalisation of divorce procedures in Scotland. Already one in three marriages end in divorce and the Study Commission on the Family estimates that one in five or six children in Britain will witness their parents' divorce before they reach the age of sixteen.[6] This does not include those whose parents live apart without resort to the divorce courts. Whether we like it or not, marriage in our society is often a temporary arrangement, whatever the intentions of the parties at the outset.

At the same time more couples are choosing to live together outside of legal marriage. In 1970 only 3% of couples getting married had previously lived together; in 1975 it was 9% and today it is more than 20%.[7] One out of every ten single women over the age of seventeen lives with a man as "husband and wife".

The continued emphasis by governments and social agencies on what they think is the "traditional" family penalises those who fall outwith this fictitious norm.

Women workers

The belief that woman's first line of defence against poverty is her husband has led to some misconceptions about women's role in the workforce. These misconceptions have been shared by many people in government, in the trade unions and even by women themselves. They have been crucial in determining the level of women's earnings and the kinds of jobs open to them. They have been used as an excuse for persuading women to accept low wages and in inhibiting active trade union negotiation to increase the wages in low-paid, predominantly female industries. Yet the low wages and lack of opportunities that are the consequence of these misconceptions are suffered by all women, married or single, with or without children.

Nearly 43% of the permanent workforce in Scotland is female. This means that almost half of our workers are women, not including the many women who work on a casual basis. Women who work are not exceptions to the norm; they are part of the norm.

It is popularly believed that the large number of women working is a fairly recent phenomenon. Yet, since records have been kept, official figures show that women have always formed a substantial part of the workforce. In 1841 26.3% of workers were female. In 1861 it was 31% and throughout this century there has never been less than a third of the adult female population at work outside the home.[8] Before the industrial revolution women, men' and children all worked in or close to the home. The introduction of the factory system forced both sexes (and children) to work outside the home and since then working-class women have continued to hold down jobs. The much vaunted "family wage" has never been a reality for the working classes. Much of the recent increase in the number of women workers is the result of middle-class women going into the professions.

The most vehement arguments against women working are usually directed towards married women who are seen as taking jobs away from unemployed men. Unfortunately this view is now shared by some male trade unionists as well. A more sophisticated version is that working married women reduce male wages because households are expected to live on two incomes rather than on one. Yet, as we have seen, married working-class women have been going out to work for centuries. The middle-class ideal that the male earned enough for all the family has never been achieved by ordinary working people, however much they have been encouraged to strive for it. Those households which have managed a comfortable life on one wage have usually depended on the man working excessive overtime with the resultant deterioration in other aspects of family life.

I am not arguing here that wages should be so low that one income is insufficient to maintain a family. Rather, I am suggesting that to idealise the one wage-one family system leaves the woman dependent economically on her husband and deprives her of the job opportunities that should be available to adults of either sex. A properly constructed support system of childcare provision and financial benefits for both the unemployed and those who have responsibility for children or the elderly would go far to provide for the financial independence of someone, of either sex, who is unable for whatever reason to take on employment. This will be discussed more fully later in the chapter.

Fifty-six per cent of married women do now work outside the home[9] and it has been estimated that the number of families which would be living below the official poverty line would increase fourfold if it were not for the mother's wages.[10] The same report by the Study Commission on the Family states that "an extra 2.5 million children would live in poverty if a woman's place was always in the home". A survey by the Office of Population Censuses and Surveys shows that 40% of women with dependent children do in fact hold outside jobs and that 26% of them have children under the age of five. This trend towards mothers working must undoubtedly be related, besides to the increase in marriage breakdowns, to the greater effectiveness and availability of contraceptive methods which free women from almost continuous childbirth and childcare. The time taken off work to have children is now only a small part of most women's working lives yet it is used as a justification for discouraging women from seeking better-paid and more interesting jobs.

Let us look at how women actually fare in the workforce. Compared to a high point in 1977, the year after the Equal Pay Act came into force, when women workers' hourly earnings were 75% of men's, women's hourly earnings were at April 1982 only 73.9% of men's.[11] This may seem like a small drop but it is a sustained drop. The previous year women's hourly earnings were 74.9% of men's. Women's full-time gross weekly earnings averaged only 65.8% of men's in 1982.

Women's earnings relative to men's are, therefore, actually dropping. More importantly, however, than the average female wages are the abysmal incomes of many individual women workers, most notably in the catering, cleaning and services industries which account for about 40%[12] of all female manual workers. Even in the non-manual section about 58% of women workers are in clerical work, an occupation not renowned for its high wages. Fred Twine's article in this book illustrates in detail the actual low wages of women in individual occupations.

In the professions women theoretically have equal pay with men but a combination of factors, such as interrupted work records because of childbirth, limited self-expectations and downright prejudice, makes them less likely to be on the upper rings of their profession.

So what have women workers actually achieved from the Equal Pay and Sex Discrimination Acts that were passed in a flurry of glory last decade? The British Equal Pay Act was severely flawed in construction and allowed women to claim equal pay only if they could show that a man doing the same or broadly similar work was being paid more. This was of no help at all to the many low-paid women employed in predominantly female industries where no man could be found for comparison purposes.

So too the Sex Discrimination Act has been unable to break down the barriers between "male" jobs and "female" jobs. Notable instances of female executives or telephone engineers, and vice-versa male midwives, have been well documented by the press but they do not represent any real breakdown of traditional occupational boundaries between the sexes. Partly this is due to traditional attitudes on the part of both sexes, partly to occupational guidance which is often still sex-biased, and partly to the difficulties inherent in the Sex Discrimination Act in actually proving that sex discrimination has taken place.

In the last few years there have been a number of successful appeals to the European Court on equal pay and sex discrimination in Britain.[13] As a result the EEC took infringement proceedings against the UK government for failing to implement Article 119 of the Treaty of Rome and a 1975 EEC Directive on equal pay for work of equal value. The government is now drawing up a Parliamentary Bill to bring UK legislation into line with EEC requirements.

Whatever the terms of the proposed legislation, and they have been criticised severely by the Equal Opportunities Commission, it will take more than a few Acts of Parliament to remove discriminatory wages policies. Even opening up "male" jobs to women begs the question of why traditionally "female" jobs are so poorly paid. Women cannot feed, clothe, amuse or house themselves any more cheaply than can men. Quite clearly, the Labour and trade union movement has not in past years fought hard enough for decent wages in these low-paid female industries because women have not been recognised as a central part of the working population.

The challenge is now on them, but it is one that must compete with the claims of the young unemployed and the wage restraints encouraged by the present Conservative government. In a time of economic recession it is hard to see how trade unions can successfully push the claims of one underprivileged group against another, especially when women low-paid workers have been so poorly organised in the past. Part of this lack of organisation is historical — until fairly recently little effort has been made to organise low-paid women workers — and part of it is due to the genuine lack of identity that many women have as workers and full members of the legitimate workforce. Many unions are now trying to overcome this problem, especially in the public sector, but the immediate threats of a Tory government are being more strongly resisted by already established highly paid "male" union sections than by emerging female, previously unorganised, workers.

The state back-up?

At June 1983 there were 323,887 people registered as unemployed in Scotland (14.5% unemployment rate). Of these only 99,654 were female (10.6%), but this is no real indication of the true numbers of women looking for work because the figures include only those who are registered as available for work. Many women do not bother to register if they are not entitled to unemployment benefit, either because of interrupted national insurance contribution records or because they were paying at the married woman's reduced rate. The married woman's reduced rate contributions are now being phased out as an option but many women are not entitled to unemployment benefit because of reduced contributions they made in the past.

In addition recent changes in registration procedures allow women with family responsibilities not to register, thus further disguising the true extent of female unemployment.

Many women, of course, choose not to work especially if they have young children, but whether women stay at home out of necessity or choice they are not adequately provided for by the social security system. Like other social institutions the rules of social security reflect the expectation that women who want or have to support themselves are exceptions to the norm. Most national insurance benefits, such as unemployment benefit and sickness benefit, still discriminate against married women in that they are not entitled to the additional allowance for dependants that men can receive. Change in this rule has been promised for the year 1984.

Other social security benefits are even more blatantly discriminatory, especially for those caring for sick or elderly relatives. Invalid care allowance, the state benefit specifically designed for people who give up work to look after sick relatives, is not available to married women despite the fact that it is usually women who are expected to give up their jobs to care for the family. A survey by the Equal Opportunities Commission[14] found that 75% of those responsible for sick or elderly relatives were women, two-thirds of whom were married. These women who have sacrificed their working lives to look after invalid relatives have to rely on supplementary benefit and if they have husbands in employment they are not even eligible for that. In the current social service spending cuts even more women may have to take on this added responsibility.

Women who are themselves invalids also face discrimination. If they are married they are entitled to the non-contributory invalidity pension only if they can show that they are incapable not only of paid work but also of normal household duties such as washing, ironing, cooking and cleaning. Married men claiming the pension do not face this double test. They need show only that they are unable to take on paid employment. This is yet another example of how married women are treated by the social security system as primarily housewives rather than workers.

Supplementary benefit is probably the most important discriminatory social benefit, mainly because so many households are now forced to rely on it. One out of every ten British households now live on supplementary benefit. The man is treated as head of the family and all benefit due to the household is paid to him. Women living with their husbands cannot get supplementary benefit in their own right, however long they may have worked outside the home beforehand. Women living on their own, whether married or single, face losing their benefit altogether if they form a steady relationship with a man. Although technically the couple must actually live as "husband and wife" before benefit is withdrawn, many women fear harassment from social security officers because of the ambiguity of this term.

The lack of an independent income for women at home forces many of them into a state of financial helplessness and dependence on their husbands. For many the only income they can call their own is their child benefit, but at £6.50 a week per child (£10.15 for single parents) it is hardly a major contribution to household income.

The single parent

Most women suffer to some extent the effects of low female wages and discriminatory social security rules but it is the female single parent who is most disadvantaged by them. Yet, as we have seen, single-parent households are growing in numbers, mainly because of the increase in divorce and separation.

More than half of Britain's single parents live on supplementary benefit.[15] They spend a higher proportion of their incomes on housing and fuel than any other group in the country (except retirement pensioners) and the lowest proportion of their incomes on alcohol and tobacco (except single women aged over 60).[16] Their straightened circumstances make them particularly vulnerable to housing or fuel debts with the consequent terrors of threatened evictions and fuel disconnections.

Many of these female single parents have little choice but to live on supplementary benefit. Even if jobs were available some of them would be unable to go out to work because of limited childcare provision. There are less than 4,000 full-time nursery places available in Scotland, catering for only about 1% of the under-fives.[17] The bulk of local authority provision is in the form of part-time nursery school places for children aged over three. Usually this involves only three hours childcare a day, making it impossible for the mother to work either part time or full time. Some working single parents have to rely on childminders but this can cost them about £20 a week, an abysmal wage for the minder but also an intolerable drain on the income of the mother if she is low paid herself. Childcare expenses are not considered a deductable allowance for tax purposes.

Some single parents also receive aliment (maintenance) from the fathers of their children but this is not necessarily to their advantage. Firstly, the amount of aliment recieved is deducted from the woman's supplementary benefit payments and so for non-working mothers there is no overall gain. Even voluntary payments made at birthdays and Christmas can be deducted. Secondly, the amounts of aliment fixed by the courts are seldom more than supplementary benefit rates and so the woman is often just as well off on supplementary benefit.

Even when a court does award aliment it is often very difficult to get the man to hand over the money. The Finer Committee Report on One Parent Families in 1974[18] quoted studies which found that 39% of maintenance orders were in arrears. This figure is likely to be substantially higher now that so many men are out of work or are suffering wage restraints. In Scotland the legal procedures for enforcing alimentary decrees are largely ineffective, though the Scottish Law Commission has now recommended changes in them. The Commission also recently drew up a draft Parliamentary Bill[19] to reform the Scottish laws of aliment and the financial consequences of divorce (restricting, for example, allowances after divorce and making the division of marital property more equitable) and the government has promised to introduce a Bill to effect the changes.

As far back as 1974 the Finer Committee recognised the unsuitability of supplementary benefit and maintenance as a regular source of income for single parents. Instead the committee recommended that a guaranteed allowance be paid by the state at a level higher than supplementary benefit.

Successive governments since then have failed to act on the proposal and in 1983, under a new Conservative government committed to cutting social security spending, it would be foolish to expect even lip service to the idea.

A step back for women
The relative position of women will undoubtedly worsen over the next few years of Conservative rule. There can be little commitment to equal pay policies, for example, when the workforce as a whole are suffering restrictions on wage rises. Redundancies and closures affect both sexes, especially in the traditional industries, but for women the chances of returning to work are very limited because of the lack of training and retraining opportunities. Mrs Thatcher's advocacy of traditional family values, in a context of savage cuts in local authority, health and social security spending, will force many women to take an undue share of the burdens of caring for the elderly, the sick and the young.

The labour movement is trying to fight back with a resistance to social spending cuts and the dismantling of British industry. It is up to us also to recognise the special disadvantages women are facing in these attacks on ordinary working people's lives. Almost every group in the country is being hit by present government policies — the young, the old, the unemployed, the sick. The needs of these groups should not be seen as competing — that would be to accept the Conservative philosophy that there is only so much cake to be shared around. What must be understood is that within each group about 50% of the people are women and that they may suffer special additional disadvantages. We cannot allow the current disastrous economic climate to lead to a return of male-dominated nineteenth-century values and priorities.

References
1   Women and Low Incomes, Equal Opportunities Commission, November 1977.
2   Social Insurance and Allied Services, Cmnd. 6404, November 1942.
3   November 1979.
4   Quoted in *Happy Families?*, the Study Commission on the Family, September 1980.
5   Civil Judicial Statistics Scotland, annually (HMSO).
6   *Families in Focus: Marriage, Divorce and Family Patterns*, the Study Commission on the Family, October 1981.
7   General Household Survey, 1979.
8   British Labour Statistics: Historical Abstract.
9   General Household Survey.
10 Quoted in *Happy Families?*, the Study Commission on the Family, September 1980.
11 New Earnings Surveys, 1977 to 1982.
12 Calculated from New Earnings Survey.
13 MacArthy's Ltd. v. Smith. Jenkins v. Kingsgate Clothing Ltd. Worringham and Humphreys v. Lloyds Bank. Garland v. British Railways Board. Burton v. British Railways Board. Summarised case reports available from the Equal Opportunities Commission.
14 *The Experience of Caring for Elderly and Handicapped Relatives*, March 1980.
15 *Social Assistance: A Review of the Supplementary Benefits Scheme*, DHSS.
16 Family Expenditure Survey.
17 Scottish Abstract of Statistics.
18 Report of the Committee on One Parent Families, Cmnd. 1529, July 1974.

Bill Clark and John Casserly

THE DISABLED

IT is ironic that the 1980s, which started with the International Year of Disabled People, should have provided the context for government policy initiatives which one commentator described as ". . . the most explicit and sustained setback in the living standards of people with disabilities since the war . . .".[1] The Thatcher Conservative government has pushed through changes in social security legislation[2] which have cut the living standards of disabled people on state benefits and eroded discretionary entitlement; has initiated proposals which will potentially end job protection for disabled people[3]; has begun the process of restricting access to benefits for sickness and injury;[4] has proposed reductions in short and possibly long-term benefits under the industrial injuries scheme,[5] and has caused marked deterioration in the level of provision of health services,[6] other personal services and housing for disabled people.

Conservative measures such as increased prescription charges and fiscal changes towards regressive, indirect taxation, have had a severe impact on the "cost of living" for disabled people. Harris's figures indicate the existence of 3,071,000 "impaired people" in Great Britain. In Scottish terms this is 274,000 people (108,000 "appreciably" to "very severely" handicapped and needing supportive services). Even allowing for the exclusion of certain groups (under-16s, mentally disordered people, those with sensory problems) this set of figures grossly under-represents numbers of disabled people. Townsend puts the UK total of people with disablement problems at between 6.5 and 7 million.[7]

Using Townsend's "conservative" figures, we would expect Strathclyde Region itself (far less Scotland) to have well over 250,000 disabled people with a condition which prevented them doing things which were "normal" for people their age. Strathclyde Regional Council recently mounted a regional door-to-door survey[8] to estimate the numbers and needs of the chronically sick and disabled in the community. Projected estimates of numbers[9] suggest something like 175,000 disabled people resident in Strathclyde. The survey team estimate something like "133,000 disabled people are in need of some kind of service available from the existing statutory and voluntary services". This means 76% of identified disabled people are in need of services or support. The survey clearly identifies the core of obvious handicap but the discrepancy between Regional estimates and Townsend's poverty survey suggests that marginal disability may not be fully represented. This is important. Disabling conditions are often progressive, and even less serious (functional) disability can have painful repercussions: the colostomy user shows no outward sign of disability but may have real difficulty in developing personal relationships. Townsend's work also indicates a strong correlation between deprivation and even minor disablement. The relationship between impairment and low levels of living standards is clearly demonstrated.

The relationship between disability and deprivation represents the key area to be explored in this paper. Current policies respond haphazardly to disability. They relate more to causes than consequences, and generally fail either at the individual or the collective level to cope with the problem of deprivation.

Poverty and Deprivation
The disabled are more than likely also to be members of other "social" minorities", such as the elderly, the unemployed, the single parents. Compared with the "non-incapacitated", they live in poorer housing, have poorer facilities, miss cooked meals, go short of fuel and winter heating, take less holidays and have more difficulty managing their income.[10] Their lack of money is dramatically illustrated by the poverty survey. More than three times as many disabled as non-disabled people live in or close to the margins of poverty (as defined by supplementary benefit plus housing cost). At the more serious levels of incapacity, something like 55% will experience low levels of income. In Scottish terms, using estimates from Townsend's figures, this would suggest around 150,000 disabled people living in or near to poverty.

Disabled people and their families have extra expense and at the same time their earning capacity is limited. The "special needs" of disabled people have been consistently and cogently argued from a number of sources. The government survey team identified one in three impaired people as having one extra source of expenditure as a result of health problems. Our own limited study in Lanarkshire[11] confirmed, on average, three extra sources of expense for each disabled person and their households. The points made in studies such as these seem self-evident — how do spastics clean windows? How do chairbound people keep warm? How does a paraplegic person stop getting pressure sores except by getting help (which might involve payment)? How long do clothes last that are subject to continual soiling and laundering? The needs are obvious and the list of corroborating studies and reviews is extensive.[12]

The income maintenance system for the disabled is largely inadequate, in scale of provision, unjust and arbitrary, and absurdly complex. In the short term it is the key to offering disabled people decent living standards and some measure of independence (one-quarter of supplementary benefit claimants have been sick or disabled for three months or more; two-fifths of supplementary pensioners are appreciably or severely disabled).

Evaluation of social security provision for the disabled has declined as a political concern. This is an insidious trend. It is based partially on complacency resulting from a decade of limited but much publicised reform. Benefits have been spawned (e.g. non-contributory invalidity pensions, mobility allowance, attendance allowance, invalid care allowance) and legislation has been enacted (Chronically Sick and Disabled Persons Acts 1970, '72, '76, '78) but reallocation of resources has been minimal.

The general impression that the disabled are justly treated does not bear close scrutiny. It has, however, provided the platform for recent government moves to cut benefits and services for the disabled. Hansard (3 June, 1980) quotes, "The disabled cannot expect to be exempted from the sacrifices necessary." We are moving, regressively, to a "minimum rights" posture for the disabled. Discretionary and conditional welfare is the order of the day.

Perhaps the severest criticism of the benefit system in terms of adequacy is its failure to respond to entire groups of disabled people. The cause of disability rather than need determines the benefit option offered.[13] One claimant in our Lanarkshire study put it succinctly: "If you are going to be a 'cripple' make sure it happens to you at work or when you are fighting for your country — that way you'll get enough money to manage on. Hard lines if you are just a stroke victim like me." In our experience, claimants with similar handicap levels had as much as 200% variations in benefit income, although their needs were the same. This kind of arbitrary treatment provides much of the impetus for reforms such as those suggested by DIG and Disability Alliance.

One central issue is that of "take-up". Inadequate benefits could partly be justified if levels of take-up were convincing. The selective approach towards welfare depends on high take-up for moral validity. Evidence suggests no room for conservative complacency. The welfare rights activity in Strathclyde Region has yielded consistent and depressing results. A Lanarkshire study[14] found that for every hundred disabled people (with appreciable to severe handicap) about £20,000 (in annual terms) of unclaimed benefit could be expected. Similar studies have now been carried out in various parts of Strathclyde Region and other parts of the UK and with different groups of clients, and the same deplorable picture of low take-up has been found.

Probably the most worrying aspect is the low take-up of attendance allowance and mobility allowance within the Region and Scotland as a whole. A study undertaken[15] by Strathclyde Welfare Rights workers of five hundred claims for attendance allowance indicated that only one in four claims were successful initially, but 405 claims were eventually awarded after advocacy. A number of factors are involved (including inappropriate medical advice to the Attendance Allowance Board), but the findings indicate that the Scottish take-up rate (second lowest of twelve DHSS regions) will not alter if left to the DHSS. In the benefits business nothing succeeds like success and systematic campaigns (involving good, accessible information and support in claiming) yield results. The recent Strathclyde Regional Council "post-card" campaign, dismissed by the government as a "cheap publicity stunt", resulted in a 300% increase in take-up of "exceptional needs payments" before the discretionary benefit was limited by Social Security reform.

The ineffectual efforts of government and DHSS policy and practice deserve examination. The poverty lobby has long concentrated on the complexity of our present social security system. The 1980 Act was a piece of consolidation legislation to bring about simplification of the Supplementary Benefit system. Donnison[16] (former chairman of the then existing Supplementary Benefits Commission) had argued for simplification at the cost of individual justice. But the reforms do not appear to have made life simple, only to have saved money and eroded discretion.

The complexity of the benefits system has left potential claimants and agencies confused. Multi-agency administration (central, local government, voluntary organisations), the mixture of entitlements, some rights-based, others discretionary, "frontier problems" of interrelationships (taxation implications, better-off calculations), medical assessments, means tests and appeals procedures are all sources of confusion. There is no single door to benefits, yet few appreciably or severely disabled people manage on one state benefit alone. The burgeoning welfare rights industry is an indication of the problems both DHSS and consumers have in exploring entitlement. Ignorance, of course, is related to complexity, and there seems to be a trend on the part of DHSS to inform the "brokers of rights" such as Welfare Rights Advisers rather than potential claimants directly.

The best leaflets are not available to the public and updating and distribution are a problem (the pamphlet *Handicapped in Scotland* has not been updated for three years). Social security payments represent a quarter of public expenditure, yet publicity and information budgets are well below other areas of government persuasion, for example, road safety (Clunk Click Every Trip), energy conservation (Save It), anti-litter campaign (Keep Britain Tidy).

Problems of access to offices and communication also impede the disabled claimant. Stroke sufferers with speech impediments do not find the telephone a straightforward means of communication; blind people do not read letters. The personalised approach to welfare rights has been proved effective. DHSS policies of centralised office bases, restrictive visiting/assessment patterns and compartmentalisation of benefits all lead, at least, to an insensitive, impersonal approach to the welfare of disabled people.

Even if all these problems could be alleviated then "take-up" would still be a problem if the present "residual model" of welfare applied to the disabled and their benefits. Stigma is an overworked concept in rights issues. It has not received adequate research and operational study, but it is still the best conceptual tool we have to encapsulate the ambivalence recipients of welfare seem to experience. Titmuss's work[17] concludes that an "infrastructure of universalist services" would do most to minimise stigma. The social reality of the disabled claimant appears to be one of perpetual loss in social exchanges. The claim itself expresses dependency.

Pinker[18] advocates that not only are universalistic frameworks required, but also the re-education of agencies and their consumers. But the deployment of DHSS staff to combat fraud still far outstrips resources allocated to assessment and encouragement of take-up. The social security system has never taken seriously this aspect of its responsibilities.

The key reform required is the introduction of a unified comprehensive disablement benefit. Almost every benefit currently available to the disabled requires "treatment" to modify inconsistency and anomalies. There is an overwhelming case for a comprehensive scheme which relates to needs (in particular extra expenses), covers interruption of earnings flexibly, does not depend on contribution records and integrates well with other benefits. What sticks in political throats is money. The futility of attempting to deal with individual benefits in isolation is well illustrated by the recent debate on the industrial injuries scheme.[19] Keith Joseph once described the income maintenance system as a "rambling Gothic pile". Heaping more on the pile is not the answer.

Work and Disability
The pattern of disadvantage is continued in employment. Unemployment is proportionately much higher amongst disabled people (14.6%). The gap is widest in England. The disabled tend to be the long-term unemployed. Their employment problems are also evident at the outset of their entry to the job market. Walker's research for the Warnock Committee[20] indicated that young disabled people were often educationally poorly qualified. The pattern of segregation and inferior education for the physically and mentally handicapped is a tradition which has little statutory support. Practical problems and prejudice have effectively ensured its continuance. In a recent White Paper,[21] the Secretary of State for Scotland outlined the main themes of the Warnock Report and recommended that the traditional distinction between "ordinary" and "special" education is no longer appropriate.

The need for job protection and positive discrimination has long been recognised in principle (if not in practice). The Tomlinson Committee's findings,[22] and post-war concern, resulted in the Disabled Persons (Employment) Act of 1944. The main form of protection has been the "quota" scheme (all firms with 20+ employees must employ 3% Registered Disabled Persons or seek permission through permits to employ non-disabled). Implementation of the scheme has not been effective and there has been a resurgence of government interest in consultation with a view to abolition (1973—the quote scheme for Disabled People, and 1980, The Quota Scheme—MSC). The renewed interest is particularly hard to accept, as there are no concrete proposals for alternative forms of protection.

The debate against abolition is well argued by Jordan[23] and Lonsdale.[24] Factors which have to be considered are the rising number of unemployed disabled people, the lack of enforcement of legislative duties (then prosecutions since 1944), and the increasing non-compliance of employers. Standard measure of quota compliance is the percentage of employers failing to fulfil quota requirements and this has moved from 38.2% (1960) to 63.2% (1978).[25] The Scottish figures are worse. In the West of Scotland the non-compliance rate is 70%. The Manpower Services Commission suggests the scheme is impractical and since 1977 (Fit to Work Campaign) they have embarked on a policy of "persuasion" to improve employers' perceptions of the disabled as workers. Employers should be levied for non-fulfilment and rewarded for co-operation, for example with tax relief. The status of an "equal opportunity employer" should confer concrete benefits. Enforcement of the quota scheme should be pursued (at present there is only one quota enforcement officer for Scotland).

Housing

The government survey[26] indicated that one in four disabled people live in housing which is inadequate for their needs. Leaving aside design issues it is apparent that local authorities do not have adequate pools of suitably built housing stock for the disabled There is also difficulty in many house-letting regulations about matching needs to available resources. Most local authorities have shirked their responsibilities by hiding behind a screen of "inadequate information". The absence of systematic identification of handicap (as envisaged by CSDP Acts) has clearly hampered adequate provision but there are other guidelines. In the *Scottish Office Housing Handbook 6*, the recommendation for Strathclyde is 53,000 houses for elderly disabled (10,000 wheelchair and 43,000 ambulant); 39,000 houses for families with disabled members (10,000 wheelchair, 29,000 ambulant); 3,500 for single people (1,500 wheelchair, 2,000 ambulant). To complete this scale of development would require £2,029 million. Other means of meeting need are available, including adaptation and conversion, but cost outlays would still be significant.

Local authorities are in severe financial difficulty for capital development. The Conservative government has applied stringent financial control on local authority funding. The 1981/82 housing support grant for District Councils in

Strathclyde was cut to £71m from £92m (this represents a 30% cut). At the same time they have been trying to persuade District Councils to lower their rate fund contributions from £57m to £29m (a cut of 54%). The task of choosing housing priorities in the face of these pressures will be difficult. Sheltered housing appears to have held its own in priority terms but the other types of housing stock required for the disabled will have to wait. (An interesting issue is the sale of council homes — disabled people asserting their right to buy would continually deplete special needs stock.)

The Built Environment
The legislation controlling buildings and development is generally either inattentive or permissive. It includes such provisions as Building Standards (Scotland) Regulation 1971; Town and Country Planning (Scotland) Act 1972; Offices, Shops and Railway Premises Act 1963; Health and Safety at Work Act 1964; Fire Precaution Act 1971 and the Chronically Sick and Disabled Persons Acts 1970, 1972, 1976 and 1978. Some of these regulations actually impede disabled people's right of access. This kind of discriminatory legislation denies the disabled full rights of citizenship. The only Act which mentions "Handicap" is the CSDP legislation, and the key clause in Section 4 stipulates that facilities (access, toilets etc.) are required ". . . insofar as it is in the circumstances both practicable and reasonable".

Greater awareness among the community of architects and planners is required, but change will only come when legislation has sanctions and ensures the design and building of appropriate premises. In the short term, use of MSC schemes for adaptations (grants of up to £6,000 per disabled employee) and access panels[27] and guides would be helpful. Improvement in building design is also necessary.

Transport
The problem of getting from place to place makes life difficult for disabled people, and has an impact on every sphere of their lives — education, work, leisure, shopping, and so on. Governments are faced with an interesting dilemma with regard to transport services. Should individuals be given the resources to opt for tailor-made market choices, or should collective public transport be developed to cater for all needs? Recent governments have tended to avoid answering the questions.

At present, transport policies have a bias towards selective help to individuals — invalid trikes and "government Minis" (being phased out after the Sharp Report[28]); mobility allowance (meshed into Motability); MSC schemes such as fares to work; and concessionary travel and parking concessions. All these benefits are dependent on medical criteria being satisfied, and probably no other issue creates more tension between claimants and agencies than the problem of defining need for help with mobility. The capital cost of converting public vehicles and converting transportation centres appears to be a daunting prospect to transport authorities. "Out of sight, out of mind" seems to be the dominant point of view. The pious hopes of Snowdon's working party, "integrating the disabled",[29] will need considerable political enthusiasm to become reality. A more modest goal would be a widening of the eligibility for mobility allowance (e.g. retired people), and a real amount of benefit to meet transport costs.

Personal Support Services

Legislation is often not the answer and this is particularly relevant when we consider those personal services available under the Chronically Sick and Disabled Persons Acts (1970, 1972 and 1978). When Alf Morris's Bill reached the statute book (albeit modified), many commentators felt the millenium had arrived and that the charter for the disabled was a living reality. The twelve or so years since the Act have not justified that optimism. The non-delivery of service, despite apparent statutory duty, has to be seen in the wider economic context. The pamphlet *Breakdown*[30] highlights the plight of local authorities. The CSDP Act gave additional powers to local authorities to help disabled people. The Acts' provisions were not compulsory, in that there is a question of justifiable need. Increasingly this has been interpreted as "if they have the resources to give such help". The present government has asked local authorities, while implementing cuts, to protect the most vulnerable. At the same time it is considering modification of Section 2 of the Act (the key section).

The Act is weak in that no qualitative standards are laid down for local authorities to inform themselves about the number of persons and their needs. Strathclyde's venture with the CSDP Survey Project provides the kind of model required. Other authorities have avoided indentifying need and thereby have not had to meet it. The Act mentions services such as domiciliary assistance (e.g. home helps), aids and adaptations, meals, telephones, leisure and educational facilities. Services often respond to demand. By playing down availability, local authorities have cushioned themselves against having to provide the level of practical assistance needed in the community. The demand is there — in a survey of Cambuslang (pop. 33,600) the CSDP Survey Team identified more than five hundred people who wished to attend day centre facilities.

The range of responses among local authorities is varied. Court cases are currently exploring the legitimacy of non-implementation by local authorities (using Section 36 of the National Assistance Act). It seems certain that as cash limits on local authorities tighten, services for the disabled will deteriorate. The Act must be strengthened and the resources made available.

Conclusion

The limited exploration in this article of the needs of disabled people and our collective social policy responses indicates that the disabled are clearly one of the more disadvantaged groups in our society. In psychological, social and economic terms, they are at the very margin. Our material and social responses to their problems are totally inadequate.

References
1 Alan Walker, "Poverty, Disability and Welfare Rights", Sheila Kay Memorial Lecture, 1980.
2 Social Security Bill (no. 2), Clause 1: changes/uprating of benefits from "better off" wages and prices to prices only. There will also be a cut of 5 per cent in increase relative to inflation (*Disability Alliance* indicate this cut could be as high as 8 per cent): " A Very High Priority", April 1980.
3 *The Quota Scheme for the Employment of Disabled People: a Discussion Document*; Manpower Services Commission, London, 1979.
4 *Income During Initial Sickness: A New Strategy*; HMSO, London, 1980.
5 *Industrial Injuries Compensation: A Discussion Document*; DHSS, London, 1980.
6 *Patients First*; DHSS/HMSO, London, 1979.
7 Peter Townsend, *Poverty in the United Kingdom (London, 1981)*.
8 G. Legg and R. Stewart, *Action on Handicap*; Strathclyde Regional Council, 1980.
9 E. Woldman, Research Paper on CSDP Survey Project, May 1981.
10 Townsend, op. cit.
11 W. Clark and J. Casserly.
12 H. Phillips and J. Glendinning, "Welfare Benefits", in *Disability Alliance*, March 1981; Alan Walker, "Living Standards in Crisis", in *DA*, 1977; Alan Walker and Peter Townsend, "Poverty and Disability", in *DA*, 1975; *National Disability Income*, Disablement Income Group Occasional Paper no. 3, 1979; P. Stowell, *Disabled People on Supplementary Benefit*; SRC, 1980.
13 F. Wright, "Rough Justice for the Disabled", in *Social Work Today*, vol. 7, no. 3, April 1976. .
14 J. Casserly and W. Clark, op. cit. This figure would now be nearer £30,000.
15 Q. Oliver and J. Laird, *Snakes and Ladders*; Strathclyde Regional Council, 1981.
16 D. Donnison, "Supplementary Benefits — Dilemmas and Priorities", Seth Memorial Lecture, 1978, *British Journal of Social Policy*.
17 R. M. Titmus, *Commitment to Welfare* (Allen and Unwin, 1972).
18 R. Pinker, *Social Theory and Social Policy* (Heinemann, London, 1979).
19 Alan Walker, "The Case for Reforming the Industrial Injuries Scheme", in *Disability Alliance*, 1980; "Industrial Injuries Scheme at Crossroads", in *New Society*, 22 January 1981.
20 *Special Education Needs*, Report of the Committee of Enquiry into the Education of Handicapped Children and Young People (HMSO, London, 1976).
21 *Special Education Needs in Scotland* (HMSO, London, 1980).
22 Interdepartmental Committee on the Rehabilitation and Resettlement of a Disabled Person.
23 D. Jordan, "A New Employment Programme Wanted for Disabled People", in *Disability Alliance*, 1979.
24 S. Lonsdale, Low Pay Report: Job Protection for the Disabled; Low Pay Unit, 1981.
25 *Hansard*, House of Lords, vol. 397, 18 January 1979.
26 J. R. Buckle, *Work and Housing of Impaired and Handicapped in Great Britain* (OPCS, 1971).
27 *Can Disabled Go Where You Go?*, Report by the Silver Jubilee Committee on Improving Access for Disabled People; DHSS, January 1979.
28 *Mobility of Physically Disabled People* (HMSO, London, 1974).
29 *Integrating the Disabled*; National Fund for Research into Crippling Diseases, Snowdon Report, 1975.
30 *Breakdown—the Crisis in your Public Services*.

Robin Cook

HOUSING AND DEPRIVATION

THE past few years have witnessed a sustained and dramatic assault by the Thatcher government on all the major policies and initiatives fashioned by previous administrations to reduce housing deprivation in Scotland.

The central thrust of this assault is a commitment almost to *halve* government expenditure on housing in Scotland over the lifetime of their administration. This target may reflect their preoccupation with reducing public expenditure in general to conform with monetarist precepts, but it must also spring from a deliberate decision that housing expenditure could most readily be sacrificed. In both England and Scotland the housing budget is providing no less than three-quarters of the total cut in government expenditure, which implies a powerful prejudice against the use of public expenditure to improve housing conditions.

Capital cuts
The worst casualty has been the allocations to local authorities for capital expenditure on housing. The total allocation for Scotland has dropped from £313m in 1979/80 to £232m in 1981/82 (1981/82 prices) — a cut of just over a quarter. The reduction experienced by individual housing authorities has often been much worse. Glasgow, which notoriously contains a quarter of all Scotland's unfit houses, has suffered a cut of over a third in its capital allocation. Both Aberdeen and Dundee have had a cut imposed in excess of 40%. The impact of such reductions on local housing need in particular local authorities is compellingly demonstrated in the recent SHELTER report, *Dead End Street*.

The scale of cuts, and the rapidity with which they have been imposed, have thrown into confusion the rolling programmes of local authorities to modernise and upgrade their housing stock. A number of councils have been obliged to halt modernisation projects that were already under way, leaving housing schemes awkwardly divided between those whose homes have been modernised and those whose homes have not. Glasgow has radically revised the amount it will spend per dwelling in modernisation contracts in order to maintain the number of units being treated, but even so believes that the present level of spending is insufficient to prevent deterioration of the housing stock. Edinburgh's own estimates suggest that at current spending levels it will be ninety years before it has tackled every council house suffering from dampness.

Nevertheless councils have attempted to preserve modernisation programmes wherever possible. Commitments which were previously given to tenants in good faith are difficult to evade even if the funds have not been forthcoming. The consequence has been to concentrate the impact of the cuts on new-build projects, which has in turn provoked what can only be described as a collapse of the council building programme. In 1980 Scottish local authorities started a mere 2,771 houses — less than half the number started as recently as 1977 and a *tenth* of the figures achieved in the record years of the late 'sixties. Most local authorities are reserving precious capital resources for special needs housing to meet particularly acute shortages, such as sheltered accommodation. For all practical purposes Scotland no longer has a construction programme of public housing for general needs.

The last Labour government's annual housing plans, under which housing authorities were required to assess housing need in their district and submit proposals for meeting the shortfalls within five years, were a standing embarrassment to the present government. They provided official evidence that the level of capital allocation was inadequate to match the housing need which each local authority had identified and the government had accepted. The government therefore issued a circular in August 1981 which sabotaged the system by requiring each authority to submit a housing plan every four years rather than annually. The pretext for shelving annual housing plans was they they had proved "unduly burdensome to some authorities". In reality it is the government that has found the cost of meeting the need the plans revealed too "burdensome".

Local authorities are not the only public agencies which have been obliged to cut back on their housing programme. New Towns have been required to observe a moratorium on housing construction projects. The SSHA has been compelled to abandon general needs housing outside Glasgow, and in Edinburgh sites that had been reserved for a SSHA scheme are now up for sale to private developers.

Housing associations now find themselves large-scale landlords of slum property which they have no immediate prospect of upgrading. In some cases, particularly in Glasgow, the delay in rehabilitation will necessitate demolition as the tenements decay beyond recall. Perhaps even more serious is the permanent loss of tenants' confidence in the new community housing associations which are unable to meet the hopes of a new deal that they had inspired.

Perversely, those housing programmes are being savaged at a time of record spare capacity in the construction industry. Between May 1979 and May 1981 unemployment in the construction industry in Scotland precisely doubled to over 25%. On Treasury figures it will cost £165 million to keep the present number of unemployed construction workers idle for a year. This is double the amount being "saved" by cuts in local authority housing programmes.

Subsidy cuts

The other major casualty of expenditure cuts has been the Housing Support Grant which is the sole fund through which central government subsidises council house rents. The 1978 Act unwisely swept aside the preceding mix of formulae for calculating Treasury payments over the lifetime of the housing stock, in favour of a system of annual grants within the gift of the Secretary of State. As a number of critics of the 1978 Act predicted at the time it was introduced, the Conservative government has ruthlessly abused its powers under the Act to enforce annual reductions in the grant. In 1979/80 Housing Support Grant met 43% of housing revenue expenditure. Two years later that proportion had fallen to 23%. At the present rate of reduction, the government will succeed in eliminating all Treasury subsidy of council housing costs within the life of this Parliament.

The inevitable corollary of the cuts in government subsidy has been dramatic increases in council rents.

Many local authorities have sought to cushion the full effect on rents of the cuts by replacing government subsidy with a contribution from the rates fund. The Scottish Office has attempted to plug even that escape hole by imposing even further reductions in capital allocations to any authority stubborn enough to use the rates to protect its tenants. The intention is to ensure that the loss of grant to the housing authority falls on council tenants alone rather than the community as a whole. The method is to blackmail the housing authority into fulfilling government policy by threatening it with an even more limited capacity to meet the claimant needs of its waiting list.

The last Conservative government justified its cuts in housing subsidy by arguing that it was more equitable to provide a rebate to the individual tenant than a subsidy to the housing stock in general. This Conservative government has produced proposals to unify rent rebates with supplementary benefit which could result in some of the poorest tenants losing up to £2 per week — in *addition* to the general cut in grant.

Nor can tenants anticipate a better service in return for higher rents. The present government inherited from its predecessors plans for a Housing Training Council to stimulate higher standards in housing management among Scottish local authorities. They scrapped the plans, apparently because Mrs Thatcher required her personal authorisation for the creation of a new quango, and no Scottish Minister was willing to dare the lion in her den over the quality of housing management. Meantime the new restrictions on direct labour organisations make it more difficult for housing authorities to maintain their own repairs service.

In stark contrast to its relentless pressure to force up council rents, the Conservatives have simultaneously obliged housing authorities to allow generous discounts to those tenants who offer to buy their home. This has the perverse, but no doubt intended, consequence that a number of tenants will find it cheaper to buy their house than rent it. In 1980 more council houses were sold by local authorities than were completed. The public sector housing stock has begun to shrink for the first time. Moreover, it is the best and most popular housing which is being sold. Out of 6,337 dwellings sold between 1 April 1980 and 31 March 1981, 87.5% were cottages and only 0.7% were maisonettes. When these houses next fall vacant they will no longer be allocated by reference to housing need but will come on the housing market at a price beyond the reach of most of those on the waiting list. Meantime local authorities will increasingly find their role confined to matching the needs of those too poor to buy with a housing stock limited to those houses too unattractive to invite purchase.

The private sector
Although the effect of housing cuts inevitably falls most severely on tenants of council houses and applicants on the waiting list, other aspects of the government's housing policy have had an equally serious impact on the private tenure groups.

The Tenants Rights etc. Act contains a number of provisions diminishing the legal protection of private tenants. Rent control is finally abolished although those who lose its protection are all elderly tenants, mostly single women, who are least likely to be able to cope with the complex maze of the rent laws into which they have now been thrust. The much larger body of tenants for whom a fair rent is registered will find that next time it is increased, the new rent will no longer be phased in over three years, but will take effect immediately. Finally, the Act creates an entirely new class of tenancy agreement, the short tenancy, which provides a device to circumvent the security of tenure that accompanies any other standard tenancy agreement, and without which few tenants will have the confidence to insist on their other rights.

Even owner-occupiers have been affected by a Conservative government, particularly because of the steep rise in housing costs resulting from record interest rates. Low income owner-occupiers have encountered new complications. The budget for local authority home loans has been placed under the same restrictions as other local housing expenditure, which has both made it more difficult for newly married couples to raise the finance to purchase a flat at the cheaper end of the market, where building societies are reluctant to lend, and trapped an equivalent number of couples with young children in overcrowded flats which they cannot sell. Should any couple succeed in obtaining a home loan against the competition, they will then find that a section in the 1980 Act obliges the council to charge a rate of interest higher than it needs to cover its own borrowing. Should the breadwinner subsequently fall unemployed and they require help from supplementary benefit with their housing costs, they may then discover themselves among the million similar low-income owner-occupiers whose assistance with housing costs has been cut in line with the proposals in the current Green Paper.

In one sense the owner-occupier has been unusually favoured by this government in that it has not tampered with the subsidy afforded by tax relief on mortgage interest. Indeed the value (and cost) of this subsidy rises with interest rates, as each additional £1 in mortgage interest automatically releases the owner-occupier from 30p in tax, or even more if he pays a higher rate of tax. Thus as government support to council rents plummeted as a direct consequence of their assault on public expenditure, government support to owner-occupiers with a current mortgage has soared as an indirect consequence of its economic policy. That is why tenants paying income tax may actually find it cheaper to buy than rent.

In Edinburgh the policies of a Conservative council and a Conservative government combined to produce a new twist in the contrast between council tenant and owner-occupier. After a prolonged rundown in expenditure on council housing Edinburgh District Council arrived at the bizarre result that *more* of its capital allocation is channelled to the private sector through home loans and improvement grants than is spent on its own housing stock.

The only group whose level of housing support has increased under this government are owner-occupiers who hold a current mortgage on the better type of property, for which they do not depend on a local authority home loan, and who have a secure income which does not render them liable to future assistance from supplementary benefit. It is impossible not to note that this description neatly fits the type of person who staffs this government and the senior civil servants who advise it on its housing policy.

The context of deprivation

In order to set these policies in the context of the existing state of Scottish housing, we must attempt to define deprivation in relation to housing.

Commentators on housing policy frequently yearn for the certainty of previous ages. The problem facing pre-war legislators was stark and convincing. The meaning of deprivation in housing was readily measured by counting the number of families living in cramped, squalid, insanitary conditions, providing a standard of accommodation so basic that the census confined itself merely to counting rooms. Refinements such as access to a fixed bath and hot water were not recorded until 1951.

The solution to the problem was to build more houses which were larger than the standard tenement flat and possessed proper plumbing arrangements. The Acts of 1930 and 1935 explicitly linked the provision of this new housing with the clearance of the old slums. Under these Acts were built Niddrie in Edinburgh, Blackhill in Glasgow, Raploch in Stirling, Ferguslie in Paisley. They were peopled with the destitute from the slums. It is these very estates which now symbolise deprivation in urban accommodation and environment and pose the most intractable challenge to those still concerned with housing. Yesterday's solution has become today's problem. Deprivation in housing plainly cannot be measured simply by adding up houses without water closets or households who are overcrowded.

The shortage of up-to-date statistics on Scottish housing inevitably limits the discussion. The data collected in the 1981 census material relates to 1971. The Department of Environment compensated for the cancellation of the 1976 sample census by sponsoring the National Dwelling and Household Survey, which investigated housing conditions in a number of selected English housing authorities. Although the survey is based on a limited sample, the results provide a fuller picture of housing need and demands than could have been obtained from the sample census. Regrettably no similar survey was initiated by the Scottish Development Department.

The difficulty is most acute in relation to physically substandard property. In 1971 just over 86% of all households in Scotland had exclusive use of hot water, fixed bath and inside WC — rather more than in England and Wales where only 82% of all households attained this standard. This would suggest that perhaps 240,000 houses were below the present tolerable standard by reason of the absence of one or more of these standard amenities. Of the dwellings identified by Scottish Housing Statistics as sub-tolerable, over a fifth are included in current Housing Action Areas. There remains a balance of at least 70,000 substandard dwellings for which there are no immediate plans. This figure is comparable to the number of dwellings to be found in a city the size of Dundee.

Statistics do not adequately describe the problem. A large proportion of those living without bath or hot water are elderly persons who find it most difficult to cope with their housing circumstances. Meanwhile local authorities close facilities, communal baths and "steamies", which were first provided to compensate for inadequate domestic plumbing, but are now underused because of the general improvement in home conditions.

Nor can it be assumed that even those sub-tolerable dwellings within Housing Action Areas will receive early treatment. The Housing Action Area procedure is proving frustratingly cumbersome and it is yet difficult to find an example where it could convincingly be claimed that rehabilitation has been completed. A review of Edinburgh's Housing Action Area programme in March 1979 revealed that five years after the programme had begun 60% of the houses due for improvement had not been touched.

The statistics on plumbing amenities may be fragile and fragmentary, but when we turn to estimating the number of tenements which are substandard because the roof is on the point of collapse or the foundations about to crumble, we find ourselves plumbing an abyss of ignorance. Such fragmentary evidence as comes to hand is frightening. In 1980 the Scottish Development Department published a report' on Housing Action Areas based on a survey carried out in 1978. This concluded that 35% of all dwellings in the Housing Action Areas suffered from structural weakness, but in two of the six areas included the proportion rose to an alarming 80%. Investigation into housing in Clydeside in 1970 found that no less than 28% of dwellings built before 1919 suffered from one or more serious external structural defects (visible subsidence, cracks in lintels, or bulging of the walls). Even more serious in its implications for the future was the state of disrepair which they discovered in the older tenements. Well over half the dwellings built before 1919 revealed six or more defects requiring repair.

We have no means of measuring what improvements may have taken place since then, or knowing whether the situation has deteriorated. Here it is relevant to draw upon the pioneering work of the Cullingworth Committee on Scotland's Older Houses which first pointed to the importance of maintenance and concluded: "The situation might not have been of such serious dimensions had corrective action been taken in time to prevent deterioration from passing a point of no return." The logic of Cullingworth's argument was that every year a fresh batch of dwellings became unfit because neglect had reduced it to a state of chronic disrepair or structural instability, and housing planners have since had to live with the unnerving possibility that the numbers falling below the tolerable standard every year may actually be greater than the numbers they cleared.

Scots tenements were by and large built by single contractors who then let each flat through common factors. This arrangement provided a structure by which repairs to mutual parts such as the roof or drains could be managed, although from an early date the private landlord ceased to invest in adequate maintenance. The drift from private letting to owner occupation brought the procedural problems associated with multiple ownership, which have greatly complicated maintenance contracts. A statutory notice is often the only means of obliging improvements to be put in hand to rescue the residents of the top floor from constant inundation from a rotting roof.

Possibly the most imperative need for action now lies not with the clearly sub-tolerable housing stock, but the much larger, though unrecorded, stock of tenements which now teeter in the twilight between acceptable accommodation and irredeemable decay. Investment in preventing further deterioration in this enormous stock of adequate accommodation is essential to provide us with a breathing space to tackle the urgent problem of the already substandard buildings. Far from encouraging such investments, we actually tax it by the imposition of VAT on building repairs, a burden which has been doubled by the present government.

Overcrowding

Another measure of physical deprivation is provided by overcrowding, which actually increased between the sample census of 1966 and the census of 1971. This rise was entirely attributable to the public sector, where the percentage of households living at a density of over 1.5 persons per room doubled from 3.9% in 1966 to 7.7% in 1971. (The parallel figures for England and Wales are not only smaller, but also show a much slower growth rate — from 1.5% in 1966 to 1.8% in 1971.) In all other tenures the degree of overcrowding actually fell. Overcrowding among private tenants in unfurnished flats was exactly the same as among council tenants in 1971 but accounted for 63% of all overcrowded households.

There are two possible explanations to account for the reappearance of the overcrowding which characterised the Victorian slums among the council estates of the twentieth century. The first is that it in part reflects the growing problem of homelessness following marital breakdown, where parents take in their daughter and grandchildren for substantial periods of time. The second and statistically more significant cause is the stark shortage of larger council houses produced by our obsession with building three-apartment dwellings to fit a regulation family of mother, father and two children (of the same sex). A clear third of all council households in overcrowded dwellings were families of five persons in three-apartment houses which they presumably had been allocated when the family was smaller and from which they were unable to obtain a transfer. The growth in overcrowding in the late 1960s coincided with the post-war peak of council house construction, but only 3% of the houses built were of five apartments or more, while 8% of all Scottish households contained six or more persons.

The General Household Survey provides more recent information on overcrowding, although the data is not comparable with the census material as it is based on the more sophisticated assessment of overcrowding provided by the "bedroom standard". This stipulates the number of bedrooms any household ought to enjoy as a benchmark against which the reality can be measured (each single adult over twenty-one is assumed to require a separate room and children past puberty are not expected to share with a sibling of the opposite sex). The figures suggest that the position has improved since 1971 and the number of households below the bedroom standard more than halved between 1965 and 1978 leaving only 8% of all households below the standard. (In England and Wales only 4% of all households fail to meet the bedroom standard.) The greatest gains have been among small households; there persists a significant shortage of larger council houses.

Although the number of households living in cramped conditions in old substandard dwellings may now be a small percentage of all the households in the nation, they do constitute a significant proportion of those communities where they remain in large numbers. This is particularly true in the inner city areas of Glasgow and its satellite burghs, where it is still possible to find rotting warrens drawn up in rectangular blocks as though designed for fortification, housing a densely packed population in flats which neither have gained modern plumbing nor retained their original capacity to keep out wind and rain, and surrounded by a back yard of unparalleled squalor.

The extraordinary concentration of such communities in Clydeside was graphically illustrated by the work of Sally Holterman on the returns from the enumeration districts of the 1971 census. This revealed that of the 1% of enumeration districts with the worst incidence in Britain of overcrowding combined with lack of a basic amenity, a staggering 94% were located in Clydeside. Similar results were obtained when either indicator of inadequate housing was correlated with the incidence of unemployment. These results are particularly striking when it is remembered that in 1971 Scotland as a whole had fewer houses lacking basic amenities than England and Wales.

The Scottish Office has since sponsored its own review of the 1971 census data which appeared in June 1980 as *A Study of Multiply Deprived Households in Scotland.* Unfortunately this document furnishes little insight for housing policy as only three out of the ten chosen indicators are related to housing conditions. Some of the indicators selected are perplexing. Most startling of all is the assumption that any household living in a dwelling with three rooms or less is thereby deprived. Once again Glasgow dominates the pattern which emerges. Not only are 40% of all deprived households in Scotland to be found in Glasgow, but even within Glasgow they are concentrated in pockets of multiple deprivation which results in the city accounting for an even higher proportion (51%) of the worst 10% of the enumeration districts in Scotland.

It is a neat question whether it is more deprived to be inadequately housed in a community whose higher standard of accommodation contrasts with your own, or to be inadequately housed amidst others whose own deprivation reinforces your own by reducing the quality of shared facilities such as shops and schools. Concentration results in the problem being dramatically more visible, but it is not necessarily a bad thing that the extent of the problem should be constantly under the nose of the policy-maker. In terms of administration there is a distinct advantage in substandard property being gathered together where it can more conveniently be treated by housing action area procedure. Whether such treatment has in fact significantly eroded the problem we will not know until the results of the 1981 census are available.

Rural housing
Paradoxically the other sector with a high proportion of substandard property

is in the remote rural areas. Indeed the proportion of substandard property in Clydeside is now probably only matched in the islands. In 1971 no less than 29% of all houses in Orkney were below the tolerable standard. Even in Bute, the island most integrated with the Central Belt, 17% of the housing stock was below the tolerable standard.

These figures come from *Housing in Rural Scotland,* a study completed by the SDD in February 1977 which since has been circulating in photocopy. It provides a fascinating insight into housing deprivation in the rural areas, where low incomes frequently collide with high housing costs. Distance and the absence of any economies of scale are largely responsible for the high costs, but they are exacerbated by the market in second homes, retirement cottages and conversions for letting to tourists. This market brings residents into competition with more highly paid incomers from the Central Belt. Some of the present second homes would simply have remained derelict had they not been acquired, but plainly there are some houses for which there is a local demand, which have been removed from the local stock. In Skye and Lochalsh there are now more dwellings occupied for less than twenty weeks in the year than there are households on the waiting lists.

In the remoter areas any housing market at all is inhibited by the policy of the building societies, who operate a rural version of the "red-lining" policy which they apply to the inner city areas where they will not lend. They say that there may be difficulty in reselling because of the remote location. The effect, as in the inner cities, is to inhibit younger families from acquiring and renovating existing dwellings.

Traditionally few council houses were built in the rural areas and such as were constructed were mostly initiated by burgh authorities. Thus two-thirds of the council houses in the entire Western Isles are in Stornoway. Local government reorganisation which merged these burgh authorities with their landward areas has resulted in a considerable stimulus to building programmes outside the burghs. Since reorganisation in 1974 the majority of houses built in the rural areas has been local authority stock, while in the rest of Scotland the balance has tilted the other way. In Orkney half of all council houses have been built since 1974.

There remains, however, a substantial backlog. In the half dozen rural districts selected by the SDD for special study, there was one applicant for every three or four houses in the council stock. The group who suffer most as a result of this backlog are those who are trapped in houses below the tolerable standard, with little realistic prospect of rehousing, most of them elderly people.

Council estates

Present government Ministers uphold the fashionable analysis that Scotland groans under a surfeit of public sector houses inhabited by tenants who seethe with dissatisfaction. Left-wing writers have inadvertently supported them by rightly campaigning for a better deal for the tenants of the worst estates, thus contributing to the media stereotype of council housing as large, soulless communities rife with social disorder. We must therefore preface an examination of deprivation on council estates with a few perspectives.

First, the range in quality of both council houses and their environment is every bit as wide as in the owner-occupier sector. Every large problem estate is matched by many smaller estates containing homes built to higher specifications than their contemporaries in the private sector and set in a well-planned environment.

Second, it is important to remember that council housing is now the form of tenure held by a majority of the population and by a large majority of socio-economic groups C, D and E. In other words most of the urban poor are now housed within the council sector. It would be naive not to expect the deprivation associated with urban poverty to surface within the public sector.

But multiple deprivation is still a feature of many council estates. There is no more eloquent testimony to this than the steadfast refusal of households in desperate housing circumstances to contemplate an offer of rehousing in certain estates. I represented an inner city area and constantly encountered pensioners who would prefer to wait on the grave, housebound in an insanitary flat up a tenement stair, than accept a ground-floor house with modern amenities in a deprived estate. I have seen a separated mother share a single room with a young family in her parents' flat in preference to a whole house in such an estate, and have witnessed the patience of parents who tolerate the overcrowding of such an arrangement rather than pressure their daughter to accept a tenancy in one of these estates.

Few of those who resist rehousing in these estates relate their reluctance to the standard of accommodation. They may even link their criticisms with an expression of appreciation for the individual housing units. They are more likely to articulate their objection as a distaste for the social composition of the neighbourhood, accompanied by fear of vandalism or violence, or concern at the lack of facilities on the estate and distance from areas where such facilities are to be found.

There is objective evidence to support the latter set of criticisms, but they would be less significant if the estates themselves had not been built without adequate attention to such facilities. Few large estates in Scotland could boast the full range of facilities appropriate to their size, partly because they were conceived as housing estates and not as new towns. To describe the result as dormitory accommodation is to understate the nature of the problem; only a minority of the population has the opportunity to escape from the estate on a daily basis and the rest are confined to it all week.

The failure to supply services is more marked on the part of the commercial sector than the public agencies. The development of the post-war estates coincided with the trend towards larger and more centralised shopping units. This reinforces the deprivation of lower income households without private transport, who have to rely on more expensive local outlets. Few of the small shopkeepers who have survived have been able to contemplate the higher rent and rates demanded for modern premises on a council estate. A similar trend can be observed in the commercial entertainment industry. The number of cinemas created since the war is negligible and it is therefore not surprising that none are to be found on the modern council estates.

Some local authorities have attempted to remedy the absence of leisure facilities by providing community centres and sports complexes. Indeed this type of expenditure has been the fastest growing item in the budget of Scottish local authorities since reorganisation and for that reason has attracted frequent peevish complaints from central government who appear incapable of comprehending its importance. But large centralised complexes, far from reflecting community aspirations or encouraging neighbourhood identity, are inevitably institutionalised and regulated. What the isolated estates desperately lack is rendezvous such as cafes where youths can find unstructured and undemanding opportunities to waste their leisure time, or the tatty huts on corner sites which provide the most suitable habitat for youth clubs and other forms of unofficial activities. There is enough spare ground on most estates to cater for such needs.

The recognition of this problem is not new. The Report on Council House Communities by SHAC in 1969 emphasised the importance of allocating open space to meet specific needs. Unfortunately it then compounded the problem with facile projections of car ownership with the result that between a third and a half of all land on new estates is now dedicated to roads, pavements, turning circles and sight lines at road junctions.

The bleak prospect of the new wastegrounds is matched by the monotony of the modern tenements which surround them. The characteristic council estate lacks variety of design and variation in housing form. It is unfashionable to criticise housing on the basis of aesthetic criteria — which is perhaps as well for the architectural profession, but the stultifying boredom of many local authority estates denies any visual interest to their tenants.

There is little that can now be done to impose variety on houses that are already built, but much can be done with the wide open spaces. We need a new age of enclosures to break the spaces up into productive units — sites for community huts, play spaces, allotments, pigeon lofts, anything to produce the fascinating clutter of a mature urban neighbourhood. None of this is likely to happen as long as the land is held and run by local authorities, which would impose standards for such developments which are too demanding for local initiatives, and which anyway find it more convenient to control and maintain the land as a barren steppe. Achieving diversity in estate management, by devolving such decisions to the tenants, is probably a precondition of obtaining variety in land use.

An invaluable survey of the relevant literature by Attenburrow, Murphy and Simms   found some commentators who deny any correlation between the physical features of an estate and the probability of its becoming a problem scheme. The only point on which common agreement emerges is that the incidence of vandalism is related to the density of the child population. There appears to be a level of child density which can only be exceeded at the cost of imposing intolerable demands on the environment. This may explain the repeated phenomenon of tenant satisfaction increasing markedly after the second decade in the life of an estate. Child density declines with the ageing of the original householders. There are implications here for allocation policy in respect of existing estates as well as for the design of the housing mix for new estates.

It is possible to identify one aspect of past policies which has helped to determine the failure of certain Scottish council estates. There is a sharp distinction between the pre-war estates, which were built for general needs under the legislation of the 'twenties, and the later estates where, under the legislation of the 'thirties, rehousing was specifically limited to residents of the deprived slum clearance areas. The former estates were let at relatively high rents which tended to confine lettings to households whose head of family was in employment. The allocation policy of the 'thirties bodily lifted populations from the slums and re-established them on the new estates.

The Morris Committee   has isolated the social problems of the depressed estates which sprang from this policy: high incidence of poverty, with associated high levels of rent arrears and other debts; high levels of unemployment; large families, with associated overcrowding and higher than average proportions of children in the population; high incidence of single-parent families; concentrations of families with problems who are known to the social work department and low levels of educational attainment.

Different types of housing are typical of differing estates. The characteristic housing unit of the 1920s was the four-in-the-block, each dwelling having a main door on its own plot of garden. By contrast the 'thirties tenement flat had a communal back-green, demanding a high level of co-operation in a community where traditional relationships had been disrupted by the process of rehousing.

The difference in the social composition of the original tenants has undoubtedly been a more powerful force for divergence than any distinction between housing forms. As has been demonstrated in work on local authority housing estates, the original social composition of each estate has been perpetuated through a combination of self-selection by applicants and housing authority allocation policy.

In one further respect allocation priorities have deepened still further the deprivation of those families with a social problem. Most housing authorities have developed a system for allocating council houses by reference to some measure of housing need, but few have found means of building into the regulations a recognition of the applicant's wish or need to be rehoused near a relative. The consequence has been a steady erosion of the social support that might otherwise have been provided through patterns of extended kinship.

Much of the property and most of the environment on the depressed estates is in urgent need of rehabilitation. It is irrelevant to ask whether rehabilitation will result in a reduction in the social problems of the residents; it is sufficient merely to show that it will improve their living conditions. Plainly though the improved living conditions will be short-lived unless rehabilitation is accompanied by a package of policies to tackle the problems of social deprivation and urban poverty, which will otherwise rapidly reduce the estates again to their present squalor. Those responsible for framing housing policy have a vital contribution to make to such a package, particularly through the refinement of more sensitive allocation procedure and through the involvement of tenants in estate management.

The damp home

Perpetual condensation is now one of the most significant sources of housing deprivation. Those who have not observed the problem at first hand may object to the use of the term deprivation in this context, but how else could we describe the plight of families living within walls black with mould and constantly discovering that clothing and bedding is infected with mildew?

The problem is particularly prevalent in late post-war housing. Accustomed to an era in which energy costs declined in real terms, architects in the 1960s appear to have given up even attempting to design houses which conserved heating. The result was a generation of homes with thermal insulation grossly inferior to the tenement slums on which they were intended to represent an advance. Many of the package systems of the late 'sixties actually incorporate features which might almost have been designed to defeat thermal insulation. Such features were adopted by architects on the assumption that all rooms would be constantly heated. The first reaction of housing authorities to the discovery of widespread condensation was to blame tenants for a "lifestyle" that falsified this assumption.

In fairness to the architects it should be added that the problem was often exacerbated by the deletion of any provision for insulation at a late stage of design, in a desperate attempt not to exceed the maxima set by the SDD. Thus the Housing Plan of Dumbarton District, discussing types of houses where condensation is rife, explicitly admits, "proposed insulation of the mass concrete was taken out to meet indicative costs".   In 1978 the Department of the Environment published a Domestic Energy Note [7] which tacitly conceded the role of government in pressing for reduction in capital costs through deletion of insulation that had been an integral part of the original design.

Long before the energy crisis it was evident that many tenants simply could not afford the "lifestyle" necessary to prevent condensation. Since the mid-1970s energy costs have increased in real terms and the number of tenants who cannot afford to turn on their central heating has rapidly multiplied. The scale of the problem is much worse in Scotland than in England because of the much higher proportion of all-electric houses. All-electric houses were attractive to housing authorities because their capital costs were lower; there was no need to provide the flue and greater ventilation required for fossil fuel combustion, but this very design feature encouraged condensation when the tenants attempted to save fuel costs by introducing alternatives such as paraffin heaters.

There is no central estimate of the extent of the matter. Dundee has identified condensation as a major problem. Edinburgh estimates that between 10,000 and 12,000 houses are affected — a fifth of the total council housing stock. In West Lothian over 10% of their houses are estimated to suffer from condensation. In Dumbarton 2,500 houses out of a total of 13,000 are affected. Other housing authorities persist in refusing to recognise condensation as a problem or treat it with breathtaking complacency. Thus Wigtown, "it is the opinion that condensation and dampness are not serious problems . . . although there are a number of complaints from tenants".

The SLASH consortium has since calculated that 150,000 dwellings — 15% of our public housing stock — is affected by condensation. They estimate that Scottish local authorities require £500 million to tackle the problem, although even this startling figure may underestimate the real need as Glasgow believes it will take £140 million to treat its 35,000 damp houses. The prognosis for funds on this scale being released to local authorities in current circumstances is dismal. In August 1981 the present government finally promised to "pay particular attention" to dampness in determining capital allocations, but greater priority within a diminishing sum is a meaningless commitment.

Housing management and deprivation

In a nation which has chosen to house over half of its population in the public sector, neglect of housing management has been scandalous. In 1967 the Scottish Housing Advisory Committee recommended that we should aim at one housing manager for every 2,000 council houses. Ten years later a further survey revealed that there were still only 137 professionally qualified housing managers employed by Scottish local authorities — one for every 8,000 houses. *Half* of all housing authorities had *no* member of staff with a qualification in housing management. Provision for training was equally rudimentary:

> Our survey showed that the only form of training which the vast majority of
> housing staff receive is "sitting with Nellie" on the job. We are in no doubt that
> this reliance on imitating the behaviour of other staff is quite unsatisfactory.

It is unlikely that the position has altered significantly since then. Indeed, as
the committee noted, the limited opportunities in Scotland to study for a
qualification in housing management make it difficult rapidly to increase the
supply of professional managers.

Much of our housing deprivation can be laid at the door of our neglect of
housing management. For a start there are all the resources that have been
wasted through failure to analyse the needs and aspirations of those seeking
rehousing. Glasgow has achieved the truly extraordinary feat of arriving at a
point where it expects within the next five years to have a surplus of 50,000
three and four-apartment houses, and a shortage of 50,000 two-apartment
and 10,000 five-apartment houses.

The problems of rent arrears and evictions in certain areas are a reflection
of the failure to act early. At one point Edinburgh was evicting twenty times as
many tenants as Dundee, a variation which can only be explained by a
difference in management practice and policy. The Scottish Office Social
Research Study on Rent Arrears concluded that in 1977/78 over a thousand
council tenants were evicted as a result of rent arrears. Its authors were
concerned to discover that visits to tenants at an early stage of arrears were
"unusual". They recommended that weekly rent payments should be
encouraged, in contrast to the current arrangement where three-quarters of
council tenants have been discouraged from weekly payments for short-term
reasons of economy.

Perhaps the principal way in which lack of imagination in management has
created deprivation is the slow pace at which it has adapted to catering for
groups other than nuclear families. This failure has borne particularly hard on
those groups who previously sought shelter of a kind in the private rented
sector, which has now contracted.

The largest of these groups is the category of single persons. Laurie
Naumann in other published work deals with their problems, and here we
need only note that many remain homeless because of the refusal of local
authorities to accept responsibility for meeting their housing needs. Lauser's
survey of thirty-eight housing authorities shows that few have any dwellings
custom-built for single people, and most have no intentions of building any.
Aberdeen and Clackmannan actually expressed opposition on grounds of
public policy to such a notion as it may stimulate the break-up of existing
households. Nor are housing authorities particularly ready to compensate by
facilitating the access of single people to the stock constructed for general
needs. Yet the subsequent survey of the housing needs of single people in

Scotland by the SPAN project estimates that over the next decade we need to provide quarter of a million new homes for single households.

Parliament has connived at the omission of single households from council plans, most notably through the Housing (Homeless Persons) Act, which deliberately excluded single persons from the priority strategies and thus denied them any practical statutory right. The figures for the first two years' operation of the Act reveals that the single homeless accounted for 58% of applicants who were rejected because they were not in "priority need".

The other obvious failing of housing management is in its apparent inability to respond with greater sensitivity to the explosion in single-parent households. In the past decade the number of such households in Scotland has increased by half as much again.

The last major review of the difficulties encountered by single parents in their search for accommodation was provided by the report of the Finer Committee in 1974. Its work was carried out in the early 'seventies, before the latest surge in the numbers of single-parent households. Finer concluded that the evidence then available "puts it beyond doubt that housing problems closely rival money problems as a cause of hardship and stress to one-parent families" (para. 6.1).

A survey of the housing circumstances of single-parent families based on the 1971 census returns from five local authority areas was carried out in connection with the work of the Finer Committee. On the basis of this research the Finer Committee noted that:

> in the measurable indices of rooms occupied, rooms and beds shared, and the level of household amenities and equipment, standards were lower in each area for one-parent families than for two-parent families. . . . It is clear one-parent families tend, through low income, insecurity and factors promoting excessive mobility, to be channelled into inferior types of accommodation (para. 6.21).

The survey revealed that compared with two-parent families far fewer single parents succeeded in remaining owner-occupiers. Even more striking was the high proportion of single-parent families who were obliged to share dwellings with other households, generally the parents of the mother.

The incidence of shared accommodation is an imperfect index of deprivation, but the wide variations in the proportion of single parents in shared accommodation clearly reveals a substantial unmet housing need. It is particularly striking that the highest incidence of unmet need should be found in Dundee, which also contained the largest proportion of local authority houses. The success of Dundee in finding separate accommodation for nearly every two-parent family in the city and its parallel failure to rehouse more than a derisory proportion of its unmarried mothers, can only be explained by some aspect of management policy.

It is impossible that the situation described by Finer may have been significantly improved by the operation of the Housing (Homeless Persons) Act of 1977, which gave homeless families a statutory right to obtain rehousing from the local authority and put single parents on the same footing as other families with children as priority groups. It is necessary for the time being to be cautious as to the effect of the Act for the good reason that compliance with the Act is by no means uniform, and some district councils have deliberately evaded their responsibility.

The generous scope for discretion is convincingly demonstrated by figures collated by the Scottish Office from local authority returns. Over the first two years of the Act's operation 42% of all applicants in Scotland obtained permanent accommodation, but in Midlothian the proportion falls to a mere 10% and in Monklands to a startling 7%. A major cause of this variation is the differing standards which local authorities bring to the assessment of "intentionally homeless".

Irrespective of the success, or lack of it, which applicants experience in obtaining rehousing, the statistics on applications under the Act confirm that single parents continue to experience grave difficulty in securing accommodation for themselves. "Dispute with spouse or cohabitee" proves to be the largest single reason for homelessness, accounting for 40% of all applicants and dwarfing all other reasons, yet in the first eighteen months of the operation of the Act only half the women who quoted domestic violence as the reason for their homelessness were successful in securing permanent accommodation. Insofar as the Act has created statutory rights for the homeless, single parents have received the greatest increase in legal status. Insofar as some district councils have failed to respect the new legal rights, it is single parents who have been most deprived.

The rudimentary state of housing management in much of Scotland has contributed to the resistance to the Housing (Homeless Persons) Act. Indeed the very need to legislate in this area reflects the failure of many district councils to adopt progressive management policies. It is striking that no less than 63% of applicants under the Act who had lost secure accommodation had been public sector tenants. In other words, the public sector itself made a disproportionate contribution to homelessness, much of which could have been avoided by more sensitive management.

David Raffe

EDUCATION AND CLASS INEQUALITY IN SCOTLAND

Education and the reproduction of inequality

IN Scotland, as in other industrial societies, education plays a large part in reproducing inequality from generation to generation. At school differences in power and advantage in society are translated into differences in educational attainment, with the children of professionals tending to come at the top and the children of unskilled workers, together with children from single-parent families or other disadvantaged backgrounds, tending to come at the bottom. When young people leave the educational system, the educational hierarchy is converted back into an occupational hierarchy; those with the best qualifications get the best jobs, and those with no qualifications get the worst jobs or, if they are even more unlucky, remain unemployed.

Happily the fit has not been perfect. Many working-class children emerge with high levels of educational attainment, and many people with few or no educational qualifications nevertheless enter relatively high status jobs. There has been social mobility, even if it is still very limited.

In this chapter I document the role which Scottish education has played in the reproduction of class inequality.[1] Inevitably my account is a selective and partial one. It focuses on one aspect of social inequality — "class" inequality as reflected in gradations within the occupational structure — and does not deal with other inequalities, for example those associated with sex or region. It also focuses on only one aspect of education — its function of grading and differentiating pupils and students by the award of formal qualifications. My discussion is largely concerned with one educational stage, the later years of secondary education after pupils have been sorted into Certificate and non-Certificate classes. Much of my evidence is taken from the Scottish Education Data Archive (SEDA) surveys of school leavers.

I first describe the link between class background and qualifications gained in secondary schools, and I then describe the link between qualifications and the future (un)employment of school leavers. In the course of these accounts I comment on the effects of some of the policy initiatives of the past two decades. In the concluding section of the chapter I touch on the more general question of whether educational policy can do more than tinker at the margins with inequality of opportunity.

I must first point out that there is a deeply rooted assumption in the Scottish educational system that education involves differentiating people, and grading or ranking them, and that education involves a hierarchy, whether of treatment or achievement. The hierarchical view of education is so deeply rooted that we often take it for granted; but it is an important precondition of the role of education in reproducing inequality, and I will start by describing its importance in Scottish secondary education.

Inequality within education

Scottish education has a strong tradition of equality.[2] This tradition was reflected in the structure of nineteenth-century university education in Scotland, with its emphasis on accessibility for able children from all backgrounds. The scale of university provision was far higher than in England; there were no formal restrictions on entry based on wealth, race or creed; the university was not collegiate or residential but open to its community, and the student was able to live (more cheaply) at home or in lodgings. The same tradition has been reflected in the structure of secondary education; the full secondary course was shorter (notionally five years compared with seven years in England), placing fewer financial burdens on poor students; more Scottish than English pupils were admitted, in the past, to selective or academic courses; very few pupils (compared with England) were educated outside the public (state) sector; and parts of the country were served by "omnibus" (or bilateral) schools, in which children of all backgrounds and abilities were taught under the same roof, if often in strictly separate departments. The folk hero who personified the Scottish tradition of equality was the "lad o' pairts", the young man of humble background (a lad, not a young master) whose talents (or parts) enabled him to rise and take advantage of all that education had to offer.

However, the concept of equality contained in this tradition was a limited one. It was a concept of equality of opportunity rather than equality of result or treatment; and it was linked to a view of education that served only the academic élite among pupils. It rested on an assumption that only a limited number of people were capable of profiting from education; equality in education meant that all members of this latent élite should have the chance to profit from academic education without prejudice of social origins.

The tradition of equality in Scottish education, therefore, has co-existed with marked inequality of esteem and treatment *within* education. It has been oriented towards an academic minority of pupils, and until recently it ignored the larger majority of pupils who did not pursue academic secondary courses or aspire to higher education. In 1965, however, the government issued Circular 600 which initiated a process of comprehensive reorganisation which is now virtually completed; eight years later, in 1973, the statutory leaving age was raised to sixteen. As a result of these two changes, and of the continuing trend for young people to remain longer in secondary education, schools have had to adjust to meet new demands from those pupils who previously formed the non-academic majority.

The result has often been that schools have attempted to extend to all pupils the education formerly offered to the academic minority. More important, the values and priorities of the old academic system have survived in comprehensive schools: even after pupils have been selected into Certificate and non-Certificate classes their treatment has been influenced by the old academic values. This can be seen in the comments of young people in the Scottish Education Data Archive (SEDA) surveys of 1977 and 1979. A leaver with Highers passes (one of the successful ones) wrote:

> Most of our teachers concentrated on bright pupils, encouraging them, which is wrong because bright people get on fine without help, while the less able pupils get moved into a lower non-certificate class and the attitude was, "we only have to put up with them until they reach SLA, we'll just keep them occupied until then", with no care about preparing them for life outside school in any way.[3]

This theme is echoed in the comments of non-Certificate leavers:

> I didn't like school as it is biased towards the intelligent people and didn't always try to help the people who were not so intelligent. The best teachers are always given to the best classes and teachers who taught the lower classes couldn't always teach them very well.

> I did not like my last year at school at all. Those who were doing a non-certificate course were asked to sit in a class with a book opened at any page at all and pretend to be reading in case the headmaster or someone like that would come into the room. If you were not interested in 'O' levels then the teachers couldn't be bothered with you.[4]

In the 1977 SEDA survey non-Certificate leavers were less likely than Certificate leavers to say that they enjoyed their last year at school. Less than one-quarter of non-Certificate leavers said that their last year at school was worth while, compared with half of the leavers who had taken O-grade but not Highers and three-quarters of leavers who had taken Highers. Non-Certificate leavers were several times more likely than the others to have extensive records of truancy.[5]

Differentiation within Scottish education is formalised in the hierarchy of examination attainments with which pupils leave school. In 1979 17% of Scottish school leavers had three or more SCE Highers passes (in principle if not always in practice this is the qualification for entrance to higher education). A further 9% had one or two Highers passes. Nearly a third of school leavers (32%) had varying numbers of O-grade awards in bands A, B or C (these are the old "pass" grades which are still informally recognised as such by teachers, pupils and indeed by government).[6] The remainder, 42% of school leavers, had no Highers or O-grade "passes". About one-third of this unqualified — or less qualified — group had sat the O-grade examination in at least one subject while they were at school;[7] most of those who did so obtained D or E awards. D or E awards were introduced in 1973; together with a category euphemistically termed "no award" they replaced the old "fail" grade, largely as a response to the declining pass rates as larger and larger proportions of pupils came to sit the examination. They lack credibility: in the 1977 SEDA survey more than seven out of ten O-grade leavers said that a D or E result at O-grade was "no use at all".[8]

Inequality in educational attainment

In this section I describe the extent to which pupils' positions in this hierarchy of examinations reflect their social background, as measured by the occupations of their fathers.

If you want to do well at school you should choose your parents carefully. In virtually every advanced society there is a strong correlation between educational attainment and the occupational level or class of a child's parents; Scotland is no exception. Class differences in educational attainment are at least as large in Scotland as in England or most other western countries.

Table 1. Class inequality for six criteria of educational attainment: 1975/76 school leavers from Fife, Lothian, Strathclyde and Tayside.

per cent reaching attainment level:

Criterion of attainment	of all leavers (i)	of middle class leavers (ii)	of working class leavers (iii)	relative class chances (ii)/(iii) (iv)	measure of inequality (v)
Any SCE award (including D or E)	67	87	59	1.5	.65
1+0 grade at A-C (or 1+Higher pass)	58	82	48	1.7	.66
1+Higher pass	27	53	16	3.4	.72
3+Higher passes	17	38	9	4.4	.73
University entrance	8	20	3	6.1	.76
Entrance to any (full-time or part-time) post-school course	47	65	39	1.7	.49

Source: SEDA; abstracted from Table 12.1 of Gray McPherson and Raffe, *op. cit.*
Notes: Independent schools excluded. The measure of inequality is represented by Yule's Q statistic; 0 represents equality and 1.0 represents maximum inequality. Figures are subject to rounding.

Table 1 shows class differences in relation, respectively, to four different "benchmarks" of examination attainment at school, to entrance to university, and to entrance to any kind of post-school education, including part-time courses. Class is defined in terms of father's occupation: children with fathers in non-manual occupations (rather less than one-third of the total) are counted as middle class;[9] children with fathers in manual occupations are counted as working class. The columns of the table show the proportion of all 1976 leavers reaching the benchmark, the proportion of middle-class leavers reaching it, the proportion of working-class leavers reaching it, the ratio of middle-class proportion to the working-class proportion (subject to rounding error), and a summary measure of inequality which ranges from zero (for perfect equality) to 1.0 (for maximum inequality).

The table shows that there are considerable differences in educational attainment between children from different classes. It is sometimes claimed that class differences in educational attainment result from class differences in ability and are therefore legitimate. It is true that when ability is measured by IQ tests or verbal reasoning tests middle-class children, on average, achieve higher scores than working-class children. However, class differences in ability are themselves part of the educational problem: differences in ability are determined at least partly by differences in the social environment, of which education is an important part.[10] For the last two decades it has widely been accepted that schools should compensate for differences in other aspects of the environment. Moreover, class differences in measured ability are not large enough to explain all the class differences in educational attainment in Scotland.[11] Other factors are at work.[12] In this respect Scotland resembles post-war England and Wales, where Halsey, Heath and Ridge have shown that class differences exceed those which would have been expected on "meritocratic" assumptions based on IQ differences between classes.[13]

The figures in Table 1 suggest that class matters more at the highest levels of attainment. The relative chances of middle and working-class children gaining any SCE award are 1.5 to 1, whereas their relative chances of entering university are 6.1 to 1. But the measure of inequality shown in the last column of the table varies much less over the different levels of attainment. This is because it takes account of the different proportions of the age group who reach the different levels of attainment, whereas the measure based on relative class chances does not. (As the proportion of the age group reaching a level of attainment approaches 100%, so do the relative class chances of reaching it necessarily approach 1 to 1, i.e. equality.) If we allow for the different proportions of the age group reaching different levels of attainment, we find that the overall level of inequality varies only slightly between most different kinds and levels of attainment.

The pattern of inequality shown by the table supports the interpretation that class differences in attainment can be attributed to differences in the advantages of resources which are available to children of different classes.[14] The main implication of this interpretation is that the problem of class inequality is diffuse and affects the entire educational system: it cannot be blamed on particular levels or stages of education. For example, class differences in education are often most visible in the strongly middle-class composition of university entrants. Yet entrance to university is no more class-related than comparable levels of school attainment which are reached by the same proportion of the age group. Similarly, the class differences in attainment that emerge at the age of 16 have been shown to be present in the earlier stages of secondary education.[15] In seeking an explanation — or a solution — to the problem of inequality we should therefore focus our attention upon the whole educational system and its relation to society, and not upon its constituent parts or stages in isolation from each other.

The main exception to the generality of class influences is the sector of non-university further education. The class differences in entry to FE are somewhat smaller than those in levels of school attainment reached by comparable proportions of the age group. However, there is evidence that class differences in entry to FE have been increasing over the last two or three decades.[16]

In 1974/5 over four thousand adult males living in Scotland were interviewed as a sample for the Scottish Mobility Study (SMS). The data collected included details of their educational attainments and their fathers' occupations. Comparisons of different age groups within the sample suggested that the link between social class and educational attainment had been remarkably persistent over the half-century since World War I. The researchers concluded that:

> the Scottish secondary education system has to a very high degree failed to enable the sons of manual workers to get as much out of their education as the sons of non-manual workers. In some important respects the more recent situation is worse than fifty years ago. In short, social class background is still a major factor in a child's chance of success in Scottish Secondary Education, despite the myth of equal opportunity.[17]

The Centre for Educational Sociology (CES) has carried out a study of trends since the war, comparing Scottish Mental Study sample members who left school in the early 1950s, with SEDA sample members who left school in 1975/6. No change in the level of class inequality was found between the two samples. Both the SMS and the CES studies looked at the effects of educational expansion (i.e. the expansion of certificates, secondary education or higher education) on class differences. The Scottish Mobility Study found that "although recently more children from all backgrounds obtained exam passes, the non-manual sons did even better out of this expansion than the manual sons". The CES study revealed that this trend has continued since the war: as more certificates, higher education places or whatever were made available, the middle class benefited from the expansion more than its proportion in the age group would suggest. Nevertheless the middle-class advantage with respect to the expansion — the extra certificates or higher education places — was slightly less than the middle-class advantage before expansion occurred.

In a sense, therefore, educational expansion has produced a very slight decline in class differences. But some of the benefits of expansion are offset by the fact that the inflation in qualifications leads to job requirements being upgraded. From this point of view what matters is the relative level of attainment: for example, reaching a level of attainment that puts one in the top ten per cent of the age group. Class differences in relative levels of attainment have not changed over the last thirty years.

Educational expansion was partly a response to government policies, whose principal aim was not social justice but a reduction in the drop-out of able youngsters from the educational system and an increase in the supply of qualified manpower.[18] Nevertheless it was believed that these changes would help to reduce class inequalities. Another government policy with rather more immediate egalitarian ends was the comprehensive reorganisation of secondary education initiated by Circular 600 in 1965. Comprehensive education has advanced more rapidly and more thoroughly in Scotland than in England, and is now virtually complete. Its effectiveness has been enhanced by the relatively small size of the independent sector, except in Edinburgh: there has been less opportunity for the creaming of able and middle-class children away from comprehensive schools.[19] But, as in England, many of the processes of selection and differentiation associated with the old bipartite system are now to be found within the comprehensive schools.[20] It is increasingly recognised that rather more than changes in selection arrangements to schools will be required if there is to be a significant decline in class inequalities.[21]

An indication of the complexity of the situation, and of the need to understand the history and traditions of education as well as its current organisation, is provided by an analyses of the SEDA data on 1975/6 school leavers. Those from "uncreamed comprehensive" schools were compared with leavers from all other schools; the latter comprised a mixed bag of schools and included senior and junior secondaries, schools making the transition to comprehensive status, grant-aided schools and creamed comprehensives.[22]

The average examination attainments of the uncreamed comprehensives were very slightly higher than those of the other pupils, but the dispersal of results was narrower with fewer pupils attaining at the very highest or the very lowest levels. More remarkably, however, class differences in attainment among the leavers from uncreamed comprehensives were smaller than among the other leavers; on a crude measure of attainment, the "class gap" between middle and working-class leavers from the uncreamed comprehensives was about three-quarters of the size of the class gap in the other schools. This difference cannot be attributed to variations in the geographical or occupational structures of the areas served by different kinds of schools; nor, it seems, can it be attributed to the post-1965 comprehensive reorganisation.

The evidence, partial though it is, suggests that the same schools which were uncreamed comprehensives by the 1970s *already* had smaller class differences in attainment in the early 1960s, before comprehensive reorganisation. Most of them were formerly "omnibus" (or bilateral) schools, typically serving all the children from the burgh, albeit in separate senior and junior sections. The omnibus schools could be reorganised most easily and were most likely to be comprehensive by the 1970s. The SEDA analysis appears to show the continuing influence of the omnibus school tradition, and of the social and educational circumstances linked to it. This tradition seems to have involved at least a marginally smaller level of class inequality than in the parts of Scotland, such as the cities and much of the west, where the omnibus school tradition never applied. It remains to be seen whether modern comprehensive schools can recreate and extend this tradition in these other areas.

Comprehensive reorganisation was an example of a policy which attempted to address the problems of inequality across the whole spectrum of the social and educational hierarchy, although the independent schools were left untouched. However, governments have often found it politically convenient to focus attention on an underprivileged minority rather than to try to deal with inequality in general, since the latter would involve a more direct attack on the privileged minority. Many policy interventions have therefore been aimed at a "disadvantaged" minority of pupils, usually concentrating on the pre-school or primary stages.

The Scottish EPA Project of 1968/71 was based on three Dundee primary schools and the areas they served, and attempted to compensate for what was perceived as social and educational disadvantage by the provision of additional teachers and equipment, curricular innovations, extra-curricular activities and improved home-school links, social work, and other measures.[23] However, the project failed to gain the wholehearted support of the regular teachers involved. "Any radical intentions which the EPA project may have held were . . . countered by a firm belief on the part of the members of the educational system that any fundamental change was not required."[24] The EPA intervention was designed and imposed from outside the schools, and the identification of the schools as being in need of extra help seemed to cast a slur upon their present work. The teachers' reactions may also have owed something to the traditionalist view of Scottish education, with its conservatism, respect for intellect and academic values, and preference for traditional methods.[25]

The EPA project team gloomily came to "the fundamental conclusion that educational deprivation, let alone societal or economic deprivation, can be tackled only in part through the educational service. . . . If radical change is desired, plans to bring it about must involve public policies relating not merely to education and 'social work', but to social, and with it economic, structure".[26] The policy of "positive discrimination" persists in some Regions in the provision of additional resources to schools which are designated as being in need of additional help. However, the extra resources made available under these policies are on a very small scale and their effect has not been evaluated.

The Dundee EPA Report also questioned, at least in relation to the circumstances of Dundee, the area approach which assumes that social and educational deprivation are geographically concentrated in areas which can be made the targets of remedial policy. Projects elsewhere have focused on small areas with some degree of success. Perhaps the most interesting feature of the Govan project, set up in 1976, is that much of the work concentrated on the parents and the community of a small housing estate, Moorpark, rather than on the school.[27] Indeed, it may turn out that the project's most lasting effects have been on the community rather than on the educational attainments of its children. There are strong arguments for a community focus in compensatory education[28] but this trend reflects a fundamental paradox of all attempts to solve social problems through educational means: educational reforms are sought in order to change society, but a change in society is needed to bring about educational reforms.

Education, employment and unemployment

The Scottish Mobility Study of 1974/5 surveyed more than four thousand Scottish men aged between 20 and 65. About one in eight of the sample members were in jobs which the researchers identified as "upper middle class". As we might expect, the men in this class had higher average levels of educational qualifications than other members of the sample. But nearly half of them had no educational qualifications or only poor ones and the upper middle class men whose fathers had not been in the upper middle class were even less likely than the others to have qualifications.[29] In other words, qualifications had not been a necessary condition for occupational success, and a number of men had been socially mobile without qualifications.

This might suggest that the preceding discussion of class differences in educational attainment is irrelevant: if qualifications do not count for much in society, or in the job market, why should we worry that the working class are not getting them? However, this ignores the fact that the vast majority of unqualified men did *not* reach upper middle class (or even lower middle class) positions; that many of those who did so had other educational advantages, such as private or state selective education; and that men who reached upper middle class jobs without benefit of qualifications tended to do so comparatively late in their working lives. Most important, it ignores the fact that the average member of the Scottish Mobility Study sample left school several decades ago, when far fewer school leavers gained qualifications of any kind. Lack of academic qualifications was the norm for most men in those generations.

For today's school leavers, however, the position has changed. The proportion leaving school with some kind of SCE award has increased over the last two decades from less than one in six to just over two-thirds. Unqualified school leavers, who used to form a large majority of their age group are now a shrinking minority; their position has accordingly become more invidious.

Table 2.   Destinations early in 1977 of 1975/6 school leavers in Fife, Lothian, Strathclyde and Tayside who entered the labour market.

		SCE attainment			
		SCE O-grades			
	no SCE awards %	D or E awards %	1-2 A-Cs %	3-4 A-Cs %	5 or more A-Cs %	any SCE Highers passes %
Boys						
white collar employment	2	4	6	13	30	60
skilled manual	16	27	35	44	41	13
less skilled	56	54	44	31	20	15
other employment	3	4	6	6	5	5
unemployed	23	10	9	6	4	8
total	100	99	100	100	100	101
unweighted n	(2038)	(510)	(1243)	(740)	(516)	(1081)
Girls	%	%	%	%	%	%
white collar employment	12	29	47	63	79	83
services	20	28	25	18	9	7
manual	42	30	20	13	7	2
other employment	2	1	2	2	2	2
unemployed	24	12	7	4	3	5
total	100	100	101	100	100	99
unweighted n	(1741)	(680)	(1071)	(737)	(400)	(1139)

Source: SEDA; from Table 7.1 of Gray, McPherson and Raffe, *op. cit.*
Note: EA schools only.

The link between qualifications and jobs among recent school leavers is shown in Table 2. This describes leavers in the 1977 SEDA survey who entered the labour market directly from school; it does not include those who went on to further full-time education or who did not seek full-time employment. The table describes leavers' destinations early in 1977, some eight months after the last of the 1975/6 leavers had left school. The first column of the table describes the unqualified leavers with no SCE awards. Nearly a quarter were unemployed, compared with about one in ten of the whole sample. Of those who were employed, most were in the less desirable jobs: the boys were mostly in "less skilled jobs" and the girls in manual jobs, most as factory machinists. Of course, qualifications were neither necessary nor sufficient conditions for occupational success: several school leavers with O-grades were in less skilled or manual jobs, and some of the unqualified leavers found white-collar or skilled jobs. Nevertheless, qualifications made a substantial difference to a school leaver's chances: even those with D or E band awards were less than half as likely to be unemployed as the unqualified leavers. Further evidence from the SEDA suggests that the link between qualifications and jobs cannot all be explained away by the tendency for better qualified leavers to have higher aspirations, by differences in behaviour, attitudes or social background, or by employers' use of their own tests. Even at the marginal levels qualifications matter, to some extent at least, in their own right.[30]

The importance of qualifications is recognised, and resented, by many of the young people themselves, especially those who have lost out through lack of qualifications. A girl, working as a machinist, wrote "When you have no O-levels, you have no other alternative but factory work".[31] An unemployed boy: "I'm very keen to be a painter and decorator but my chances are next to none because I've got no O-levels. In my own opinion I don't really think you need O-levels to be a tradesman as it never happened in days gone by."[32] Another boy wrote: "Scrap O-levels and make everything equal."[33]

The most pressing aspect of the link between education and the labour market is the link between qualifications — or the lack of them — and unemployment. The level of youth unemployment in Scotland has been rising almost continuously since 1973, and unqualified school leavers have been the worst affected. There has also been increasing comment in the last couple of years about the growing numbers of qualified school leavers who find it hard to get work. However, although the absolute levels of unemployment have risen in all categories, the qualified leavers have increasingly taken the jobs which would otherwise have gone to the unqualified, and the relative disadvantage of unqualified leavers has persisted. In May 1981, the unemployment rate among the previous year's leavers ranged from 12%, among those with five or more O-grades A-C, to 49%, among those with no SCE awards.[34]

Figures can be misleading if they suggest that unemployment is an all-or-nothing experience: you either find a job or you become unemployed. In practice, spells of unemployment alternate, at least for the lucky ones, with spells of employment; for every young person on the unemployment register at any one time there is another who has either recently left it or will soon join it. One way or another unemployment affects a much larger proportion of young people than those who are unemployed at any one point in time. Yet both the average frequency of spells of unemployment, and the average length of those spells are considerably higher for the unqualified that for other young people.[35]

Adrian Sinfield has written of unemployment that "its distribution, as well as its scale, is central to any sociological analysis of the issue of unemployment, influencing both who bears the heaviest burden and the ways in which the public, the state and significant groups within society perceive and react to both the issue and the troubles it may bring".[36] The unequal incidence of youth unemployment was noted by the 1977 Holland Report on *Young People and Work:*

> It is the unqualified and least able amongst unemployed young people who need most help and are least adequately understood and provided for at present. It is they who experience the longest periods of unemployment, they who are prone to repeated spells of unemployment not just when they are young but in later years, and they who, later in life, are most likely to become the long-term unemployed.[37]

The Holland Report contained plans for the Youth Opportunities Programme (YOP), which was set up in 1978 to replace existing job creation and work experience schemes with a more integrated programme of work experience or training for unemployed young people. Emphasis was given to providing opportunities for the least qualified of the unemployed.

Since 1978 the numbers of young people entering YOP in Scotland have grown year by year: 23,600 in the first year (1978/9), 36,300 in 1979/80, 49,300 in 1980/1 and an estimated 70,000 in 1981/2.[38] Nearly all entrants are aged 16 or 17, and a majority have not had a regular job since leaving school. The scale of the programme is indicated by comparing the planned number of entrants in 1982/3, a staggering 90,000, with the number of young people expected to enter the labour market from school, which is less than 75,000.[39] Even allowing for substantial double counting among young people who enter more than one scheme, this suggests that a majority of young people entering the labour market from school can expect to pass through the programme.

YOP has been less than wholly successful in meeting the needs of the unqualified. In May 1981 more than half of the previous year's school leavers who were still looking for work were unqualified, with no SCE awards at any level. However, only 45% of unemployed leavers with no SCE awards were on special schemes at the time of the survey, compared with 57% of leavers with SCEs.[40] The quality of the schemes on offer, and the value of the training they provide, has come under frequent attack, but the schemes have helped some individual young people to find jobs. Up to the end of 1980 the MSC's own follow-up surveys found that a fairly consistent six out of ten YOP trainees found regular employment on leaving their scheme, but in 1981 this proportion fell to about one in three.[41] The 1979 SEDA survey showed that the rate of employment among ex-YOP trainees was higher than among comparable groups who had not been employed.[42] Of course this does not necessarily mean either that the schemes have had much effect on the aggregate level of youth employment or even that they increase the skills or productivity of the young people who attend. There is evidence that many employers use schemes as a means for recruiting regular employees, so the extra employment opportunities available to former YOP trainees must at least partly be set against a decline in the opportunities available to other unemployed young people.

When employers use YOP as a means of recruitment, they need to rely less on educational qualifications as criteria for selection. In the 1979 SEDA survey employment chances among young people who had been on YOP were less strongly linked to taking O-grades than among young people who had not been on YOP.[43] So even if YOP does not have a large impact on the level of youth employment it has at least a marginal impact on its distribution: it offers a second chance to some of the young people who left school with no qualifications and no prospects.

Conclusion: Can education solve the problems of inequality and poverty?

To an individual born in poverty or deprivation, education offers one of the best means of escape from disadvantage. If he or she can only cut the knot that ties educational attainment to social background and obtain educational qualifications, then those qualifications hold out a good chance of relative occupational success in the future. Over the years the residual influence of social background upon life chances has become smaller and smaller among people with comparable educational qualifications.

For some individuals, therefore, education offers a solution to the problems of poverty, deprivation or unemployment. However, it is not a solution which is readily accessible to all young people. The links between social background and educational attainment are strong, and the various interventions designed to weaken those links have met with limited success.

Moreover, although education may provide an individual with an answer to the problems of poverty, deprivation and unemployment, it is unlikely that education can provide society with answers to these problems. The education system helps to determine the *distribution* of advantage and disadvantage within society, but it has little influence on their *level*. I suggested above that YOP, while undoubtedly influential in helping individual young people find jobs, may not have significantly affected the total number of jobs available. The same may be true of more explicitly educational kinds of provision. Interventions such as the EPA scheme ultimately rest upon the assumption that if fewer children from poor or disadvantaged backgrounds themselves become poor or disadvantaged when they grow up, the total level of poverty and disadvantage in society will fall. However, there is little evidence to link education with the overall level of inequality in society: education may affect an individual's chances of escaping poverty, deprivation or unemployment but it seems to have little influence on the overall level of these things.[44]

The most that current forms of educational intervention can expect to achieve is a marginal increase in equality of opportunity, not an increase in social equality as such. This is not to deny the importance of equality of opportunity: although some see it as an ideological front for an unequal society, others regard it both as desirable in itself and as an indirect means to social equality. If policy makers or influential groups in society knew that their own children (or they themselves) had no better than an average chance of avoiding poverty, deprivation or unemployment, they would probably attack these problems with much more determination than at present.

Educational policy alone, however, cannot achieve greater equality. As the EPA Report pointed out, "radical change" requires public policies relating to "social, and with it economic, structure": in other words, political change.[45] Perhaps the main role of education is to help us to learn how to make that change.

References
1   Much of the empirical evidence in this chapter is from the Scottish Education Data Archive (SEDA), which contains data from surveys of Scottish school leavers. Many of the analyses summarised in the chapter are contained in J. Gray, A. McPherson and D. Raffe, *Reconstruction of Secondary Education: Theory, Myth and Practice in Scotland since the War*, published in 1982 by Routledge and Kegan Paul. I gratefully acknowledge the contribution of my two co-authors to the analyses reported in this chapter, and thank Andrew McPherson for comments on an earlier draft. The SEDA surveys have been funded by the Social Science Research Council, the Scottish Education Department and the Manpower Services Commission.
2   For further discussion of the Scottish tradition in education, see Gray, McPherson and Raffe, *op. cit.,* Part II.
3   L. Gow and A. McPherson (eds.), *Tell Them From Me: Scottish School Leavers write about school and life afterwards* (Aberdeen University Press, Aberdeen, 1980), p. 100.
4   *Ibid.*, pp 30, 29.
5   *Ibid.*, pp 114, 115.
6   These figures are calculated from Table 2 of Scottish Education Department, *Young People Leaving School*, Statistical Bulletin No. 10/E3/1980, November 1980. Consistent with my observations on the informal recognition of A to C band awards as "passes", this Bulletin does not report on D or E band awards held by school leavers.
7   Estimate based on the 1979 SEDA survey.
8   See Gray, McPherson and Raffe, *op. cit.,* chapter 8.
9   See Office of Population Censuses and Surveys *Classification of Occupations 1970* (HMSO, London, 1970). Classes I, II and III N are counted as non-manual (middle class); Classes III M, IV and V are counted as manual (working class).

10   Even extreme hereditarians accept a partial influence of environment on ability; at the other extreme some environmentalists deny any influence of heredity. Between these extremes the "heredity versus environment" debate concerns the relative share of the two factors in explaining individual variations in ability.

11   See Gray, McPherson and Raffe, *op. cit.*, chapter 12.

12   For an account arguing that Scottish society *is* relatively meritocratic see K. Hope, *As Others See Us* (Nuffield College, Oxford, 1977, Mimeo).

13   A. Halsey, A. Heath and J. Ridge, *Origins and Destinations: Family Class and Education in Modern Britain* (Clarendon Press, Oxford, 1980).

14   The analysis on which this argument is based is contained in Gray, McPherson and Raffe, *op. cit.*, chapter 12.

15   A. Ryrie, "Social Class, Examination Success and School Differences", in *Scottish Educational Review*, 13, 1, May 1981.

16   Gray, McPherson and Raffe, *op. cit.* See also, D. Raffe, "Social Class and Entry to Further Education", in *Scottish Educational Studies*, 9, 2, November 1977, pp 100-111.

17   Scottish Mobility Study, *Scottish Education Fact Sheet No. 1: Social Class and Success in Secondary Education*, Department of Sociology, University of Aberdeen, 1976. The Centre for Educational sociology's study is published in Gray, McPherson and Raffe, *op. cit.*, chapter 12.

18   *Ibid.*, especially chapter 1 and Part V.

19   The NCB's study shows how in the early 1970s comprehensives in England were creamed to the point where the social and intellectual composition of their intake was indistinguishable from that of secondary modern schools. See J. Steedman, *Progress in Secondary Schools*, National Children's Bureau, London, 1980.

20   See, for example, J. Ford, *Social Class and the Comprehensive School* (RKP, London, 1969). For accounts of the processes of differentiation within Scottish comprehensive schools see Gow and McPherson, *op. cit.*; A. Ryrie, A. Furst and M. Lauder, *Choices and Chances* (Hodder and Stoughton, Sevenoaks, 1979); and A. Ryrie, *Routes and Results* (Hodder and Stoughton, Sevenoaks, 1981).

21   For an account of the changing context of policy debate see *Equal Opportunity in Education,* H. Silver (ed.), (Methuen, London, 1973), especially Part 3 and the introduction, pp 251-8.

22   Uncreamed comprehensives included all schools which had comprehensive intakes and offered Highers courses by 1970, and which were judged to be sufficiently far from the nearest selective school (EA, grant-aided or independent) not to be significantly creamed. The comparison group included all other schools except independent schools, which were excluded from the analysis. (Only one per cent of leavers in 1976 were from independent schools.) For further details see Gray, McPherson and Raffe, *op. cit.*, chapter 14.

23   *Educational Priority Volume 5: EPA–A Scottish Study*, C. Morrison (ed.) (HMSO, Edinburgh, 1974).

24   *Ibid.*, p 184.

25   *Ibid.*, chapter 11.

26   *Ibid.*, p 209.

27   E. Wilkinson, D. Grant and D. Williamson, *Strathclyde Experiment in Education, Govan Project: A Public Report*, Strathclyde Regional Council and University of Glasgow, 1978.

28   See, for example, chapter 1 of *Educational Priority Volume 1: EPA Problems and Policies*, A. Halsey (ed.) (HMSO, London, 1972).

29   G. Payne and G. Ford, "Social Mobility and the Upper Echelons", in SMS Working Paper No. 9, Department of Sociology, University of Aberdeen, 1977.

30   Gray, McPherson and Raffe, *op. cit.*, chapter 7.

31   Gow and McPherson, *op. cit.*, p 96.

32   *Ibid.*, p 95.

33   *Ibid.*, p 95.

34   Provisional figures from the 1981 SEDA survey. The percentages quoted include those on special schemes as unemployed and are based on labour market entrants.

35   Gray, McPherson and Raffe, *op. cit.*, chapter 9; Manpower Services Commission, *Young People and Work* (the Holland Report), London 1977, p 17.

36   A. Sinfield, "Unemployment in an Unequal Society", in *The Workless State*, B. Showler and A. Sinfield (eds.) (Martin Robertson, Oxford, 1980), p 126.

37   Manpower Services Commission, *op. cit.*, p 29.

38   Manpower Services Commission, *Annual Report 1980/81*, London, 1981, p 45; the 1981/82 figures are a provisional estimate.

39   The estimate for YOP entrants is given in Manpower Services Commission, *Plan For Scotland 1982-1986*, Edinburgh, 1982, p 21; estimates of school leavers entering the labour market are contained in Scottish Education Department, *op. cit.* (see note 6), Table 2.

40   Provisional figures from the 1981 SEDA survey.

41   Manpower Services Commission, *Review of the Third Year of Special Programmes*, London, 1981, p 7, and subsequent surveys.

42   D. Raffe, "Special Programmes in Scotland: the first year of YOP", in *Policy and Politics*, 9, 4, 1981, pp 471-487.

43   *Ibid.*, pp 484-485. See also D. Raffe, "Education and Unemployment: does YOP make a difference (and will YTS)?", in *Youth Training and the Search for Work*, D. Gleeson (ed.) (Routledge and Kegan Paul, London, 1983).

44   See, for example, L. Thurow and R. Lucas, *The American Distribution of Income: A Structural Problem*, Joint Economic Committee, Congress of the United States, 1972; J. Coleman, "Equality of Opportunity and Equality of Results", in *Harvard Educational Review*, 43, 1, February 1973. On the causes of youth unemployment see P. Makeham, *Youth Unemployment: An examination of evidence on youth unemployment using national statistics*, Research Paper No. 10, Department of Employment, 1980.

45   C. Morrison (ed.), *op. cit.*, p 209.

John Hubley

POVERTY AND HEALTH IN SCOTLAND

Introduction

POVERTY and ill health form a vicious circle: the poor are more likely to be ill and die prematurely; loss of earning power through ill health is likely to plunge a low-income family even further into poverty. Despite a marked decline in death rates from many former killer diseases in Britain over this last century, inequalities in health between different social groups persist.

The report *British Births 1970*,[1] which surveyed the babies born throughout Britain during one week in 1970, compared its findings with previous surveys in 1946 and 1958 and concluded that, despite overall improvements, "there is nothing to contradict and everything to support the theory that social class differences in health are widening rather than diminishing". This is confirmed in more recent data published by the Register General on social class differences in Scottish infant mortality (deaths in first year of life) reproduced in Table 1. While all infant mortality rates have improved in the last thirty years, rates for social class V continue to be about double the rates for social class I.

Table 1.

CHANGING INFANT MORTALITY AND SOCIAL CLASS
IN SCOTLAND

Social Class	Infant Mortality Rates (infant deaths/1,000 live births)			
	1950	1960	1970	1977
I Professionals	25.9	15.7	12.2	9.2
II Employers	24.2	21.5	11.9	12.6
III Skilled non-manual and manual	37.0	24.3	18.6	14.2
IV Semi-skilled manual	43.8	30.9	22.2	15.3
V Unskilled manual	53.6	33.8	31.8	21.5
Ratio V/I	2.07	2.15	2.61	2.34

Source: Annual Report for 1977 of the Registrar General for Scotland Vol. 1, HMSO, 1978.

Scotland's health

The poor health of the Scottish people has been much publicised. Death rates from heart disease and lung cancer in Scotland are among the highest in the world. Infant mortality is a sensitive indicator of the state of health of a society and here also Scotland has lagged behind the improvements that have taken place in many industrialised countries. In the table of international comparisons in the most recent report of the Register General for 1977, nineteen countries, including Sweden, USA, England, and poorer countries such as the Irish Republic and Spain, had better infant mortality rates than Scotland.

In Table 2 some health statistics compare Scotland and the United Kingdom as a whole. In 1977 the life expectancy of a man in Scotland was 1.2 years less and for a woman 1.1 years less than for England and Wales.

Table 2.

COMPARISON OF HEALTH IN SCOTLAND WITH ENGLAND
AND WALES AND UNITED KINGDOM

Health Indicator	Scotland	England & Wales
Infant mortality 1977 (deaths/1,000 live births)	16.8	13.8[1]
Peri-natal mortality 1977 (deaths/1,000 total births)	18.3	17.0
Expectancy of life at birth	m 68.3[2]	69.5
(years, 1976 Scotland, E&W 1973-75)	f 74.6	75.74
Standardised mortality ratios:[3] (UK 100, 1976)		
Ischaemic heart disease	m 119	
	f 124	
Malignant neoplasms (cancers) of lung, bronchus	m 116	
and trachea	f 113	
Influenza	m 146	
	f 116	
Cirrhosis of the liver	m 162	
	f 149	
Cerebro-vascular diseases	m 133	
	f 127	

Source: Scottish Health Statistics 1977, HMSO, 1978.
1   Figures quoted as provisional.
2   m male, f female.
3   "The standardised mortality ratio shows the number of deaths in Scotland registered in 1976 as a percentage of those which would have been expected in that year had the mortality experience in the whole of the United Kingdom operated on the population of Scotland. Where the ratio is more than 100, mortality in Scotland for that cause is higher than the UK." (Extract from Scottish Health Statistics, 1977.)

Social class differences in health in Scotland

The real divide is not between Scotland and the rest of Britain but between different social groups in both countries. But these social inequalities are obscured in the routine publications of Scottish health statistics which rarely distinguish between social classes.

Table 3 brings together some recent health indices for Scotland analysed by social class. The ratio of deaths for social class V to social class I is calculated. The infant mortality rate for unskilled manual workers is double and the post-neonatal mortality rate almost 3.5 times that for the professional class. The post-neonatal mortality rate is a particularly sensitive measure of the effect of the environment as it is concerned with deaths between the fifth week and the eleventh month of life, when the infant is exposed to potential hazards in the home. The striking social class differences reflect the adverse home environment of the social class V population. A simple calculation shows that if the lower mortality and still-birth rates of social class I applied to all the 62,342 babies born that year, then 626 unnecessary deaths could have been prevented.

The death rate for lung cancer in Scotland is the highest in the world and a recent social class analysis by Kemp and Ruthven showed that a social class V male is almost four times as likely to die from lung cancer.[2]

Reviews of social inequalities in health by Townsend, Brotherston, Hart and Morris,[3] while drawing mainly on data from England and Wales, catalogue the long list of causes of death which are more prevalent among social classes IV and V. These include heart disease, strokes, respiratory disease, lung cancer and even suicides. One cause of death which merits special attention (because of its origin in environmental hazards) is accident, the commonest single cause of children's deaths. A study by Adelstein and White, of children under fourteen in England and Wales, surveyed the 23,418 child deaths between 1959 and 1963 and showed that 27% were from accidents. Social class gradients for accidents were greater than for all other causes of childhood deaths and the death rate from accidents for social class V children aged between one and four years was 4.7 times higher than for the social class I child. The analysis of childhood deaths in the Registrar General's decennial supplement showed that the death rate for the social class V child through being knocked down by motor cars was *ten times higher* than for a social class I child. These death rates are a tragic reflection of the differences in living environment and availability of safe play facilities to the different social classes.

Death rates are dramatic and always recorded but are only the tip of the iceberg. The remaining mass of illness goes largely unrecorded in official statistics and is rarely broken down by social class. The General Household Survey provides a way of examining differences in illness between different social groups by asking each respondent to record his or her illness experience

Table 3.

SOME SOCIAL DIFFERENCES IN SCOTLAND

SOCIAL CLASS	Still Birth Rate deaths/1,000 live and still births	Infant mortality rate 1977 deaths/1,000 live births	Post-neo-natal mortality rate 1977 deaths/1,000 live births	Lung Cancer registration rates 1972-4 cases/100,000 population		Heights of school children at age of 14 years 1973 (cm)	
				Male	*Female*	*Male*	*Female*
I Professionals	5.6	9.2	2.5	740	227	158	156
II Employers/managers	7.1	12.6	3.7	1140	303	156	156
III Clerical & skilled manual	8.9	14.2	4.0	2000	371	155	155
IV Semi-skilled manual	10.0	15.3	4.5	2094	388	154	154
V Manual worker	11.4	21.5	7.0	2888	554	152	153
Ratio 1/V	2.04	2.34	2.8	3.9	2.4		

Source: Infant mortalities, still births and post neo-natal mortalities from Register General for Scotland Annual Report for 1977; lung cancer rates from I. W. Kemp and H. E. Ruthven (1978), Cancer of the Lung in Scotland, Health Bulletin 36, 259-268; heights quoted in J. Brotherston (1976), "Inequality, is it inevitable?" in *Equalities and Inequalities in Health*, eds. C. O. Carter and J. Peel (Academic Press, London).

during a two-week period. One of the puzzling features about this data source is that despite the well-documented higher death rates and days of sickness benefit per person in Scotland compared to England, rates of self-reported sickness as revealed by the GHS are *less* in Scotland. An explanation may be that the people of Scotland have come to take their worse state of health for granted.

The social inequalities in self-reported illness show themselves when data in the General Household Survey is analysed by occupational group. Table 4 gives the respondents in 1975 and 1976 reporting a "limiting long-standing illness" or "chronic handicapping illness" (i.e. those giving the answer yes to two questions: "do you suffer from any long-standing illnesses, disability or infirmity?", and "does it restrict your activities compared with most people of your age?"). Manual workers suffer most from chronic handicapping illnesses. Rates of chronic handicapping illness were greater for the 65-plus groups compared to the 15-44 group. Ill health is particularly serious for the elderly as it can hamper their mobility and ability to fend for themselves, thus forcing them to rely on institutional care. What the General Household survey tells us is that it is the working-class elderly who are most affected, and the percentage of elderly among the population of Scotland is rising.

Table 4.

CHRONIC SICKNESS: BY SOCIO-ECONOMIC GROUP,
AGE AND SEX, 1975 and 1976

People reporting limiting long-standing illness:	Great Britain			Rates per 1000		
	Males aged:			Females aged:		
	15-44	55 or over	all ages	15-44	55 or over	all ages
Professional	60	238	86	64	266	81
Employers & Managers	78	346	126	76	402	127
Intermediate and junior non-manual	85	392	149	80	430	158
Skilled manual and own account non-professional	94	430	151	89	436	141
Semi-skilled manual and personal service	93	403	169	96	455	205
Unskilled manual	99	440	231	29	460	282
All persons	88	398	148	87	440	164

Source: General Household Survey, 1975 and 1976.

Brotherston's review of inequality in health[4] presents an analysis of data on the health of Scottish schoolchildren by social class in 1973, and his figures for heights of children at the age of fourteen are contained in Table 1. The Scottish

Home and Health Department, in the discussion on nutrition and childhood within its report for 1978 on the Health Services in Scotland, confirms that the shorter stature of social class V children persists. A preliminary report in 1977 of the findings of the Scottish Survey of Short Stature, by Vimpani, Vimpani and Farquhar, showed that short stature was twice as prevalent in Glasgow children as elsewhere, and that the highest levels of short stature were found in areas of social deprivation. Short stature was nine times more common in children from state schools than in those from private schools. In Glasgow, 47% of the short children had single parents or a father who was unemployed, 56% lived in overcrowded conditions (more than 1.5 persons per room) and 47% had four or more siblings.

Brotherston's 1973 school health data also showed social class differences in vision and tooth decay: 8.6% of social class V five-year-old schoolchildren had an "uncorrected refractive error in eyesight" (i.e. needed glasses) compared with only 3.7% for social class I children and over three times as many social class V children as social class I children had tooth decay (2.2%; 6.7%). This steep social class gradient in dental decay of Scottish schoolchildren extends to later life. A survey in 1972 of adult dental health in Scotland[5] showed that 44% of all Scots over the age of 16 years had lost all their natural teeth and that there were considerable social class differences, particularly in the younger age groups.

Poverty and social class in Scotland
The greater ill health of the Scottish people is the result of a higher concentration of working-class people and poverty. Ill health is more concentrated in poor areas, as is shown in Table 5, which compares some health indicators for local authority districts in Scotland. Both Glasgow City and Inverclyde have high concentrations of multiple deprivation and this is reflected in their correspondingly higher infant mortality, peri-natal mortality and post-neonatal mortality, compared with the Scottish average. The overall death rates for the entire population standardised for age and sex are also higher in these two areas. By way of comparison, examples are given of two other urban areas, Edinburgh and Aberdeen, showing mortality figures below the national average.

Unfortunately the data collected by the NHS is not analysed to a more detailed level than that of the district level. Laborious *ad hoc* surveys are necessary to show how health is divided within the districts. Few studies of small-area statistics and health have been carried out in Britain but an important one was carried out in Glasgow by McIlwaine, who mapped by electoral ward the 462 peri-natal deaths which occurred in 1970 and showed that they closely followed the social class distribution of the population.[6] A more recent study by Marr looked at indices in the "Areas for Priority Treatment" (APT) identified in the Strathclyde Regional Council's urban

Table 5.

HEALTH INDICES FOR FOUR SCOTTISH LOCAL AUTHORITY
DISTRICTS IN 1977

	Inverclyde	Glasgow City	Edinburgh	Aberdeen	Scotland
Estimate home population	103,245	832,097	463,923	208,340	1,195,600
Total live births in 1977	1,253	9,425	4,625	2,097	62,342
Infant mortality (deaths/1,000 live births)	18	20	14	14	16
Peri-natal mortality (deaths/ 1,000 live births)	27	22	14	17	18
Post-neonatal mortality (deaths/ 1,000 live births)	7	6	4	4	5
Standardised death rates (deaths/ 1,000 pop.)	13	13	11.2	11.3	12

Source: Annual Report of the Register General for Scotland, 1977, HMSO, 1978.

deprivation programme.[7] She examined infant mortality rates over a three-year period from 1975 to 1977 in APTs within Renfrew and Inverclyde health district, and found that infant deaths were running at 30.3 per thousand live births — almost double the rates in the rest of the districts.

Another *ad hoc* survey by Dunnet and Stansfield compared fifty babies in another Strathclyde APT, Blackhill, with a control area, Carntyne.[8] The babies from Blackhill had a lower birth-weight, were more likely to be born premature and had grown less in both weight and length in the first nine months of life.

Social inequalities in health and NHS policy
While there is some controversy about whether the use made of curative services is in proportion to need, there is general agreement that people in social classes IV and V under-utilise preventive services such as ante-natal care, family planning, child health clinics, immunisations, cervical screening and dental services. The report of the 1973 working party, *Towards an Integrated Child Health Service*, makes the frank admission:

What is certain is that our preventive health services are failing to reach out adequately to the families most in need of help.[9]

Other reasons for the small uptake of preventive services will be discussed in a later section, but one reason may be the lower availability of services in areas of highest need. The Court Report, *Fit for the Future* (1976), on the child health services in England and Wales[10] was an impressive overview on a scale that has not been produced for Scotland, and contained this sweeping condemnation of the child health services:

> Poverty and ill health are fellow travellers, while health services tend to travel in the opposite direction. The inverse care law still operates and there are fewer GPs, home nurses and health visitors in the areas where they are most needed.

In his report on the health services in Scotland for 1975 the Secretary of State for Scotland noted the publication of the Court Report and admitted that much of it was relevant to Scotland.[11]

A comparison of manpower resources in 1977 from the *Scottish Health Statistics* for Lothian and Glasgow Health Boards is revealing. Despite the poorer level of health in Glasgow, there were fewer GPs (58.9 GPs/100,000 population in Glasgow Health Board cf. 63.9 for Lothians and 59.5 overall for Scotland) and fewer health visitors (25.7 health visitors/100,000 population or 3,892 persons per health visitor for Glasgow cf. 27.5 and 3,635 for Lothians). The greater concentration of highly qualified medical manpower in the Lothians is also revealed by the percentage of consultants and community medicine specialists with distinction awards. While 43% of those eligible in the Lothian Health Board had distinction awards, the figure for Glasgow was 40%.

Such a comparison, of course, ignores the way services are deployed in areas of high poverty within the Glasgow and Lothians Health Boards. Unfortunately, while a lack of social amenities is a well-known characteristic of multiply-deprived areas in Scotland, there have been few studies of availability of health services in these areas. McIlwaine's study of peri-natal mortality in Glasgow,[12] having highlighted the high rates in the Provan area, comments that:

> This area is known to be socially deprived yet there is no co-ordination of medical help. There is not even a health centre in the area and there is a great shortage of health visitors; concentrations of resources, both manpower and money, would reap enormous benefits for the population in that area.

The only systematic study of the inverse care law in Scotland is Knox's analysis of the geographical location of GP surgeries in the cities of Aberdeen, Dundee, Edinburgh and Glasgow.[13] He qualified his conclusions by remarking on the absence of surgeries in newer owner-occupied housing estates and the concentration of surgeries in deprived inner city areas, but by developing an index of accessibility which took into account the proportion of the population owning cars and the distance from home to the GP surgeries, he found the lowest levels of accessibility in all cities in the most deprived areas:

> The lowest levels of accessibility (in Glasgow) are found mainly in peripheral suburbs which in Glasgow happen to consist almost entirely of public housing. These include Easterhouse, Balornock, Thornliebank, Drumchapel, Nitshill and Castlemilk districts which encompass some of the most notorious of the city's problem estates.

> The city's (Edinburgh) worst served areas correspond depressingly with deprived local authority estates: Granton-Pilton-Drylaw in the North and Sighthill-Stenhouse in the West and a large uninterrupted tract in the East stretching from Lochend through Duddingston and Craigmillar.

A similar inverse relationship of accessibility with socio-economic status was found in Aberdeen and Dundee.

Resource allocation

The Scottish Health Authorities Revenue Equalisation Report (SHARE)[14] was published in 1977. It failed to introduce any weighting for either the social class composition or the extent of multiple deprivation within a health board; thus for the health boards containing the Inverclyde and Glasgow East Districts, whose poor health statistics are shown in Table 5, the SHARE report called for a *decrease* in the proportion of total NHS finance going to the Greater Glasgow Health Board (containing Glasgow East) from 28.36% to 27.52% of total revenue allocated, and only for a slight increase to the Argyll and Clyde Health Board (containing Inverclyde), from 7.12% to 7.27%. This "equalisation" is to be phased in over the next ten years.

The irrelevance of the SHARE report to the health of the poor is made even more apparent by its failure to discuss how funds should be allocated to areas of need *within* health boards and between different parts of the Health Service.

Prevention

While Health Service facilities may be poorer in areas of multiple deprivation, it does not follow that positive discrimination will necessarily remove social inequalities in health without an accompanying shift in the style of service towards prevention. Available evidence suggests that social class and area differences in health in Scotland have environmental rather than innate genetic origins and could therefore be prevented. In her survey of peri-natal deaths in Glasgow during 1970, McIlwaine found that two-thirds of the deaths could be attributed to environmental effects on the mother rather than obstetric factors.[15] A similar figure of 77% was found by Marr who, in her survey of infant and peri-natal mortality in Inverclyde and Renfrew health districts, suggested that poor housing, unemployment, financial problems, poor spacing of pregnancies, larger families, concealed pregnancies and smoking were responsible.[16] Environment and personal behaviour play a crucial role in many health problems,[17] including the peri-natal period to the post-neonatal period where infants are vulnerable to hazards at home.

Health education

One of the most important preventive measures is health education. Since the Cohen Report in 1964[18] there has been a real increase in expenditure on health education in Scotland with the establishment of the Scottish Health Education Unit and the setting up of health education departments in most of the Scottish health boards. The consultative document *Prevention and Health – Everybody's Business* (1976),[19] the Scottish NHS Policy Document *The Way Ahead* (1976)[20] and its DHSS counterpart *Priorities for Health and Personal Social Services* (1976)[21] together with *Prevention and Health* (1977), which was the government's response to the House of Commons Select Committee on Expenditure's report on prevention and health, all spell out an apparent shift in emphasis towards prevention and individual responsibility for health.

The reality is quite different. The lack of importance the NHS attaches to prevention is illustrated by the breakdown in Health Service expenditure in Table 6, showing the overwhelming bias towards services in hospitals, rather than preventive measures in the community such as immunisation, screening, health visiting and health education. Even within the hospital sector there are inequalities. The expenditure in the hospital sector of the Health Service in Britain is biased towards acute curative high-technology medicine rather than long-stay chronic patients such as the elderly and the physically handicapped.[22]

Table 6.

CAPITAL AND REVENUE EXPENDITURE OF THE NATIONAL HEALTH SERVICE IN SCOTLAND 1977/1978

Total Expenditure £755.39 millions

HOSPITAL SERVICES	70.40%
COMMUNITY HEALTH SERVICES	5.62%
FAMILY PRACTITIONER SERVICES	17.79%
(includes expenditure on GPs, drugs, dental and optical services)	
OTHERS	6.19%
(includes central administration, Common Services Agency, Information Services Unit, Research etc.)	
Total	100%

Source: "Health Services in Scotland" Report for 1978 (HMSO, 1979).

While there have been increases in health education staff in Scotland, the number of officers in post by May 1979 was only forty-one compared with the SHHD's recommended figure of 108.[23] The number of health visitors is also below the recommended level. The 1973 report *Towards an Integrated Child Health Service* admits that for deprived groups:

> Health visitors have a particularly valuable role to play . . . but to function effectively a large amount of visiting will be required and a large proportion of health visitor's time will be spent with a small minority of children.

The ratios of 3,892 people per health visitor, for the Greater Glasgow Health Board, and 4,159 per health visitor, for Scotland as a whole, in 1977, are well above the 3,000 recommended in a SHHD circular.[24] This figure was accepted by the Joint Report of the Scottish Advisory Committee for the Education and Training of Health Visitors (1973) as a "realistic first target which would permit health visitors not only to carry out their present function but also to extend their field of activity both with the high risk population groups and health education".[25]

The Scottish Health Education Unit is part of the Common Services Agency with a budget in the 1978/79 year of about £1.1 million.

Prevention—for whom?

While any shift to prevention would be a welcome step forward, a simple expansion of the existing preventive measures may actually *increase* social inequalities in health. The poor take-up of preventive health services by social classes IV and V has already been described above.

A frequently cited success story for health education, in reducing levels of smoking, also reveals its weakness. Tobacco Research Council survey data showed that in 1961 smoking in Britain was equally prevalent between the different social classes. However, by 1972 a pronounced social class gradient had developed. While the percentage of smokers during this period for social class I had dropped from 53% to 30%, the figure for social class V males had only dropped from 62% to 58%. Although the percentages of women smokers among social class I had decreased from 45% to 31%, the percentage of women smokers from social class V had actually *increased* during this period from 43% to 46%.[26]

The large body of literature on the professionalisation of medicine highlights barriers that exist between the medical profession and the social class IV and V population, hindering effective communication. Some of these studies will be briefly summarised below.

There is a close relationship between the poor utilisation of antenatal services and peri-natal mortality. In their 1972 study of the under-use of maternity services by working-class women in Aberdeen, McKinlay and McKinlay showed a common lack of permanent accommodation, overcrowding, marital instability, financial difficulties and frequent sickness in their families.[27]

Wedge and Prosser's *Born to Fail* study explored the relationship between health, housing, income and single-parent family status. Richards' 1971 review of infant mortality in Scotland analysed the effect of housing on infant death rates in Glasgow in 1967.[28] In the post-neonatal period from the second to the twelfth month of life, death rates decreased in proportion to the number of rooms in a house, the use of one room exclusively as a bedroom and the possession of their own WC and hot water supply. The post-neonatal mortality for infants of families living in one-room houses was thirteen deaths per thousand live births, more than double that in houses with four or more rooms (5/1,000 live births).

In her study of attenders at ante-natal clinics at York,[29] Graham questions the assumption that mothers are to blame for the low take-up of ante-natal care and sees the inadequacies of the services as the reason because of their location, their timing and the impersonal conveyor belt approach to which the expectant mothers are subjected during examination. A similar criticism was expressed by "Mrs A" in her account of the problems of bringing up a family in a council housing estate in the West of Scotland.[30]

A Scottish study by Buchan and Richardson (1973)[31] showed that their sample of GPs spent an average of 6.1 minutes with social class I patients and 4.4 minutes with those from social class V. In this shorter period underlying social causes for a patient's complaint may not reveal themselves.

A survey of drug prescribing by Scottish GPs showed that in the eight years from 1967 to 1974, the numbers of prescriptions for tranquillisers and anti-depressants increased considerably from 6.1% to 9.4% of all medicines prescribed.[32] The work of Brown's group in England on mental illness in women (the main recipients of psychotropic drugs) points to the need to deal with the social causes,[33] showing that working-class women suffered most from mental illness. 25% of his sample of working-class women had had a recent or chronic psychiatric disturbance compared with only 5% of middle-class women. The group of working-class mothers who were most affected were those with a child under five years old, 42% of whom were mentally disturbed (by his set of criteria). More recently he has extended his work to the investigation of childhood accidents and has shown a connection with ill health, marital tensions and shortages of money in the family.

A new approach to health

A new approach is required by the Health Service. Considering the abundance of evidence that there is more ill health among the poor, it is remarkable how little the NHS has participated in the UK poverty programmes of the last decade. Rather than laying the blame on the poor for not doing the right things, the Health Service itself must be reorganised to meet their needs. This would involve a genuine shift towards community-based services and prevention, without neglecting the Service's caring function for chronic long-stay patients among the elderly and the mentally and physically handicapped.

In addition to the expansion of community services such as health visiting and health education, other special outward-reaching services could be developed, including occupational health services, domiciliary family planning services (such as those that have been operating in Glasgow) and mobile child health clinics (like those operated in Teesside and Southwark). At present the opposite is taking place: GPs are making fewer home visits[34] and there is a threat that accessible local clinics will close with the opening of new health centres.[35]

Health education is potentially important, but will need to do more than just beam messages as if the problem lies with the poor themselves. An alternative model of health education, going beyond the limited horizons of the "culture of poverty" and "cycle of deprivation", might allow for health workers helping to demystify the workings of the Health Service. It might also show how environment and life-style play a crucial role in moulding health and could develop the power of community and trade union groups to control these factors. This could be done through identification with local actions on issues such as better social amenities, pre-school facilities, dampness, improved housing quality, safer working places, public transport, traffic controls and more employment opportunities.

In this alternative model of health education, nealth workers could pass on relevant information about housing and public health legislation, about patients' rights to health care and free social security benefits, and about work hazards and rights under the Factory and Health and Safety at Work Acts. They could encourage community groups to campaign for better services in their area and work for a change in attitude of the policy-makers within the Health Service to make it more responsive to the needs of the poor.

While there is considerable scope for action by the Health Service, social class and area inequalities in health cannot be removed by the efforts of the NHS alone: they require an integrated attack on the whole spectrum of poverty. The *Report of the Working Party on Relationships Between Health Boards and Local Authorities* produced by the Scottish Home and Health Department in 1977 called for the setting up of joint consultative committees[36] and one of the tasks of these committees was envisaged as:

> To achieve liaison, co-operation and joint action on broad issues such as tackling urban areas of multiple deprivation, preparation of planning reports by health and local authorities etc.

An important outcome of such joint committees would be the active encouragement of workers from health, education and social work departments to collaborate at all levels in programmes to tackle poverty. Two key agents at a local level with whom health workers might collaborate are community development and community education workers.

Attempts to introduce a proper health education syllabus into schools (as outlined in Scottish Education Department Curriculum Paper 14)[37] must be backed up with measures to deal with educational disadvantage among the children of the poor. In the conclusions of the recent paper by H.M. Inspectors on *Health Education in Primary, Secondary and Special Schools in Scotland* (HMSO, 1979), there was no discussion of the need for such positive discrimination measures. The Strathclyde Regional Council has a representative from the five health boards within the region on its "Urban Deprivation Officers Group", and has included the health boards among the services to be linked by the area co-ordinators in its "Area of Needs" area management policy.[38] The contributions of the health boards to these poverty programmes must be critically assessed in any evaluations carried out on the effectiveness of these programmes.

The way ahead?

The Way Ahead was published by the Secretary of State for Scotland in 1976 to provide guidelines for the development of the health services in Scotland up to 1979 and 1980.[39] In the foreword the Secretary described the main points in the document:

> I am anxious that the Health Boards, the Common Services Agency and all those engaged in the Health Service should take account of six main principles which are developed in detail in the memorandum:
>
> (1) The need to operate the services within the budgets available which allow for a limited measure of growth.
>
> (2) The need to promote health care in the community through the progressive improvement of primary care services and community health services.
>
> (3) More positive development of health services for families in areas of multiple deprivation.
>
> (4) Lessening the growth rate of the acute sector of the hospital service in order to finance essential developments in other sectors.
>
> (5) Continued improvements in hospital and community health services for the elderly, the mentally ill, the mentally handicapped and the physically handicapped.
>
> (6) Encouragement of preventive measures and the development of a fully responsible attitude to health on the part of the individual and the community.

If the last five points are considered without the first, this document would seem to indicate a remarkable and enlightened shift in health service policy for Scotland. However, the "limited measure of growth" (i.e. cuts!) referred to in the first principle of *The Way Ahead* severely undermines the credibility of the document.

Equally unlikely to be implemented are the recommendations in the report of the Royal Commission on the NHS which finally appeared in July 1979. While the report fails to give serious attention to the problems of social inequalities in health some of its recommendations are relevant: the expansion of health education, the abolition of Health Service charges, special schemes for staffing NHS facilities in deprived inner city areas and the provision of further resources to local health councils so that they can liaise more effectively with the public.

While I have criticised the NHS in this review for its emphasis on cure and its lack of responsiveness to the needs of the poor, others such as the British Medical Association and the provident associations (e.g. BUPA) do so to promote their own vested interests. Implementation of the proposals made by the BMA, in their evidence to the Royal Commission, for more private medicine and increased NHS charges, will make health care even more inaccessible to the poor.

Cuts in public expenditure will only exacerbate the ill health of the poor both through their effects on the NHS and on vital local authority support services. As the Royal Commission on the NHS points out, Britain actually spends *less* of her public funds on health as a percentage of her gross domestic product than many other countries. In the debate about the future of the NHS, Scotland's poor, whose health is so bad, command little attention compared to the powerful interest groups such as the BMA, the Royal Colleges, BUPA and the pharmaceutical industry.

In the introduction of *Towards an Integrated Child Health Service* in 1973, the subcommittee of the Scottish Joint Working Party on Integration of Medical Work stated:

> There is a need to find means of levelling up these unacceptable differences. . . . To make the least favourable health statistics approximate to the best must be a priority task of the reorganised National Health Service.

Nine years on, the NHS in Scotland has yet to back this up with action.

References

1   G. Chamberlain, *British Births 1970*, Vol. 1, *The First Weeks of Life* (Heinemann, London, 1975).

2   OPCS, *Occupation Mortality 1970-72*, Decennial Supplement (HMSO, London, 1978).

3   See Peter Townsend, "Inequality and the Health Service", *Lancet* I, 15 June 1974, pp. 1179-90; Sir James Brotherston, "Inequality: Is It Inevitable?", The Galton Lecture 1975, in C. O. Carter and J. Peel (eds.), *Equalities and Inequalities in Health* (Academic Press, London); N. Hart, *Health and Inequality*, Occasional Paper, Department of Sociology, University of Essex, 1978; J. N. Morris, Social Inequalities Undiminished, *The Lancet*, 13 January 1979, pp. 87-90.

4   Brotherston, op. cit.

5   J. E. Todd and A. Whitworth, *Adult Dental Health in Scotland*, 1972, OPCS (HMSO, Edinburgh, 1974).

6   G. M. McIlwaine, *Social and Obstetric Factors in Relation to Peri-natal Mortality in Glasgow*, Ph.D. thesis, University of Glasgow, 1974.

7   Reported in "Infant Mortality Mirrors Deprivation", in *The Health and Social Service Journal*, July 1978, p. 750.

8   M. C. Dunnet and J. P. Stanfield, "A Survey of Infant Nutrition, Growth and Development in Glasgow — Preliminary Report", in *Nutr. Metab.* 21 (Supplement 1), pp. 220-2.

9   Report of Joint Working Party on the Integration of Medical Work (chairman, Sir John Brotherston), *Towards an Integrated Child Health Service*, SHHD, 1973. Many of the studies on the uptake of preventive services have been reviewed in I. Waddington, "The Relationship between Social Class and the Use of Health Services in Britain", in *Journal of Advanced Nursing* (2), 1977, pp. 609-19.

10 Court, *Fit for the Future*, Report of the committee on child health, Cmnd. 6684 (HMSO, London, 1976).

11 *Health Services in Scotland: Report for 1976*, SSHD (HMSO, Edinburgh, 1977).

12 McIlwaine, op. cit.

13 P. L. Knox, "The Intra-urban Ecology of Primary Medical Care: Patterns of Accessibility Policy Implications", in *Government Planning* 10, 1978, pp. 415-35; P. L. Knox, *The Accessibility of Primary Care to Urban Patients: a Geographical Analysis*, J. Roy, College of General Practitioners, 29, 1979, pp. 160-8.

14 Scottish Health Authorities Revenue Equalisation (SHARE), *Report of the Working Party on Revenue Resource Allocation*, SHHD (HMSO, Edinburgh, 1977).

15 McIlwaine, op. cit.

16 *Health and Social Services Journal*, op cit.

17 See the evidence on the importance of prevention in the DHSS' *Prevention and Health: Everybody's Business* (HMSO, London, 1976).

18 Lord Cohen of Birkenhead, Health Education, *Report of a Joint Committee of Central and Scottish Health Service Council* (HMSO, 1974).

19 DHSS, op. cit.

20 SHHD, *The Way Ahead* (HMSO, Edinburgh, 1976).

21 DHSS, *Priorities for Health and Personal Social Services in England* (HMSO, London, 1976).

22 For example, the critique of DHSS, op. cit., by the Radical Statistics Health Group, *Whose Priorities?*, 1976, and the writings of the Unit for the Study of Health Policy, *The NHS in the Next 30 Years: a New Perspective on the Health of the British*, 1978.

23 Figures quoted for health education manpower from a summary dated May 1979, published by the Scottish Health Education Unit. The staffing guidelines for health education departments within Scottish Health Boards were laid down in Scottish Home and Health Department, *NHS Reorganisation in Scotland, Memorandum No. 1*, 1974, on health education in Health Boards.

24 SHHD, *Towards an Integrated Child Health Service*, op. cit.

25 Joint Report of the Scottish College of GPs and the Scottish Advisory Committee for the Education and Training of Health Visitors, 1973.

26 See P. J. Capel, "Trends in Cigarette Smoking in the United Kingdom", in *Health Bulletin* 36, 1978, pp. 286-94; J. Townsend, "Smoking and Class", in *New Society*, 30 March 1978, pp. 709-10.

27 J. B. McKinlay and S. M. McKinlay, "Some Social Characteristics of the Lower Working Class Utilizers and Underutilizers of Maternity Care Services", in *Journal of Health and Social Behaviour* 13, 1972, pp. 369-82.

28 I. D. G. Richards, "Infant Mortality in Scotland", in *Scottish Health Service Studies*, 16, 1971, SHHD.

29 A paper by H. Graham entitled "Problems in Ante-natal Care", reported in an account of the proceedings of a joint conference held by the Child Poverty Action Group and the Secretary of State for Social Services in England by Ruth Lister, "Ante-natal Care and Child Health Services — Reaching the Consumer", in *Poverty*, no. 40, 1978, pp. 5-10.

30 J. Hubley, "Mrs A Speaks Out! An Interview with a Mother from a Deprived Council Housing Estate in the West of Scotland", in *Community Education*, no. 1, 1978, pp. 1-8.

31 I. C. Buchan and I. M. Richardson, "Time Study of Consultations in General Practice", in *Scottish Health Service Studies*, no. 27, 1973, SHHD.

32 SHHD, *Health Services in Scotland: Report for 1976* (HMSO, Edinburgh, 1977).

33 See G. W. Brown, M. N. Bhoolcham and T. Harris, "Social Class and Psychiatric Disturbance among Women in an Urban Population", in *Sociology*, 9, 1975, pp. 225-54; G. W Brown and S. Davidson, "Social Class, Psychiatric Disorder of Mother and Accidents to Children" in *The Lancet*, 18 February 1978, pp. 378, 340.

Ronald Young

A LITTLE LOCAL INEQUALITY

1. Out of the Ordinary

ON a clear day the view would have the estate agents sharpening their epithets for a killing. The Clyde Estuary at your feet — and the sweep of the Argyll peaks beyond putting Ben Lomond to shame. This, however, is Strone-Maukinhill — a council house scheme of 10,000 people, 40% of whose male population is unemployed. There is no killing for estate agents because about two-thirds of the households are (or should be) on rent rebate and the few who could afford a mortgage don't fancy the houses or the area. Only half a dozen council houses have been sold.

The shipyards have been the traditional source of employment for the area: they once employed 10,000, are now at half strength and face immediate extinction. The gaunt cranes you can see from Riverside Road are generally idle. So are the teenagers who have joined the long-term unemployed listlessly around the rubble of the shop units opposite the Day Nursery and Community Complex both of which arrived in the 1970s. On one side an off-licence and chippy and across the road—leading ironically through the rolling Renfrew hills to stockbroker Kilmalcolm—a general store. The town centre is two miles and a £1.00 bus ride away — when, that is, you can find a bus — as the mothers stress, who, after two years' campaign, have persuaded an insensitive health service to reinstate a part-time health clinic. 25% of families are single parent and the Social Work case load from the area is the largest in the town.

Over the last seven years the housing stock has been slowly modernised — with somewhat dubious effects for the quality of life. Only £4,000 a house was spent on rewiring, heating and external painting work as against the £5,000 recommended and some £15,000 in many other local authorities.

Some comparisons

Strone-Maukinhill is one of Strathclyde Regional Council's 74 "areas of priority treatment" — but by no means the hardest hit. Not only does that view give it an open outlook but there is little of the urban dereliction one normally associates with APTs. Its two primary schools may not be all that progressive about parental involvement but the last ten years have seen major developments in pre-five facilities — a new day nursery and nursery school — and community action has produced various developments such as an informal education project, the community complex and an information and advice project run by local people. Many APTs are worse — take, for example, West Carntyne in Glasgow.

Table 1.

	Strone-Maukinhill	West Carntyne
Male Unemployment	34%	60%
Female Unemployment	24%	29%
Single Parent	25%	38%
Car Ownership	23%	7%

But many areas are better. Take Bearsden, for example.

Table 2.

	Bearsden
Male Unemployment	5%
Female Unemployment	4%
Single Parent	7%
Car Ownership	80%

(1981 Census)

While most people will be shocked by the stubborn continuation of the disparity between privileged and poor areas they will probably be fatalistic about it. What else, they will say, do you expect with such unemployment around? We have always known it affected the poor more. Such fatalism, however, betrays a short memory — and a misunderstanding of the nature of the problem in the West of Scotland.

2. What is the problem?
It is almost ten years to the day since the National Children's Bureau document *Born to Fail?* brought home to the Scottish public just how relatively large a share of urban poverty seemed to be concentrated in the West of Scotland. One in 14 children "Born to Fail" in the UK: one in six here. The NCB gave kids that designation on the basis of their living in households which had a combination of poor housing, low income and were over-crowded. As Scotland had few houses which were then classified as deficient this result was all the more surprising — and caused essentially by the scale of unemployment in 1971 and by the extent of overcrowding. The Census Indicators on Urban Deprivation from the Department of Environment fuelled the fire of concern in 1974 just as the new local authorities were being created. Some 90% of multiple deprivation in Britain was apparently, if one

believed the newspapers, to be found in Clydeside. While that created the conditions for a new attack on urban problems in the West of Scotland — both by traditional methods (the Labour government's creation of GEAR to deal with the scar of Glasgow's East End) and by more novel political and social programmes embodied in Strathclyde Region's deprivation strategy of 1976 onwards — it was in fact a false perception confusing the question of the *scale* of urban poverty with that of its spatial *location and intensity*. The two reports measured different things — one the extent of family disadvantage, the other its geographical concentration. Appropriate action on problems does require some clarity on their precise nature! Urban poverty is very much an issue for central government — although the scope for local government action is clearly greater than the people imagined. Where, however, poor people live is governed by operation of the local housing market and this in turn affects the treatment meted out by public agencies and the labour market generally. Clearly the causes of poverty are deeply engrained in our socio-economic processes although the labelling which occurs in the interaction between professionals and clients can intensify it. But the *concentration* of families with similar characteristics in certain geographical areas is more obviously an avoidable/political bureaucratic problem. Certainly the level of service received in such areas has been clearly inferior to other areas — not least because of staff attitudes and turnover.

It is surely not a coincidence that such "apartheid" was most evident in that part of Britain in which "the local state" was so dominant: some people have got round recently to characterising local authorities in the West of Scotland as "Stalinist bureaucracies"[1] as if:

(a) such a perception of local government behaviour in working-class areas was novel; and

(b) nothing had even been attempted in recent years by at least certain authorities to transform the way local government operates.

A later section attempts to describe the critique of local government which underpinned Strathclyde Region's deprivation strategy in 1976 and which currently is being strengthened. What, however, is crucially important to grasp at this stage is that until the latter part of the 1970s no coherent critique of local government was even on offer — let alone one which had clear and practical implications for the different services of local government at their different levels.[2] Perhaps more to the point it is only in the last few years that we have been able to cut through the swathes of obfuscation — deliberate or otherwise — to develop a language with which to understand the very disparate models of human behaviour and therefore of action which lie behind the bewildering range of programmes we have seen in the last decade (modestly relating generally to something called "the Inner City" problem rather than to urban poverty!). I well remember how helpful after four years of confusion I found Bob Holman's classification[3] of thinking about urban

Table 3. DIFFERING EXPLANATIONS OF URBAN PROBLEMS

Theoretical model of problem	Explanation of the problem	Location of the problem	Type of change aimed for	Method of change
Culture of poverty	Problems arising from the internal pathology of deviant groups	In the internal dynamics of deviant groups	Better adjusted and less deviant people	Social education and social work treatment of groups
Cycle of deprivation	Problems arising from individual psychological handicaps and inadequacies transmitted from one generation to the next	In the relationships between individuals, families and groups	More integrated self-supporting families	Compensatory social work, support and self-help
Institutional malfunctioning	Problems arising from failures of planning, management or administration	In the relationship between the disadvantaged and the bureaucracy	More total and co-ordinated approaches by the bureaucracy	Rational social planning
Maldistribution of resources and opportunities	Problems arising from an inequitable distribution of resources	Relationship between the underprivileged and the formal political machine	Reallocation of resources	Positive discrimination policies
Structural class conflict	Problems arising from the divisions necessary to maintain an economic system based on private	Relationship between the working class and the political and economic structure	Redistribution of power and control	Changes in political consciousness and organisation

problems (and their policy consequences) which indeed I included in my contribution to the 1975 *Red Paper on Scotland* and, in a more detailed way, in the article the following year which described Strathclyde's Urban Strategy.[4]

Urban areas in Scotland have in recent years experienced many programmes reflecting, with greater or less degrees of coherence, such approaches. Strone/Maukinhill has probably run the gamut: and it is worth looking briefly at its experiences.

3. An everyday story of indifference, good intentions and reaction

Greenock is in many respects like other towns in the West of Scotland.[5] Its values and community networks are, however, reinforced in the evening newspaper which has kept alive a Liberal tradition. The Liberals here, however, are Gladstonian rather than modern and radical! The west end is a beautifully laid out part of the town — egalitarianism of recent decades has meant simply that the boundary between privilege and poverty has moved two or three blocks west. Labour generally hold political power (although the Liberals controlled the local authority from 1966 to 1972 and in 1977 to 1980) but the local "establishment", which includes the bureaucracy, is very much in charge. And only the defection of the Labour MP to the SDP and the bankruptcy of the Labour Party's Social Club ironically has begun to restore some vigour to a fairly typical ailing local Labour Party.

It had ten years ago the usual range of stigmatised, peripheral council estates which characterise any West of Scotland town. In 1971 the Rowntree Trust funded a seven-year community action project in Strone-Maukinhill which gave it its own community worker — that not only helped produce a very impressive informal adult education project[7] (designing its own curriculum and bringing into the area lecturers from the F.E. College in the centre of the town) but paved the way for a three-year Urban Aid funded "community planning team" of a planner and community worker. Such a project was created largely because of the apparent need thrown up by an earlier positive discrimination attempt in another housing scheme for longer "lead time" before the physical rehabilitation of the area being undertaken by the local authority — to ensure that this process reflected genuine community concerns and ideas.[8] Unfortunately not only did local government reorganisation remove the key supporters for this approach from the local housing and planning authority but they left behind them a political and social culture essentially unsympathetic to attempts to redistribute resources let alone political influence.[8]

The project effectively died after reorganisation, but the corpse was perversely kept alive to ensure the frustrations of community activists were maximised when the housing committee, for example, treated with contempt the ideas which emerged. It was only when the Liberals took control in 1977 that the exercise was given an indecent burial.

From here on two things happened — first, any pretence at consultation was thrown out of the window. Quite patently for the Liberals it raised expectations which the council was not prepared, financially or politically, to respond to. Secondly, the District refused to join with the Region in the Area Initiatives it was trying to negotiate (see 5.3 below) — building on the lessons of both successes and failures in the West of Scotland as a whole. Before we pick up that strand, however, let us complete the review of activities in the area in the last decade.

Relationships in such areas have never been easy — caring agencies which get involved in community work soon get sucked into and indeed compound internal community jealousies and rivalries. The danger indeed is that the different ideological and organisational systems of Community Education, Social Work, Community Work, Leisure and Further Education can add a whole new dimension to community rivalries and stymie any real progress. It is perhaps an understandable phenomenon — when one is working in such difficult circumstances with very little support it is useful to have a visible scapegoat for one's failure to make an impact — particularly if it comes from someone who has a very different ideological approach to the situation. Certainly in this area from the mid-1970s most projects turned sour for such reasons. And the area did not really benefit from Strathclyde Region's subsequent deprivation strategy.

The problem was simply that many of the professionals were being too ambitious — casting their net too wide and finding it getting entangled with other nets rather than catching fish! In the 1970s one of the real successes in the area was by a small tenant action group in a row of grim tenements dubbed "unfit for human habitation" by some European MPs who were persuaded to visit them. They were demolished as a direct result of the pressures of that small neighbourhood group working closely with their councillor who helped orchestrate their campaign. This much more limited canvass of activity is evident in current work in the area — it is as if local officials and residents, left largely to their own devices, have recognised that if *they* cannot achieve working relationships (let alone solidarity) all will be lost.

Community Action
HEALTH ACTION GROUP
In February 1981 a bright new health centre opened to the west of Greenock's town centre. As part of the package a part-time local health clinic for east end mothers closed — to the consternation of mothers in Strone-Maukinhill who immediately started a campaign, again involving an appropriate local official and the local councillor. Their efforts were initially treated with contempt even after a special survey (mounted with the help of a student on placement) demonstrated a serious drop in attendance of mothers at the health facility.

Only an offer late in the day from Strathclyde Region to locate the two- to three-hour-a-week facility (which was all that was being demanded from the Board!) in a new Social Work office to be opened in 1985 eventually persuaded the Health Board to concede to the two-year campaign. The whole episode was very revealing of the health system's insensitivity, insouciance and ignorance. They "rubbished" the women: they didn't know where Strone-Maukinhill was: they clearly didn't begin to appreciate the problems of mothers with young children making expensive bus journeys, having to return in time to collect other children from school — nor certain problems about the new health centre (not being allowed to take prams in: being shouted advice in a crowded room) nor the effects of the new "practice" base to health visitors which not only broke the community link of that crucial service but somehow had resulted in considerably reduced visits. The whole episode indeed serves not only to demonstrate how much the health service is failing the working class, it also showed how little has changed elsewhere. For when the design plans of the new office for the area — to involve 30-odd Social Work staff and some Housing staff — were examined it was to discover that no attempt had been made to think about the reception process and to provide informality and creche facilities — let alone some form of community management to ensure that buildings, facilities and resources were clearly there as a help to the area rather than to control it!

4. Strathclyde's Deprivation Strategy: 1977 to the present

Strathclyde Region's deprivation strategy has been *area based* — operational in 45 areas (most council estates) judged serious enough to warrant priority treatment. This simply because of the geographical polarisation which was such a feature of the West of Scotland. We were appalled by the myths about money being poured into these areas and by the patronising attitudes of many people to the competence of the residents of the areas which seemed to place the blame for the poverty on the poor themselves. The reality was administrative, political and professional neglect creating a group of second-class citizens.

We had more sympathy with the view which pinned the blame on the government — with its responsibility for economic policies and social security. But as these areas always had unemployment running at two or three times the regional average, which in turn was twice the national average, we could not accept that central government action, if and when it came, would be sufficient to overcome the deep-rooted problems of these areas.

We were convinced that local authorities — particularly one as large as Strathclyde — *could* and *should* do more within its existing resources and skills to ameliorate conditions in these areas. *When* and *how* such resources and skills were made available was the crucial question which local government seemed to have ignored — thereby ensuring that it compounded rather than ameliorated the effects of inequality.

In 1976 the Regional Council drew up its strategy to tackle multiple deprivation. This has five basic elements:

(1)   To bring pressure on central government and its agencies — the DHSS, the Health Boards, the Gas and Electricity Boards — to deal with the problems of poverty.

(2)   To pressure the government and — through our own efforts — to tackle the severe unemployment problems of the poorer parts of Strathclyde.

(3)   To encourage district council housing departments, the Scottish Special Housing Association and the new towns to stop concentrating disadvantaged families in selected areas. We also asked them to try to achieve a more balanced community mix.

(4)   On our part we would try to make sure that the services we provided in the poorer areas were as good as — if not better — than those in the better-off places. These services would be run well, more accessible and relevant to the people's needs.

(5)   Finally, we would back up communities which wanted to plan and run their own projects to help their own areas.

What we were asking our staff to do in 1976 was to accept that fairly simple things were needed from them in the first instance: not massive spending but just a commitment, firstly to those who lived in these areas, secondly to attempting new relationships both with their colleagues in other departments and with residents. We were also asking for a bit of imagination and courage, in encouraging staff to bring forward proposals for better practice despite the discouragement we knew they would encounter from the rules, traditions and prejudices which seemed deeply engrained in certain departments.

Even then, we had examples of good practice developing in some localities by dint of individual officers, politicians or activists being prepared to roll up their sleeves and try something different. In some places it had been police initiatives; in others adult education and in yet others health initiatives. In many cases, these were accompanied by rapid improvements in the indices of social malaise. The tragedy, however, is how isolated such simple initiatives were — and how many obstacles seemed to be placed in their way. We always seem to be wishing to reinvent the wheel.[10]

5. Its critique of local authority management—and consequences

Behind all this *lay a fairly coherent* critique of *local authority management* which it is important to spell out: it came very much from the experience of councillors and officials struggling in the early 1970s with rehabilitation schemes and has found expression — in a rather bland and diluted way — in such different national documents as the Seebohm and Paterson Reports.[11]

—The boundaries between local authority departments are too strongly defended;

—the professionals who inhabit them are too blinkered in their perceptions of problems; and too casework orientated;

—the departments are too hierarchical (and therefore oppressive of initiatives);

—it is the better-off who make most use of our services and are quickest to articulate demands for more.[11]

Since 1977 Strathclyde Region has been involved in a range of apparently unrelated innovations which have, however, all stemmed from this simple critique, and a belief that unless that machine was fundamentally changed socialist programmes would be distorted out of all recognition.

These activities have been:

> Urban Programme activities;
> Community Development;
> Area Initiatives;
> Member/Officer working groups.

The following section will look briefly at each.

5.1 Urban Programme

Since 1968 central government has made available special 75% funding to local authorities for projects relating to social problems: in such areas they require to be individually approved by the Scottish Office and are then funded for three to five years. Thereafter if they are to continue, they become part of the local authority's normal rate-borne expenditure. Prior to reorganisation this fund was not really used by Scottish local authorities. Since 1976 Strathclyde Region has changed all that and is now guaranteed about £6 million each year for new projects in its areas of priority treatment. While this is:

(a)   a small fraction of what we have lost in central government financial support recently;

(b)   considerably less than we were promised in the 1977 White Paper on Inner Cities;

(c)   small beer compared with Strathclyde annual budget of £1,500 million;

its significance should not be underestimated.

It constitutes, after all, a major part of the development money at the Region's disposal and, properly used, can exercise important "leverage" in changing traditional practices, policies and resources allocations of departments. Almost 1,500 staff are employed on 600 schemes in Strathclyde's urban programme.

There have, however, been various problems associated with it.

(a) *Types of projects:* in theory we have adopted a "bottom up" approach, viz. projects were to come from local staff and community groups in APTs. In fact, for various reasons, the programme was in the early years used more as an alternative source of funding for main line activists[12] and some considerable difficulty has been experienced in attracting well-designed, innovative projects for areas where the need was greatest.

(b) *Support:* those projects which were clearly innovative have not always received adequate management support.

(c) *Staffing:* many of the urban programme posts are the most demanding in the Region, yet salaries and conditions (limited contracts) have been such as generally to recruit only inexperienced (however committed) staff. Naturally, as a project approaches the end of urban aid funding and uncertainty arises about its absorption by the Region, staff tend to leave for more secure jobs — and considerable difficulty is experienced in replacing them. The subsequent underspending is then flaunted at local authorities by central government as proof that they are at the limit of their spending!

(d) *Timing:* looking at the most appropriate way of responding to local problems in APTs is time consuming — not least because of inter-departmental tensions. A lot of people have to be consulted, premises found, architectural briefs for conversion jobs agreed and leases negotiated. Then the submission has to survive the various hurdles of council and Scottish Office approval.

5.2 Community Development

"Inside every fat man," Cyril Connolly once wrote, "is a thin man struggling to get out." For such a large authority Strathclyde has a major commitment to local action. It has:

—established in 1978 a Community Development Committee which has acted as a "friend at court" for community groups and organisations;[13]

—appointed an increased number of community workers;

—set aside more than £1 million a year for community projects;

—established 20 area development teams;[14]

—organised six community conferences during 1982 to feed into a major review of the deprivation strategy.[15]

The "community approach" has become a fashionable phrase which conceals more than it reveals.[16] There seems to be a consensus about the desirability of something called community development/involvement/ participation. But behind that consensus lies confusion. At one extreme it may reflect a deliberate or unconscious attempt to ensure a more orderly acceptance of the agency's policies and services,[17] at another it might express a genuine desire to shift the balance of political power. In between there is a lot of confusion — and no little paternalism with assumptions that it is communities, or groups within communities, who need changing or developing.[18] Table 4, for which I am indebted to Alan Barr of Glasgow University, is a useful exploration of some of those meanings. As far as Strathclyde Labour councillors have been concerned it was the institutions, policies and procedures of *government* that needed changing or developing. In espousing community development we were recognising simply that in such an endeavour we needed the active support of residents. Support here does not mean harmonious consensus. Many people in local government seem to think that clients of statutory services should have a subservient and grateful relationship to local government and that collective organisation and protest is impertinent and unseemly. What they seem to want from community involvement is public approval if not applause! By "support" *we* mean strong collective organisation to press from below — whether by example or by argument — for the sorts of improvements we indicated in 1976 we wished to see from our nominal positions of power. Because what many of us have recognised is the illusion of being able to use such power or authority to engage *on our own* in significant change.[19]

In as much as community workers were a group of staff whose training, role and location identified them closely with our commitment, they have tended to be seen as the "front line" troops in the strategy. It is here, however, that dangers lie. Many of them are young and inexperienced and working in the most difficult jobs! They are not necessarily familiar or even sympathetic to the detailed workings of bureaucracy. In many cases they lack supportive management and have been left to fend for themselves. In some cases they are just glorified youth workers and some serious questions have to be asked about their qualifications. We have expected too much of them. The time has come to ensure they work in a clearer policy and management framework and receive more support.

5.3 Area Initiatives

Since 1978 the Region has established at a local level a variety of neighbourhood structures (Area Initiatives: Area Development Teams) to break through bureaucratic inertia and professional myopia in particularly the APTs.

Table 4.

THREE MODELS OF COMMUNITY WORK

Model	Community Organisation/Care	Community Development	Community Action
Explanation of cause of poverty	Social Pathology Inadequate Service Delivery Economic and Social Structure		
Style of problem and solution	Consensual (Collaborative)	Conflictual (Campaign)	Confronting (Contest)
Primary conception of community	Neighbourhood Issue		
Evaluation of community condition	Limited Analysis	Systematic/ Rational Analysis	Assessment of local feeling (rhetoric)
Fear of community activity	Internalised	Participatory	Externalised
Objectives of workers for communities	Domestication Liberation		
Workers' roles	Direct service provision and support to self-help services	Interactive roles: enabling advocacy brokerage, planning educational	Support to locally determined initiatives and actions. Enabling educational. Organising.
Political framework	Conservative	Reformist	Radical reformist (Revolutionary)
Examples of good practice	Direct services with volunteers. Self-help services and recreational activity, e.g. lunch clubs, playgroups, co-ops, TAs etc.	Self-help and investigative activity as an educational basis for democratic participation and campaigning, information services, co-ops, lunch clubs.	Aggressive political action as a tool for direct changes and radical political education, e.g. squatting, claimants, unions, action groups, TAs.

In January 1978, as a result of negotiations with the six District Councils who indicated their agreement with the Regional Strategy, seven joint Area Initiatives were established on an experimental basis — in the first instance for three years. They reflected a belief that many field officers were frustrated in their desire to work with one another and local people in a more creative search for relevant solutions to local problems by petty administrative controls and over-sensitivities about "setting precedents". Area Initiatives were, in one sense, invitations to local staff and residents to think creatively to take initiatives without being hamstrung about precedent and to demonstrate more effective ways of running services which might have implications elsewhere.

Each Area Initiative had certain common features, viz:

—an Area Co-ordinator;

—appointed by the two respective Chief Executive Officers;

—with special links to the Policy Committees;

—and to senior levels of the relevant departments;

—a support group of local officers;

—and a reasonable guarantee of Urban Programme support for the new projects.

Lessons from the subsequent five years' experience of these initiatives are at various levels — first, about the precise shape of such interventions: second, about the detailed implications of that experience for policy, procedures and structures in local government generally and, finally, about the nature of — and potential for change within — local government.[20]

The second level lessons are incorporated in a later section: at the most fundamental level it could be rather cynically said that the Area Initiatives served merely to confirm our analysis of the essential obstructiveness of the present administrative system within local government. A couple of years ago Robin Hambleton of the School for Advance Urban Studies reviewed the British Inner City Programme and the following excerpt should be pinned to the noticeboard of politicians and officials who profess their commitment to such programmes:

> Area approaches, like the American Model Cities Programme and the current British Inner City Initiative, by attempting to build positive discrimination in favour of specific areas into existing services, by insisting on a more co-ordinated approach to the problems of these areas and by attempting to open up the processes of decision-making, challenge three fundamental organising principles of urban government — *uniformity of service division, functional service management* and formal political and departmental *hierarchies of control.*

In these circumstances it is inevitable that new initiatives will be faced with formidable opposition from entrenched interests. Whilst some opposition may take the form of hostile resistance, a more subtle and probably more widespread response is to absorb the threat — to defuse, dilute and redirect it.[21]

5.4 Member/Officer Groups

In the last few years a large number of proposals for change have derived from reports produced in the Region by small working groups of councillors and officials in such areas as Child Care, Addiction, Disablement, Further Education, Community Business, Pre-Fives and the first two years of the secondary schooling. Generally after the approval of the recommendations in the reports, monitoring groups had been established to oversee the translation of the recommendations into practice — whether by negotiation with such agencies as Education, Health and Housing (and government and social work staff) or by extra finance for new programmes — and to monitor their implementation. This experience breaks with local government convention on at least three counts:

(i) Members and officers are working as equals in a task-oriented framework.

(ii) New policies are assumed to derive from such a *joint search* and not from circulars, professional or political prejudice.

(iii) New emphasis is given *politically* to the process of implementation.[22]

Such structures reflected the discontent in the Region in the mid-1970s with the committee system and departmentalisation which was sustained by it.

The committee process itself, with its predetermined agendas, its rules of procedure, focuses upon itemised decision-making at the expense of policy-making, becomes a substitute for real action. It does little to encourage constructive communication between the two main participants — councillors and officials, let alone the public at large — or to bring together and exploit their special skills and experience.

The other criticisms we were making in 1976 of the committee system related to:

(a) *Size.* An average of 15-20 councillors plus twelve or so other officers gives three times the effective number for creative exploration of issues.

(b) *Role.* To take decisions. Councillors become impatient with colleagues who question fundamental issues and are generally keen to move on to "next business".

(c) *Collusion* of chairman and chief officers. Basic political loyalties, if not whips, can be guaranteed to carry the day for predetermined recommendations.

(d)   *Inertia.* Officers can generally rely on the caution of the average member to act as a brake on the dangerous, radical idea.

(e)   *Professional control.* Committees relate to and are controlled by a single department organised around a set of professional skills and perceptions.

(f)   *Cinderella issues.* Those issues which are low in the priority of professionals or overlap with other departments create rivalry and therefore fall into the cracks between departments and committees.

This last point is particularly the case with the problems experienced in working-class areas.[24]

6. What has the rest of the machine been doing?

These have, of course, been *special* initiatives, attempting to change by various means — persuasion and exhortation, financial incentives, new structures and grassroots pressures — not just specific policies and resource allocations but the whole basis of professional thinking about, and response to, urban poverty. One of the most important areas has been the way officials see their own and others' role and expertise.

There is still too easy an assumption that only those with certificates from professional training schools can solve problems: that individual therapy and treatment is as much as one can or should offer: that the residents of areas such as Strone have no skills to offer.

Having said this one must recognise the valiant attempts made by departments to reallocate resources and to make their services more relevant.

The Education Department has moved, since reorganisation, towards providing comparable or better staffing in the APTs than other areas. The effect of declining rolls and the ability to recruit and deploy staff across the whole Region have helped the Education Department to eliminate part-time education and achieve national standards of staffing in APTs. In addition the extra staffing provided through the Urban Programme have been entirely deployed in areas of need ensuring a slightly better pupil/teacher ratio in most schools serving APTs.

Other progress has been made largely through use of the Urban Programme—thus new nursery schools, home/schools link teachers, extra careers staff and the development of community centres have all been largely dependent upon the Urban Programme. The development of Community Education services, particularly in the field of adult education, has been considerable and largely funded through mainline resource provision.

On the other hand the combination of threat of school closures and the new Parents' Charter has in some cases lessened rather than increased social mix. Equally there is still too much of an inclination in the system to blame problems of uptake on behaviour of people in these areas rather than on attitudes, structures and practices within the educational system.[24]

The *Social Work* Department has also been able, in a period when the basic grade establishment has increased from 289 to 712, to divert staff to the APTs. Again they often started well behind but areas now have a better level of staffing per head of population than other areas — not that this is totally adequate as the scale of problems is dependent on factors other than the total population. Unlike Education, Social Work has been growing during the five years since the strategy was introduced. Community Work and Welfare Rights have expanded almost ten-fold and the majority of the new staff have been deployed in the APT areas. Other developments, mainly funded through the Urban Programme, include Children and Family Centres, Social Group workers, Family Aides, Homemakers and a number of projects aimed at special client groups such as the Single Homeless, Battered Wives and Alcoholics.

On *poverty* we mounted a series of massive campaigns to make sure that people were getting their full rights from the DHSS.

For example, we distributed tens of thousands of claim postcards which put £4 million into the pockets of people who hadn't been claiming their rights.

We sent "Benefit Buses" into every APT to show people how to get their entitlements. As a result the image of the unemployed as "scroungers" has taken a severe knock.

Regarding employment, with unemployment of over 200,000 or 19% of the working population, the need to retain and create new jobs remains a key objective of the council. The Policy and Resources Committee of the council has established an Economic Strategy Subcommittee and has launched a *Strategy for Joint Economic Initiatives* for twelve areas of the Region. The council have also pioneered a £2 million *Employment Grants Scheme* using the European Social Fund, and has taken an active role in defending the loss of jobs in steel and shipbuilding. The council also blazed a national trail in the development of *Community Businesses*.[25]

7. What has been happening to people between 1971-1981?

All that makes interesting reading no doubt: and it certainly keeps quite a few of us busy and stimulated. The basic question, however, is what difference it all makes to the people of Strone-Maukinhill — later sections indicate what lessons some of us have learned from the work of the past five years. The hard reality, of course, is that life has become much worse for people in areas such as Strone.

So much of current government action strikes at such areas:

—the factory closures;

—the slashing in half of council house capital expenditure (at a time when Inverclyde District, for example, needs at least £4 million to cope with the dampness in its existing houses);

—the selective withdrawal of modernisation grants from those districts who don't raise rents high enough;

—the legal penalties on over-spending authorities such as Renfrew and Glasgow Districts (and if Strathclyde's £83 million "overspend" were judged "excessive and unreasonable" by the Secretary of State, the obvious targets would be school transport, meals and milk and concessionary fares, all of which are crucial to the areas of priority treatment);

—and even more insidiously and dishonestly are the effects on these areas of the government drive towards parental and tenant choice;

—which reinforces rather than eases the differences between APTs and non-APTs.

Such trends don't show up too readily or quickly on statistics. Nonetheless, the change in Strone-Maukinhill registered in the 1971 and 1981 censuses is shocking.

Table 5.	1971	1981	
Population under 15	38%	27%	
Large households	23%	12%	
Male unemployment	14%	34%	
Female unemployment	9%	24%	
Single parents	10%	25%	
Car ownership	20%	23%	
Rent	£47.00	£381.00	(RPI 371)

Recently too — and for the first time — DHSS published statistics showing local trends in supplementary benefits claimants between 1979 and 1982 which have allowed us to identify locally the number of people at or below the official poverty line.

The three-year period has seen an increase in Strathclyde of 58.7% in the number of claimants (compared with 33% for the rest of Scotland): due largely to the increase in unemployment claimants which rose in Renfrew and Lanark Divisions by an astonishing 165% and 162% respectively (i.e. more than three times in that period!).

More to the point when one adds an estimate of the non-claimants and dependants (but still excluding the low paid in employment) we get the horrific picture detailed in Table 6 that 25% of the population of Strathclyde are at or below the official poverty level: and in some places in Glasgow it is 50%.

Table 6. SUPPLEMENTARY BENEFIT CLAIMANTS, ELIGIBLE NON-CLAIMANTS AND THEIR DEPENDANTS, 1982

DIVISION	DHSS Local Office	Eligible Non-Claimants	Total Claimants and Non-Claimants	Total Non-Claimants	Claimants, Non-Claimants and Dependants	Total population at or below SB level %
Argyll/Dumbarton	Campbeltown	1203	515	1718	2893	13.3
	Clydebank	4761	2038	6799	11450	22.2
	Cumbernauld	8296	3551	11847	19950	16.4
	Dumbarton	7406	3170	10576	17810	20.2
	Oban	1662	711	2373	3996	11.8
	Total	23328	9985	33313	56099	18.7
Ayr	Ayr	12572	5381	17953	30233	19.3
	Irvine	11026	4719	15745	26515	26.8
	Kilmarnock	8422	3605	12027	20254	24.9
	Total	32020	13705	45725	77002	22.9
Renfrew	Greenock	9812	4200	14012	23596	24.3
	Paisley	13634	5835	19469	32786	21.8
	Paisley West	7013	3002	10015	16865	21.3
	Port Glasgow	4156	1779	5935	9995	37.0
	Total	34615	14816	49431	83242	23.6
Lanark	Airdrie	6233	2668	8901	14989	24.9
	Bellshill	5380	2303	7683	12938	24.7
	Coatbridge	4624	1979	6603	11120	23.1

Table 6—CONTINUED

Lanark—contd.	East Kilbride	5190	2221	7411	12480	15.2
	Hamilton	13068	5593	18661	31425	22.5
	Motherwell	10056	4303	14360	24182	20.7
	Total	44551	19067	63619	107134	21.5
Glasgow	Anniesland	9302	3981	13283	22369	34.6
	City	7475	3199	10674	17975	38.2
	Cranstonhill	1949	—	—	—	—
	Maryhill	10217	4373	14590	24570	26.3
	Partick	6097	2610	8707	14663	25.5
	Springburn	8959	3834	12793	21543	45.4
	Craigton	10415	4458	14873	25046	38.6
	Queen's Park	3028	1296	4324	7282	16.7
	South Side	11755	5031	16786	28268	20.5
	Bridgeton	2018	864	2882	4853	53.4
	Dalmarnock	1941	831	2772	4668	52.0
	Laurieston	7426	3178	10604	17857	38.2
	Parkhead	11156	4775	15931	26828	35.0
	Provan	12645	5412	18057	30408	41.5
	Rutherglen	11539	4939	16478	27749	30.9
	Total	115922	48781	162754	274079	31.4
STRATHCLYDE	Total	253469	107201	357670	602316	25.5
Rest of Scotland	Total	171531	73415	244946	410285	14.8
Scotland	Total	422000	180616	602616	1009382	19.5

On the face of it all the energies of local residents, politicians and professionals over the last five years or so seem to have been pointless. If the West of Scotland no longer stands out so dramatically in the statistics it is not so much because of the effects of any positive action as because the rest of Britain has "risen" to our unemployment levels.

8. What do we expect of local government?
We didn't expect as a local authority to make any impact — certainly not in five years — on basic economic problems. What we attempted to do was to break the vicious circle of hopelessness and cynicism which prevailed in so many of the areas and to generate *understanding* within local government of the nature of the problem and *commitment* for moving against these problems with more vigour than before. All this suggests two basic tests whereby the activities should be measured.

8.1 Community action
How many more people are now prepared to fight for their rights? Are they more knowledgeable? Are they being given a chance to work in partnership with the local authority? Do they have access to appropriate advice and resources?

8.2 Take-up of services
Are resources going to those who most need them? At long last through Area Profiles, the Social Work Needs and Resources reports and Member/Officer group reports this test can now be strictly applied. They are certainly showing the stubbornness with which existing patterns of disadvantage are being maintained.

Take, for example, two local services — home helps and pre-fives services.

Within the Renfrew Division the Social Work needs/resources analysis has shown that the *best* service in the Division is in Clarkston with 271 elderly cases per 1,000 vulnerable elderly covered — whereas Strone-Maukinhill has only 90 such cases covered, *one-third of the service* (although some people point to this figure proudly as an indication of the strength of community networks).

Pre-five statistics have to be treated with great care — since the relevant provision ranges from nursery schools and children's centres through day nurseries to pre-school playgroups and childminders — and children attend on different bases. Nonetheless the provision in Strone — despite the major development in recent years — seems to be only *one-half* that of the Renfrew Division average.

Pre-fives have been on everyone's agenda for more than a decade.[26] The importance of these early years is understood and the relevance of Educational, Health and Social Work input accepted. But the area remains

Table 7.

1981 CENSUS OF POPULATION: COMPARATIVE INDICATORS OF DEPRIVATION

	Unemployment		Large Households (3+Children)	Single Parent Families	Lacking or sharing use of a bath	With no car
	Male	Female				
CENTRAL CLYDESIDE CONURBATION[1]	17.3	7.7	8.6	2.4	2.8	57.8
Tyne and Wear Metropolitan County	16.5	5.8	6.3	2.4	1.7	56.5
South Yorkshire Metropolitan County	12.0	4.9	6.5	1.9	2.3	49.6
West Yorkshire Metropolitan County	11.3	4.9	7.3	2.4	2.4	47.4
West Midlands Metropolitan County	15.7	6.3	8.4	2.4	2.0	44.3
Greater Manchester Metropolitan County	12.6	5.9	7.5	2.5	2.9	47.2
Merseyside Metropolitan County	17.8	7.2	8.4	2.5	3.6	50.1
Greater London	9.3	4.6	6.4	2.7	5.8	44.7
Outer Metropolitan Area	6.2	2.9	7.2	1.8	2.3	26.6
CLYDESIDE'S RANK (Out of 9)	2	1	1	4 Equal	4	1
England	10.0	4.5	6.9	2.1	3.1	38.6
Wales	13.3	5.6	7.2	2.1	4.4	38.0
Scotland	13.0	6.1	7.7	2.3	2.6	48.7
Rest of Scotland excluding Clydeside	10.8	5.3	7.3	2.2	2.6	44.2

Note: 1 Bearsden and Milngavie, Clydebank, Cumbernauld and Kilsyth, East Kilbride, Eastwood, Glasgow, Hamilton, Monklands, Motherwell, Renfrew and Strathkelvin Districts.

Source: 1981 Census—O.P.C.S. Monitor—G.B. National and Regional Summary (CEN 81 CM 57).

under-resourced and peripheral and, like most such areas, fraught with ideological tension between such groups as Education, Social Work and the pre-school playgroup movement. For two years a Member/Officer group has wrestled in the Region with the various issues and is clear that the present services are:

—too compartmentalised;
—unfairly distributed;
—inflexible;
—insufficiently known about.

And that structures are needed to sort this out at both central and local level.

The key is local link groups of all workers concerned, resource centres and pre-school animateurs — working within a more committed framework of ensuring the provision of the appropriate service to the child and family.

In youth services, a not dissimilar situation exists. Everyone pays lip service to the problems of youth unemployment: and behind that lies deep concern about the effects not so much on "blighted lives" as on social order.[27] But surprisingly little is actually being done — particularly in areas such as Strone-Maukinhill — perhaps because of the realisation of those in positions of authority that they don't begin to understand the feelings, interests and problems of youth generally, let alone those in such areas. Literally almost they don't speak the same language and those with responsibilities for youth services patently do not reach the vast majority either because of the institutional setting they offer or because of their own attitudes and background. Clearly the work in Intermediate Treatment has been seen as threatening by many schools: it has, however, profound lessons.[28]

We do not have the space here to talk about developments (or rather lack of them) in the crucial areas of Health and Housing. It has frankly been difficult to get such agencies even to pay lip service to positive discrimination and community development let alone appreciate what the practical consequences of such commitments would be.[29] While more inter-agency work could certainly pay dividends, more confrontational tactics also clearly have a role to play.

9. The lessons from six years of Strathclyde's strategy

Strathclyde has, over the past 18 months, been intensively reviewing its deprivation strategy: with the active involvement of activists in APTs.

The review has thrown up *negative* and *positive* lessons.

9.1 Negative

—The good intentions of some projects/programmes failed to be realised because of insufficient support (particularly at managerial and political level).

—Despite the number of projects/programmes they have remained peripheral to the operations of the various agencies—easy to isolate/deflect.

—And that very diversity has been a source of confusion.

—Many staff could not see the implications of the strategy for their work.

—Every APT is different—not only in the intensity of its problems and the nature of its needs but in the opportunities for change offered by local circumstances, whether staff or community.

—The "man and dog" approach is irrelevant when the decline of an estate has gone beyond a certain point.

9.2 Positive

—The way ahead is through simple devices rather than complex programmes of organisational change.

—It involves being clear politically about *what* we want and about the *most effective means* of achieving this.

—Information is power—particularly about the unfair distribution of resources. Hence the compilation of Area Profiles.

—While special projects are necessary, staff as a whole somehow have to have the strategy built into their job specification. It is not someone else's responsibility: everyone has to ask where their practices and attitudes perhaps don't compound the problem of inequality.

—Political leadership at HQ and local level is crucial.

—As is proper training and back-up.

—And above all accountability.

Local government tends to oscillate between two extreme models of policy management — "non-directive" (waiting for local initiatives) and "directive" (assuming that the centre knows best). What is needed is a mixture of these two models: *clear guidance* from the politicians on priorities and considerable scope for *local negotiation, within that framework,* of local developments and improvements in particular areas of priority treatment for which *local staff* can then be held accountable.

10. Some prerequisites

The policies, resources, structures and skills thrown into a genuine fight against urban poverty must be *appropriate*.

POLICIES must distinguish between the needs of the most disadvantageous groups and areas on the one hand and the more marginal on the other. To date no such distinction has been made — which makes local authorities vulnerable to the accusation of "gilding the ghetto".

Policies need to avoid the patronising and labelling dangers of the normal local authority approach. Youth, elderly, or pre-fives, are not homogeneous groups: multi-purpose prepackaged kits off the professional shelf will generally be irrelevant and encourage the inter-professional jealousies evident in so many areas.

Policies, finally, should build on good practice — which is generally community based.

RESOURCES should be allocated according to need — a good socialist principle observed more in the breach.

STRUCTURES should be established to ensure that the deprivation strategy is taken as seriously by officials as traditional structures. Three types are needed:

(a)   *at the centre* — to pursue and monitor the issues of strategic concern detailed below;

(b)   *at a local level* to ensure collaborative work between officials, councillors and local people for the improvement of particular services within that strategic framework;

(c)   *at an inter-agency* level to ensure the proper response of health, housing and ad hoc agencies.

SKILLS: such work will involve people in new challenges and roles. A lot of these skills are around although under-used but they need proper development and this has major implications for "training".

11. The fundamental challenge

What then does all this experience mean for a relevant local authority strategy? There are many who have seen positive discrimination as meaning the charitable dropping of a few crumbs from the table for the poor underneath once the rest have had their fill. And who now take the view that when the "collective belt is being tightened" they need the crumbs for themselves! That is to say that the reduced resources of local government makes the fairly limited fight which has so far been conducted against urban poverty at a local level both financially and politically impossible. I cannot accept this; it paradoxically underestimates both the scale of emasculation the government is inflicting on local government and the political potential such a development offers.

First the bad news; local authorities have not only had legal shackles placed on their individual spending levels and patterns through the Miscellaneous Provisions Act and their revenue and capital grants (particularly housing) seriously reduced.[30] Privatisation has been going on apace — without the term being used — in areas other than Cleansing. Local authorities, for example, have virtually ceased being housing agencies — apart, that is, from their landlord functions (and the Sale of Council Houses policy is attempting to restrict even that to APT ghettoes). The huge expansion of MSC has been at the expense of education authorities — even before the Parents' Charter further compounded the problems of APTs. And even the Labour-conceived SDA has recently been usurping the traditional local authority role of local environmental improvements.

The paradox emerges from the insufficiently appreciated point that local authority power is not to be equated with resources and responsibilities. Many European local authorities don't have anything like our resources and functions and yet wield far more influence — simply because their elected representatives do not see themselves as surrogate managers to be manipulated by skilful professionals controlling the local population[31] but as politicians supplying the local link in the national chain of policy-making.[32]

The Strathclyde initiatives have indicated the pay-off which can be achieved if only objectives are properly detailed and real political muscle is put behind them by the development of *appropriate machinery and skills* and more joint endeavours particularly between Labour councillors of different authorities, community activists and party members. This, it should be said, doesn't come from simplistic rhetorical calls to battle for the retention of the status quo but from patient analysis of present trends, identifying opportunities and constructing suitable alliances.[33]

Of course, local government cannot ignore the realities of international economic forces — let alone Thatcherism. But in the past five years a range of significant initiatives have been taken by Strathclyde in such fields as welfare rights, continuing education, community business and other self-help endeavours between which it is important to make connections. The Labour movement is too dismissive of many of these as insignificant and "peripheral" — or alternatively as potentially threatening. We really do have to make up our mind about whose side we are on: the big battalions of non-accountable professionals[34] or the public who elect us. One of the interesting features of the Urban Programme in Strathclyde is the democratic way every project has to be designed, the critical questions that are subsequently posed about it before approval and the sustained evaluation councillors then carry out as it approaches the end of three and five years of its life. The partnership this entails between councillors, professionals and the public is simply not replicated elsewhere in local authority (or public) services. With proper accountability and budgetary systems more can be done for and in APTs than at present.

One of the difficulties, it must be said, is an analytical one. The landscape of work and public agencies has changed so dramatically since the mid-1970s and local government has never seen it as within its competence to make judgements about the nature and consequences for its services of socio-economic changes.[35] For too long there has been an assumption that "normal service will be resumed shortly". And while local authorities remain the largest employers in their localities, very large purchasers and large investors of capital (even apart from their major role in the "informal economy") so far there has been all too little creative thinking about how their influence could be used to help local people confront and cope with the new problems of the 1980s.[36] It is significant, for example, that the initiative for Local Enterprise Trusts has come generally from Chambers of Commerce. It is time that local government seized the initiative (while appreciating the dangers of too all-embracing a role) — particularly on behalf of the "evicted from the formal economy". Some "mapping" of the effects of what is currently being done in the locality by various agencies is needed — as well as a matching of community needs with the variety of special funds available.[37] This involves making the connections I've spoken about between activities all too often seen as separate and peripheral. I am indebted to Colin Ball for the following schemata:

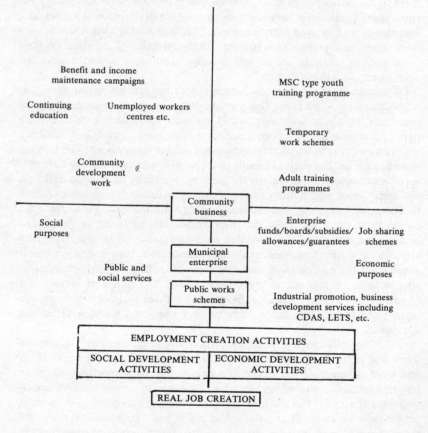

12. The way ahead

In late summer 1983 Strathclyde Region published a crucial document outlining the lessons it had learned from the various activities and developments since it had first indicated, seven years earlier, how seriously it was taking the attack on urban poverty.

More positively the report identified what it called "strategic areas of concern" to which particular priority should be given (services to the unemployed, pre-fives, youth provision, the elderly, continuing education and single parents) through simple but nonetheless powerful devices which should become the focus for the council's energies, viz:

(a)   *Local structures* led by the Regional Councillor for every APT — their remit being to negotiate relevant improvements as suggested by Area Profiles and the strategic areas of concern, using urban aid and other developmental monies.

(b)   All within a framework set by the five *Divisional Deprivation Groups* who, on the model of the pre-five work[39] would be inviting specific APTs to indicate how they would repair particularly serious deficiencies; after agreement local staff would be held accountable for the outcomes.

(c)   Some twenty or so housing schemes, however, are so problematic as to require stronger organisational support — with an inter-agency element — building on the lessons of the Area Initiatives.

(d)   The intensive work involved in all this would be serviced by a *new unit* of experienced and committed workers — seconded for the most part from other departments to DDGs and particular projects.

(e)   Although 1983 saw the pulling together of regional experience in such areas as community business, pre-fives, elderly and youth work by "short, sharp" member/officer groups meeting virtually every three days or so, more such work is required at a *regional level*. Equally more politically led inter-agency work is needed on the basic themes of unemployment, health, poverty and housing.

It all sounds simple; but as the Hambleton quote[21] indicated it challenges basic tenets of local government.

The test of the Labour movement locally — as well as that of local government — as far as the people of Strone-Maukinhill are concerned — is whether we will rise to that challenge.

References

1   "Urban Policies: A New Approach", D. Donnison,|Fabian Tract 487 (1983).

2   First in the field were John Dearlove (see his article in *Community Work One*, edited Jones and Mayo) and John Benington: *Local Government becomes Big Business* (CDP, 1976). For a critique of the literature see particularly G. Kirk's *Urban Planning in a Capitalist Society* (Croom Helm, 1980), and P. Dunleavy's *Urban Political Analysis* (Macmillan, 1980).

3   In his *Socially Deprived Families in Britain*.

4   In "The All Embracing Problem of Multiple Deprivation", *Social Work Today* (October 1976).

5   Interestingly it has produced in recent years not only the author Alan Sharp (of *Green Tree in Geddes* fame) but also playwriters Bill Bryden and Peter McDougall, who drew on the Strone area for several of his TV plays.

6   See the contribution by Charlie McConnell to *Community Development, Adult Education and Positive Discrimination*, by Jones and Mayo.

7   See the contribution by the author to *Participation in Urban Renewal*, published by the Council for European Municipalities (1982).

8   See Stuart Hashegan's "Making and Breaking the Rules", in *Strathclyde Studies in Community Work II*.

9   See paragraph 10 for an excerpt from S. M. Miller's "Reinventing the Broken Wheel". It is also salutary to reread the classic *Dilemmas of Social Reform*, published in 1968 by Marris and Rein.

10 *The Reorganisation of the Social Services* (HMSO, 1968); *The Management of Scottish Local Authorities* (HMSO, 1973).

11 Studies on this phenomenon have reached saturation point: they range from the seminal book *Conviction*, edited by Norman McKenzie in 1959, through Townsend's work to Julian Le Grand's recent book on equality.

12 See the book on the Urban Programme by Edwards and Batley. The best critique, however, of the British approach to urban strategy probably still remains Joan Higgins' *The Poverty Programme*.

13 This was the result of a councillor review group on Community Development

14 The establishment of these teams requires a submission to be made by a regional councillor with local staff to the Community Development Committee of the Region who must be satisfied that there is a manageable task for such a team to perform which is not properly being carried out by existing machinery. It is a simple but powerful device for cutting through inter-agency inertia and departmental hierarchies!

15 See the special August 1982 issue of Strathclyde's *Digest* for details.

16 See, for example, the confused debate which arose during 1982 following on the publication of the Barclay Report on Social Work: the June/July issues of *Social Work Today* contain a particularly interesting debate.

17 One of the best surveys of a complex and confusing literature on participation is Peter Hain's *Neighbourhood Participation* (Temple Smith, 1980). *Public Participation in Local Services* by Boaden et al (Longman, 1982) is also a useful overview of the different forms participation has taken in Britain in the last decade. It is, however, salutary to read the Fabian Tract 419 of 1973, "Toward Participation in Local Services".

18 See the author's article, "Community Development: its administrative and political challenge" originally published by *Social Work Today* in February 1977 and incorporated in *Readings in Community Work*, edited by Henderson and Thomas (Allen and Unwin, 1981). Again it is salutary to look at Fabian Tract 400 on *Community Action*, edited by A. Lapping, which appeared in 1970.

19 See the author's "Must the System always win?" in *Community Care*, September 1977.

20 An evaluation of four of these initiatives was carried out by the Institute of Operational Research.

21 R. Hambleton, "Inner City Policy—Reflections from Experience", *Policy and Politics*, Volume 9, No. 1 (1981).

22 This is taken from the author's "The Management of Political Innovation — The Strathclyde Experience of New Devices for Policy Making", *Local Government Studies*, November/December 1981.

23 A neglected report on this issue was that from Southwark CDP, "The management of deprivation".

24 For a critical look at the Scottish Educational System, see T. Worthington's "Life Long Learning: The Enemy Within", in the *Times Educational Supplement for Scotland*, February 1981.

25 A copy of the Region's review of the nature of future support for Community Business is available from the Chief Executive's Department. More than three-quarters of community enterprise projects in UK are to be found in Strathclyde — due in no small measure to the Local Enterprise Advisory Board headed by John Pearce and located at the Local Government Unit, Paisley College.

26 See Strathclyde Region's Interim Report on Pre-Fives (1981).

27 A particularly useful book is *Law and Order: Arguments for Socialism* by Ian Taylor (Macmillan, 1981).

28 Again a particularly useful book is *Out of Care: Community Support of Juvenile Offenders* by Thorpe et al (Allen and Unwin, 1980).

29 For a very useful overview of a community-based approach to health problems see the paper commissioned by Strathclyde Region from Community Projects Foundation *Health and Community Development*.

30 From a small article by S. M. Miller, *Reinventing the Broken Wheel: lesson learning in social policy*.

31 The most succinct critique are the two documents issued by COSLA in 1981/82 — the *COSLA Critique* and *A time to listen: a time to speak out*.

32 Which is, expressed simplistically, the argument of Marxist urban sociologists who have in recent years turned their attention to local government — and produced some of the most insightful studies yet. G. Kirk's *Urban Planning in a Capitalist Society* (Croom Helm, 1980) is a good review of the literature. See also the SAUS paper on *The Local State* (1980).

33 For a fascinating (if somewhat long) comparative study of local government systems which challenges a few of our myths, see *British Dogmatism and French Pragmatism*, Douglas Ashford (Allen and Unwin, 1982).

34 While writing this piece I have been rereading Hugh Stretton's neglected *Capitalism, Socialism and the Environment* (Cambridge University Press, 1976) and would strongly urge change agents to read it — particularly pp. 150-157 — as an antidote to the strident counterproductivity of so much left politics.

35 One of the best reviews of this area is a paper delivered by Pollitt at the 1982 RIPA Summer Conference. The present situation has moved even Ken Livingstone to issue a public blast.

36 As far back as 1978 Ray Pahl was beginning to do this: see his piece "Will the Inner City problem ever go away?" in *New Society*, February 1978. The most helpful book is Charles Hardy's recent *Taking Stock* (BBC Publications, 1983).

37 A useful review of the various activities of local government in this field is available from School of Advanced Urban Studies at Bristol. See also the small article in the Local Government Unit's 2nd issue of Forum.

38 For a development of this point, see the author's contribution to a collection of papers on Urban Economic Regeneration edited by CURS (Glasgow University, 1983).

INDEX

Aberdeen, custom-built dwellings for single people 187; cuts in allocation for housing expenditure 172; location of GP surgeries 213; mortality figures 211; opposition to custom-built dwellings for single people 187; under-use of maternity services by working women 216

Age concern, report 1974 138; study of pensioners' assets 140

Areas for Priority Treatment 211-2; education in 237-8; effect of Parents' Charter 247; ghettoes 246; involvement of activists 244; social work 238; see also Strone-Maukinhill

A Study of Multiply Deprived Households in Scotland 180

Attendance Allowance Board 165

Ayrshire, mining in 44; shelving of health projects 73

baby boom 55, 58

benefits, see under child, National Insurance, unemployment, supplementary etc.

Bevan, Aneurin 73

Beveridge Report (1942) 13, 16, 18, 134, 137, 152

birth rate, fall in 15, 41, 60, 62; fluctuations in 54-5; historically high in Scotland 71

Black Report 16

Born to Fail 217, 223

Bosanquet, N. 83

Breakdown 169

British Births 1970 206

British Medical Association 220

bronchitis, higher incidence of 16

Building Standards (Scotland) Regulation 1971 168

BUPA 220

cancer, death rates in Scotland 207, 208; more common among those on low incomes 73; prevalence of 16

Census Indicators on Urban Deprivation 224

Centre for Educational Sociology 195

Changing Patterns of Care for the Elderly 14

children, child benefit 15, 18, 131, 147, 150, 158; born to fail 223; disadvantaged 11; educational attainment of children of unskilled workers 190; govt. financial support for 14; in care in Strathclyde 101, 102; increase in poor 31; in poverty 15; minimum costs of raising 145, 146; need for increased provision of child-minding etc. 15, 155, 159; provision for under Supplementary Benefits Scheme 100; Scottish Office report (1930) 70; survey—Children in Adversity 11; relation between vandalism and child density; see also education

Chronically Sick and Disabled Persons Act 164, 168, 169

Circular 600 191, 196

Citizens' Advice Bureaux, Edinburgh, increase in queries regarding redundancy and unemployment 101

Clydebank, growth of 66; rise in unemployment 101

Clydeside, overcrowding 180; shipbuilding 44

Cohen Report (1964) 215

community care, burden to fall on women 19, 153; need for development of 143

Conservative government, administrations in 1950s and early 1960s 73; annual reductions in Housing Support Grant 174; attacks on policies to reduce housing deprivation 172; argument for lower wages and benefits 18; changes in social security legislation 161; commitment to cutting social security spending 160; decisions 17; discounts to tenants who offer to buy own homes 175; effects of four years Conservative administration 35, 37; future under Conservatives 16; manifesto (1983) 13; long-term philosophy 36; policies undermining women 152; scrapping plans for Housing Training Council 174; wage restraints 157

Court Report 213

Crops, West Highland failure of (1923) 70

Cullingworth Committee 178

dampness, a source of housing deprivation 185-6; see also Edinburgh, Dundee, Inverclyde

Dead End Street (Shelter) 172

dementia, Scottish pensioners suffering 143; see also pensioners

Department of Employment 52, 53, 119

deprivation, comparative indicators (1981) 243; cycle 80, 87; disabled 163-6; housing 86, 87, 172-89; who are the deprived? 86-8; see also urban/multiple deprivation under Strathclyde Regional Council etc.

DHSS, deployment of staff to combat fraud 166; disabled claimants 165; informal complaints from staff 98; official statistics of number of poor in Scotland 28, 32; pensioners 137; proposal by review team for raising of benefits 100; studies undertaken 99; unpublished data regarding unemployment; see also benefits, social security, Strathclyde Regional Council, single-parents, unemployment, women

disabled 15, 31, 32, 33, 34, 161-71; dependent on national insurance benefits 30; Disability Allowance 164; Disabled Persons' (Employment) Act 166; Disablement Income Group 164; increase in numbers 29; International Year 161; moves to cut benefits and services, Hansard 164; selling off of homes for 19; see also Strathclyde Regional Council survey

Doeringer, P. 83

dole, introduction of a statutory minimum 68; lengthening of queues 91

Donnison, Professor 149, 165

dual labour market thesis 84, 85, 86

Dumbarton District Housing Plan 185

Dundee, cuts in allocation for housing expenditure 172; damp houses 186; evictions 187; failure to meet single-parent housing need 188; location of GP surgeries 213; Scottish EPA project in primary schools 197-8; specialisation in textiles 44; study of redundancies 97

earnings, abolition of related supplement 29, 37; average weekly of men in Britain 107

Edinburgh, capital allocation for housing 176;